Covering bin Laden

Covering bin Laden

Global Media and the World's Most Wanted Man

EDITED BY SUSAN JEFFORDS
AND FAHED AL-SUMAIT

UNIVERSITY OF ILLINOIS PRESS
Urbana, Chicago, and Springfield

Library of Congress Control Number: 2014958351
ISBN 978-0-252-03886-0 (hardcover)
ISBN 978-0-252-08040-1 (paperback)
ISBN 978-0-252-09682-2 (e-book)

Contents

INTRODUCTION

After bin Laden

Osama bin Laden.

It would be difficult to find someone for whom this name does not evoke images, emotions, memories, desires, beliefs. Even years after his death in 2011, Osama bin Laden's name conjures up a complex array of narratives and representational structures. Depending on one's location—geographically, politically, religiously—the name invokes stories of evil, bravery, destruction, retribution, deception, truth-telling, cowardice, courage. The name—"Osama bin Laden"—goes far beyond the man—Osama bin Laden—and extends well beyond his death.

In 1998, American Broadcasting Company journalist John Miller wrote that "the American people, by and large, do not know the name Usama [sic] bin Laden, but they soon will."[1] With tragic prescience, Miller's prediction chronicled the passage of Osama bin Laden from a relative unknown to one of the world's most immediately recognized figures.

Before the attacks of September 11, 2001, on the World Trade Center, the Pentagon, and a third target in Washington, D.C., Osama bin Laden's name was known in limited circles. Within Saudi Arabia, he was known as one of four children of the pious and hardworking Mohammed bin Awad bin Laden, a billionaire construction magnate who earned his wealth by constructing some of Saudi Arabia's most iconic buildings. In response to the Soviet invasion of Afghanistan in 1979, Osama bin Laden went to Pakistan, where he became known in broader circles as a wealthy supporter of the anti-Soviet Muslim forces in

Afghanistan, eventually earning a reputation for himself on the battlefield. In 1998, as the founder of Al Qaeda—"the base"—he became known more broadly through the work done by Al Qaeda, most vividly in the attacks in 1998 on U.S. embassies in Tanzania and Nairobi, and then in 2000 on the USS *Cole* as it sat anchored in a harbor in Yemen, resulting in combined deaths of hundreds of people.

For many around the world, however, his association with 9/11 was the first they had heard of Osama bin Laden. On September 11, 2001, CBS News journalist Jim Stewart linked Osama bin Laden's name as a probable source of the attacks as early as 9:17 a.m. (EST), a mere thirty-one minutes after the first World Trade Center attack. During that same period, bin Laden was mentioned on Howard Stern's radio show in connection with the World Trade Center attacks.[2] With an unprecedented rapidity made possible by media and the Internet, Osama bin Laden soon became "the most wanted man in the world," going from being "the world's most notorious terrorist into one of the leading newsmakers—indeed *the* leading newsmaker."[3]

If bin Laden was not broadly known to media audiences before 9/11, it was not through a lack of effort on his part. Christina Hellmich remarks that bin Laden "was vying for attention . . . from the early 1990s," while Andrew Hill notes that bin Laden was making himself "available to Western journalists," using video appearances "to seek to sway Western public opinion."[4] Hellmich points to the period preceding 9/11 as particularly media-focused for bin Laden: "interviews with Western-based journalists, fatwas, open letters and public statements aired via Al Jazeera, by which bin Laden was attempting to establish a public image."[5] Whether, indeed, bin Laden was the "leader of a global terrorist network at this point," Hellmich concludes, "it is clear that this was precisely the image he wanted to communicate to both journalists and the wider audience."[6] By all accounts, bin Laden was very conscious of the role that media played in the achievement of his goals, and he intentionally used media—whether interviews, video-taped speeches, or distributed statements—to achieve those ends. An Al Qaeda associate remarked that "Sheikh Osama knows that the media war is not less important than the military war against America."[7] Analyst Jeremy White concluded that bin Laden's "status as the most wanted man on the planet was enough to get him airtime on every major news network whenever he wished."[8] Indeed, it can be argued that global media made Osama bin Laden possible. Some associates of bin Laden even worried that he gave too much attention to the media. Mustafa Setmaerian (Abu Musab Al Suri) wrote in an email to bin Laden on July 19, 1999, that he "has caught the disease of screens, flashes, fans, and applause."[9]

Perhaps the most powerful indication that bin Laden was aware of the role that media would play on 9/11 was the timing of the two airline collisions with the World Trade Center towers, an event in which, to use Brigitte Nacos's words, "9/11 terrorists outperformed Hollywood."[10] Indeed, the seventeen minutes between the attack on the North and South Towers insured that, while media did not telecast the first crash, they were riveted by the second. By the time the second plane flew into the South Tower, both CNN and MSNBC, along with local New York networks, were televising the scene at the World Trade Center, positioning millions of viewers to watch the second plane fly into the South Tower. Real-time images were transmitted beyond the United States, with the BBC showing the World Trade Center on its website, making the attacks a global media event in real time. Peter L. Bergen reports that bin Laden told his companions who were watching the televised images: "If he [the newsreader] says: 'We have just received this . . .' it means the brothers have struck." Knowing that the second attack was to come, he advised them, "be patient."[11]

Bin Laden was not, of course, the first to understand the symbiotic relationship between media and terrorism. Ayman Al Zawahiri, named leader of Al Qaeda after bin Laden's death, wrote in a personal letter in 2005 that "we are in a battle, and that more than half of this battle is taking place in the battlefield of the media."[12] Senior Al Qaeda strategist al-Suri (Mustafa Setmariam Nasar) stated that jihad itself was best understood "as a comprehensive war, where its soldiers employ military, political, media, civil and ideological tools."[13] Citing a manual of the Afghan Jihad used in Al Qaeda training camps, Brigitte Nacos remarks that "publicity was (and most probably still is) an overriding consideration in planning terrorist acts."[14] As Ibrahim Seaga Shaw summarized, "the relationship between terrorism and media [is] one of "symbiosis," in which terrorism's primary aim is media coverage."[15] Bin Laden himself is reported to have told the Taliban leader Mullah Omar that "up to 90 percent of his battle was fought in the media."[16] Indeed, an Al Qaeda writer celebrated the cost-saving impact of media in propagating the end point of terrorism—the creation of fear: "The giant American media machine was defeated in a judo strike from Sheikh bin Laden. CNN cameras and other media dinosaurs took part in framing the attacks and spreading the fear, without costing al-Qaeda a dime."[17]

A few days after September 11, 2001, while on a visit to the Pentagon, President Bush declared: "I want justice. And there's an old poster out west, that I recall, that said, 'Wanted, Dead or Alive.'"[18] Revealing that bin Laden was not the only political actor to understand the value of conveying messages through the media, he followed these words by saying, "The Taleban [*sic*] must take my statements seriously."[19] Osama bin Laden's death on May 2, 2011, was the culmination of almost a decade of efforts by the U.S. government to find him, "dead or alive." Tony Blinken, Vice President Biden's chief of staff, pointed to the importance of bin Laden in the U.S. government's political calculus when he said that "a number of people felt that half—if not more—of the success we would achieve [in capturing or killing bin Laden] would be the world knowing that bin Laden was gone."[20] The final raid of bin Laden's house in Abbottabad was itself a carefully orchestrated media event. The highly controlled nature of the mission by the now-famous U.S. Navy SEAL Team 6 included a mindful decision about how to confirm bin Laden's death through a series of photographic images taken on-site before the team left Abbottabad. The power of bin Laden's image was a conscious factor in determining that there was a need for proof of death that was not itself an incitement to vengeance.[21] The U.S. government claims to have fifty-nine photos of bin Laden dead. Legal controversy surrounds these photos, with claims for their release becoming the subject of decisions by the U.S. District Court and now the U.S. Court of Appeals for Washington, D.C.[22] A search on the Internet quickly shows a photo of bin Laden—dead, beaten, and bloodied. However, the image, which circulated online for more than two years after bin Laden's death, is a fake, an amalgamation of a photograph of the face of another man who had been beaten and the face of bin Laden.[23] The "real" bin Laden continues to be elusive even after his death; in Andrew Hill's words in this volume, bin Laden continues to "haunt" the Internet in ambivalent versions of himself.

Bin Laden's continued power as a cultural and political icon is shown in the conspiracy theories about his death that populate the Internet. Numerous voices in the media ask, "Is bin Laden really dead?" Political commentator Glenn Beck, on the day after bin Laden's death was announced, offered on his radio show this rambling speculation:

> There is something bothering me and it has to do with the helicopter crash. Getting Osama Bin Laden out, and the fact that we know that Wikileaks says that al-Qaeda has nukes. And here we have the head of al-Qaeda and we shoot him. Reports coming from the Pentagon, he was unarmed. Now why would we shoot a guy? Did we get the information? Could we have done anything with that? Were poll numbers involved, or are we seeing a show? Is it possible that Osama Bin Laden has been ghosted out of his compound, and we're seeing a show at this point? Watch the other hand. Watch the other hand.[24]

While Beck wonders if bin Laden was actually killed, others believe that bin Laden had been dead for some time and that he was "re-killed" on May 2. Antiwar activist Cindy Sheehan posted a lengthy blog about bin Laden in which she asserts the "re-killing" of bin Laden: "I have written over and over on my Facebook wall since this whole farce began that, even though I don't believe one word of the story yesterday, there are many things that OBL could be, but being killed yesterday by Navy SEALS was not one of them."[25]. Radio talk show host and blogger Alex Jones has claimed for some time that bin Laden died in 2002 and that "his corpse would be dragged out at the most politically expedient moment."[26] Irish pop musician Jim Corrs even created a parody movie poster: "Osama Zombie 6: They dug him up and killed him again."[27]

Global Media

In slightly over twenty years, Osama bin Laden went from being a relatively unknown wealthy Saudi to the world's "most wanted man." Global media made this shift—and the impact of bin Laden's actions around the world—possible.[28] Whether through the dissemination of bin Laden's ideas to those who followed and were inspired by him, or the provocation of fear among those who witnessed the terrorist attacks he organized, global media played the part of both witness and actor in the Global War on Terrorism. We can rephrase what Rohit Chopra says of Barack Obama to apply to bin Laden, that "media have been central to the processes by which the world and bin Laden have come to know each other."[29] The essays in this volume do not attempt to show how the global media represented bin Laden accurately or inaccurately but instead to use the figure "Osama bin Laden" as a window into the operations of global media in its relationship to the Global War on Terror.

There are numerous (contesting) biographies available that attempt to narrate bin Laden's life, whether from the point of view of how he came to lead Al Qaeda, of explaining "what went wrong" (how did the son of a successful Saudi family come to lead the world's most famous terrorist group), of how he was influenced by others (Zarkawi), of what he was like with his family, and so on. An increasing number of books are dedicated to the events surrounding bin Laden's life and death, and there are books that contain bin Laden's speeches and statements.[30]

It is not the intention of the essays in this volume to "define" Osama bin Laden. Indeed, representations of bin Laden are contradictory and shaped by the political, social, economic, cultural, and religious contexts of their authors. In looking at bin Laden's biography, Christina Hellmich asks: "Was Osama bin Laden an engineer, a business-school graduate, a playboy or a university dropout?"[31] Media representations cross the spectrum: as leader of Al Qaeda, was he "the most wanted man in the world" or a "beatific" leader?[32] While the dominant narrative in Western countries was of bin Laden as evil, Pew Research polls in the world's six predominantly Muslim countries showed majority favorable impressions of bin Laden in the years after 9/11: 72 percent in the Palestinian Territories, 59 percent in Indonesia, and 56 percent in Jordan.[33] The ambivalent nature of bin Laden's presence is captured on a T-shirt for sale in New York soon after 9/11. Next to the popular "Bin Laden—dead or alive" phrase was one that declared "Bin Laden—dead and alive."[34] The competing perceptions of bin Laden in the global media have led to a sense that his representations in media are themselves indistinct. Matt Frei of BBC1 called bin Laden "Al Qaeda's spectral anchorman," and Andrew Hill refers to bin Laden's "shape-shifting capacities."[35]

While it is one of the premises of this volume that there is not a single, knowable bin Laden, it is also not the case that the essays in this volume subscribe to a strategy of confusion; instead they focus on location and specificity. As authors in this volume show, media depictions of bin Laden not only diverge but often contradict each other depending upon the media provider (U.S. news or Al Jazeera), the global location of the viewer (United States, Europe, Pakistan, or India), the viewer's religious perspective and context (Muslim or Christian), or the media format (mainstream journalism versus gaming). These essays show that there are not multiple "bin Ladens" but instead multiple locations for representing and receiving "bin Laden." These multiple locations participate in what Arjun Appadurai has called "mediascapes," referring both to "the distribution of the electronic capabilities to produce and disseminate information . . . And to the images of the world created by these media," meaning that they "involve complicated inflections, depending on their mode . . . , their hardware . . . , their audiences . . . and the interests of those who own and control them."[36] Several essays pointedly compare the representations of bin Laden across national boundaries, religious perspectives, and media formats, concluding that who bin Laden is depends very much upon who controls the media coverage about him.

W. J. T. Mitchell reminds us that "images have social lives," and that "they are capable of detaching themselves from pictorial support and finding—potentially limitless—new hosts."[37] The authors in this volume underscore this point about images—of bin Laden, his wives, of other global figures—showing how their "lives" are taken up by seemingly contradictory producers and audiences. In approaching images, Mitchell advises us that if we wish "to locate them, give them an address, then the challenge is to place them, and to see them as landscapes or spaces."[38] By contributing to the articulation of the "landscapes" that are "Osama bin Laden," the essays in this volume inform our understanding and critique of today's global media landscape.

Why does this matter? Savvy users of the Internet today know that there are few individuals, issues, or images that have only one story associated with them and that media outlets themselves often present very different versions of the same events (think Fox News and MSNBC in the United States). What makes the stories about bin Laden distinctive is that these conflicting images and narratives are not just confusing or distracting; they have profound impacts on actions and policies around the world. In the Global War on Terrorism, Helga Tawil-Souri reminds us, "certain representations have become dominant and hegemonic, and shape the way in which reality is imagined and acted upon" to the extent that "it has become increasingly impossible to conceptualize reality in other ways."[39] This is a point reiterated by several authors in this volume. The impact of this conceptualization of reality is that nations, armies, citizens, and communities are mobilized, located, and reconfigured in their relationship to the Global War on Terrorism that has redefined the world since 9/11, with Osama bin Laden as the iconic thread that weaves these narratives together. Bin Laden's images and narratives are used to shape, motivate, justify, and rewrite the stories that are told around the world about terror and the actions that are taken as a result. Consequently, understanding the landscape that is "bin Laden" is more than a media exercise—it is a necessary component of understanding, critiquing, and rethinking the Global War on Terrorism.

More than just being vehicles for representing the Global War on Terrorism, the global media are themselves participants in this war. Donald Rumsfeld marked the distinctive change that media meant for the post-9/11 Global War on Terrorism: "In an era of e-mails, blogs, cell phones, BlackBerrys, Instant Messaging, digital cameras, a global Internet with no inhibitions, hand-held video cameras, talk radio, 24-hour news broadcasts, satellite television. There's never been a war fought in this environment before."[40] In the face of this new media context, André Nusselder argues that the Global War on Terrorism "is to a large extent a virtual war of images" that is "above all a conflict over the symbolic ordering of the world."[41] Media have become instrumental in this "virtual war" not only because of their pervasive presence but also because, as Ashley Marie Nellis and Joanne Savage remind us, Americans—and, indeed, many audiences around the world—"rely exclusively on the media for terrorism-related information."[42] Few have direct contact with terrorists, terrorist attacks, or those who are victims of them. Andrew Hill astutely calls such audience members "waiting subjects" because of the relationship that terrorism fosters in the media:

The waiting subject is a subject that is prey then to visions and imaginings in ways they attempt to ascertain what is to happen to them. How in the case of Western publics does the waiting subject imagine, conceive of, and comprehend the "distant places" which have figured as pivotal sites in the War on Terror? . . . How do these publics come to conceive of the relationship . . . between "the homeland" and the "faraway place"? And in turn, how do these publics come to comprehend the terms in which these faraway places have come to constitute a source of the threats they await?[43]

Consequently, media play an exceptional role in shaping understandings about who terrorists are (Al Qaeda? The United States?), why they should be feared ("pure evil" or "the Great Satan"), and what kind of fear audiences should feel.

Collectively, the essays in this volume speak to larger academic debates about the communicative relationships between political actors, media, and society. There exists robust research into the normative principles underlying these relationships from areas like political communication and critical terrorism studies. The unique vantage point of this volume, however, arises from using bin Laden and those associated with him as consistent "objects" of analysis across a range of contexts. In doing so, the authors provide opportunities for comparison across media formats, national boundaries, and political viewpoints, revealing in the process the complex operations and intersections of global media. Furthermore, the chapters bring into conversation various disciplinary fields (political science, media studies, cultural studies, comparative literature, etc.), and theoretical angles (such as critical terrorism studies, postcolonial theory, genre theory, feminism, representation, framing, social categorization theory, and narrative theory, to name a few) with the goal of encouraging readers to consider the complexity of debates surrounding bin Laden and the multiplicity of analytical tools with which his legacy is interpreted. By bringing together contributors from around the world who are writing about multiple media formats, from assorted disciplinary perspectives and with varying critical approaches, this volume contributes to increasing our understanding of the role of global media in a post-9/11 world. Because, as W. J. T. Mitchell puts it, "We not only think *about* media, we think *in* them," it is imperative that we hone our understanding of how media produce, disperse, mimic, target, sustain, recall, and figure and disfigure those who become the objects of its attentions.

Part I. Defining Political Actors

The essays in this volume underscore the point that there is no single "knowable" narrative about Osama bin Laden, Al Qaeda, and terrorism. The nature of that unknowability is not a result of yet-to-be-discovered evidence, but rather of limitations in the structures of knowledge that underpin the ways in which we think about and come to "know" terrorism. Global media contribute to those structures of knowledge, not only by disseminating the opinions of others but by structuring and restructuring images and narratives and by contributing to the construction of what comes to be seen as "fact" and "evidence."

Essays in the first section take on the question of how Osama bin Laden is positioned within structures of meaning that define, target, and enable him. It is here that the epistemology of bin Laden is most directly brought into question. Bin Laden captured the attention of the Western media and politicians by both promoting himself as a political actor and by fitting the expected notions of an individual at the head of a complex organization that is led by a charismatic individual. By looking at him as a political actor, Aditi Bhatia and Andrew Hill examine the force of bin Laden's own words, both in terms of his direct statements and in terms of the rhetorical structures that inform them. In contrast, Richard Jackson's essay on the meaning of bin Laden requires that we question the very practice of thinking through political actors. Jackson focuses on the adequacy of the epistemologies that the West has used to define who bin Laden is and, based on these definitions, determine how to act in relation to him.

Richard Jackson's defining essay, "Bin Laden's Ghost and the Epistemological Crises of Counterterrorism," opens this volume because of its seminal framing of analyses about Osama bin Laden and the media. In what may initially seem a counterintuitive move, Jackson argues that bin Laden's death is meaningless. Jackson's observation goes beyond what might seem an obvious fact—bin Laden's death has not meant the disappearance of Al Qaeda, and terrorism did not stop as a result of it—to make a broader and more important point about the way in which knowledge about terrorism is constructed, disseminated, and acted upon: that there is an "epistemological crisis" surrounding the construction of meaning about bin Laden and Al Qaeda.

In the post-9/11 period, Jackson points to the multiple and conflicting narratives of bin Laden and Al Qaeda as evidence of the difficulties of constructing meaning. As he points out, these conflicting narratives result from the use of different sources of evidence and, more importantly, from the ontological conceptions that dictate the kinds of data that are selected. Given the unprecedented global resources that have been committed to "knowing" Al Qaeda, it is astounding that, as Jackson puts it, it remains "an essentially unknown entity." Consequently, Jackson argues that there is an "adoption of ontological uncertainty as a fundamental condition of terrorism knowledge." One of the most significant implications of Jackson's argument is that this uncertainty is more than simply a lamentable situation; it has consequences for political actors. By accepting these uncertainties—what Donald Rumsfeld called the "unknown unknown"—as a "fact" of terrorism, political actors are limiting the kinds of information they are willing to consider in decision making. For Jackson, such limitations include "the knowledge generated within the military-intellectual system that anti-American terrorism is primarily caused by U.S. military intervention overseas," or the conclusion that "terrorists are no longer understandable as political actors."

A direct result of this epistemological crisis is, Jackson argues, the opening of the space of fantasy as a form of "knowing." The lack of firm knowledge about bin Laden and Al Qaeda has led to the projection of fantasies to make up for the lack of confirmed meaning. Because bin Laden and Al Qaeda took the world by surprise once, how might they surprise again? Such fantasies—usually the stuff of Hollywood films and thriller novels—show up in Western security practices that respond to imagined terrorist activities such as airport searches of baby diapers or protection of candy machines that could be used by terrorists to spread contaminated food. Jackson puts it most powerfully: "Once it is accepted that we essentially do not know where, when or how terrorists might strike . . . then the only way to detect and deal with them is to try to *imagine* what they might do." To return to the subject of this volume, Jackson argues that bin Laden's death may heighten the use of fantasy and speculation as tools of analysis and forms of response to terrorism. Without the figure of bin Laden as a focal point of the Global War on Terrorism, and without bin Laden's own media statements to provide a scaffolding for terrorism narratives, speculation as a mode of thinking may increase.

Aditi Bhatia argues in her chapter, "The Discursive Portrayals of Osama bin Laden," that the Global War on Terrorism is largely a metaphorical battle whose sides can be represented by the figures of Osama bin Laden and George W. Bush. While others have also examined the rhetorical similarities between these two men,[44] Bhatia revisits these ideas to remind readers of the Manichaean tendencies prevalent in both religious and political discourse. Focusing on three dominant dichotomies—*Good* versus *Evil, Civilization* versus *Barbarism*, and *Moral Justice* versus *Retribution*—Bhatia shows how the rhetoric used by both figures shows similar structure and patterns, with each side positioning the other as evil, barbaric, and immoral. Because global media remain dominated by the West and by the narratives employed by its producers, Bhatia's essay is an important reminder that "the other" not only has a voice but also articulates its positions in similar dichotomies.

Bhatia's chief focus in her essay is on the ways in which both bin Laden and Bush use religious discourse to achieve similar goals: "the objectification of their individual, ideologically simulated conceptualizations of reality." Bin Laden's use of Islam and Bush's use of Christianity create similar foundations from which each draws his objectification of the other. Importantly, Bhatia concludes that the "battle" between the sides represented by bin Laden and Bush cannot be defused without a deep understanding of the "cultural contexts, political histories, and affiliations" that inform the logic of each side. Expecting one side to "win" this rhetorical battle reveals a limited understanding of the dense structures of meaning that inform each set of arguments.

In highlighting the use of religious discourse as a focal point for her essay, Bhatia makes more complex our understanding about the role of political actors in the Global War on Terrorism. By focusing on religious references in the rhetoric of bin Laden and Bush, she shows how difficult it would be to sever either of these individual political actors from the cultural discourse they employ in their rhetoric. In doing so, Bhatia furthers Jackson's argument about the "meaninglessness" of bin Laden's death; the rhetorical dichotomies that underlie the Global War on Terrorism did not disappear with bin Laden (or, for that matter, with the election of Barack Obama). Without a better understanding of the rhetorical structures that underlie discourses on terrorism, the role of political actors and the media cannot be well understood.

In his evocative chapter, "The bin Laden Tapes," Andrew Hill looks back to the time before Osama bin Laden's death and then reflects on the period after his death. The exercise reminds us of the intimidation factor bin Laden wielded—through both his media ubiquity and his simultaneous physical elusiveness. Hill examines Bin Laden's video and audio appearances after the September 11 attacks in order "to scrutinize both the means by which these appearances have allowed bin Laden to continue to intervene in the War on Terror, and the terms in which they have served to shape perceptions in the West of the nature of the enemy faced in this conflict." Although bin Laden functioned "as a metonym for Al Qaeda and the enemy more broadly in the War on Terror," his death did not eliminate the threats—real or perceived—posed by Al Qaeda. Indeed, Hill argues that the West can be said to have "exorcised" Osama bin Laden by shifting the narrative from that of hunting for the world's leading terrorist to that of "Obama got Osama."

As discussed repeatedly in this volume, most people know bin Laden only through his mediated presence. For years, bin Laden goaded his opponents with threats and accusations through his video appearances. Each release served as a potent reminder of his enemies' inability to find him despite conducting the most intensive manhunt in history. As Hill describes, "bin Laden's video appearances acquire an added aura of defiance, demonstrating that despite the measures taken to achieve a sighting of him, he can persist in making himself seen across the globe—apparently if and when he so wishes—without being captured or destroyed." Hill argues that bin Laden acquired a type of demonic, spectral presence: "the absence of the hard Real of his physical presence allow[ed] him to remain beyond the grasp of his captors." Until his death, bin Laden existed largely as a malevolent voice and disembodied form; the object whose physical presence—a precondition for his capture or killing—seemed beyond the reach of the world's most powerful nations. "Locating Bin Laden in these terms serves to illuminate the scale of the fears associated with him, in suggesting he is able to enact a form of total or universal haunting from which it is impossible to escape." And yet, with his death, escape appears to have come. In terms of the extent to which bin Laden continues to constitute a rallying figure for his followers and future supporters, the evidence is uncertain. When he was alive, bin Laden created a "sense of ontological indeterminacy associated with the ghostly [. . . that] constituted a key element in the fears and fantasies associated with the threat both he and the enemy more generally [were] conceived as presenting to the West." The significance of his death then, argues Hill, occurred on two levels. "In addition to a biological death—death in the Real—it is possible to speak of another type of death—death in the Symbolic, the death of a subject's signifying status, and the capacity of their name and actions to continue to register in the way they had once done." The Obama administration's decision to refuse the release of any images of bin Laden's death (or burial) might be "understood as striving to bring about his second, Symbolic death. [. . .] It is in this attempt to bring about bin Laden's Symbolic death that Operation Neptune Spear can be said to constitute a type of exorcism." Indeed, bin Laden himself may have contributed to his own symbolic exorcism due to his lack of visibility and seeming inability to carry out attacks either personally or through Al Qaeda during his final years. Hill points to the last images we have of bin Laden—sitting on the floor wrapped in a blanket and watching himself on TV—to underscore the shift in who is haunting whom: "in these video excerpts a monstrous source of evil is revealed as nothing more than a frail, lonely figure, sitting alone in a room."

Part II. Comparing Global News Media

Political actors play a fundamental role in defining a figure like Osama bin Laden and his perceived significance on the world stage. But as with the messages of bin Laden himself, most people's exposure to the perspectives of political actors is indirect; that is to say, it is mediated. This mediation comes through many channels and is continually shaped in the process by issues such as language, context, geography, and media form. The second section of this volume examines the interplay between context and media in representing bin Laden and the Global War on Terrorism, paying particular attention to the news media. News media are a distinctly important link in the process of political communication due to their power as intermediaries between political actors and the rest of society. Their contributions to discourse, both actively and passively, have deep-seated impacts on social perceptions and political decision making.

It may be a modern truism to declare that people experience global events and actors primarily through media. Less obvious, however, are the contradictions and consequences of today's mediated environment. Media bring the world closer to us, yet their very use illustrates how removed from events we really are. Media inform us and depict what we cannot see for ourselves, yet their representations are, by nature, selective and habitual. Media provide us with unprecedented tools for collective awareness, yet individuals are increasingly overwhelmed by information and entertainment flows. Osama bin Laden was surely "known" to most people only through his media representations, making him a particularly useful case for examining these distinct conditions of our contemporary mediated environment. It is certainly another truism that bin Laden and his network were at the center of a discourse on terrorism that has reshaped geopolitics in the twenty-first century. Examining the media's role in crafting and circulating this discourse—especially the news media—contributes to a greater understanding of public perceptions and the policies that followed from them after September 11, 2001.

The extraordinary circumstances connected to Osama bin Laden's life and death bring to the fore issues of geography and intimacy, media production and representation, spectacle and sense making. Chapters in the second section speak to each of these elements within our contemporary mediated environment by examining important relationships between Osama bin Laden—the phenomenon—and the diverse global news media that represented him. For years, bin Laden was simply "out there" in an unknown location, geographically removed from the experiences of ordinary citizens. Though his physical whereabouts remained a mystery for many years, as a globally mediated figure he was always intimately accessible. This was no coincidence. As noted previously, bin Laden himself labored to get maximum exposure by exploiting both the Internet's growing reach and terrorism's reciprocal relationship with the news media. He did manage to transcend physical boundaries, but his messages always remained subject to the myriad of contexts through which they cascaded. By applying comparative approaches, each author in this section uses variations in context as analytical devices to explore contrasting representations of bin Laden. Whether comparing Al Jazeera to Al Qaeda, German and British tabloids, bin Laden's wives in Anglo-American and Arab news coverage, or bin Laden's death with those of Saddam Hussein and Muammar el-Qaddafi, these four chapters illustrate how specific social, political, cultural, and communicative contexts can impact our perceptions of global actors and the events surrounding them.

In addition to the issues of geography and intimacy, the mechanics of media production and representation are other recurrent themes in this section. Factors such as media routines and news norms shape content in significant ways. In turn, that content shapes social perceptions and attitudes. As discussed in the previous section, political actors on all sides operated from the premise of media's capacity to shape social perceptions and often exploited these conditions in an effort to influence media representations for their own political advantage. During the Global War on Terrorism, battlefronts were fought with tenacity both on the ground and through the media. News media professionals, of course, are not simply slaves to routine and manipulation. They are also actors in their own right, serving as a kind of distillation point for social discourse. News and information flow through them and are actively shaped in the process. In the wake of 9/11, for example, Hellmich describes how "virtually overnight, journalists became the most influential commentators in the field . . . because their words and their analyses of the situation reached many people first."[45] Even after distillation, the amount of information and "news" about bin Laden and his associates became simply overwhelming in volume. This was largely driven by the public's heightened interest in him. Regardless of one's affiliations, for years there existed a global audience for information about bin Laden's activities and whereabouts. His case is therefore instructive for what it says about the ways in which political actors, news media, and society interact under exceptional circumstances.

Despite the extraordinary circumstances that produced bin Laden himself as an object of media, however, a study of bin Laden and global news media may actually reify more normative principles than exceptions. Across time, space, format, and focus of inquiry, many embedded principles of media operation and attraction reveal themselves in these four chapters. The authors demonstrate such phenomena as the news media's tendency to echo Manichean political narratives, and they exhibit how intimacy, horror, and voyeurism underpin terrorism's mediation. The use of social categorizations (in-groups and out-groups), narratives, framing devices, and the penchant for spectacle are familiar themes in all the examined media—in addition to the persistent issues of context, media production, and representation previously discussed. It is especially telling that such similarities arise considering the significant differences between the four essays in this section. As a collective, the authors examine language and imagery, primary and secondary political actors, and different times and locations. They cover a broad spectrum of media formats, including tabloids and broadsheets, print and broadcast journalism, as well as text, images, and video. They also look at news products in different countries and languages. Even bin Laden himself is not always the central focus: Al Jazeera, Al Qaeda, bin Laden's wives, Saddam Hussain, and Muammar el-Qaddafi feature prominently in the respective essays. Ultimately, this breadth speaks to the vast configuration of signs and symbols associated with bin Laden, which the authors skillfully reassemble in different contexts to show important relationships between social discourses and the sense-making process.

In her chapter, "Words and War: Al Jazeera and Al Qaeda," Courtney C. Radsch explores globalization, resistance, and identity as forces shaping the relationship between Osama bin Laden and the Qatar-based Al Jazeera news network. As powerful alternatives to the American status quo, the two networks are bound up in each other. Like many of the other authors in this volume, Radsch describes a dominant friend/enemy paradigm in the years following 9/11 that pitted Al Qaeda's terrorists against America and the West: It reflected an ideological dichotomy of fundamentalism versus neoliberalism, which replaced the Cold War's communism-versus-liberalism paradigm as the central grand narrative. Actors on both "sides" encouraged this black-and-white narrative, and Al Jazeera both suffered and benefited from this condition. Self-branded as an alternative to Western news hegemony and offering exclusive access to people and places close to America's conflicts, it was not long before many people inexorably linked Al Jazeera with Al Qaeda. Radsch notes that, although damaging in some contexts, the controversies surrounding Al Jazeera's relationship to Al Qaeda simultaneously contributed to the station's meteoric rise.

Through the paradigm of this bipolar world order, one's enemies seemingly come into clear focus. On one side, bin Laden and his supporters effectively portrayed the United States and its allies as the purveyors of discontent. Conversely, after the attacks of 9/11, George W. Bush and his allies "used the concept of the enemy to create social solidarity and reconstruct collective conscience to allow [the United States] to invade Iraq and restrict civil liberties." In short, Radsch contends, "radical Islamists and neoliberals served each other's political needs since each group was strengthened and identified in opposition to its ideological Other." Like much of the global news media, Al Jazeera amplified these dichotomous characterizations through their coverage. Unlike their American counterparts, however, Al Jazeera portrayed these conflicts more in line with Arab public opinion, tying them closely with the Israeli-Palestinian conflict, the invasion of Iraq, and the U.S. military presence in the Arabian Peninsula. Al Jazeera's representations were distinct manifestations of its particular geography and context. In turn, this influenced how people around the world made sense of the station and its content. Given the prevalence of Manichean thinking at the time, it seems almost inevitable that Al Jazeera's practices—indeed its very existence—situated it clearly in the counter-hegemonic camp by people on all sides of the conflict.

Ultimately, Radsch argues that psychological factors can prove more significant than numerical or physical superiority in such ideological conflicts. It is here that both Osama bin Laden and Al Jazeera may have had their biggest impact on the world stage. By simply questioning U.S. moral leadership and its role as the sole superpower, they have added fissures to the perceived authority of the United States. She argues that if hegemony derives power from operating on an unquestioned basis, then foregrounding such fissures can contribute to a decline in U.S. hegemonic power. "The use of force, in Iraq and elsewhere, undermined consent and the legitimacy of values, norms, and other such intangibles. Al Qaeda brought this contestation to the forefront while Al Jazeera ensured the world was aware of these challenges." Even with the death of bin Laden, efforts to present an ideological alternative to U.S. hegemony continue. "Although it will take a lot more to destroy America than a few attacks," concludes Radsch, "the U.S. and Western *response* to Al Qaeda's terrorism and Al Jazeera's coverage may be what ultimately undoes American hegemony by weakening America's moral authority and consent to its normative ideals." Meanwhile, Al Jazeera's legacy as either a villain or a hero is still being negotiated on the airwaves and in the presses. To see this battle in action, one needs only to look at the recent controversy surrounding Al Jazeera's 2013 purchase of Al Gore's cable station, Current TV. Dichotomous characterizations, heightened emotions, and political opportunism are familiar themes as the station tries to enter the U.S. media market more than a decade after the 9/11 attacks.

Alexander Spencer's chapter, "Metaphorizing Terrorism: Al Qaeda in German and British Tabloids," also deals with ideology and hegemony, though he moves the discussion from issues of geopolitics and media production to the power of words. He declares that "until fairly recently there has been little interest in the perception of terrorism and role of language and discourse in the construction of 'the terrorist.'" Specifically, he focuses on metaphors as mechanisms that project "understandings from one conceptual area, such as war, to a different area, such as terrorism, [... thus naturalizing] specific countermeasures while placing other options outside of the mainstream debate." In doing so, he argues that the influence of metaphors extends into both the realm of public perception and policymaking.

Spencer illustrates this by examining metaphors about bin Laden that dominated in German and British tabloids following four large Al Qaeda attacks: September 11, 2001; the 2002 bombings in Bali; the 2004 train bombings in Madrid; and the 2005 London Underground attacks. He identifies four particular "metaphorization[s] of terrorism" that cross both time periods and borders: Terrorism is war; Terrorism is crime; Terrorism is uncivilized evil; and Terrorism is a disease. Each suggests a particular frame for interpreting these terrorist acts, which in turn works to confine the locus of discussion and its ensuing policy responses. For example, Spencer reminds us that constituting terrorism as "war" calls for a military response, as was conducted against Afghanistan, Iraq, and elsewhere under the grand metaphor of the War on Terror. His second conceptual metaphor, that terrorism is "crime," helped naturalize certain judicial responses. Certainly, news media frequently framed controversial changes in domestic policies and the debates over international terrorism laws through such a metaphor. Third, Spencer claims that the metaphor of terrorism as "uncivilized evil" provided a psychological basis for "concrete and clear polarization, as it outcasts the actor and his or her actions and dichotomizes and antagonizes *them* (the out-group) and *us* (the in-group)." He contends that this social categorization "increasingly constructs the terrorist as something 'other' and generally alien and foreign, which then makes counterterrorism measures—such as tighter border and immigration controls—possible and appropriate in order to keep such elements out." Finally, as with the metaphor of "evil," that of "disease" confers terrorists as people beyond reason. The implication is that nonmilitary options for response or prevention are ultimately fruitless.

Spencer cautions that "there is no one-to-one relationship between reality and metaphors, as we cannot observe physical events directly but do so in a particular interpretative context and through discourse." That is—reinforcing one of the key themes of this volume—experiences of empirical events shape discourse, and discourse shapes experiences. This mutually constitutive relationship compels us to consider the role of language in our understanding of a subject with terrorism's gravity. Spencer examines both the mediated specter of bin Laden as the central protagonist representing Al Qaeda, and Al Qaeda as the archetypical terrorist organization. Spencer's chapter provides insights into some of the linguistic mechanisms by which tabloid media told this global drama in two different Western contexts, thus illuminating some of the important discursive backdrop to bin Laden's story. Spencer's analysis reminds us again how issues of geography, representation, and sense making come together within our contemporary mediated environment to shape how audiences "know" a figure like bin Laden.

In the third essay of this section, "The Myth of the Terrorist as a Lover: Competing Regional Media Frames," Noha Mellor examines media coverage of Osama bin Laden in Anglo-American and Arab news sources. Like the other contributions in this section, Mellor's international scope illustrates geographical variations, the content she examines underscores issues of representation, and her analysis explores the process by which meanings about bin Laden are constructed. Mellor's particular angle is in her attention to intimacy and spectacle. Mellor focuses exclusively on coverage about bin Laden's relationships with his wives. She describes how bin Laden's sexuality and personal relationships—often no more than speculation—were used in Anglo-American contexts to further demonize him as barbaric and primal. Of course, sex also sells: "Indeed, the focus on sex and sexuality is one strategy of the tabloid journalists to attract readers' attention." However, Arab media appears to have covered bin Laden's partners in quite a different light. Arab journalists focused more often on the societal circumstances surrounding bin Laden's family and depicted his wives' loyalty as acts motivated by their faith, rather than by sexuality or blind obedience.

Mellor discusses common practices in the news-making process that underlie the circulation and interpretation of these stories among different communities. "Because news communicates through narrative, it rests on the construction and dissemination of known cultural myths, understood not as false tales but as narratives that are grounded in specific cultural values and ideologies. Such narratives then reflect a certain (cultural) view of the world, and it inevitably includes archetypes such as heroes, villains, and victims." Journalists utilize these conventional storylines to reduce the complexity of news into short vignettes. The continual retelling of cultural myths in such a way thus naturalizes certain interpretations of events, facts, and characters to make them appear commonsensical. The power of myth in the news is particularly noteworthy because it rests on journalistic claims of objectivity and factuality, even when drawn from predefined narratives. The circulation of myths through the news may be a common factor of production in any environment. However, the content of the myths themselves is highly contextual. Mellor's analysis of the myths embedded in news coverage of bin Laden's wives is provocative for the questions it raises about the disparate ways of "knowing" between world regions and communities.

Bin Laden's wives are perhaps supporting characters in a larger story, but they did receive notable coverage in both Arab and Anglo-American media—especially his last wife, Amal Assadah. What is most telling, however, is not the quantity of coverage about these women, but rather the qualitative differences between their representations in Arabic and English media. Arab news used humanitarian narratives, telling such stories as the tragedy of "mothers and widows detained in a foreign country and in need of help from the Arab states, particularly Saudi Arabia, to facilitate their release and their return to Saudi Arabia." By contrast, Mellor shows that Anglo-American media chose to focus on bin Laden's wives as mostly objects at the control of a sexual being. Such depictions contributed to—and also reflected—the broader myth of bin Laden as "neurotic evil." Media fascination with the Al Qaeda's women is likely to continue for years to come. Mellor's attention to bin Laden's wives gives us some indication of how this attention will be shaped by media in different regions of the globe.

The final chapter in this section addresses the significance of visual communication. What we "know" and how we know are not just functions of words and language; they are also influenced profoundly by imagery. In their piece, "Images of our Dead Enemies: Visual Representations of bin Laden, Hussein, and el-Qaddafi," Susan Moeller, Joanna Nurmis, and Saranaz Barforoush provide a comparative analysis of visual representations surrounding the killing of today's most infamous tyrants. The variation in their analysis is not so much one of geography, but rather of person. The subject of death and the manner of its visual portrayal (or lack thereof) accentuate the issue of intimacy over proximity. Here again, media norms and social context dictate the representation of events. Minutes after President Obama's announcement of bin Laden's killing, "news outlets across the world scrambled to cover the story of the decade. With no immediately forthcoming photos of bin Laden's corpse . . . [they] had a set of decisions to make about what kind of image to select to accompany the announcement." This chapter examines how those choices helped frame bin Laden's death for a watching world and directed the public to a particular understanding of it.

Today, journalists are increasingly framing news using digital information and visuals that come from nontraditional sources. Moeller and her colleagues describe how these tangled connections blur "the lines between 'mainstream' journalism and 'citizen' journalism, between breaking news that is first reported by professional journalists, and 'news' that is published via YouTube, Twitter, or Facebook by people who happen to be 'on location.'" In today's fast-paced, digitalized news environment the public expect immediate access to uncensored information—though with instances of death and destruction, news media must still negotiate a careful balance between explicit portrayals and public sensitivities. Where they draw the line, Moeller and her coauthors point out, depends significantly on who the dead are. "When someone has died who is believed to be guilty of violent aggression, war crimes, or crimes against humanity, all too often a blood lust rises among those who consider themselves to be victims, even victims by proxy. Audiences want to see the formerly all-powerful persecutor 'taken down.'" Osama bin Laden is an instructive example of such a situation where digital convergence, expedience, and blood lust intersected on a grand scale. Without official visual evidence of his death, however, the media were compelled to draw upon other sources in framing the story. In evaluating the choices they made at that time, this chapter argues that it is instructive to consider the deaths of Saddam Hussein in 2006 and Muammar el-Qaddafi five years later. The histories of these three men as "enemies of the West," and the literal circumstances of their capture and deaths, provide instructive cases about the powers of visual representation. In each situation, citizens—as audiences and occasionally "news sources"—had profound impacts on how the news media framed these stories.

Moeller and her colleagues situate their analysis within broader conceptual debates about the very nature of evidence and the perennial question of whether seeing (in person or virtually) is believing. The authors ask, "if the fact of a death really matters—politically, militarily, even emotionally—is it enough to take someone else's word for it, to just simply hear (or read) a narrative account of that death?" Indeed, a photograph appears to provide relatively neutral "evidence" when portraying a death. Video footage can have similar believability, especially when shot on scene. Both place the viewer intimately within, but at a safe distance from, the events they appear to represent. Nevertheless, viewers are simultaneously aware these representations are only simulacra for direct visual knowledge. Using the cases of Osama bin Laden, Saddam Hussein, and Muammar el-Qaddafi, the authors address such deep-seated contradictions of our mediated environment and remind us again that "framing is one of the most inevitable, yet at the same time most complex, of all media actions."

News media, however, do not comprise the totality of media forms. Expressions of popular culture also provide significant reflections of social experience as manifested through various media outlets, like films, posters, bumper stickers, and video games. Where the news media boast objectivity, popular culture exudes subjectivity. This window into popular expression is the subject of the final section in this volume.

Part III. Engaging Popular Cultures

Osama bin Laden was not a movie star, a pop singer, or a television celebrity. Why, then, focus critical attention on bin Laden and popular cultures? "Terrorism," as Susan Moeller says, "is about getting the public's attention."[46] A popular culture analysis of Osama bin Laden and terrorism reminds us that there are multiple ways in which to get and sustain "attention" and that "attention" itself takes multiple expressive forms. While Osama bin Laden is responsible for orchestrating the most effective attention-getting act of terrorism in history in the attacks on the World Trade Center, the televised images of the attacks are not the only ways in which messages about terrorism—and specifically characterizations of the figure held responsible for the 9/11 attacks, Osama bin Laden—were disseminated in global cultures. In addition to news media, posters, blogs, cartoons, speeches, film, video games, and word-of-mouth all contributed to how people learned of events surrounding Osama bin Laden—and, indeed, about bin Laden himself. The essays in this section affirm Maura Conway's point that, while "it is through media consumption that a majority of individuals learn about terrorism . . . it is not through 'news media' alone that this learning takes place."[47]

More importantly, while audiences learn information about Osama bin Laden, terrorism, the "Ummah," or the World Trade Center attacks through more than news media, audiences *process* what they see and learn through the popular narratives that provide sense and meaning to events that otherwise may seem disjunctive, overwhelming, or fearful. Renata Salecl explains that "When people feel uncertain and afraid they are in search of clear images of their enemies."[48] Both the "beatific" images of bin Laden that appeared on T-shirts "throughout the Muslim world" and the poster of bin Laden being anally penetrated by the Empire State Building that appeared in New York a few days after 9/11 provide popular meaning for audiences by signaling sense-making narratives: bin Laden as the "religious Robin Hood" who brought justice to those who suffered from American military actions or bin Laden as the object of violent, sexualized retribution for the 9/11 attacks ("The Empire Strikes Back . . . So you like skyscrapers, huh, bitch?"[49]).

What Andreas Behnke and Benjamin de Carvalho argue about international relations scholarship—that it "is not about whether popular culture is relevant . . . but about how it is relevant"[50]—stands as the theme for this third section: that it is not a question of whether popular culture should be considered in an examination of bin Laden and global media, but instead a question of how popular culture across the globe is used as a mechanism for disseminating, comprehending, and making sense of the globally recognized persona, "Osama bin Laden."

Television, magazines, newspapers, films, posters, T-shirts, cartoons, websites, blogs, comic books, video games, signs, caricatures—around the world, images of Osama bin Laden were disseminated widely across media formats. Indeed, bin Laden's image was so widely propagated that his image itself became less a representation of a person than a cultural object in its own right, carrying less value as a depiction of a person than as an icon with broad and varying symbolic value. Whether as a "terrorist" or a "hero," as an object of hatred or reverence, "Osama bin Laden" as a cultural image carried broad meanings that varied across audiences and publics the world over. These signifiers captured many of the emotional tenors that surrounded the cultural object of bin Laden: anger, reverence, fear, hero worship, revenge, to name a few. Most importantly, popular culture images intersected with news discourse and political rhetoric to provide underlying sense-making narratives.

Within today's global media context, Osama bin Laden has been one of media's most recognized figures. In the ten weeks after 9/11, for example, bin Laden's image appeared in the United States on the covers of *Time* and *Newsweek* five times, more than President Bush.[51] A Google search in 2014 of the name "bin Laden" turns up 150,000,000 references, with an additional 116,000,000 images, indicating the degree to which Osama bin Laden's name has become a part of global media culture. He was called "the most hunted and arguably hated person this century" with "one of the most famous faces in the world."[52]

The cultural icon "Osama bin Laden" was propagated in other forms as well. Australian artist Priscilla Bracks sparked controversy by using popular morphing imagery to merge bin Laden's image into that of Jesus Christ, while other morphing games allowed players to change bin Laden's image themselves.[53] In the United States, bin Laden was the object of jokes by comedians and humorists. Late-night talk show host and comedian David Letterman offered one of his standard "top ten reasons" jokes about bin Laden: "Top Ten Ways bin Laden can improve his image. 10. There's no way he can improve his image. He's a murdering, soul-less asshole."[54] (The remaining nine items on the list are blank.) Entire web pages are devoted to jokes about bin Laden. Others are devoted to cartoons.[55] One internet list even includes anagrams of bin Laden's name ("do a samba, Lenin").[56]

Through video games, audiences were invited to join in the hunt for bin Laden. In "Kill Osama bin Laden," players are instructed to "snipe terrorists and take out Osama bin Laden. Once dead, cut off his head for proof to the government."[57] What Ian Bogost has called "tabloid games" also feature bin Laden. "Ogama Ben Ladder," for example, has players control a falling bin Laden, trying to avoid dangerous objects or, as one reviewer put it, "hit them. The rag doll Bin Laden likeness bruises, loses limbs and bleeds as he hits objects during the fall, until he finally succumbs to his injuries."[58] With even more graphic opportunities to harm bin Laden, games such as "Osamagotchi" offer players the chance to "do with him what you want, even throw missils [sic] and knifes [sic], very original."[59] The magazine *Political Humor* lists some of the "humorous" games that enable players to box with bin Laden ("put him down for the count"), "fire missiles and splatter bin Laden all over the desert" ("Bend Over bin Laden"), or to take him as a prisoner and ponder "how will you treat him" (Alquaidomon).[60]

Bin Laden's dead body—real or imagined—is so frequently referenced that it constitutes a category of its own, with over three million images available on the Web. In perhaps the ultimate confirmation of its allure, bin Laden's dead body was used as bait for a computer scam, with an email message inviting recipients to view bin Laden's captured or hanged body as a lure to download a computer virus.[61] In the days immediately after bin Laden's death, hackers took advantage of the attention the story was getting to develop multiple internet scams. "This is one of those rare opportunities that can build you a great list and a couple of zeros in your profit," an anonymous hacker crowed. "Use it while the news of Bin Laden killed by US forces is hot. I just started one and it had 600 likes in 2 minutes."[62]

In her analysis of "Osamakitsch," Tracey J. Potts argues that, in dealing with cultural objects, one has to be "mindful of the specific manner of their production and consumption."[63] To that end, the essays in this section begin the project specification of how "Osama bin Laden" has been produced as a cultural object and for what purposes. We begin with an examination of video games before moving into cinema and then popular culture writ large. The section ends with an exploration of grand narratives about bin Laden, terrorism, and Islam as expressed through U.S. popular culture to highlight some of the broad social implications of such totalizing expressions.

In "Congratulations! You Have Killed Osama bin Laden!!" Simon Ferrari posits that the fact that the field of video games—as both a product and an object of critique—has not yet been codified makes it an appropriate location for studying the political and cultural narratives surrounding bin Laden and the Global War on Terrorism, since these too are areas in which critique and, indeed, product has yet to be solidified. An examination of bin Laden video games provides a glimpse at short-term cultural "sense-making." While cultural products such as film, television, or written narrative take time to process and produce, the video games that Ferrari highlights are—often with low quality and without industry support—a short-term response to cultural events. In his essay for this volume, Ferrari looks particularly at a segment that he calls "newsgames," those video games that perform "one of the functions or goals of journalistic endeavor."

Ferrari introduces readers to the gamut of newsgames about bin Laden. The first game, entitled "Bad Dudes vs Bin Laden," was produced just three days after 9/11. The action of the game is straightforward: bin Laden is tracked by a Secret Service agent to a "Middle Eastern marketplace" where the player can deliver a series of punches and kicks to the bin Laden figure, culminating in a "Finish Him" kick that removes bin Laden's head. In the years following 9/11, games continued to feature such retributive attacks on bin Laden's person, adding elements of torture that, as Ferrari points out, prefigure some of the images later seen from Abu Ghraib. The production of bin Laden newsgames resurged after the news of his death, shifting to more documentary games that place players in the compound in Abbottabad. Continuing to emphasize the rapidity of response to events, Ferrari points to the version of the popular "Counter-Strike" series that adds a segment, "Fight Yard Abbottabad," in which multiplayer teams fight "terrorists" in a simulated likeness of the compound in which bin Laden had been living for six years.

In addition to providing an opportunity to understand a newer form of global media, Ferrari's essay foregrounds an aspect of global media that is mentioned in other essays in this volume—the creation of "news" by those who are not journalists. Importantly, Ferrari points out that these contributions often enable expressions that are deemed inappropriate for mainstream media, such as the blood and gore of the violent games that target the "real" figure, Osama bin Laden. In the end, Ferrari points out, such newsgames "are about how he made us feel, about us rather than him."

Returning to the issue of bin Laden's "ghost" as discussed separately by both Jackson and Hill in part I of this volume, Purnima Bose's chapter, "Without Osama: *Tere Bin Laden* and the Critique of the War on Terror," analyzes an Indian independent film, *Tere Bin Laden*, in which bin Laden never actually appears but in which his image, speeches, and actions impact all of the film's main characters.[64] The film is a critique of global media, the Global War on Terrorism, the U.S. security state, and the aspiring middle class in Pakistan, and its plot revolves around a series of fake bin Laden tapes manufactured by an Indian journalist who has been mistakenly placed on a terrorist watch list and who hopes that the profit from selling the videos will enable him to purchase a falsified passport that will gain him entry to the United States. Bose's trenchant analysis reveals the ways in which the icon, "Osama bin Laden," has both literal and cultural currency across the globe. As she explains, "In the mediated landscape of the twenty-first century, Osama bin Laden exists as a handy empty signifier that multiple agents can manipulate for different kinds of economic, professional, and geographic mobility." Bose's essay reminds us that conversations about global media are about more than media formats, representational choices, and narrative styles but instead are deeply intertwined with global economic flows, national power, and geographies of both individual and regional positioning.

Most pointedly, Bose shows how individuals across the globe use global media to profit from bin Laden, even (and perhaps especially) a fake bin Laden. Whether the Pakistani journalist who ends up emigrating to the United States, the man who faked bin Laden's voice who ended up founding the Communist Party of Pakistan, or the U.S. director of Intelligence who participates in the final fake bin Laden tape rather than admit he was fooled by it and is subsequently promoted to secretary of defense—all achieve successful careers for themselves as a direct result of their participation in the manufacturing of "bin Laden" as a media product. Through her critique of this satirical film, Bose reminds us that the global media version of "bin Laden" has become an industry in its own right, whether in the United States, Pakistan, India, or elsewhere around the world.

In "Obama bin Laden [*sic*]: How to Win the War on Terror #likeaboss" Ryan Croken speaks directly to the sense-making role of popular culture in his analysis of the cultural "confusion" that existed in the United States between Osama bin Laden and Barack Obama. Croken uses the cultural slippages (Obama/ Osama), conspiratorial elisions (Obama is Osama), and religious assumptions (Obama, like Osama, is Muslim) that surround Osama and Obama as points for analyzing racialized dynamics that underlie narratives of U.S. exceptionalism, military power, and global dominance. Croken's essay points us to some of the myriad streams through which popular culture effects its messages: T-shirts, web tools (photo morphing), memes, hip-hop, tweets, YouTube videos, and the like. Attending to these media formats is an essential component of examining sense-making across the complexities of U.S. cultures. In contrast to the mainstream media, which is more unidirectional in its distribution, the popular media formats examined by Croken are most often user-generated. In using what he calls "digital minstrelsy ventriloquism," for example, Croken shows how users create new meanings from existing videos (for example, of Obama's walk to the podium to make the announcement about bin Laden's death) by editing the videos and adding sound tracks from existing songs ("Like a Boss").

Importantly, Croken uses this focus on the negotiations and creations of meaning in popular narratives to argue that the "confusion" between Osama and Obama is more than just difficulty with name pronunciation, lack of familiarity with Islam, or merging of nonwhite skin color, but is instead a complex negotiation of racial intersections with national narratives. The interplay in U.S. cultural meanings between nonwhite African Americans and nonwhite Arabs positions African Americans to be aligned with U.S. national goals in opposition to the Muslim Other, a narrative in which Obama can redeem his own "Americanness" and put to rest questions about his own national belonging by killing his "brother," Osama bin Laden.

Brigitte L. Nacos reminds us in her essay, "Muslims in America and the Post-9/11 Terrorism Debates: Media and Public Opinion," that there are intimate intersections between popular culture, mainstream media, and political actions. In her discussion of representations in U.S. media of bin Laden, terrorists, and Muslims, she focuses on the "post-9/11 'us' versus 'them'" narrative structures that enable the positioning of Muslims as the enemy. She argues persuasively that depictions of Muslims as enemies were not only a commonly shared trope across mainstream media and popular culture, but that these depictions themselves shaped the attitudes toward and practices of torture of presumed Muslim terrorists by the U.S. military. As Nacos concludes, "How we view the world around us, how we think and talk about issues and problems . . . is not only affected by the information we receive as news but also by the words, ideas, images, and stereotypes presented in different types of mass media." By looking at one of the most famous examples of "Hollywood terror fiction"—the television program 24—Nacos is able to show the overlaps between popular narratives, mainstream media, and political discourses. With politicians, judges, and newscasters all using the program's star, Jack Bauer, as an example of what to do to stop future terrorist attacks, it is clear that the boundaries between forms of media are permeable and cross-pollinating.

Nacos returns us to questions about the epistemological structures of media's engagement with terrorism by reminding us that what the media chooses not to say is just as important as what it does. Focusing on media's ability to both "communicate" and "excommunicate," Nacos analyzes the ways in which portrayals of Muslims changed after 9/11 and the decade following. By choosing not to "communicate" information about Muslims who opposed bin Laden and terrorism, U.S. media effectively enabled negative representations of Muslims to dominate the mediascape. Importantly, Nacos argues that such omissions are not merely oversights or mistakes on the part of a busy media but instead are framing moments for cultural understanding and action. Nacos links media's negative portrayals of Muslims to subsequent actions in the Global War on Terrorism. In particular, she points to acts of torture such as those at Abu Ghraib as implementations of the "excommunication" epistemologies employed in media.

Conclusion

The essays gathered in this volume contribute to our understanding of global media in multiple ways. By taking a common focal point for their discussions—Osama bin Laden—the authors give us an opportunity to compare media perspectives across national and regional boundaries, across media formats, and across methodologies, theories, and disciplinary practices. In so doing, they provide a case study on contemporary media analytical methods. In addition, by writing about perspectives both in and outside the West, the authors provide insight into the complex terrain that is global media, an arena in which the same "object" has multiple and frequently conflicting meanings, depending upon the frameworks within which audiences interpret media products. Simultaneously, the essays in this volume remind us that there is no stable "object" of global media. Osama bin Laden—enemy, hero, fiend, visionary, egotist, mastermind, husband, father, murderer, savior—is variously a certainty—"we know who he is" (a necessary precondition in order to hunt and kill him)—and he remains a ghost who haunts the discourses of the Global War on Terrorism.

In addition to serving as a focal point for understanding the operations of global media, bin Laden is an important figure of analysis because he is a key participant in the global tensions around the nation-state, with global media transecting these debates. Bin Laden was himself an advocate of the dissolution of states and replacing them with the Ummah, the nonstate-based Muslim community around the world. He was also the symbolic leader of a movement that took on the most powerful state in the world—the United States—and revealed its vulnerabilities. Simultaneously, the global media that he used to communicate with the world and that made him a globally recognized figure is itself becoming decreasingly state-based, with the rise of multinational media conglomerates and media outlets such as Al Jazeera that are designed to serve cross-national populations. As Rohit Chopra explains, "the category of the national itself has been profoundly altered in a global world, and media both contribute to and reflect this change."[65]

The authors in this volume collectively encourage an engagement with the media that would 1) seek comparative readings of the news from other media outlets, whether in other national contexts or other media formats; 2) look not only at what media says, but also at what it does not say—what voices are being left out, what information is being excluded, and what stories are not being told; and 3) understand how media both uses and is used by individuals and groups, whether they be political actors, nations, individual and corporate profit seekers, or nonnational movements. Global media have changed dramatically since Osama bin Laden became a world figure. By studying how he used media and how media used him, we can gain a greater understanding of global media "after bin Laden."

Notes

1. John Miller, "Usama bin Ladin: 'American Soldiers Are Paper Tigers,'" *Middle East Quarterly* 5, no. 4 (December 1998): 73–79.

2. "Howard Stern 9 11 Broadcast Show," September 11, 2001, http://www.wcqj.com/howard-stern-9-11-broadcast-show/.

3. Brigitte Nacos, "The Terrorist Calculus behind 9-11: A Model for Future Terrorism?," *Studies in Conflict and Terrorism* 26, no. 1 (2003): 1–16; quote from 8.

4. Christina Hellmich, *Al-Qaeda: From Global Network to Local Franchise* (New York: Zed Books, 2011), 85; Andrew Hill, *Re-Imagining the War on Terror: Seeing, Waiting, Travelling* (New York: Palgrave, 2009), 60.

5. Hellmich, *Al-Qaeda*, 46.

6. Ibid., 47.

7. Qtd. in Manuel R. Torres Soriano, "Terrorism and the Mass Media after Al Qaeda: A Change of Course?" *Athena Intelligence Journal* 3.1 (2008): 1–20; quote from 14.

8. Jeremy White, "Virtual Indoctrination and the Digihad: The Evolution of al-Qaeda's Media Strategy," *Small Wars Journal*, November 19, 2012: 6, http://smallwarsjournal.com/jrnl/art/virtual-indoctrination-and-the-digihad.

9. Mustafa Setmaerian, qtd. in Alan Cullison, "Inside Al Qaeda Hard Drive," *Atlantic Monthly*, September, 2004, http://www.theatlantic.com/magazine/archive/2004/09/inside-al-qaeda-s-hard-drive/303428/.

10. Nacos, "Terrorist Calculus behind 9-11," 3.

11. Peter L. Bergen, *Manhunt: The Ten-Year Search for bin Laden from 9/11 to Abbottabad* (New York: Crown, 2012), 23.

12. "Letter from al-Zawahiri to al-Zarqawi," http://www.globalsecurity.org/security/library/report/2005/zawahiri-zarqawi-letter_9jul2005.htm; qtd. in David Ensor, "Al Qaeda Letter Called 'Chilling,'" CNN, October 12, 2005.

13. Al-Suri, qtd. in White, "Virtual Indoctrination."

14. Nacos, "Terrorist Calculus behind 9-11," 4.

15. Ibrahim Seaga Shaw, "Stereotypical Representations of Muslims and Islam following the 7/7 London Terror Attacks," *International Communication Gazette* 74, no. 6 (2012): 509–24, quote from 515.

16. Bergen, *Manhunt*, 143.

17. Ibid., 58.

18. "Bush on Bringing bin Laden to Justice," *Washington Post*, September 17, 2001, http://www.washingtonpost.com/wp-srv/nation/specials/attacked/transcripts/bush091701.html.

19. Brian Knowlton, "Terror in America: 'We're Going to Smoke Them Out': President Airs His Anger," *New York Times*, September 19, 2001, http://www.nytimes.com/2001/09/19/news/19iht-t4_30.html.

20. Bergen, *Manhunt*, 175.

21. Craig Whitlock and William Wan, "U.S. Cautious on Releasing Proof of bin Laden's Death," *Washington Post*, May 2, 2011, http://www.washingtonpost.com/national/bin-ladens -secret-sea-burial-adds-to-the-mystery-of-his-life/2011/05/02/AF4uEPZF_story.html.

22. Michael Doyle, "Bin Laden Death Photos Might Not See the Light of Day," January 10, 2013, *McClatchy DC*, http://www.mcclatchydc.com/2013/01/10/179536/bin-laden -death-photos-might-not.html.

23. Amelia Hill, "Osama bin Laden Corpse Photo Is Fake" *Guardian*, May 2, 2011, http://www.guardian.co.uk/world/2011/may/02/osama-bin-laden-photo-fake. See also Moeller, Nurmis, and Barforoush in this volume for a more detailed description.

24. "Glenn Beck Claims Osama bin Laden Is Not Really Dead," *Politicus USA*, May 3, 2011, http://www.politicususa.com/glenn-beck-bin-laden.html.

25. Cindy Sheehan, "I'm Not the Deather," *Cindy Sheehan's Soapbox*, May 2, 2011, http://cindysheehanssoapbox.blogspot.com/2011/05/im-not-deather-by-cindy-sheehan.html.

26. Alex Jones, "Insider Exposes bin Laden Death Book Hoax," Infowars.com, August 24, 2012, http://www.infowars.com/insider-exposes-bin-laden-death-book-hoax/.

27. Jennifer Harper, "Without Photo Proof, Is bin Laden Really Dead?" *Washington Times*, May 4, 2011, http://p.washingtontimes.com/news/2011/may/4/without-photo -proof-is-bin-laden-really-dead/?page=all.

28. We define "global media" as media that is multinational and multiregional and that is characterized by the convergence of media technologies that has taken place since the end of the Cold War, resulting in the creation of transnational media conglomerates. We subscribe to both macro and micro analytical frameworks that examine both the globalization of media organizations and technologies and the localization of media interpretation.

29. Rohit Chopra, introduction to *Global Media, Culture, and Identity: Theory, Cases, and Approaches*, ed. Rohit Chopra and Radhika Gajjala (New York: Routledge, 2011), 2.

30. Biographies of bin Laden include the following: Peter Bergen, *The Osama bin Laden I Know: An Oral History of al Qaeda's Leader* (New York: Free Press, 2006); Yoseef Bodansky, *Osama bin Laden: The Man Who Declared War on America* (Rocklin, CA: Forum, 1999); Steve Coll, *The Bin Ladens: An Arabian Family in an American Century* (New York: Penguin Books, 1999); Steve Coll, *The Bin Ladens: Oil, Money, Terrorism and the Secret Saudi World* (New York: Penguin Books, 2009); Thomas R. Mockaitis, *Osama bin Laden: A Biography* (New York: Greenwood Press, 2010); Michael Scheuer, *Osama bin Laden* (Oxford: Oxford University Press, 2011); Najwa bin Laden, Omar bin Laden, and Jean Sasson, *Growing Up bin Laden: Osama's Wife and Son Take Us inside Their Secret World* (New York: St. Martin's Griffin, 2010).

31. Hellmich, *Al-Qaeda*, 2.

32. Bergen, *Manhunt*, jacket cover copy, 35.

33. "Osama bin Laden Largely Discredited among Muslim Publics in Recent Years: Al Qaeda Too," Pew Research Global Attitudes Project, May 2, 2011, http://www.pewglobal.org/2011/05/02/osama-bin-laden-largely-discredited-among-muslim-publics-in-recent-years/; the remaining three countries are Egypt, Turkey, and Lebanon; these numbers have since declined.

34. Qtd. in Renate Salecl, *On Anxiety (Thinking in Action)* (New York: Routledge, 2004), 3.

35. BBC1, *News at 10 O'Clock*, October 30, 2004, qtd. in Andrew Hill, *Re-imaging the War on Terror: Seeing, Waiting, Travelling* (New York: Palgrave Macmillan, 2009), 104, 141.

36. Arjun Appadurai, "Disjuncture and Difference in the Global Cultural Economy," *Theory, Culture and Society* 7 (1990): 295–310; quote from 298–99.

37. W. J. T Mitchell, *What Do Pictures Want? The Lives and Loves of Images* (Chicago: University of Chicago Press, 2005), 84.

38. Ibid., 208.

39. Helga Tawil-Souri, "The 'War on Terror' in the Arab Media," in *Media and Terrorism: Global Perspectives*, ed. Des Freedman and Daya Kishan (London: Sage, 2012), 241–55; quote from 252.

40. "New Realities in the Media Age: A Conversation with Donald Rumsfeld," Council on Foreign Relations, February 17, 2006.

41. André Nusselder, "Virtual war and repolitization in visual culture," *Cambridge Review of International Affairs* 25, no. 3 (Spring 2012): 451–61; quote from 452, 455.

42. Ashley Marie Nellis and Joanne Savage, "Does Watching the News Affect Fear of Terrorism? The Importance of Media Exposure on Terrorism Fear," *Crime and Delinquency*, September 10, 2012: 1–21; quote from 3–4.

43. Hill, *Re-imaging the War*, 89.

44. See, for example, Bruce Lincoln, *Holy Terrors: Thinking about Religion after September 11* (Chicago: University of Chicago Press, 2006); and Mark Juergensmeyer, *Terror in the Mind of God: The Global Rise of Religious Violence*, 3rd ed. (Berkeley: University of California Press, 2003).

45. Hellmich, *Al-Qaeda*, 4.

46. Susan D. Moeller, *Packaging Terrorism: Co-opting the News for Politics and Profit* (New York: Wiley-Blackwell, 2008), 18.

47. Maura Conway, "Introduction: Terrorism and Contemporary Mediascapes—Reanimating Research on Media and Terrorism," *Critical Studies on Terrorism* 5, no. 3 (2012): 445–53.

48. Salecl, *On Anxiety*, 150.

49. Bergen, *Manhunt*, 35, 145; "Empire," cited in Jasbir Puar, *Terrorist Assemblages: Homonationalism in Queer Times* (Durham, NC: Duke University Press, 2007), 1.

50. Andreas Behnke and Benjamin de Carvalho, "Shooting War: International Relations and the Cinematic Representation of Warfare," *Millennium: Journal of International Studies* 34, no. 3 (August 2006): 937–49.

51. Nacos, "Terrorist Calculus behind 9-11," 8.

52. "Osama bin Laden Killed in US Raid on Pakistan Hideout," *Guardian*, May 2, 2011, http://www.guardian.co.uk/world/2011/may/02/osama-bin-laden-dead-pakistan.

53. Elizabeth Fortescue, "Artist Defends Osama-as-Jesus," *Advertiser* (Adelaide), August 29, 2007, http://www.adelaidenow.com.au/news/national/artist-defends-osama-as-jesus/story-e6frea8c-1111114298967?nk=4f87ba9467717c3a5083df2c1130c6f0.

54. *The Late Show with David Letterman*, November 27, 2001.

55. For listing of bin Laden cartoons see Daniel Kurtzman, "Osama bin Laden Cartoons," Political Humor, About.com, n.d., http://politicalhumor.about.com/od/osama binladen/ig/Osama-Bin-Laden-Cartoons/.

56. Daniel Kurtzman, "Top Anagrams for Osama bin Laden," Political Humor, About. com, n.d., http://politicalhumor.about.com/library/jokes/bljokeanagrams.htm.

57. "Kill Osama bin Laden," Free Online Games, Gameslist.com, n.d., http://www.games list.com/playonline/Kill-Osama-Bin-Laden-Game.

58. Brian Crecente, "Bin There, Done That: Video Games Let You Kill, Abuse Osama," Kotaku, May 2, 2011, http://kotaku.com/5797601/video-games-let-you-kill-abuse-osama.

59. Osama Games, Dailygames.com, n.d., http://www.dailygames.com/search/Osama .html.

60. "Osama bin Laden Games," Political Humor, About.com, n.d., http://politicalhumor .about.com/od/binladengames/Osama_bin_Laden_Games.htm.

61. FBI warning: "Malicious Software Features Usama bin Laden Links to Ensnare Un-suspecting Computer Users," Federal Bureau of Investigation, May 3, 2011, http://www .fbi.gov/news/pressrel/press-releases/malicious-software-features-usama-bin-laden -links-to-ensnare-unsuspecting-computer-users; "Osama is dead, watch this exclusive CNN video which was censored by Obama Administration due to level of violence, a must watch" (Robert McMillan, "Bin Laden Video Is a Virus, FBI Warns," in *PC World*, May 4, 2011, http://www.pcworld.com/article/227039/Bin_Laden_Video_Is_a_Virus _FBI_Warns.html.

62. Qtd. in Greg Keizer, "Fake AV Makers, Scammers Exploit bin Laden News," *Com-puterworld*, May 2, 2011, http://www.computerworld.com/s/article/9216330/Fake_AV _makers_scammers_exploit_Bin_Laden_news?source=CTWNLE_nlt_pm_2011-05-02.

63. Tracey J. Potts, "'Dark Tourism' and the 'Kitschification' of 9/11," *Tourist Studies* 12, no. 3 (December 2012): 232–45; quote from 237.

64. Abhishek Sharma, dir., *Tere Bin Laden*, Walkwater Media, 2010.

65. Chopra, introduction, 9.

PART I

Defining Political Actors

1

Bin Laden's Ghost and the Epistemological Crises of Counterterrorism

RICHARD JACKSON

As we know,
There are known knowns.
There are things we know we
know.
We also know
There are known unknowns.
That is to say
We know there are some things
We do not know.
But there are also unknown
unknowns,
The ones we don't know
We don't know.

—Donald Rumsfeld, February 12, 2002

Osama bin Laden remains one of the most recognized figures of this century. At the height of the war on terror, he received more media coverage than his opponent, President George W. Bush, and likely more than any other single newsmaker over the past ten years.[1] At the same time, the United States government invested billions of dollars and vast human and material resources in the attempt to bring him to justice, arguing that as the mastermind, symbolic leader, and financier of the global jihadist movement and the individual most directly responsible for the 9/11 attacks, his death or capture was critical to winning the Global War on Terrorism. Given the intensity of this focus on the figure of Osama bin Laden, it is not surprising that the global media went into overdrive when he was killed by U.S. Special Forces in Pakistan in May 2011. Since then, a vast number of news stories, commentaries, articles, documentaries, books, comics, children's books, and even a feature film have been produced that describe and speculate on the meaning surrounding his death and its aftermath.

In this chapter, I argue that despite all the media attention, punditry, scholarly analysis, and official commentary, Osama bin Laden's death remains an essentially meaningless (non-)event or what Jean Baudrillard calls a simulacrum.[2] That is, it is an event that at first appears to be a real, meaningful moment in world politics, whereas, in fact, closer analysis reveals that it is merely a symbolic *imitation* of a meaningful event—notwithstanding the "real" people killed and affected. This is evident, in part, in the way the events played out as a kind of espionage movie that the administration viewed like a regular film audience, while the global media in turn viewed the administration viewing the events. In what follows, I argue that Osama bin Laden's death is meaningless or without consequence in two main senses of the word.

First, it is most obviously meaningless in real-world strategic and material terms. For example, as a direct consequence of bin Laden's death, no counterterrorism programs have been scaled back or ended, counterterrorism laws repealed, military or security funding reduced, security agencies scaled down or closed, foreign training programs ended, overseas military forces withdrawn, or military bases closed. Instead, the global counterterrorism effort remains completely unchanged by his death and continues on as it has for the past ten years. It could even be argued that, if anything, the War on Terror continues to expand and intensify. Certainly, the secret drone program aimed at eliminating terrorists has grown over the past few years, new counterterrorism laws are regularly passed, surveillance programs and counterradicalization programs continue, security measures are rolled out into ever more areas of social life, and levels of spending on counterterrorism remain extremely high.

Second, and perhaps more importantly, I argue that bin Laden's death has, among other things, generated so many divergent meanings that it has been rendered ultimately meaningless in terms of its analytical consequences, symbolism, and epistemological significance. Popularly, it is frequently asserted that events speak for themselves and that their meanings are obvious. The reality, however, at least in this case, is that no one knows what bin Laden's death at the hands of U.S. Special Forces really means. Does it signal the destruction of Al Qaeda and the jihadist movement? Does it mean the War on Terror has finally been won? Does it represent the administration of justice for the 9/11 victims? Is it a strategic blow for Al Qaeda and its allies, or merely a symbolic blow? Or, alternately, does it mean that the jihadist movement now has a potent new symbolic martyr to inspire it? Does it signal that Al Qaeda has morphed into a new form and is as deadly as ever? What does it say about Pakistan's role as an ally in the war on extremism?

The uncertainty surrounding the interpretation of bin Laden's death—as well as the not insignificant uncertainty about the manner of his death[3]—can be seen in the often ambivalent or even contradictory statements about what it really means for the ongoing struggle against terrorism and, more broadly, the Obama administration's handling of national security issues. For example, not long after bin Laden's death, an official report stated that "U.S. counterterrorism officials are increasingly convinced that the killing of Osama bin Laden and the toll of seven years of CIA drone strikes have pushed al Qaeda to the brink of collapse." However, the same report concluded that "al-Qaeda might yet rally and that even its demise would not end the terrorist threat."[4] In other words, officials are fundamentally unsure whether bin Laden's death is a significant blow to the group or, even if it is, whether this means that the threat of terrorism will decrease.

Of course, this argument does not negate the numerous ways in which politicians and security officials have attempted to exploit the death of the Al Qaeda leader for political—particularly, electoral—capital or the way many U.S. citizens chose to interpret it as a kind of moral victory.[5] From this perspective, the death of bin Laden has been enormously significant for political elites and sections of the public, and reflects a genuine desire to construct the events as meaningful. However, as I suggest below, efforts to *construct* the event as important and meaningful do not necessarily resolve the deeper epistemological crises the events inevitably demonstrate.

This puzzle—why there is little consensus on the meaning and significance of bin Laden's death, how it can be claimed to be both significant and insignificant at the same time, and the political struggle to imbue it with meaning—provides the analytical focus of this chapter. It is my contention that this profound ontological uncertainty, and the essential meaninglessness of Osama bin Laden's physical death in any material or strategic sense, were inevitable or at least highly probable. This is because the particular counterterrorism paradigm constructed and institutionalized after 9/11 made real knowledge and meaning about Al Qaeda and Osama bin Laden impossible. The central reasons for this are that bin Laden's death occurred in the midst of two key epistemological crises: first, the epistemological crisis surrounding Al Qaeda and the figure of Osama bin Laden himself; and second, the deeper and more pervasive epistemological crisis affecting counterterrorism more generally. In other words, I am arguing that in a context in which we do not really *know* what Al Qaeda is or signifies and, more importantly, what terrorism itself is or signifies, it was therefore always going to be impossible to *know* what the death of the world's most famous terrorist meant or signified.

Unknowing Al Qaeda

As Christina Hellmich has incisively demonstrated, there has never been a clear consensus on what Al Qaeda actually is at the ontological level—what its nature and threat actually consist of.[6] Is it a structured organization, a diffused network, a franchise, an ideology, or a figment of the Western imagination? Does it pose an existential threat, a strategic threat, or is it really little more than an irritant? Is it driven by religious extremism, nationalism, or political grievances? In other words, officials, security practitioners, and terrorism experts have never been able to agree on what the term "Al Qaeda" represents or means in real-world material, strategic, or political terms, and they have put forward ontologically opposing descriptions and explanations of this thing called "Al Qaeda." For example, government officials in many countries, especially the United States, as well as terrorism experts like Rohan Gunaratna and Bruce Hoffman, have put forward the view that Al Qaeda consists of a hierarchically organized inner core leadership, surrounded by a second level of loyal cadres and a wider network of supporters and links to other groups.[7] In this view, Al Qaeda is an organization in the traditional understanding of the term, and Osama bin Laden was its charismatic leader.

A second perspective comes from terrorism experts like Jeffrey Cozzens and Magnus Ranstorp, who argue that Al Qaeda is not a hierarchically organized group, but rather a diffused and amorphous functional network with numerous nodal points and genuine adaptability.[8] Marc Sageman's notion of "leaderless jihad" is a variant of this perspective, suggesting that Al Qaeda primarily consists of self-motivated individuals and small cells linked largely by ideology and aims.[9] These scholars point to the spread of Al Qaeda branches around the world and the growing number of plots perpetrated by self-radicalized individuals. Ontologically, a diffused network or leaderless resistance is something quite different to a formal organization. Within this perspective, Osama bin Laden played a relatively insignificant role in the actions and continued existence of Al Qaeda, and therefore his death is probably of minor significance.

A third perspective from terrorism experts such as Peter Bergen and Fawaz Gerges views Al Qaeda as one branch of a much broader international jihadist movement, but suggests that it is by now a spent force within that wider movement.[10] While it may have once been quite influential and effective, it is today largely irrelevant and impotent, regardless of its real form or actual capabilities. This viewpoint is based on the observation that the group has failed to launch or claim any major attacks for several years now and presently appears to rely solely on amateurish plots by lone self-radicalizers such as Abdul Farouk Abdulmutallab, the Detroit Christmas Day bomber. It is also based on an analysis of the so-called Arab Spring in which it has been noted that Al Qaeda and jihadist groups like it have played virtually no role and have been politically marginalized.

A fourth perspective shared by a few experts such as Jason Burke and Christina Hellmich views Al Qaeda as part of a broader pan-Islamist movement upon which it is parasitic, and which it tries to inspire and lead, to greater or lesser effect.[11] From this perspective, Al Qaeda is more of an ideological framework and source of inspiration, rather than a structured and materially embedded organization or network.

Other crucial areas of disagreement among experts include the nature of Al Qaeda's ideological drivers and its broader aims and goals. Most officials and a great many scholars and terrorism experts argue that Al Qaeda is a religiously motivated, anti-modern, extremist actor with essentially otherworldly goals and aspirations related to converting the world to Islam and reestablishing the Caliphate.[12] Others suggest that it is a completely modernist project and is driven primarily by concrete political grievances related to Western foreign policy.[13] Similarly, while many scholars and officials still consider Al Qaeda to be a significant threat to Western society, others argue that recent terrorist plots demonstrate that jihadists are, for the most part, "incompetent, ineffective, unintelligent, idiotic, ignorant, unorganized, misguided, muddled, amateurish, dopey, unrealistic, moronic, irrational and foolish," and that Al Qaeda "has only a handful of individuals capable of planning, organizing and leading a terrorist organization," and "its capabilities are far inferior to its desires."[14]

The key point is that these different perspectives deploy different data and evidence to support their claims and, more importantly, rely on competing ontological conceptions of what Al Qaeda actually is. Moreover, such radically divergent understandings of Al Qaeda clearly have profound consequences for counterterrorism policy: if Al Qaeda is a diffused nodal network with genuine capabilities to cause destruction, for example, it will require completely different counterterrorism strategies than if it is a broader ideology without a central material organization or the capability to launch physical attacks. Such differences are also consequential for assessing the impact of bin Laden's death: if he is the leader of a functional organization, for example, his death will be of greater significance than if he is only a symbolic figurehead in a dispersed global network.

In the end, these divergent explanations and understandings of one of the most studied and targeted groups in the world provide clear evidence that there is an epistemological crisis regarding Al Qaeda.[15] It is, despite all the research and study by all the experts and special agents assigned to countering it, an essentially unknown entity. In the words of Donald Rumsfeld quoted at the start of this chapter, Al Qaeda is one of the "known unknowns" of the current terrorist threat: we know it exists, but we do not know exactly how dangerous it is or what they really want. This is the first epistemological crisis that makes the death of Osama bin Laden a non-event and essentially meaningless. If experts and counterterrorism officials do not know what Al Qaeda really is, then they cannot know what role bin Laden played in the organization/network/franchise/ideology; and if they do not know what role he played, then they cannot know what significance or meaning his death has.

The Epistemological Crisis of Counterterrorism

It could be argued that the inability of terrorism experts and officials to determine what role Osama bin Laden played in Al Qaeda and what his death signifies is simply normal intellectual disagreement about actors and a phenomenon that is shrouded in secrecy and a lack of hard data and information. However, the sheer volume of analysis on Al Qaeda over the past ten years and the profound ontological basis of the disagreement would appear to throw doubt on such a simplistic explanation. Instead, I argue that this lack of consensus is, together with a range of other examples of profound uncertainty and unknowing about terrorists and the threat they pose, *emblematic* of the broader counterterrorism paradigm that has been in operation since the 9/11 attacks. This is the second epistemological crisis within which the death of Osama bin Laden occurred, and it further helps to explain why his death remains essentially meaningless.

In addition to the uncertainty of officials and experts about Al Qaeda's nature described above, the prevalence of *fantasy* in counterterrorism thought and practice is another indicator of the current epistemological crisis of terrorism.[16] As a number of scholars have recently shown, fantasy, exaggeration, hypercaution and even forms of magical realism are now central themes in counterterrorism and security practice, and bizarre fantasy-imbued behavior by security officials seems to occur on a daily basis.[17] For example, in addition to examples of security officials at airports searching very elderly passengers and babies' diapers, and re-x-raying any book considered suspicious, serious discussions have taken place about the possibility that terrorists could introduce biological weapons into the water supply through fire hydrants, that they might use hang gliders to deliver suicide bombs into urban areas, that candy machines might be vulnerable to terrorists, and that hundreds of American amusement and water parks are all vulnerable to terrorist attack.[18] What these and many other cases illustrate is the key role of *fantasy* in counterterrorism; that is, officials imagining unrealistic—or at least exaggerated or reality-enhanced—possible terrorist scenarios and then treating them as real threats requiring a material response from officials.

What I am suggesting is that the prevalence of fantasy and magical thinking in counterterrorism flows directly from the profound lack of knowledge that officials and experts have about terrorism and the real threat it poses; it is therefore symptomatic of an epistemological crisis. In this crisis, terrorism is perceived as fundamentally unknown, incalculable, and unpredictable—what Donald Rumsfeld referred to as an "unknown unknown." In other words, there are aspects of terrorism such that we do not even know what it is that we do not know. Once it is accepted that we essentially do not know where, when, or how terrorists might strike, or what potential danger they may pose (conventional, nuclear, chemical, biological), then the only way to detect and deal with them is to try to *imagine* what they might do—which, of course, inevitably leads to fantasy in counterterrorist thought and practice.

How did this epistemological crisis—the condition where *lack of knowledge* is the main thing we *know* about the terrorist threat—first arise? I propose that it occurred in six key steps or social developments. First, as Behnke and Hellmich remind us, the 9/11 terrorist attacks by Al Qaeda were constituted as an "event" in the Derridaian sense that exceeded existing cognitive and discursive frameworks and thus created a "void of meaning."[19] In particular, the difficulty of interpreting the attacks through traditional Western concepts of politics and political action enveloped Al Qaeda and its enigmatic leader in a web of uncertainty. In other words, once 9/11 itself was seen as an event beyond meaning, then the perpetrators of 9/11 (Al Qaeda, Osama bin Laden, and "terrorists" more generally) similarly became wrapped in the same web of unknowing. Crucially, constructing 9/11 in this way served to sever connections to previous understandings of terrorists and terrorism. As a number of terrorism scholars argued, the September 11 attacks wiped the slate clean and rendered previous terrorism knowledge obsolete.[20]

Second, and directly related to the epistemologically paralyzing effects of 9/11, terrorism as a form of political violence had been subject to a discursive reconstruction by terrorism scholars and experts since the early 1990s. The "new terrorism" thesis argued that contemporary terrorism could not be understood through the prism of previous research and understandings, because unlike the "old terrorism," the "new terrorism" was motivated by religious extremism rather than politics, unconstrained in its targeting of civilians and thus willing to employ weapons of mass destruction, and organized in nonhierarchical, fluid networks.[21] This meant that we could no longer be sure that terrorists would behave according to previously predictable patterns or follow previously identified pathways. It meant previous data and analysis relating to terrorism was largely obsolete, and we no longer knew where, when, or how terrorists might strike, or what kind of threat they really posed. At the same time, popular cultural production of depictions of "new terrorists" attacking with nuclear bombs, chemical weapons, and biological agents in an effort to effect maximum civilian casualties proliferated across the media. Thus, severed from previous forms of knowledge and evidence, and fed by media images, the "new terrorists" became the nightmare specter haunting the Western imagination.[22]

Third, as the sociologist Ulrich Beck and others have demonstrated, over the past few decades the social paradigm of traditional risk analysis has been replaced by precautionary thinking, and public officials have come to be preoccupied with the *possible* over the *probable*.[23] That is, they have come to prioritize and be concerned about the potential terrible *consequences* of risks, rather than the very low statistical *probability* of those risks actually materializing. For public officials, what *could* happen in future acts of terrorism now assumes greater significance than what *has* happened over the past centuries of terrorist violence or what might actually happen in a probabilistic sense. At the same time, officials have come to believe that society expects them to adopt a zero-risk approach to public safety: no level of risk, even a one percent risk, can now be tolerated.[24]

Fourth, as the Donald Rumsfeld quotation aptly illustrates, security officials have come to focus on the "unknown" element of terrorism, particularly the "unknown unknowns"—those things we do not even know we do not know about the terrorism threat. This represents the adoption of ontological uncertainty as a fundamental condition of terrorism knowledge, in effect, severing links to previous empirical evidence, analytical frameworks and knowledge, and remaking terrorism as an unlimited, infinite risk. As Donald Rumsfeld also said, "Absence of evidence is not evidence of absence."[25] In other words, if terrorism is now defined primarily by what is unknown, then there is no reliable empirical evidence or data from the past that can help us "know" terrorism in the present. In consequence, this means, among other things, that there is no basis or imperative for officials to conduct empirical evaluation or cost-benefit analysis of current counterterrorism measures.[26] After all, what could they tell us about an unknown and ultimately unpredictable danger? More importantly, if terrorism is conceptualized in terms of a lack of knowledge, then its threat becomes limitless because there are no set limits to ignorance.[27]

Fifth, as I have argued elsewhere, a process of "knowledge subjugation" in regards to terrorism has also taken place over the past decade.[28] This is the condition of what in Donald Rumsfeld's formulation might be called, "unknown knowns," or those things we "know" but which we do not wish to "know." As Christopher Daase and Oliver Kessler imagine another verse of Donald Rumsfeld's poem:

> Finally, there are unknown knowns
> The knowns
> We don't want to know.[29]

Others have described this situation as "the politics of anti-knowledge" or the "active refusal of explanation itself."[30] Anthropologists Joseba Zulaika and William Douglass argue that the moral status of terrorists as evil and irrational proscribes intimate knowledge of them, making the search for real knowledge of terrorism taboo.[31] Certainly, as a great many analysts have noted, with only a handful of notable exceptions, little effort has been made by terrorism experts and officials to try to understand terrorist motivations by listening to their own words and messages and seriously engaging with their subjectivity.[32] This is especially the case with Al Qaeda, where the voice of Osama bin Laden, despite a vast corpus of open letters, interviews, propaganda videos and statements, has remained largely unheard among Western audiences.[33]

This condition of willful ignorance is achieved by forgetting, suppressing or repressing evidence, knowledge, and perspectives that challenge accepted ideas (or, in this case, accepted ignorance), for example, such as the knowledge generated within the military-intellectual system that anti-American terrorism is primarily caused by U.S. military intervention overseas, or that the violent suppression of terrorism is less effective than conciliation-oriented approaches like dialogue.[34] Consequently, officials, the media, and many terrorism experts frequently assert that we simply do not know why terrorists attack or what causes their actions: their motives are inexplicable and unknown to us, despite the existence of terrorists' own explanations for their actions.[35] Moreover, because the terrorists are a dangerous taboo, they cannot and should not be known: "the Western audience has largely been shielded from the voice of bin Laden, almost as if hearing him unedited posed a threat to the national wellbeing."[36] For counterterrorists and terrorism experts, this has meant: "Rather than rely upon the creation of knowledge about terrorism, the dominant approach has rejected the very possibility of knowing terrorists."[37]

Finally, at the same time as terrorism has been constructed as unknowable and unpredictable, and officials have become preoccupied with the possible over the probable, they have also embraced the impossibility of ever completely securing society against terrorism. This is evident in the Prepare strand of the United Kingdom's CONTEST counterterrorism strategy, for example.[38] In 2012 the Home Office stated, "**Prepare is the work stream of the counterterrorism strategy that aims to mitigate the impact of a terrorist incident where it cannot be stopped.**" In other words, official UK counterterrorism policy—and that of most other Western states—is based on the assumption that terrorist attacks will inevitably occur regardless of any of the measures currently undertaken to prevent such an outcome. This assumption, that no matter what they do to deter or protect, or what they ultimately know about terrorism, they will never be able to prevent future terrorist attacks, has the paradoxical effect of rendering any (little) knowledge we hold about terrorism impotent. In the end, the only thing we know for sure is that more terrorist attacks are inevitable, and no amount of knowledge or action can prevent them all from occurring.

It is easy to see that, in combination, these six developments have created a profound crisis of knowledge about terrorism—an epistemological crisis and a void of meaning—which in turn results in an endless and incomplete search for useful knowledge about terrorism. That is, faced with a profound lack of knowledge and a seemingly intractable condition of uncertainty, counterterrorism officials are forced to employ their imaginations to try to detect, prevent, and deter terrorist attacks before they occur. Employing imagination rather than empirical evidence, data, and scholarly analysis, officials inevitably end in fantasy thinking. In other words, in a field defined by a deep and profound epistemological crisis about the nature and threat of terrorism, often bizarre and ever-expanding and intrusive counterterrorism practices are not exceptions; they are normal. They are the inevitable outcome of the condition of unknowing.

More importantly for the topic under investigation in this volume, the direct consequence of the dual epistemological crises relating to Al Qaeda and terrorism more generally is that it was always highly likely, if not inevitable, that the death of Osama bin Laden would be a meaningless (non-)event or simulacrum. In other words, we have to ask: in a context where terrorist attacks such as 9/11 are essentially incomprehensible, where terrorists are no longer understandable as political actors and their motives are inscrutable, and where risks and dangers are no longer calculable, is it reasonable to believe that the death of the world's most famous terrorist can be rendered comprehensible and meaningful?

Conclusion

Although it is beyond the scope of this chapter, it must be noted that the mainstream domestic and international media have played a key role in both constructing and maintaining the dual epistemological crises of Al Qaeda and terrorism more generally. Similar to the mythology the media constructed around Carlos the Jackal in the 1970s and 1980s,[39] the media have constructed Al Qaeda and Osama bin Laden as a global network possessing extraordinary capabilities relentlessly plotting apocalyptic destruction, in the vein of a James Bond film. More importantly, they have largely reproduced and reinforced exaggerated depictions of terrorist capabilities and intentions and, with only a few exceptions, have failed to report and discuss terrorism in an informed, analytical, and sober manner. In this respect, as the primary institution of public education and communication, they have done nothing to mitigate the epistemological crisis of terrorism and have instead contributed directly to it. In either case, the media battle over the meaning of bin Laden's death cannot resolve the epistemological crises of Al Qaeda and terrorism. Rather, the battle is itself symptomatic of these crises and one of the arenas in which the crises are acted out.

To conclude, what are some of the main consequences—analytical, political, and normative—of the epistemological crises and ultimate meaninglessness of the death of bin Laden that I have described here? As suggested, the first consequence is that the (non-)event of bin Laden's death is largely inconsequential to the continued real-world Western prosecution of the Global War on Terrorism. In part, this is due to the material interests that have grown up around the counterterrorism field operating in the West and that would make its dismantling extremely difficult under any circumstances.[40] However, I would argue that it is primarily the epistemological impossibility of discerning whether bin Laden's death has any substantive impact on Al Qaeda and its ability to launch serious attacks that explains why it cannot be a significant factor in determining (or changing) real-world counterterrorism policy or approaches. As Daase and Kessler express it, "It is the relationship between what we know, what we do not know, what we cannot know and what we do not like to know that determines the cognitive frame for political practice."[41] In the counterterrorism field, this relationship is in crisis.

In addition, from an analytical perspective, it means that officials, analysts, and scholars can never hope to finally *know* who or what Al Qaeda is, or what the death of bin Laden ultimately means—even while they attempt to generate political capital from the death of its leader. As Behnke and Hellmich argue, this means that the questions "how is al-Qaeda known?" and "what are the political consequences of these different interpretations of what al-Qaeda is?" are probably of greater import at the present juncture than "what do we really know about al Qaeda?"[42] In other words, the current epistemological crises preclude the procurement of secure ontological knowledge about Al Qaeda and its threat. Until analysts and scholars reassess the foundations of terrorist knowledge—by, for example, abandoning the "new terrorism" thesis, replacing precautionary risk analysis with traditional risk approaches, re-appropriating historical knowledge of terrorism, and desubjugating relevant terrorism-related knowledge in other fields—they will remain trapped in the knowledge impasse.

Third, the dual epistemological crises and the inherent meaninglessness of bin Laden's death means that imagination, fantasy, and the endlessly incomplete search for meaning and practical knowledge continue to be the defining characteristics of the counterterrorism field. Knowing that devastating attacks by Al Qaeda and other terrorists are inevitable but not knowing exactly where, when, or how they might attack, the authorities are forced to imagine the possibilities and take steps to close off any and all potential avenues. This permanent condition of "waiting for terror"[43] means that we are likely to see the continued spread of Western counterterrorism measures and programs into ever more areas of social life, and ever more regions of the world, in a bid to stay one step ahead of the unknown, threatening terrorists that Western audiences imagine. The spread of surveillance programs and technology, counterradicalization programs, the enlistment of the public in counterterrorism initiatives, and the spread of the CIA's drone-launched killing program to new countries are all examples of this expansionary tendency.

A final important consequence of the dual epistemological crises—particularly as it relates to the danger posed by unknown terrorists—is the institutionalization of a politics of fear.[44] In the atmosphere of the terrorism moral panic, threat levels are raised and lowered by officials, often without explanation, and public fear is manipulated for electoral gain and the promotion of nonterrorism-related political projects. In the process, the interplay of knowledge and ignorance transforms a public fear of terrorism into a general epistemic fear. Closely related to the politics of fear is a new exceptional normality, or the so-called state of exception, in which the purported existential threat of terrorism necessitates the suspension of normal politics. In the shadow of the ever-present "specter of the terrorist apocalypse," counterterrorists are thus "forced" to employ exceptional measures, such as using rendition and torture to thwart the proverbial terrorist ticking bomb, or the remote killing or preventive detention of individuals who might be preparing terrorist attacks or at least harboring terroristic intentions. From this perspective, one of the primary normative consequences of the dual epistemological crises has been the extensively documented litany of human rights abuses in the War on Terror.

In the end, the killing of Osama bin Laden and the struggle to understand the meaning and significance of the events surrounding his death, including the debates in this volume, are evidence of the dual epistemological crises in which Western counterterrorism is currently trapped. Certainly, bin Laden's death does not take us any closer to resolving these crises; in fact, there is the possibility that his death may even compound the crises by removing the one recognizable symbol and analytical focus of Al Qaeda's ongoing threat. That is, without bin Laden's regular media appearances and public announcements, counterterrorism officials and media analysts will be increasingly reliant on imagination and speculation to discern the future intentions and capabilities of Al Qaeda. Moreover, with his removal as the focal point of the Global War on Terrorism, it will no longer be quite so clear where counterterrorist efforts ought to be directed. In the end, until we find a way back from the current knowledge impasse, we are likely to be haunted by bin Laden's ghost for some time yet.

Notes

The quote in the epigraph was reprinted as a poem in Hart Seely, *Pieces of Intelligence: The Existential Poetry of Donald H. Rumsfeld* (New York: Free Press, 2003).

1. See Brigitte Nacos, "The Terrorist Calculus behind 9-11: A Model for Future Terrorism?," *Studies in Conflict and Terrorism 26, no. 1 (2003):* 1–16.

2. Jean Baudrillard, *Simulacra and Simulation* (Ann Arbor: University of Michigan Press, 1994).

3. Peter Bergen, "Sense and Nonsense about Obama and Osama," CNN online, August 29, 2012, http://edition.cnn.com/2012/08/29/opinion/bergen-obama-osama-books/index .html, accessed August 30, 2012.

4. Greg Miller, "Al-Qaeda Could Collapse, U.S. Officials Say," *Washington Post*, July 26, 2011, http://www.washingtonpost.com/world/national-security/al-qaeda-could -collapse-us-officials-say/2011/07/21/gIQAFu2pbI_story.html, accessed 2 September 2012.

5. I am grateful to the editors for pointing this out.

6. Christina Hellmich, *Al-Qaeda: From Global Network to Local Franchise* (London: Zed, 2011). See also Christina Hellmich and Andreas Behnke, eds., *Knowing al-Qaeda: The Epistemology of Terrorism* (Farnham: Ashgate, 2012).

7. Rohan Gunaratna, *Inside Al Qaeda: Global Network of Terror*, 2nd ed. (London: Hurst, 2003); Bruce Hoffman, *Inside Terrorism*, rev. ed. (New York: Columbia University Press, 2006). See also Bruce Hoffman, "The Myth of Grass-roots Terrorism: Why Osama bin Laden Still Matters," *Foreign Affairs* 87, no. 3 (May/June 2008): 133–38.

8. Jeffrey B. Cozzens and Magnus Ranstorp, "YES: The Enduring al-Qaeda Threat: A Network Perspective," in *Contemporary Debates on Terrorism*, ed. Richard Jackson and Samuel Justin Sinclair (Abingdon, UK: Routledge, 2012).

9. Marc Sageman, *Leaderless Jihad: Terror Networks in the Twenty-First Century* (Philadelphia: University of Pennsylvania Press, 2008).

10. Peter L. Bergen, *The Osama bin Laden I Know: An Oral History of Al Qaeda's Leader* (New York: Simon and Schuster, 2006); Fawaz A. Gerges, *The Rise and Fall of al-Qaeda* (Oxford: Oxford University Press, 2011). See also Fawaz A. Gerges, *The Far Enemy: Why Jihad Went Global* (Cambridge: Cambridge University Press, 2005).

11. Jason Burke, *Al-Qaeda: The True Story of Radical Islam* (London: Penguin Books, 2004); Hellmich, *Al-Qaeda*.

12. The religious terrorism literature is described and critiqued in detail in Jeroen Gunning and Richard Jackson, "What's So 'Religious' about 'Religious Terrorism'?," *Critical Studies on Terrorism* 4, no. 3 (2011): 369–88; and Richard Jackson, "Constructing Enemies: 'Islamic Terrorism' in Political and Academic Discourse," *Government and Opposition* 42, no. 3 (2007): 394–426.

13. See Faisal Devji, *Landscapes of the Jihad: Militancy, Morality, Modernity* (Ithaca, NY: Cornell University Press, 2005); Robert A. Pape, *Dying to Win: The Strategic Logic of Suicide Terrorism* (New York: Random House, 2005).

14. John Mueller and Mark G. Stewart, "The Terrorism Delusion: America's Overwrought Response to September 11," *International Security* 37, no. 1 (2012): 88, 91. See also John E. Mueller, *Overblown: How Politicians and the Terrorism Industry Inflate National Security Threats, and Why We Believe Them* (New York: Free Press, 2006).

15. Behnke and Hellmich argue that it is "an epistemological problem" rather than a crisis. In either case, they argue that it is "a problem of knowledge and interpretation." See Andreas Behnke and Christina Hellmich, "Introduction: Al-Qaeda and Terrorism as a Challenge to Knowledge, in Hellmich and Behnke, *Knowing al-Qaeda*, 3.

16. Richard Jackson, "Fantasy and the Epistemological Crisis of Counter-terrorism," *Richardjacksonterrorismblog*, http://richardjacksonterrorismblog.wordpress.com/2012/08/22/fantasy-and-the-epistemological-crisis-of-counter-terrorism/, accessed August 30, 2012.

17. Joseba Zulaika, "Drones, Witches and Other Flying Objects: The Force of Fantasy in US Counterterrorism," *Critical Studies on Terrorism* 5, no. 1 (2012): 51–68; Charlotte Heath-Kelly, "Can We Laugh Yet? Reading post-9/11 Counterterrorism Policy as Magical

Realism and Opening a Third-Space of Resistance," *European Journal on Criminal Policy and Research* 18, no. 4 (July 11, 2012), http://rd.springer.com/article/10.1007/s10610-012 -9180-4, accessed August 30, 2012.

18. See the story recounted in Richard Jackson, "How Bizarre: Book-Burning, Magic and the Logic of Counter-terrorism," *Richardjacksonterrorismblog,* May 9, 2012, http:// richardjacksonterrorismblog.wordpress.com/2012/05/09/, accessed August 30, 2012; Sylvia Cooper, "Fire Hydrant Anti-terrorism Project OK'd, *Augusta (GA) Chronicle,* May 8, 2007, http://chronicle.augusta.com/stories/2007/05/08/met_127596.shtml, accessed August 30, 2012; Alan Clendenning, "Paragliding Terror Suspects' Arrest in Spain Put Paragliding in Spotlight," *Huffington Post World,* August 7, 2012, http://www.huffington post.com/2012/08/07/paragliding-terror-suspects_n_1751191.html?utm_hp_ref=world, accessed August 30, 2012; Kareem Fahim, "Where Candy Machines Are Eyed with Suspicion," *New York Times,* October 12, 2007, http://www.nytimes.com/2007/10/12/ nyregion/12gumballs.html?_r=2&pagewanted=print, accessed August 30, 2012; Department of Homeland Security, "Infrastructure Protection Report: Amusement, Theme, and Water Parks," October 7, 2009, http://publicintelligence.net/infrastructure-protection -report-amusement-theme-and-water-parks/, accessed August 30, 2012.

19. Behnke and Hellmich, "Introduction," 2–3. For "void of meaning" see David Campbell, "Time Is Broken: The Return of the Past in the Response to September 11," *Theory and Event* 5, no. 4 (2001); and James Der Derian, "*In Terrorem*: Before and after 9/11," in *Worlds in Collision: Terror and the Future of Global Order,* ed. Ken Booth and Tim Dunne (New York: Palgrave Macmillan, 2002).

20. See Hoffman, *Inside Terrorism.*

21. See Isabelle Duyvesteyn and Leona Malkki, "NO: The Fallacy of the New Terrorism Thesis," in Jackson and Sinclair, *Contemporary Debates on Terrorism*; and Martha Crenshaw, "The Debate over 'New' vs. 'Old' Terrorism," in *Values and Violence: Intangible Aspects of Terrorism,* ed. Ibrahim Karawan, Wayne McCormack, and Stephen E. Reynolds (Dordrecht: Springer, 2009).

22. For an interesting discussion of the kind of data metrics used by the U.S. government in the War on Terror, see Rashmi Singh, "Measuring al-Qaeda: The Metrics of Terror," in Hellmich and Behnke, *Knowing al-Qaeda.*

23. Ulrich Beck, "World Risk Society as Cosmopolitan Society? Ecological Questions in a Framework of Manufactured Uncertainties," *Theory, Culture and Society* 13, no. 4 (1996): 1–32; Ulrich Beck, *Risk Society: Towards a New Modernity* (London: Sage, 1992); Christopher Daase and Oliver Kessler, "Knowns and Unknowns in the 'War on Terror': Uncertainty and the Political Construction of Danger," *Security Dialogue* 38, no. 4 (2007): 425–26.

24. Frank Furedi, *Culture of Fear: Risk-taking and the Morality of Low Expectation,* rev. ed. (London: Continuum, 2002).

25. Rumsfeld, qtd. in Daase and Kessler, "Knowns and Unknowns," 428.

26. See John Mueller and Mark G. Stewart, "Balancing the Risks, Benefits, and Costs of Homeland Security," *Homeland Security Affairs* 7, article 16 (August 2011), http://www .hsaj.org/?fullarticle=7.1.16, accessed August 30, 2012.

27. See Daase and Kessler, "Knowns and Unknowns," 419.

28. Richard Jackson, "Unknown Knowns: The Subjugated Knowledge of Terrorism Studies," *Critical Studies on Terrorism* 5, no. 1 (2012): 11–29.

29. Daase and Kessler, "Knowns and Unknowns," 412.

30. Lisa Stampnitzky, *Disciplining Terror: How Experts Invented "Terrorism"* (Cambridge: Cambridge University Press, 2013). Stampnitzky's analysis relies on James Ferguson, *The Anti-politics Machine: "Development," Depoliticization, and Bureaucratic Power in Lesotho* (Minneapolis: University of Minnesota Press, 1994).

31. Joseba Zulaika and William A. Douglass, *Terror and Taboo: The Follies, Fables, and Faces of Terrorism* (New York: Routledge, 1996).

32. Hellmich assesses this largely as a failure of academic process by the terrorism expert community, an approach not incompatible with the notion of "knowledge subjugation." See Christina Hellmich, "Here Come the Salafis: The Framing of al-Qaeda's Ideology within Terrorism Research," in Hellmich and Behnke, *Knowing al-Qaeda*.

33. Behnke and Hellmich, "Introduction," 3. The language barrier and dependence on translation from Arabic plays a role in this condition, although it should not be overstated. A great many interviews, letters, and statements by bin Laden have been produced in English and are available in magazines and newspapers, on the Web, and as published books.

34. Ivan Eland, "Does U.S. Intervention Overseas Breed Terrorism? The Historical Record," CATO Institute Foreign Policy Briefing no. 50, December 17, 1998, http://www .cato.org/pubs/fpbriefs/fpb-050es.html, accessed September 5, 2011; Richard English, *Terrorism: How to Respond* (Oxford: Oxford University Press, 2009); Bader Araj, "Harsh State Repression as a Cause of Suicide Bombing: The Case of the Palestinian-Israeli Conflict," *Studies in Conflict and Terrorism* 31, no 4 (2008): 284–303.

35. See, for example, "Full Text: Bin Laden's 'Letter to America,'" *Guardian*, November 24, 2002, http://www.guardian.co.uk/world/2002/nov/24/theobserver, accessed September 2, 2012; and Bruce Lawrence, *Messages to the World: The Statements of Osama Bin Laden*, trans. James Howarth (London: Verso, 2005).

36. Behnke and Hellmich, "Introduction," 3.

37. Stampnitzky, *Disciplining Terror.*

38. UK Home Office, n.d. The Counter-terrorism Strategy, http://www.homeoffice .gov.uk/counter-terrorism/uk-counter-terrorism-strat/, accessed August 30, 2012.

39. See David A. Yallop, *To the Ends of the Earth: The Hunt for the Jackal* (London: Jonathan Cape, 1993).

40. Some of the core material interests that are now invested in the continuation of the War on Terror are detailed in Richard Jackson, "Culture, Identity and Hegemony: Continuity and (the Lack of) Change in US Counter-terrorism Policy from Bush to Obama," *International Politics* 48, no. 2/3 (2011): 390–411.

41. Daase and Kessler, "Knowns and Unknowns," 412.

42. Behnke and Hellmich, "Introduction," 1.

43. Zulaika and Douglass, *Terror and Taboo.*

44. For extensive analyses of the politics of fear see, among others, Richard Jackson, "The Politics of Terrorism Fear," in *The Political Psychology of Terrorism Fears*, ed. Samuel Justin Sinclair and Daniel Antonius (Cambridge: Cambridge University Press, 2013); and Richard Jackson, "Playing the Politics of Fear: Writing the Terrorist Threat in the War on Terrorism," in *Playing Politics with Terrorism: A User's Guide*, ed. George Kassimeris, ed. (New York: Columbia University Press, 2007), 176–202.

2

The Discursive Portrayals of Osama bin Laden

ADITI BHATIA

This chapter attempts to illustrate how the creation of illusive categories and perceptions through the use of religious metaphor among other rhetorical tools culminated in the inevitable dichotomy in the way the world perceived Osama bin Laden. It thus conceptualizes bin Laden's discourse as a set of discursive illusions, in which the dual faces created of and by him turn out to be two sides of the same coin.

Drawing on a combination of analytical tools, which include the historical approach, membership categorization analysis, and discourse as metaphor,[1] this chapter analyzes a selection of speeches by Osama bin Laden and George W. Bush in an attempt to illustrate how both parties use almost identical forms of discourse in order to produce diametrically opposed conceptualizations of reality. The following sections attempt to illustrate how Osama bin Laden played the role of both the evil terrorist and the brave champion of Islam through the creation of discursive illusions.[2]

Good versus Evil

The War on Terror, for the most part, was a metaphorical battle (refer also to the chapter "Metaphorizing Terrorism" by Spencer in this book), rousing intense emotions and violent actions though the whirlwind of extreme rhetoric.[3] The key figureheads in this rhetorical war were Osama bin Laden, regarded then as the key face and motivating factor of the international terrorist network Al Qaida, and former American president George W. Bush. Both borrowed from a similar pool of rhetorical resources to draw followers toward their cause and as a result suffered from dual identities: the terrorist and the champion.

The most prominent role that bin Laden played and attributed to others was that of an evil entity. Evil opens up a range of religious imaginaries, invoking concepts of good and evil. Many Western nations portrayed bin Laden in terms of "the very worst of human nature," and as part of a group of people that "don't represent an ideology, they don't represent a legitimate political group of people. They're flat evil."[4] (Spencer in another chapter in this book makes a similar assessment about the media's portrayal of terrorists.). Bin Laden, in return, sculpted "the West" in much the same terms—casting the mold even wider, to include all infidels and non-Muslims, reiterating the evilness of the other. If one were to accept bin Laden's conceptualization of reality,[5] then it was predominantly Western nations championed by America and those who were seen by bin Laden as supporting their quest, such as the House of Saud, that were evil:

> Bush and his gang, with their heavy sticks and hard hearts, are an evil to all humankind. They have stabbed into the truth, until they have killed it altogether in the eyes of the world.
>
> Bin Laden, October 18, 2003 (Al Jazeera)

> The Islamic Nation that was able to dismiss and destroy the previous evil Empires like yourself; the Nation that rejects your attacks, wishes to remove your evils, and is prepared to fight you.
>
> Bin Laden, November 24, 2002 (Al Jazeera)

> The occupation of Iraq is a link in the Zionist-crusader chain of evil.
>
> Bin Laden, January 6, 2004 (Al Jazeera)

In the above extracts bin Laden vilifies "Bush and his gang" in a mafia and murder metaphor making them the killers of "the truth," their truth, the truth supporting, and emerging from, their perspective, subsequently correlating evil with lies and deceit. Of course, people that bin Laden's followers deem as gang members and thugs would be viewed by audiences allied with America as proactive Western nations, championing freedom. Regardless, the realizations of evil are made more intense through the invocation of history, through the comparison of Bush's administration with previous "evil Empires," possibly a reference to the Romans, or the British, and in doing so bin Laden effectively historicizes the Islamic Nation's struggle as perennial and severe. Further metaphorizing of the occupation of Iraq by the "Zionist-crusader" in terms of a "chain of evil" attributes an almost franchise-like status to the spread of terror by Western nations (again, this metaphor would be interpreted as such by those who allied themselves with bin Laden's cause and ideology). Bin Laden attempts to justify his actions and beliefs as resistance to this oppression suffered due to these evil regimes that attack with their "heavy sticks and hard hearts." Evil acts can thus be seen as

> necessarily the products of evil dispositions; or the evilness of states of affairs is a sufficient condition of the evilness of the acts that bring them about; or having evil dispositions is a necessary, and maybe sufficient, condition of being an evil person.[6]

In the rhetoric of both bin Laden and Bush above, evil is presented as a *type* categorization, denoting a certain *type* of people.[7] While for Western nations the adverb *very* in conjunction with the adjective *worst* portrays terrorists as the opposite of everything that the nation of "good folks" stand for, bin Laden typifies them in return as "an evil to all humankind."[8] Both figureheads flesh out the *evil other* with typically associated characteristics and actions: Bush disassociates bin Laden from any sort of ideology or political grouping, thereby denying him, and affiliated group members, the opportunity for justification. Evil becomes a part of the *character* of these *types* of people. The adjective *flat* further emphasizes the extreme evil of terrorists without allowing them any grounds for explanation; they are evil by nature, not consequence. The adjective adds value to the term *evil* by giving it a sense of intensity or, more specifically, by assigning to it a level of degrees. As J. S. Mackenzie notes, an advantage in the use of value is that "it enables us, without any difficulty, to recognize *degrees*."[9] In this case, however, it is difficult to differentiate between degrees of evil, since "what we regard as evil are just those actions that, to some greater extent, more seriously offend our deeply-held moral sentiments or that produce much more harmful consequences."[10] Evil in this regard already is the higher-intensity value of something not good or bad. Evil is already a valued-laden term judged differently "in terms of degree or intensity, from commonplace wrongdoing."[11] Bin Laden, on the other hand, sketches the *actions* of *evil* including stabbing "into the truth, until they have killed it altogether," and occupying Islamic nations. While for Bush, evil is an inherent trait, cognitively ingrained, a state of being, for bin Laden it is a rectifiable state of affairs, which the Islamic Nation can "dismiss and destroy," which it "rejects," and which it "wishes to remove" and "fight." Interestingly, Bush's metaphorical conceptualization of evil does not allow bin Laden to cease to be evil if he were to stop engaging in terrorist activity, because evil is viewed as an inherent trait. However, according to bin

Laden's conceptualization of evil, if Western nations are to stop engaging in undesired actions, they cease to be evil; it is more a result of social action. As R. M. Hare says, "our ultimate moral principles can become so completely accepted by us, that we treat them, not as universal imperatives, but as matters of fact; they have the same obstinate indubitability."[12]

In both cases, the figureheads generate discursive illusions of fury, injustice, a detrimental state, and a general war cry. Bin Laden, while rapidly climbing the ladder on the world's most wanted list, was able to summon support from sympathizers, admirers, and followers alike, through the *enemification* of evil Western nations.[13] Borrowing from the same discourse that was used to characterize himself, bin Laden flips the coin to proliferate the opposite image of himself and his enemies.

Civilization versus Barbarism

The psyche of the *evil* person is further explicated through an explanation of his *barbaric* nature, further escalating the war to one not simply between evil and good, but between civilization and barbarism (see also Spencer in another chapter in this book for a discussion of the media's concept of terrorism as an "uncivilized evil"). Bush made constant correlations between "those evil-doers, those barbaric people," emphasizing the "great divide in our time—not between religions or cultures, but between civilization and barbarism . . . People of all cultures wish to live in safety and dignity . . . Our enemies reject these values."[14] Here barbarism is given the same intrinsic quality that is ascribed to evil. Barbarism is distinguished from the behavior of civilization, since it does not respect the values of the civilized, who "wish to live in safety and dignity."

Bin Laden, as a terrorist, is outcast from civilization and civilized society, which is aligned with the United States and its allies, and anyone against them is against the world: "The civilized world is rallying to America's side," and Bush further explicates, "No nation can be neutral in this conflict, because no civilized nation can be secure in a world threatened by terror."[15] This sentiment is echoed by then British prime minister Tony Blair in addressing citizens of targeted countries, "Our enemy is not you, but your barbarous rulers."[16] America, as the champion of the civilized world, metaphorizes the War on Terror to its allied audiences into a political campaign or election, in favor of which the civilized world is "rallying," thus creating positive self-presentation, emphasizing the goodness of America, and furthering the illusive us-versus-them divide between the civilized (or all those on the side of America) and the "enemy," the uncivilized and barbaric. However, true to the nature of discursive illusions, participants often share *double contrastive identities*, whereby bin Laden and his affiliates, who are portrayed as barbaric by America, in turn accuse Americans of being "the worst civilization witnessed by the history of mankind," the superlative "worst" depicting a powerful negative-other presentation of the opposite side.[17] What the model of discursive illusions spotlights here is the conflict between contested versions of reality, the different, but both subjective, conceptualizations of reality put forward by elite figureheads in the pursuit of specific sociopolitical objectives.

The clash between civilization and barbarism emphasizes the illusive us-versus-them division between a civilized and an uncivilized population. It would be an easy assumption to make if one were to say that it was a decisive demarcation between the East and the West, but there is so much history to consider attached to this assumption that such a nominal division is not possible. Instead, both bin Laden and Bush supplant notions of cultural divides, typically present in discourses on clashes between civilizations, by drawing on organized religion.[18] Although Bush often reiterated, "Our war is not against a religion. Our war is against evil," and "We do not fight Islam, we fight against evil,"[19] constant referencing to the Islamic faith and Christianity gave a contrary impression: "let me quote from the Koran itself: In the long run, evil in the extreme will be the end of those who do evil"; "The terrorists practice a fringe form of Islamic extremism"; "those who commit evil in the name of Allah blaspheme the name of Allah . . . trying, in effect, to hijack Islam itself."[20] Bush invokes religion constantly, quoting the Koran itself, giving the impression that despite not being a follower of the Islamic faith he is aware of the teachings of the Koran.

There is a recurrent implication in Bush's rhetoric that terrorism arises from Islam, and as a result the pending war seems not to be between terror and peace but more specifically between Islam and the Western world, further deepening the us-versus-them divide. This very demarcation is also acknowledged and reiterated by bin Laden, who claims, "These incidents divided the entire world into two regions—one of faith where there is no hypocrisy and another of infidelity, from which we hope God will protect us," and through implication of "us" bin Laden associates himself with the first region of people.[21] The bi-propositional nature of religious discourse becomes apparent here when bin Laden quotes the same principles as Bush; however, typical of such illusion, we find both Bush and bin Laden displaying "double contrastive identities" where the roles of *us* versus *them*, good versus bad, moral versus immoral, are reversible depending on which side's perceptions are taken into account.[22] While Bush portrays bin Laden as leading the army of the Antichrist against God, bin Laden, quoting a passage from the Koran, regards Bush and his followers as "those who disbelieve, fight in the cause of *Taghut* [anything worshipped other than Allah, e.g., Satan]. So fight you against the friends of Satan; ever feeble is indeed the plot of Satan."[23]

Bin Laden also appears confident of his victory because "Allah, the Almighty, legislated the permission and the option to take revenge," and furthermore, victory is assured because "they" are "(true) believers."[24] The discursive illusions surface here in the contested versions of reality. Who is fighting which battle from which side? It is a matter of perspective. As Bruce Lincoln says, the speeches by Bush and bin Laden seem to mirror one another, offering narratives of the aggressors and aggrieved, but while "Bush preferred to define the coming struggle in ethico-political terms as a campaign of civilized nations against terrorist cells . . . Bin Laden, in contrast, saw it as a war of infidels versus the faithful."[25]

Nevertheless, as mentioned before, this clash between the East and the West, more specifically between the West and Islam, is not a random disorder; it does not surface from disjointed history but rather has grown over time, and the conflict between these two "distinct cultures" is often portrayed as having evolved for 1300 years.[26] Such perceptions of geographies/civilizations have long been socially constructed and are often narrated to be in conflict with one another. It is possible then to say that the understanding of these two cultures, and their shared relationship, has been inherited over time, gradually naturalizing into the fabric of society, and thus becoming part of our habitus.[27] These perceptions have come to exist, and in certain cases are even treated, as straightforward facts from various facets of history, some incidents of which include the eleventh and thirteenth Christian Crusades and the rule of the Ottoman Turks between the fourteenth and seventeenth centuries, which further divided and strengthened the illusive us-versus-them criteria.

The West has for a long time enjoyed its power, its global domination in various aspects, and consequently what is commonly understood as the East or Orient, and all related prejudices, stereotypes, and categories, are "generated out of strength" and in that sense are constitutive of the Orient and the Orientals.[28] This can be understood as the control and depiction of reality by the powerful in society. Powerful voices determine to a large extent how society interprets the Orient, the West, the evil, the terrorist, in accordance with their individual sociopolitical agendas. Practices of the strong and the dominant are commonsensical and objective, but those of their opponents are subjective, illogical, and random.

Discursive illusions, born out of subjective conceptualizations of reality, are based on an individual's ideological histories and past experiences; thus one's rhetoric is often reflective of his or her part-and-parcel subjectivity.[29] Appeals to history in Bush's rhetoric are indicative of how discursive illusions draw on past experiences to determine the present and become grounds for future actions: "History will record our response, and judge or justify every nation in this hall."[30] Appeals to history provide a sense of continuity; they bring about coherence in one's perceptions. Appeals to history in this sense also legitimize our way of thinking because they illustrate our thoughts, opinions, and ideologies, which, through this continuity, appear less random and arbitrary, more like objective fact. The personification of an abstract concept such as history into a judge or someone who will "record our responses" can be seen as an appeal made to a higher form of authority: time. Appeal to time is persuasive because it emphasizes how perennial the struggle against evil is, and thus how important it is to take action against it.

Employing the same rhetorical strategy, bin Laden too makes an appeal to history, reminding the world that "our nation has been tasting this humiliation and contempt for more than 80 years," and that the "blood of the children of Vietnam, Somalia, Afghanistan, and Iraq is still dripping from their teeth," metaphorizing America and allied blocs into a monster, reinforcing an earlier claim that American policies and imposition are "monstrous, destructive."[31] Bin Laden further mentions "the [U.S.] defense minister stated that this is our right. It is their right to annihilate people so long as they are Muslims and non-American."[32] Bin Laden presents himself and fellow Muslims as victims and those in the West as aggressors, giving rise again to discursive illusions.

A principle characteristic of discursive illusion is its bi-propositional nature, whereby participants in any sort of conflict or in any category pairing have a

> double, contrastive identity. Bin Laden, for instance, is an incumbent of the category "us" as he formulates it (defenders of Islam). He is also an incumbent of "them" as it is formulated by his enemy (terrorists). The same is the case for his enemy: President Bush is one of "us" (we who defend freedom and democracy) and he is one of "them" (crusaders attacking Islam). The category pairs are united in an opposition by the way in which the conflict is framed—as a religious war, on the one hand, and a war between civilization and barbarism, on the other hand.[33]

While Bush may portray terrorists as evil and barbaric as per his conceptualization of reality, Louise Richardson argues, however, that terrorists "are neither crazy nor amoral . . . They come from many walks of life . . . They come from all religious traditions and from none. One thing they do have in common. They are weaker than those they oppose."[34] The crucial point for consideration here is that the depiction of terrorists as barbaric, uncivilized, or evil can be interpreted as part of the discourse of illusion, where not only do the more powerful voices in society categorize groups and individuals into *types* of people according to their perceptions, but those who the *us* group categorize as *others* and evil in turn perhaps deem *us* as evil, since the assignment of *evil* to one group automatically denotes its equal and opposite "verbal form—Good and *Bad*, Good and *Evil*, and again Better and *Worse*."[35] Again, these labels are extreme, especially since *good* is "too suggestive of something absolute and unquestionable."[36] R. M. Hare further argues that the principal function of *good* is to commend, and in commending actions as moral or immoral one is indirectly or directly commending people.[37] In this equation *good*, *ought*, and *right* form a triangle, whereby *right* and *ought* share the supervening character of good. Hare argues that *ought* and *good* share similar descriptive and prescriptive forces, they aim to prescribe or instruct without conveying any information. In this case, bin Laden and Bush take turns to command this esteemed position, affiliating with the *good* side in opposition to the *evil* other.

Bush in the extracts mentioned above portrays himself and America as a contrast to the evil they are fighting. The "worst" in human nature is met by the "best in America." Again, we go back to what was mentioned earlier, the notion of good evokes something absolute and unquestionable. However, Daniel M. Haybron explains that *evil* is not always a superlative but is used to denote the opposite of good.[38] It is for this reason that J. S. Mackenzie says *value* is a more appropriate term to describe evil, as it "does not suggest anything absolute or unqualified . . . Value is a much more fluid and adaptable expression."[39] Let us regard evil as a *value* in this chapter, and as a value it is the equal and opposite of good. Value comes across as relatively more all-encompassing of morality, religion, and the politics that they source, and hence being more reflective of the subjectivism that discursive illusions represent, rather than treating evil simply as an intensifier or adjective.

Moral Justice versus Retribution

Once it is established who evil is, and that it leads to barbaric and uncivilized acts, it seems important to bring this evil to justice or serve it with revenge. What we find thus emerging in the discourse of both leaders are the themes of justice and retribution, which also draw on religious imagery. Bush's rhetoric seems to reflect a more orthodox view of Christianity whereby evil must be defeated and not merely separated. Bush's rhetoric is aggressive and retributive, which negates his many claims that all he wants is justice: "They find holes to get in and we will do whatever it takes to smoke them out and get them running"; "American people do not seek only revenge, but to win a war against barbaric behavior"; "Ours is a nation that does not seek revenge, but we do seek justice."[40]

Use of the phrase "smoke them out of their holes," repeated at various points during different speeches, enforces the Manichaean principles of light and dark, with "holes" being representative of darkness, secrecy, going underground. The conflict between light and dark is illustrated in a hunter-hunted analogy and on some level is even reminiscent of smoking a snake out of its hole, with the "hills" providing a nature context. The hunter metaphor also gives the impression that Bush is more interested in retribution than justice and brings to mind the previously mentioned statement by bin Laden when he represents America as a monster. Bush's next statement, "there is a desire by the American people to not seek only revenge, but to win a war against barbaric behavior," confirms this observation, whereby revenge is justified by depicting terrorists as "barbaric." This statement can be contrasted with one made exactly ten days later: "Ours is a nation that does not seek revenge, but we do seek justice." As Thrasymachus mentions in Plato's *Republic*, "the just is nothing other than the advantage of the stronger."[41] Retribution in the form of justice often stems from a religious basis, where believers of a particular faith are out to punish those who have wronged them and devalued their faith. Inherent in this definition of justice is the *individualism*, or rather the sense of unilateralism present, which might gain collective consent, but the basis of which seems fundamentally driven by emotions rather than a sense of rational objectivity. The end goal seems thus more in line with doling out punishment to the wrongdoer than establishing some form of justice. Retribution here comes with more consequences than lawful justice since it sparks the *eye for an eye* cycle. The noun retribution itself has very emotive undertones invoking various emotions—fear, anger, desire, and demanding immediacy of action. While the noun *justice* gives the impression of trials, lawyers, policies, legislation, rules, and regulations, *retribution*, however, seems to depict erratic behavior, urgency, impatience, and determination, and any actions taken in the state of retribution are rarely interpreted as objective or just.

Bush's rhetoric on retribution and justice can be contrasted with the tone of revenge utilized by bin Laden, who states:

> It is *commanded by our religion* and intellect that the *oppressed have a right to return the aggression*. Do not await anything from *us* but Jihad, resistance and *revenge*. *Is it in any way rational* to expect that after *America has attacked us for more than half a century*, that *we* will then leave her to live in security and peace?!!
>
> Bin Laden, November 24, 2002 (Al Jazeera)

I say to the American people *we will continue to fight you and continue to conduct martyrdom operations inside and outside the United States* until you *depart from your oppressive course . . . we* will *fight you as long as we carry guns. And if we fall, our sons will take our place. And may our mothers become childless if we leave any of you alive on our soil.*

Bin Laden, October 18, 2003 (Al Jazeera)

In the extracts above, bin Laden puts forward arguments similar to Bush; however, as is typical of discursive illusions, the roles of both parties are reversed. In this case America is portrayed negatively, as oppressive, while in a more positive self-representative manner sympathy is evoked by illustrating terrorists as victims of this oppression. They are not terrorizing but rather resisting. Their form of revenge is not terrorism but instead a right due to being "attacked" for "more than half a century." Bin Laden illustrates his motives for revenge as stemming from his "religion and intellect" perhaps in an attempt to justify and consequently objectify his conceptualization of reality. He goes as far as to pose in a rhetorical question whether it is "in any way rational" to expect "anything from us but Jihad, resistance and revenge." Bin Laden appears almost reasonable in his categorical logic. However, emotive language in the form of the warning "may our mothers become childless if we leave any of you alive on our soil" negates the rationality of the previous statement, appearing almost as an ultimatum in the topos of threat.[42] Stating that if they should fall then their sons will take their place gives the impression that this struggle will be long-drawn-out and violent, since they "fight" as long as they "carry guns." Bin Laden also makes much use of the pronouns *we*, *us*, and *our* in an effort to unite Muslims and fellow radicals. A point to consider here would be that although bin Laden's call for revenge seems to originate from some quasi-religious purpose, and Bush's more out of ego or rather secular politics, thus by default rendering bin Laden's motive comparatively more acceptable, it is still bin Laden's rhetoric that appears aggressive and portentous.

J. P. Larsson argues that "religious violence is on many levels *more* logical and rational than purely secular forms of political violence . . . [it] motivates and inspires followers to fight for a particular cause and it is furthermore capable of sustaining that motivation, until death for the believer and for generations to come, if necessary."[43] Consequently, it is possible to say that because bin Laden seemed so organized in his thought process, because he seemed so rational and logical, his threat was taken more seriously by his audiences, including targeted nations, as compared to the remarks of Bush, who seemed almost caught up in an influx of emotions. Religious discourse in this sense did not seem fanatical, but because of the historical grounding that bin Laden provided his plight, his religious logic seem justified, whereas Bush's religious logic often came across as retributive in terms of present-day events.

It would seem that there is more threat in religious rhetoric because there is a greater amount of consistency to it. The principles followed are decreed and appear to the followers of that religion as objective facts, based furthermore on an absolute cosmic dualism of good and evil, which is "another element of the logic of religious violence that is most prevalent . . . It is because of this absoluteness of cosmic dualism that concepts such as 'holy war' . . . have developed within every religion."[44] To people like bin Laden, who were seen by Western nations to be following a "fringe form of Islamic extremism," it is possible to understand *extremism* not as fanatic or violent but rather as groups of believers who "take concepts of cosmic war literally as a divine precept or decree."[45] As a result the threat posed by bin Laden conveyed via religious rhetoric was taken more literally by audiences as well.

In conclusion, this chapter attempts to reveal how both bin Laden and Bush drew on religious discourse alongside various other rhetorical tools in order to achieve the same goal—the objectification of their individual, ideologically simulated conceptualizations of reality. However, both versions of reality indicted the *other* to be evil, immoral, and barbaric. The construction of terrorist and vanguard, consequently, became even less defined and instead confined by a series of discursive illusions that, depending on one's sociocultural positioning, could come to mean a various number of things. The predominance of religious imagery within the rhetoric of these two key figureheads also indicated that a whole plethora of cultural contexts, political histories, and affiliations were needed on part of audiences to see through the number of shadows that were cast on societies' perceptions and understanding of what constituted a terrorist, a freedom fighter, a war, and a just cause.

Notes

1. The historical approach draws on Layder's historical analysis, which traces historical antecedents of the social phenomenon being investigated and Wodak's discourse-historical model, which looks at inconsistencies in the relations between discourses and the historical contexts within which they are embedded. Derek Layder, *New Strategies in Social Research: An Introduction and Guide* (Cambridge: Polity Press, 1993); Ruth Wodak, "The Discourse Historical Approach," in *Methods of Critical Discourse Analysis*, ed. Ruth Wodak and Michael Meyer, 63–94 (London: Sage 2002). Membership categorization analysis makes sense of people, relationships, and experiences through category work, which depicts types of people based on moral, religious, and social characteristics. A useful approach for the investigation of metaphors and the categorizations that they can

engender, which is not, however, a primary focus in this chapter, is membership categorization analysis. Lena Jayyusi, *Categorization and the Moral Order* (Boston: Routledge and Kegan Paul, 1984). See also Annita Lazar and Michelle M. Lazar, "The Discourse of the New World Order: 'Out-casting' the Double Face of Threat," *Discourse and Society* 15, no. 2–3 (2004): 223–42; Ivan Leudar, Victoria Marsland, and Jiří Nekvapil, "On Membership Categorization: 'Us', 'Them' and 'Doing Violence' in Political Discourse," *Discourse and Society* 15, no. 2–3 (2004): 243–66. For discourse as metaphor see Jonathan Charteris-Black, *Corpus Approaches to Critical Metaphor Analysis* (Hampshire, U.K.: Palgrave Macmillan, 2004). See also Jonathan Charteris-Black, *Politicians and Rhetoric: The Persuasive Power of Metaphor* (New York: Palgrave Macmillan, 2005).

2. Although many scholars and academics have tried to define what we understand by the term *discourse*, in this chapter we employ the notion of discourse in the Foucauldian sense of the term, where emphasis is placed on context and history in relation to discourse. For Foucault, discourse is not simply a linguistic practice; it is about the representation of reality, the practice of it. Discourse in turn is made of statements, which for Foucault are atoms of discourse, the way sentences are of a text: "At first, the statement appears as the ultimate, undecomposable element that can also be isolated and introduced into a set of relations with other similar elements. . . . [It] can be located in planes of division and in specific forms of groupings. A seed that appears on the surface of a tissue of which it is the constituent element. The atom of discourse." Michel Foucault, *The Archaeology of Knowledge and the Discourse of Language* (London: Tavistock, l972), 80. Foucault further argues that discourse is, from start to finish, historical. As individuals, however, we cannot discern the historicity from which our statements and discourses originate, since they are so intrinsically entrenched in us, akin in a way to a fish not being able to look at itself from outside a fishbowl. The historicity that lies behind the statements we make and the discourses we create should not be seen as a sudden burst of reference to our habitus whether or not we can identify coherences within our discourses. Rather these discourses are an attempt to reconstruct and represent reality in its entirety. The changes over time in our perceptions of the world, and thus the influence of them on the discourses that we construct, do not contribute to a disjointed history of experiences but instead are the reason for constant growth and development in our process of the reconceptualization of social reality and our skills as communicators. The discourse of illusion is grounded in a sociocultural mesh of beliefs and ideas about what the world is like and what it should be like. It illustrates how particular groups view the world, consistent with their culture and history, and what actions they take to change the world to be consistent with their perceptions of the world.

3. Metaphor enables the creation of new and alternate realities, generating the paradoxical combination of clarity and ambiguity necessary to present a biased conceptualization of the world as impartial. Through its relatively emotive character it succeeds largely in making otherwise unfeasible correlations feasible. Metaphor is regarded in this chapter as a means of perceiving one domain in terms of another in order to make issues and constructs more relatable to an audience, extracting perspectives and situations from their familiar

and orthodox settings and manipulating them within more unconventional and unfamiliar contexts. It is also important to note here that the interpretation of any metaphor is largely sociocultural and context driven, whereby the same metaphor can be subject to multiple interpretations depending on the receiver's ideological background and social reality.

4. George W. Bush, "Text of Bush's Address to the Nation," CNN, September 11, 2001, http://edition.cnn.com/2001/US/09/11/bush.speech.text/; "President George W. Bush in a Meeting with Muslim Community Leaders in the White House—9/26/01," in "Wikiquote: Transwiki/Terroriam (disambiguation)/Evil Doers," n.d., http://en.wikiquote.org/wiki/Transwiki:Terrorism_(disambiguation)/Evil_Doers.

5. As human beings we inhabit dual realities—our subjective conceptualizations of reality, or what Kant distinguishes as *phenomena*, which is what "appears to be," the reality we know and live, stemming from empirical observation; and our objective conceptualizations of reality, or what Kant refers to as *noumena*—an object represented in abstraction. Kant points out that our minds are active participants in the construction of reality. It is through the act of thinking that we construct, interpret, and structure the world around us, and our experiences within that world. The construction of this world is ideologically and culturally simulated; it is a product of our habitus, which Bourdieu describes as our dispositions, mannerisms, and belief systems, through which we construe the meaning of reality, and which eventually naturalize into consciousness. Subjective conceptualizations of reality offered to us by powerful social groups and figureheads often tend to be perceived as objective when they achieve collective consent, seeping into a collective consciousness as factual and truthful. Collective illusions are to a large extent writer/speaker-based; the audiences are given very little opportunity to develop their own interpretations. One reason for this is that illusion is correlated with social action and a social view of the world. Therefore, in talking about illusion we are moving to larger areas of social context and social reality. See Immanuel Kant, "The Active Mind: The Judgements of Experience," in *Philosophy in the Age of Crisis*, ed. Eleanor Kuykendall (New York: Harper and Row, 1970), 346–55; and Pierre Bourdieu, *The Logic of Practice* (Cambridge: Polity Press, 1990).

6. Hillel Steiner, "Calibrating Evil," *Monist* 58, no. 2 (2002): 183–93.

7. Samuel P. Huntington, "The Clash of Civilizations?," *Foreign Affairs* 72, no. 3 (1993): 22–49. One consequence of objectifying particular subjective conceptualizations of reality is the emergence of stereotypes and categories, which, when generated through discursive illusions, carry the function of organizing one's reality and experiences, in addition to complementing continually changing social roles, group conflicts, and distribution and retention of power. Gal and Irvine aptly point out that certain features of language combined with various forms of rhetoric can be understood to echo the cultural values and images inherent within peoples' habitus. See Lütfiye Oktar, "The Ideological Organization of Representational Processes in the Presentation of Us and Them," *Discourse and Society* 12, no. 3 (2001): 313–46; and Susan Gal and Judith T. Irvine, "The Boundaries of Language and Disciplines: How Ideologies Construct Difference," *Social Research* 62, no. 4 (1995): 967–1001.

8. "President George W. Bush in a Meeting."

9. J. S. Mackenzie, "The Meaning of Value," in *An Anthology of Recent Philosophy: Selections for Beginners from the Writings of the Greatest 20th Century Philosophers*, ed. Daniel Sommer Robinson (New York: Thomas Y. Crowell, 1929), 248–61; quote is from 250.

10. Ernesto V. Garcia, "A Kantian Theory of Evil," *Monist* 85, no. 2 (2002): 194–209, quote from 194.

11. Ibid.

12. R. M. Hare, *The Language of Morals* (Oxford: Oxford University Press, 2001), 165.

13. Lazar and Lazar, "Discourse of the New World Order," 223–42.

14. "Bush: 'There's No Rules,'" CNN, September 17, 2001, http://edition.cnn.com/2001/US/09/17/gen.bush.transcript/; George W. Bush, "Commemorating September 11," U.S. Department of State, Archive, September 10, 2002, http://2001-2009.state.gov/coalition/cr/rm/2002/13356.htm.

15. Pierre Tristam, "President Bush Declares 'War on Terror,'" About.com, September 20, 2001, http://middleeast.about.com/od/usmideastpolicy/a/bush-war-on-terror-speech_3.htm; George W. Bush, "No Nation Can Be Neutral in This Conflict," White House, Office of the Press Secretary, November 6, 2001, http://georgewbush-whitehouse.archives.gov/news/releases/2001/11/20011106-2.html.

16. Tony Blair, "Tony Blair's Address—20/03/2003," BBC Today, Focus on Iraq, http://www.bbc.co.uk/radio4/today/iraq/library_blairspeech.shtml.

17. Leudar, Marsland, and Nekvapil, "On Membership Categorization," 243–66; Osama bin Laden, "Bin Laden's 'letter to America,'" *Guardian*, November 24, 2002, http://www.guardian.co.uk/world/2002/nov/24/theobserver.

18. Huntington, "Clash of Civilizations?," 22–49.

19. George W. Bush, "Remarks Announcing the Most Wanted Terrorists List," http://www.presidency.ucsb.edu/ws/?pid=73422; George W. Bush, "Remarks by President George W. Bush to the Warsaw Conference on Combating Terrorism," in "Backgrounder: The President's Quotes on Islam," White House, http://georgewbush-whitehouse.archives.gov/infocus/racomadan/islam.html.

20. George W. Bush, "The President's Speech at the Islamic Center of Washington, DC on September 17, 2001," SoundVision.com, http://www.soundvision.com/info/terrorism/bushspeech.asp; George W. Bush, "President Bush Declares 'War on Terror,'" About.com, September 20, 2001, http://middleeast.about.com/od/usmideastpolicy/a/bush-war-on-terror-speech.htm; George W. Bush, "Address to Joint Session of Congress Following 9/11 Attacks," American Rhetoric: Rhetoric of 9-11, http://www.americanrhetoric.com/speeches/gwbush911jointsessionspeech.htm.

21. Osama bin Laden, "Bin Laden's Warning: Full Text," BBC News, October 7, 2001, http://news.bbc.co.uk/2/hi/south_asia/1585636.stm.

22. Illusion can conceptually differ from a number of other concepts—such as a lie, a hallucination, an exaggeration, and an error—because there is an element of intellectual deception in illusion. Unlike in the case of a lie, which generally involves knowing the truth and withholding it, the intention of telling the truth, even if subjective, is crucial in the creation of an illusion. For "double contrastive identities" see Leudar, Marsland, and Nekvapil, "On Membership Categorization."

23. Bin Laden, "Bin Laden's 'Letter to America.'"

24. Ibid.

25. Bruce Lincoln, *Holy Terrors: Thinking about Religion after September 11* (Chicago: University of Chicago Press, 2002), 27.

26. Huntington, "Clash of Civilizations?"

27. Pierre Bourdieu, *The Logic of Practice* (Cambridge: Polity Press, 1990).

28. Edward W. Said, *Orientalism* (London: Penguin, 2003), 40.

29. Simply defined, the discursive illusions are the product of a subjective conceptualization of reality, emerging from a historical repository of experiences embodying various linguistic and semiotic actions, often leading to intended sociopolitical consequences.

30. George W. Bush, remarks to the UN General Assembly, November 10, 2001, http://www.un.org/webcast/ga/56/statements/011110usaE.htm.

31. Bin Laden, "Bin Laden's Warning"; Osama bin Laden, "Message to US October 2003," Aljazeera, October 18, 2003, http://www.aljazeera.com/archive/2003/10/2008410102930678183.html.

32. Osama bin Laden, "Excerpt: Bin Laden Tape," *Washington Post*, December 27, 2001, http://www.washingtonpost.com/wp-srv/nation/specials/attacked/transcripts/binladen tape_122701.html.

33. Leudar, Marsland, and Nekvapil, "On Membership Categorization," 262.

34. Louise Richardson, *What Terrorists Want: Understanding the Terrorist Threat* (London: John Murray, 2006), 38–39.

35. Mackenzie, "Meaning of Value," 248–51.

36. Ibid.

37. Hare, *Language of Morals*.

38. Daniel M. Haybron, "Moral Monsters and Saints," *Monist* 85, no. 2 (2002): 260–84.

39. Mackenzie, "Meaning of Value," 248–51.

40. George W. Bush, "President Urges Readiness and Patience," White House, Office of the Press Secretary, September 15, 2001, http://georgewbush-whitehouse.archives.gov/news/releases/2001/09/20010915–4.html; George W. Bush, "'We're in a War We're Going to Win': Tells FBI It Will Get Tools It Needs to Fight Terrorism," American Embassy Press Section, http://www.usembassy-israel.org.il/publish/peace/archives/2001/september/09266.html.

41. Plato, *The Republic*, ed. Alan Bloom (New York: Basic Books, 1991), 338c: 15.

42. Ruth Wodak et al., *The Discursive Construction of National Identity* (Edinburgh: Edinburgh University Press, 1999).

43. J. P. Larsson, *Understanding Religious Violence: Thinking outside the Box on Terrorism* (Hants, UK: Ashgate, 2004), 106–8.

44. Ibid., 113–15.

45. Bush, "Address to Joint Session of Congress"; Larsson, *Understanding Religious Violence*, 115.

3

The bin Laden Tapes

ANDREW HILL

If Osama bin Laden, in the position he assumed in relation to the spectacle of
the assault on Afghanistan, can be conceived as constituting an "anamorphic
ghost"—as will become evident across the course of this chapter—the conception of bin Laden as a type of ghostly presence reveals much about the role
he has continued to play in the War on Terror in the midst of a hunt for him
claimed to be the largest ever undertaken for an individual.

This chapter takes as its focus bin Laden's video appearances since the September 11 attacks (while also discussing aspects of the audio material from this
period that purports to feature him)[1]—to scrutinize both the means by which
these appearances have allowed bin Laden to continue to intervene in the War
on Terror and the terms in which they have served to shape perceptions in the
West of the nature of the enemy faced in this conflict.

To Be Seen, to Remain Unseen

These video appearances can be understood as emanating above all from the
desire of bin Laden, in the midst of the War on Terror, to sustain a visible presence for both his opponents and supporters. As Clifford Geertz has argued,
such a presence has figured as crucial to the authority of diverse types of leaders
across history, proving of particular significance to the version of a charismatic

leader—delineated by Max Weber—that bin Laden exemplifies.[2] As Terry Smith, writing in 2003 in the *Critical Quarterly,* has contended:

> Bin Laden remains the spiritual guru and strategic guide for many thousands of Muslim militants around the world; every time he demonstrates that he is alive and can still make a forceful presentation on tape, he can be assured of more recruits to his cause of global jihad.[3]

In Western media coverage, the content of bin Laden's verbal statements in these video (and audio) recordings has been accorded comparatively limited attention, with interest focused instead on bin Laden's visibility—the fact that he has reappeared and been seen again (or, in the case of the audio recordings that his voice might have been heard again).[4]

These video appearances have provided a means by which bin Laden has sought to issue a reminder of the threat he continues to present to his opponents. The visibility he achieves in these recordings presents a further instance of the technique of intimidation in terms of the "overvaluation" the subject tries to attain at the Imaginary over and above the threat they constitute at the Real. In the case of these video appearances it is bin Laden's own visible profile that functions in such terms, presenting to his opponents the image of their most wanted adversary accusing, threatening, and goading them, having harmed them already and declaring he will do so again, and having resisted the attempt to capture and destroy him. At the same time, though, such has been the degree of attention focused upon bin Laden as the head of Al Qaeda—in part thanks to these very video appearances—that he has come to function as a metonym for Al Qaeda and the enemy more broadly in the War on Terror, as charismatic leaders in general have a tendency to do for the groups they lead. While maintaining a visual presence has been crucial to bin Laden in his attempts to continue to play a role in the War on Terror (and to maintain his position as the recognized head of Al Qaeda), the issue of his visibility possesses another, quite different dimension—lying at the heart of the attempts to hunt him down and capture or destroy him.

In an era of weapons technology, the sighting of a target is intimately linked to the capacity to strike at it. Where, as Paul Virilio states, "once you can see the target, you can expect to destroy it," and where "winning is keeping the target in constant sight," the technology deployed to identify and assassinate bin Laden relies crucially upon making a successful sighting of him.[5] This is evident in previous attempts to strike at him. On August 20, 1998, in response to the bombing of U.S. embassies in Kenya and Tanzania, the United States launched sixty Tomahawk cruise missiles at a suspected chemical weapons factory in Khartoum and a training camp in Khost, Afghanistan. Bin Laden was identified as being in the latter only an hour before the missiles landed, and yet he managed to escape, thanks, it is thought, to a tip-off.[6] In February 2002, an unmanned Predator drone equipped with sophisticated observation technology able to provide high-quality, live video surveillance monitoring fired on a group of fifteen to twenty individuals moving between the border of Afghanistan and Pakistan who appeared as if they were Al Qaeda fighters and might contain bin Laden. However, DNA samples from the dead suggested that the party did not contain bin Laden or any senior Al Qaeda figures.[7] Events such as these serve to emphasize that until a verifiable sighting is made of bin Laden, he is unlikely to be captured or killed. In an acknowledgment of this, in the spring of 2004 the U.S. military augmented a system of twenty-four-hour "constant surveillance" of the region in which bin Laden was suspected to be hiding out—on the Afghanistan-Pakistan border—combining U-2 spy planes, Predators, and ground sensors, linked by satellite transmissions, measures that have failed to yield a sighting of him.[8]

In the context of this hunt, bin Laden's visibility evokes the linkages Sartre outlines in *Being and Nothingness* between the desire for knowledge, seeing (in this instance seeing bin Laden and knowing where he is), and devouring (in this sense destroying) him.[9] In the face of this hunt bin Laden's video appearances acquire an added aura of defiance, demonstrating that despite the measures taken to achieve a sighting of him, he can persist in making himself seen across the globe—apparently if and when he so wishes—without being captured or destroyed. While providing bin Laden with the means of maintaining a presence at the Imaginary, these video appearances present bin Laden in a disembodied, dematerialized form, allowing him to retain an absence at the hard Real (as a physical, embodied being)—when it is precisely his presence at the latter that constitutes a precondition for his capture or killing.

Ghostliness, Haunting, the Objet Petit a

The dematerialized form bin Laden assumes in these video appearances accords with the conception of bin Laden as a type of ghostly presence outlined in my previous work.[10] Indeed, the ghostliness of bin Laden's appearance in portions of this footage has been repeatedly remarked upon, with his typically wan pallor (the result, it has been rumored, of life-threatening liver problems) combining with the low quality of portions of this footage—that blurs and distorts his appearance—serving to call to mind the association of poor picture quality in television of the 1950s as evidence of phantoms inhabiting the medium.[11]

While the sense of ontological indeterminacy associated with the ghostly is evocative of the difficulties that underpin the hunt for bin Laden, at the same time the quality of ghostliness and the sense of indeterminacy associated with it has constituted a key element in the fears and fantasies associated with the threat both he and the enemy more generally are conceived as presenting to the West. Indeed, as I discuss elsewhere, the enemy has repeatedly been depicted as constituting a ghostly or spectral presence.[12] The type of fears to which this ghostliness can give rise are invoked in Henry James's *The Turn of the Screw*—a work that pivots on the very question of the presence of ghosts. When the narrator responds to Mrs. Grose's question about the identity of the being that is haunting them with the retort, "What *is* he? He's a horror." "A horror?" comes Mrs. Grose's reply, to which the narrator replies, "He's—God help me if I know *what* he is!"[13]

This sense of the uncertain ontological status of bin Laden and the attendant sense of not knowing the specific type of threat he might present at any one time (as in not knowing what his present activities are and what he might be plotting or planning) are suggestive of the affinities between the position Bin Laden has come to assume for the United States and its allies, and Lacan's notion of "the Thing" ("Das Ding"), developed in Seminar 7: The Ethics of Psychoanalysis.[14] The Thing constitutes the abject locus of the subject's primary incestuous desire—that the subject is at once drawn toward and repelled by—that exists in "the beyond-of-the-signified" of the Real and as such remains unknowable and unreachable.[15] (The term is also evocative of the title of certain horror films—there is a 1982 John Carpenter film called *The Thing*. Indeed, Slavoj Zizek outlines how the Thing has repeatedly figured as central to narratives of Horror.[16]) Yet, it is the notion of "the objet petit a"—developed out of the notion of the Thing—that provides a further, more nuanced conception of the position bin Laden has come to assume for his opponents in the wake of the September 11 attacks.

The objet petit a occupies a pivotal position in Lacan's work, denoting the object cause of desire—that which sets desire in motion—much like, in the aftermath of the September 11 attacks, bin Laden was situated as the force behind the attacks, with his capture or killing coming to constitute a principal objective of the United States and its allies. And yet, the objet petit a remains elusive—while it may constitute desire's catalyst, it can never be possessed, remaining perpetually beyond the subject's grasp—and as such ensuring the sustenance of desire. As such, the object is at once redolent of the inability to seize Bin Laden and the terms in which (as will be discussed in a moment) he can be said to have become "uncapturable." The unobtainability of the object petit a derives in part from its rooting in the Real—a position that at once overlaps with the conception of bin Laden as a type of ghostly or monstrous presence, according with the position he assumed in regard to the bombardment of Afghanistan as an anamorphic ghost. Indeed, while the object petit a serves to provoke scopic desire, as Lacan outlines, it remains beyond the field of the visible, only registering there in the form of the blot—of which the anamorphic ghost presents one version.[17]

As the objet petit a can be located as haunting the subject—constantly present, yet forever out of reach—so the conception of bin Laden as a type of ghostly presence serves to position him as haunting the West, in a process that is revealing about the type of threat bin Laden and the enemy more broadly are conceived as presenting. This sense of haunting is eerily evoked in Ben Langlands and Nikki Bell's computer-generated projection *The House of Osama bin Laden*.[18] In October 2002 the artists visited Afghanistan and pursued rumors of a house occupied by bin Laden in the late 1990s. They located the building west of Jalalabad and used the material they gathered there to construct a virtual model of the house and its immediate surroundings that is then projected onto a gallery wall, with a joystick provided for navigation through the virtual abode. The experience of moving through this environment bears close similarity to that of playing a first-person shooter game, in which the player moves through an enemy's lair, confronting and destroying them.[19] The process of being able to wander through one of bin Laden's former abodes as if about to confront him, aware that he had once been there but now remains out of sight, is evocative of the type of threat bin Laden has come to assume in the midst of the hunt for him.

Haunting, in many of its forms, suggests the capacity of the being that haunts to appear as and when it wants—including at unexpected junctures and moments of particular resonance—and indeed the tactical value of this ability has been exploited by bin Laden in the timing of his video appearances. The first of these to occur in the wake of the September 11 attacks took place at the same time as the opening of the U.S. strikes on Afghanistan in October 2001, serving to distract attention away from and disrupt the spectacle of this assault. A similar sense of timing was evident in the footage broadcast days before the 2004 U.S. presidential election, which was widely perceived as an attempt to intervene in the election. Furthermore, the anniversary of the September 11 attacks has been accompanied by the release of video footage purporting to feature the voice of bin Laden (in 2002) and video footage of bin Laden himself, as well as Al Zawahiri.[20]

The sense of bin Laden haunting the West, and the sense of threat associated with this process, carries over into the series of audio recordings purporting to feature his voice that have circulated alongside these video appearances. In these recordings, the absence of a visible profile itself comes to constitute a source of anxiety, with bin Laden assuming a disembodied presence, issuing threats and inciting attacks while remaining out of sight. In so doing, the presence bin Laden assumes in these recordings conforms closely with Zizek's portrayal of the type of threat the enemy more generally in the War on Terror is conceived as presenting to the West, as he outlines in a discussion of Srdjan Dragojevic's Yugoslav civil war film *Pretty Village, Pretty Flame*.[21] In one sequence of the film a group of Serbian troops is trapped inside a tunnel by Bosnian Muslim forces who are heard but remain unseen until the end of the sequence. As Zizek discusses, the presence of the Bosnian troops takes the form of "vulgar insults or wild half-animal shouting which are not (yet) attributed to particular visually identified individuals, and thus acquire an all-powerful *spectral* dimension."[22] Zizek notes how such a narrative device has figured as a feature of a number of film genres "in which a group of sympathetic characters is encircled by an invisible Enemy who is mainly heard and seen only in the guise of fleeting shadows and blurred appearances."[23] This is an analysis that is equally applicable to bin Laden's video appearances, and in particular those in which the picture quality renders bin Laden's visual profile somewhat distorted, while at the same time pointing to the position the United States and its allies perceive themselves more broadly to occupy in the War on Terror in regard to the difficulties in achieving a sighting of the enemy.

If we apply the analysis Michel Chion develops in *The Voice in Cinema*[24] to the audio recordings that purport to feature bin Laden, bin Laden can be said to constitute a type of "acousmêtre": a being that speaks but is not seen. In the cinema such a creature has repeatedly figured as a source of fear, having been associated with a series of powerfully malevolent beings, imbued with four principal attributes: the ability to be everywhere, to see all, to know all, and have complete power (ubiquity, panopticism, omniscience, and omnipotence).[25] Locating bin Laden in these terms serves to illuminate the scale of the fears associated with him, in suggesting he is able to enact a form of total or universal haunting from which it is impossible to escape.

The Demon, Metamorphosis

For many in the West, bin Laden can be seen to have developed into a specific type of ghostly or spectral presence—a demon, the personification of evil that exists in similar forms across a host of cultures, and typically combining an intense capacity for malevolence with the type of shifting ontological profile that characterizes the ghost. Indeed, as Marina Warner has observed, historically, in the West at least, the devil—the supreme demon—has been portrayed as "a mimic, an actor, a performance artist," an illusionist able to play with and reconjure his image and appearance.[26] In his video appearances bin Laden displays similar powers, assuming the form he wishes to take—be it, at the opening of the assault on Afghanistan, dressed in military fatigues with a Kalashnikov by his side or, on the eve of the 2004 U.S. presidential election, as a statesman seated behind an office desk.

This ability to change appearance draws attention again to the terms in which the type of visual presence bin Laden assumes in these recordings has contributed to the threat he has come to be perceived as presenting to the West. In responding to bin Laden's appearance on the eve of the presidential election, one commentator noted that the video "could prove almost as damaging" as an attack, a reference to the propaganda power of this particular appearance that also serves to suggest the sense in which bin Laden's image has metamorphosed into a type of weaponry, not unlike that assumed by the video in Hideo Nakata's film *Ringu*, in which whoever views it dies exactly a week later.[27]

Bin Laden's gaze can be located as constituting a particular point of focus for the sense of threat associated with his image. In these video appearances Western audiences are not only confronted with bin Laden's visible presence; they are made aware that he possesses a gaze and that while they can see him, at the same time he possesses the capacity to see them. Such fears build upon the long running notion that—as Walter Benjamin discusses in "A Short History of Photography"—the figures that gaze out from images are able to see the spectator.[28] Indeed, the sense in which bin Laden's gaze constitutes a type of threat echoes the repeated anxieties associated with the Other's gaze—as evident in associations as various as "the evil eye," Sartre's conception of the voyeur, the motif Zizek observes in Hitchcock's films in which "the Other's gaze . . . epitomizes a lethal threat," and in Michael Haneke's 2004 film *Hidden*.[29] The emphasis placed here, and in bin Laden's video appearances, on the significance of being seen by the Other, accords with Lacan's formulation of the gaze as constituting not the subject's own point of view, but the subject's awareness of inhabiting an abstract field of the visible in which the subject is seen by the Other.[30] (Indeed, in *Seminar X*, Lacan locates this as a key domain in which anxiety emerges.[31]) These fears are given added weight by the sense in which bin Laden constitutes a type of demonic-monstrous presence—that he possesses what Zizek in discussing horror films calls "an absolute gaze," in which "what is truly horrifying about a monster is the way it seems to watch us all the time"[32]—a conception of bin Laden that accords with the panopticism associated with the acousmêtre. Indeed, the subject who watches bin Laden's video appearances can be located in terms of Barbara Creed's analysis of horror films and the way in which the spectator repeatedly assumes the "victim position," identifying with "the masochistic look."[33]

However, while it is as a type of demonic presence that bin Laden is most starkly perceived as presenting a threat to the West, at the same time the configuration of bin Laden in these terms has proved profoundly useful to the proponents of the War on Terror. As Anustup Basu has noted, nations "like Afghanistan, Iraq, Iran and North Korea, and spectacular profiles like that of Osama bin Laden indeed make a reassuring world picture of evil, because evil that cannot be re-presented cannot be governed" or, it should be added, acted against.[34] And as Zizek contends in discussing the predominant conception in the West of the enemy in the War on Terror, "The enemy is by definition always (up to a point) *invisible*: it cannot be directly recognized because it looks like one of us, which is why the big problem and task of the political struggle is to provide/construct a recognizable *image* of the enemy."[35]

In the Manichean terms in which the War on Terror has been configured by the Bush administration, the conception of bin Laden as a type of demon provides a primary justification for the conflict of global dimensions the War on Terror has developed into—by suggesting the United States and its allies face an opponent so monstrously evil that it cannot be reasoned with in any other way than to be hunted down and destroyed. Furthermore, with surveys suggesting that a high proportion (68 percent) of the adult population of the United States believe in the existence of the devil, and with a host of popular preachers seeking to equate bin Laden and his supporters with this figure—including Pat Robertson, who in March 2006 spoke of radical Islamists as inspired by "demonic powers"—this is a conception of bin Laden that should not be considered too farfetched or empirically distant.[36]

Indeed, the configuration of Bin Laden as a type of demonic being can be located as symptomatic of the type of attitude held by both sides that led to the September 11 attacks in the first place. As Alex Schmid cautions in a commentary on the proliferation of weapons of mass destruction written prior to the attacks, that now reads like something of a warning:

> The best defense is not to give offence. Continuous constructive dialogue and pragmatic compromise with actual and potential political opponents at home and abroad must be sought in order to prevent unilateral or mutual demonization and dehumanization which is one of the preconditions for mass murder with a "clean" conscience. With the given limitations of physical deterrence, there is no effective substitute for conflict prevention.[37]

Since the September 11 attacks, conflict prevention is something the Bush administration has had little time for, seeking to marginalize it as a strategy of the morally weak. Rather, the fact that a force of evil of bin Laden's supposed magnitude remains "out there" has proved of considerable value to the administration and supporters of the War on Terror in contributing to the justifications for the type of global struggle the conflict has developed into. Without a leader of bin Laden's infamy, the threat posed by the enemy might be perceived as significantly diminished. Indeed, the fact that bin Laden remains uncaptured, and that this figure of profound evil remains "at large," has served as a support for the panoply of contentious measures—both at home and abroad—through which the Bush administration has pursued this war. Such an analysis can be extended to the U.S. allies in the War on Terror, who may have their own uses for bin Laden continuing to evade capture, with, for instance, repeated doubts cast on the desire of the Pakistani authorities to apprehend him.[38]

As Homi Bhabha has asserted, though, in discussing conceptions of community and otherness, "paranoid projections 'outwards' hold the capacity to return to *haunt* and split the place from which they are made."[39] Indeed, the type of paranoid imagining that lies behind the conception of bin Laden as constituting a kind of demonic-spectral being that haunts the West can be understood as having brought about a splitting in Western societies in regard to the relationship of Muslim communities to the rest of society—with the potential ramifications of this process evident in the July 7, 2005, attacks on London. Here, one of the bombers, Mohammed Siddique Khan, in a videotape recorded prior to the attacks (that, to extend this chapter's concern with the spectral and the monstrous, Tariq Ali has described as "the ghoulish video tape"[40]), declared that the attacks were motivated by disgust at the United Kingdom's foreign policy: "Your democratically elected government continuously perpetuate atrocities against my people and your support of them makes you directly responsible."[41] In so doing this splitting—born from the perceived need to take on the enemy in the guise of Iraq—can be located as contributing, quite directly, to this attack.

The Uncapturable?

The conception of bin Laden as a type of demonic, spectral presence accords with the U.S. failure to have achieved a definite sighting of him—despite the scale of the hunt for him. While in these video appearances bin Laden is able to continue to assert his presence at the Imaginary, the absence of the hard Real of his physical presence allows him to remain beyond the grasp of his captors.

In doing so bin Laden accords with the conception of specter Derrida offers as existing "beyond the opposition between presence and non-presence, actuality and inactuality, life and non-life, of thinking the possibility of the specter, the specter as possibility"—with bin Laden's metamorphosis into a type of ghost having multiplied the possibilities of the role he is able to play in the War on Terror, while remaining beyond his opponent's reach.[42]

On flyers shaped as dollar bills distributed in early 2003 by the U.S. military on the border of Afghanistan and Pakistan, there appears three images. In the first, bin Laden is preaching, a finger raised; in the second, appears a pile of dollar bills overlaid with an arrow that points to the third image—that of bin Laden caged behind bars. In relation to the question of visibility, so crucial to bin Laden's capture, the phantasy laid out in this sequence of images accords with the sense—as Stephen Baker asserts in his study of "the postmodern animal"—that the cage provides a means of better seeing and monitoring a creature, by restricting its ability to move out of sight.[43] In the case of bin Laden, once caged he would no longer be able to appear and disappear as and when he wishes, but would instead be rendered perpetually visible as he languishes in his cell.

However, as an interviewee suggests toward the end of *I Met Osama bin Laden*—a documentary screened by the BBC in March 2004—for his admirers and followers bin Laden is regarded primarily as a spiritual figure (again the spectral allusions of such conception can be noted) and as such imbued with a transcendental relationship to space and time.[44] Such a conception of bin Laden points to the terms in which he can be said to have assumed the status of the uncapturable and the unkillable. Even if a successful sighting were made of him that led to his seizure or death, he would continue—for an indefinite time—to present a potentially threatening presence, not least thanks to his video appearances and the means they provide for his supporters to continue to be guided and counseled by him. Aware of such possibilities, as one commentator has suggested, bin Laden may have already videotaped his will for posterity.[45] In a still more uncanny development, it may be that bin Laden has already died, but prior to his passing away stockpiled a selection of video recordings that allow him to continue to appear from time to time to reassert his presence. In either instance, bin Laden's capacity to continue to cast his shadow over the War on Terror is clear.

The "impossibility" of destroying bin Laden adds a further dimension to the critique of the United States and its allies for instigating a conflict of the scale of the War on Terror against an adversary of bin Laden's nature. While ghosts may not be able to be captured or killed, they might, as Derrida contends, be negated, dissipated, or exorcized—processes that entail seeking to remove their presence through addressing the causes of their coming into being.[46] And yet, in the period since the September 11 attacks, addressing the processes through which bin Laden has come to assume the status he has for many in the Muslim world has been accorded far less importance than confronting and destroying him. A more subtle strategy "would have exorcised the ghost by depriving it . . . of any interstice, lodging, or spacing favorable to haunting."[47] Yet, it is the opposite strategy that has been pursued.

Addendum: An Exorcism?

On May 2, 2011, at a little after 1:00 a.m. local time, U.S. Navy SEALs engaged in Operation Neptune Spear stormed a three-story mansion in Abbottabad, Pakistan.

After a brief firefight, in which bin Laden was shot and killed, his body was flown to Bagram airbase, then on to the supercarrier USS *Carl Vinson*, where it was placed in a body bag and slid into the North Arabian Sea.

The man the United States had been searching for since 1993 had been captured and killed.

The chapter reproduced above was written in 2007. Here, by way of a brief addendum, I would like to return again to the notion of bin Laden having constituted a type of ghostly presence that has haunted the West and raise the question of in what sense the finding and killing of him can be said to have constituted a type of exorcism.

In the aftermath of Operation Neptune Spear no images were released to confirm bin Laden had been located and killed, an absence that contributed to the proliferation of questions, doubts, and conspiracy theories about whether this had indeed taken place. (An image purportedly showing the bloodied head of a dead bin Laden, that first appeared in April 2009 and recirculated in the wake of his killing, was revealed as a fake.[48])

While such images do reportedly exist, the White House decided not to release them. As President Obama declared in an interview on CBS's *60 Minutes* three days after the announcement of bin Laden's death, in response to a question about the absence of such imagery: "We don't trot out this stuff as trophies," adding that he wanted to ensure that "very graphic photos of somebody who was shot in the head are not floating around as an incitement to additional violence, or as a propaganda tool. That's not who we are."[49]

The decision not to release any images of the dead bin Laden can be taken as revealing about the way in which, beyond the capture and killing of bin Laden, the Obama administration sought to utilize Operation Nepture Spear to perform another function as well—namely, a kind of exorcism of the type I quote Derrida as adumbrating at the very end of the chapter above, in terms of seeking to deprive the ghost, "of any interstice, lodging, or space favourable to haunting."[50]

What, in the case of Bin Laden, does it mean to talk about his exorcism? Lacan's conception of the "two deaths," as reworked by Slavoj Zizek, serves to illuminate this.[51]

In addition to a biological death—death in the Real—it is possible to speak of another type of death—death in the Symbolic, the death of a subject's signifying status, and the capacity of that subject's name and actions to continue to register in the way they had once done.

Rather than seeking to simply bring about the biological death of bin Laden, in refusing to make public any images of bin Laden's death (or his burial at sea), the Obama administration can be understood as striving to bring about his second, Symbolic death. For, as President Obama acknowledges in the statement just quoted, in refusing to release these images, the administration sought to limit the capacity of bin Laden's death to figure as a means by which he was further discussed and venerated, and hence for him to go on signifying the type of threat to the West and rallying point for his followers that he had done since, and indeed prior to, the September 11 attacks. In so doing the Obama administration can be understood as trying explicitly to counter the way in which—as suggested in the chapter reproduced above in regard to his video appearances—imagery of bin Laden might help to render him "uncapturable" and "unkillable," in providing a means by which he is able to continue to appear to his supporters long after his biological death. (And in this respect the particular potency of images of bin Laden's capture and killing, in positioning him as a type of "martyr," is worth highlighting.)

In this way, in the aftermath of the announcement of bin Laden's biological death, the administration can be understood as seeking to limit bin Laden's ability to occupy what has been called "the zone between the two deaths"—the space between his Real and Symbolic deaths, that constitutes the archetypal domain in which a monstrous and/or ghostly being lives on and continues to haunt its victims.[52]

It is in this attempt to bring about bin Laden's Symbolic death that Operation Neptune Spear can be said to constitute a type of exorcism. As the etymology of the latter word makes clear—combining the Greek *ex*, "out of," with *horkizein*, "cause to swear" (from *horkos*, "oath")—this is a process that takes place and is directed toward the Symbolic, the order of language, where it seeks to remove something from this realm.

The extent to which the finding and killing of bin Laden achieved this is open to debate. In one respect the decision not to release any visual evidence of bin Laden's death ran the danger of provoking the type of accusations it did—that bin Laden had not been located or killed at all, that his biological death had not even taken place. This was a risk the Obama administration was clearly willing to take, underlining the significance attached to trying to make sure his killing did not become a means via which bin Laden could live on in the Symbolic and continue to haunt his opponents.

How successful has this tactic been? This is a difficult question to answer. In what sense is it possible—or will it ever be possible—to delineate with any clarity the ways in which bin Laden, and his video and audio recordings, have or haven't continued to constitute a source of inspiration and reference for current and future supporters and fellow travelers? (Indeed, in what sense would any assessment offered now be rendered irrelevant by future events?) In terms of bin Laden's own direct ability to continue to haunt the West, though, it is possible to argue that something has shifted, as evinced in a slogan that circulated in the wake of his death, appearing on T-shirts, bumper stickers, ties, bags, mugs, badges, and in a thousand web images: "Obama got Osama." Yes, these are only three words. Yet their utterance and circulation as a meaningful statement would not have been possible prior to Operation Neptune Spear, and they quite clearly denote a shift in the position bin Laden has come to occupy in the register of the Symbolic. "Osama" has moved from the active subject who does the haunting, who preys upon the West, to the victim, the object of what "Obama" has done to him. He has become the one who has been "got."

There is another aspect to this process, though, that is also worth raising—the way in which, prior to his death, bin Laden can be said to have contributed to his own exorcism.

As outlined in the chapter above, in the aftermath of the September 11 attacks bin Laden's video appearances offered a critical means by which he sought to haunt his opponents, presenting a figure who appeared seemingly as and when he wanted and yet was unable to be captured or killed. In contrast, the period prior to his death witnessed the absence of any such video appearances. The last piece of video material to show Bin Laden actually speaking, and hence to provide some means of being able to date when it was recorded, appeared on September 7, 2007 (although there were questions about precisely when this footage was produced).[53] Since then a series of audio recordings have appeared purportedly featuring the voice of bin Laden that, it could be contended, in part due to the absence of any accompanying video material, registered a significantly reduced impact.

We might ask why this has been the case. It seems unlikely that the technological and logistical means of producing and distributing video material lay beyond the capacities of bin Laden and his associates. He could have used such appearances to continue to issue threats and warn of the possibility of future attacks, or to have chided the United States and its allies for having failed to capture him. He could have prepared a video in readiness for his killing, denying this had taken place, to be circulated in the aftermath of the assertion that he had been killed. (He could also, as suggested in the chapter above, have videotaped his will for posterity). None of these things were forthcoming though.

He might have pursued a rather different tactic as well. He might have sought in the very act of his death to have attempted to cheat his exorcism. He might have chosen to die as a martyr in an attack on U.S. forces, be it in the form of a suicide mission or otherwise, with an announcement, again in video form, shortly afterward, recounting what had taken place. Such a gesture would have served to locate his death as the ultimate proof of his commitment to the cause he espoused and a means of ensuring his ongoing veneration by his supporters and sympathizers. And yet this didn't happen either.

It is almost as if, after years in hiding and on the run, bin Laden had lost the willingness, the energy, and the belief in his own capacities to continue to haunt his opponents.[54]

The last images we have of bin Laden only serve to encourage this assessment. In the week following the announcement of his death the Pentagon released extracts from a series of "home videos" taken from the Abottabad mansion. As one news report noted, these deliberately sought to portray bin Laden "in an unflattering light" and, so we could say, further ensure his exorcism.[55] Here, bin Laden is shown as "someone obsessed with his own image," as he sits on the floor, remote control in hand, repeatedly watching stories about himself that include footage of the man responsible for his forthcoming death, Barack Obama, and a younger version of himself from one of his prior video appearances.[56]

From the position of the one who reduces others to the role of passive spectator, be it via his video appearances or in the spectacle of the September 11 attacks, bin Laden has in this footage come to assume the position of spectator. Replaying a well-worn trope of gothic and horror narratives, in these video excerpts a monstrous source of evil is revealed as seemingly nothing more than a frail, lonely figure, sitting alone in a room. As one report stated, "looking like an elderly grandfather with a cap on his head and blanket around his shoulders," bin Laden appears transformed. "Gone is the gun-toting rebel or the scholarly sheikh dictating messages to the outside word. Instead he is shown with greying hair and a grey beard, rocking back and forth as he watches stories about himself on al-Jazeera."[57]

Perhaps this is a fitting endpoint to the megalomaniac-narcissistic logic that underpinned the haunting of his opponents. That in the end this process had—in a development again evinced in multiple gothic-horror stories—turned back on bin Laden, and he had come to haunt himself.

Notes

Adapted from the chapter in Andrew Hill, *Reimagining the War on Terror: Seeing, Waiting, Travelling* (Basingstoke, UK: Palgrave Macmillan, 2009). The first part of this paper was written prior to bin Laden's death, while the epilogue was written after it.

1. For an overview of the video and audio material featuring bin Laden, see Simon Jeffrey, "Timeline: The al-Qaida tapes," *Guardian*, June 30, 2006, http://www.theguardian.com/alqaida/page/0,12643,839823,00.html, accessed December 29, 2007.

2. Clifford Geertz, "Centers, Kings, and Charisma: Reflections on the Symbolics of Power," in *Culture and Its Creators: Essays in Honor of Edward Shils*, ed. Joseph Ben-David and Terry Nichols Clark (Chicago: University of Chicago Press, 1977), 150–71; Max Weber, *Economy and Society: An Outline of Interpretive Sociology* (Berkeley: University of California Press, [1922] 1978), 241–45.

3. Terry Smith, "The Dialectics of Disappearance: Architectural Icon Types between Dashing Cultures," *Critical Quarterly* 45, nos. 1–2 (2003): 33–51.

4. Robert Fisk, "We Should Have Listened to Bin Laden," *Independent* (London), July 2, 2005, 31. "Might" is used as there has been extensive debate over which of these audio recordings actually feature bin Laden's voice.

5. Paul Virilio, *War and Cinema: The Logistics of Perception* (London: Verso, 1989), 4, 2.

6. Jane Mayer, "The Search for Osama: Did the Government Let bin Laden's Trail Go Cold?," *New Yorker*, August 4, 2003, 26–34, quote from 32.

7. Ibid., 33–34.

8. "High-tech Snooping for bin Laden," CNN, March 5, 2004, http://www.cnn.com/2004/WORLD/asiapcf/03/04/binladen.search/index.html.

9. Jean Paul Sartre, *Being and Nothingness: An Essay on Phenomenological Ontology* (London: Methuen, [1943] 1957), 578–80.

10. Andrew Hill, *Reimagining the War on Terror: Seeing, Waiting, Travelling*, (Basingstoke, UK: Palgrave Macmillan, 2009), from which the majority of this chapter is taken.

11. See, for example, Jane Corbin, *The Base: Al-Qaeda and the Changing Face of Global Terror* (New York: Pocket Books, 2003), 267; Susan Willis, "Empire's Shadow," *New Left Review* 22 (2003): 59; Matt Frei's report for BBC, *News at Ten O'Clock*, October 30, 2004, in which bin Laden is described as Al Qaeda's "spectral anchorman"; Jeffrey Sconce, *Haunted Media: Electronic Presence from Telegraphy to Television* (Durham, NC: Duke University Press, 2000), 124–66.

12. Hill, *Reimagining the War*.

13. Henry James, *The Turn of the Screw and Other Stories* (London: Penguin, [1898] 1975), 35.

14. Jacque Lacan, *The Ethics of Psychoanalysis: The Seminar of Jacques Lacan*, book 7, 1959–60 (London: Routledge, 1992), 43–70.

15. Ibid., 54. Susan Willis speculates that in the wake of the September 11 attacks the quantity of mail addressed to bin Laden from the United States "would have included love letters to him." Susan Willis, *Portents of the Real: A Primer for Post-9/11 America* (London: Verso, 2005), 74. Pejk Malinovski's "Dreaming of Osama" sound-piece, broadcast on BBC Radio 3 on November 24, 2007, includes accounts of dreams in which bin Laden figures as an object of desire.

16. Slavoj Zizek, "The Thing from Inner Space," in *Sexuation*, ed. Renata Salecl (Durham, NC: Duke University Press, 2000), 216–59.

17. See, for example, Jacques Lacan, "The Seminar of Jacques Lacan: Anxiety," book 10, unpublished (1962–63), translated by Cormac Gallagher from unedited French manuscripts.

18. Mayer, "Search for Osama," 26–34; Langlands and Bell, *The House of Osama bin Laden*, http://www.langlandsandbell.com/the-house-of-osama-bin-laden-video.html, 2003. The profile of the latter work was heightened by it being shortlisted for the 2004 Turner Prize, an annual prize awarded to a British visual artist.

19. In fact, in the absence of the successful sighting of bin Laden, the U.S. military had to make do "with practicing using Predators to destroy replicas of Bin Laden's house in the Nevada desert." Mayer, "Search for Osama," 33.

20. See "Timeline: The al-Qaida Tapes," *Guardian*, n.d., http://www.theguardian.com/alqaida/page/0,12643,839823,00.html; David Teather, "New 'Bin Laden' Videotape Warns of Battle to Come," *Guardian*, September 11, 2003, http://www.theguardian.com/world/2003/sep/11/september11.alqaida; Declan Walsh, "Pakistan Bombs Suspected al-Qaida Camp," September 10, 2004, http://www.theguardian.com/world/2004/sep/10/pakistan.alqaida; "Bin Laden Alive Claim Is from Old Video," December 7, 2005, http://www.theguardian.com/world/2005/dec/07/alqaida.terrorism; "Al Qaeda Releases 9/11 Anniversary Message," CNN, September 11, 2006, http://www.cnn.com/2006/US/09/11/zawahiri.911/index.html?eref=yahoo; James Sturcke, "Bin Laden Releases Video on 9/11 Anniversary, *Guardian*, September 11, 2007.

21. Srdjan Dragojevic's Yugoslav civil war film *Pretty Village, Pretty Flame* (Cobra Film Company, 1996).

22. Slavoj Zizek, *Welcome to the Desert of the Real* (London: Verso, 2002), 38 (my emphasis).

23. Ibid., 38.

24. Michel Chion, *The Voice in Cinema* (New York: Columbia University Press, 1999).

25. Ibid., 24–27.

26. Marina Warner, "The Desert of the Real," *Guardian*, September 25, 2004, sect. G2, 13–14.

27. Ewan MacAskill, "Intervention That Substitutes for a Bombing," *Guardian*, October 30, 2004, 17; Hideo Nakata's film *Ringu* (1998), remade in a Hollywood version by Gore Verbinski as *The Ring* (DreamWorks, 2002).

28. Walter Benjamin, "Kleine Geschichte der Photographie," in *Gesammelte Schriften*, ed. Rolf Tiedemann and Hermann Schweppenhauser, vol. 2, bk. 1 (Frankfurt, 1977), 375; translated as "A Short History of Photography" by P. Patton in *Classic Essays on Photography*, ed. Alan Trachtenberg (New Haven, Conn.: Leete's Island Books, 1980), 206.

29. Teresa Brennan, "The Contexts of Vision from a Specific Standpoint," in *Vision in Context: Historical and Contemporary Perspectives on Sight*, ed. Teresa Brennan and Martin Jay (London: Routledge, 1996), 217–30, quote from 219–21; Jean Paul Sartre, *Being and Nothingness: An Essay on Phenomenological Ontology* (London: Methuen, 1957), 259–60; Slavoj Zizek, "In His Bold Gaze My Ruin Is Writ Large," in *Everything You Ever Wanted to Know about Lacan . . . (But Were Afraid to Ask Hitchcock)*, ed. Slavoj Zizek (London: Verso, 1997), 211–72, quote from 214.

30. Jacques Lacan, *The Four Fundamental Concepts of Psychoanalysis* (London: Penguin, 1994), 67–119.

31. Lacan, "Seminar of Jacques Lacan," book 10.

32. Zizek, "In His Bold Gaze," 256.

33. Barbara Creed, *The Monstrous-Feminine: Film, Feminism, Psychoanalysis* (London: Routledge, 1993), 154.

34. Anustup Basu, "The State of Security and Warfare of Demons," *Critical Quarterly* 45, no. 1–2 (2003): 11–32, quote from 12.

35. Slavoj Zizek, "Are We in a War? Do We Have an Enemy?," *London Review of Books*, May 23 2002, 38, http://www.lrb.co.uk/v24/n10/slavoj-zizek/are-we-in-a-war-do-we-have -an-enemy.

36. "The Religious and Other Beliefs of Americans," Harris Interactive Poll Research, February 26, 2003, www.harrisinteractive.com/vault/Harris-Interactive-Poll-Research -The-Religious-and-Other-Beliefs-of-Americans-2003-2003-02.pdf; "Top US Evangelist Targets Islam," BBC News, March 14, 2006, http://news.bbc.co.uk/2/hi/americas/ 4805952.stm.

37. Alex Schmid, "Terrorism and the Use of Weapons of Mass Destruction: From Where to Risk?," *Terrorism and Political Violence* 11, no. 4 (1999): 106–32, quote from 122.

38. Mayer, "Search for Osama," 28–31. See also Justin Huggler, "They Seek Him Here, They Seek Him There," *Independent* (London), Review section, August 4, 2004, 2–3.

39. Homi Bhabha, *The Location of Culture* (London: Routledge, 1994); Jeremy Black, *War since 1945* (London: Reaktion, 2004); Maurice Blanchot, *The Writing of the Disaster*, trans. Ann Smock (Lincoln: University of Nebraska Press, 1986), 149 (my emphasis).

40. Tariq Ali, *Rough Music: Blair, Bombs, Baghdad, London, Terror* (London: Verso, 2005), 52.

41. Mohammed Siddique Khan, qtd. in ibid., 53.

42. Jacques Derrida, *Specters of Marx: The State of the Debt, the Work of Mourning, and the New International*, trans. Peggy Kamuf (London: Routledge, 1994), 12.

43. Steve Baker, *The Postmodern Animal* (London: Reaktion, 2000), 129–32.

44. *I Met Osama bin Laden*, screened on BBC2, March 28, 2004.

45. Rahimuulah Yusufzai, "War of Words," *Guardian*, October 9, 2001, sect. G2, 4–5.

46. Derrida, *Specters of Marx*, 128, 170, 129.

47. Ibid., 129.

48. Amelia Hill, "Osama bin Laden Corpse Photo Is Fake," *Guardian*, May 2, 2011, http://www.guardian.co.uk/world/2011/may/02/osama-bin-laden-photo-fake.

49. "Obama on bin Laden: The Full '60 Minutes' Interview," CBS News, May 8, 2011, http://www.cbsnews.com/8301-504803_162-20060530-10391709.html.

50. There has been some debate about whether capturing bin Laden alive was ever an aim of the operation; for the reasons discussed here, I would suggest it was not. Derrida, *Specters of Marx*, 129.

51. Jacques Lacan, *The Seminar of Jacques Lacan: Book VII, The Ethics of Psychoanalysis, 1959–1960* (London: Routledge, 1992), 243–87. It is the latter who locates these two deaths explicitly in terms of the Real and the Symbolic. See, for example, Slavoj Zizek, *The Sublime Object of Ideology* (London: Verso, 1989), 134–35.

52. Lacan, *Seminar: Book VII*, 320. As Zizek contends, depending on the specific case, either one of these deaths can precede the other. Zizek, *Sublime Object of Ideology*, 135.

53. A video that appeared a few days later, on September 11, 2007, claimed to feature bin Laden's voice but showed only a still image of him.

54. Here it's worth bearing in mind the rumors of bin Laden's health and his weakened physical state, which had been circulating for a number of years.

55. Lolita C. Baldor, "Videos Show bin Laden Watching Himself on TV," Associated Press, *Guardian*, May 7, 2011, http://www.guardian.co.uk/world/feedarticle/9634693.

56. Ibid.

57. Paul Harris, "Bin Laden Videos Give a Remarkable Insight into Life in His Lair," *Guardian*, May 7, 2011, http://www.guardian.co.uk/world/2011/may/07/bin-laden-video-abbottobad-seals-death.

PART II

Comparing Global News Media

4

Words and War

Al Jazeera and Al Qaeda

COURTNEY C. RADSCH

On September 11, 2001, members of Osama bin Laden's Al Qaeda terrorist network blew up the Twin Towers in New York City. Less than a month later on October 7, Al Jazeera swooped onto the world stage by scooping the major international media. Al Jazeera was the only news outlet in Kabul, Afghanistan, when the United States launched its war against the Taliban, and it aired an exclusive videotape of Osama bin Laden, who was seen as the mastermind for the 9/11 attacks. Its coverage was rebroadcast on leading outlets around the world, and the pan-Arab network became the leading news channel in the Middle East.[1] It compelled Arab media to compete according to a new logic and became a competitor on par with the leading global news networks.[2]

The story of Al Jazeera's meteoric rise is tied up with bin Laden, Al Qaeda, and the so-called War on Terror. Both Al Qaeda and Al Jazeera are phenomena at the nexus of globalization, resistance, and identity. Both Al Qaeda's and Al Jazeera's rise to global prominence were also made possible by globalization and networked transnational media, namely the Internet and satellite television. Al Jazeera was often credited with building a new public sphere and pan-Arab identity while at the same time providing an Arab perspective on the series of U.S.-led incursions in the Middle East that became known as the War on Terror.[3] Its rise happened to coincide with Al Qaeda's rise and occurred amid extensive American forays into the Middle East, which were widely opposed in the region and thus not surprisingly led to highly critical coverage of a range of U.S. actions and policies toward the region and toward Muslims. Al Qaeda is primarily known to the outside world through the media and to its ideological adherents through mediated networks on the Internet and social media. Al Jazeera was primarily known to the non-Arabic speaking world through global, Western news media until it launched an English channel in 2005 and could communicate directly to the West. Both mediatized global networks represented a powerful alternative to the U.S.-dominated narrative even as they leveraged the technologies and platforms spurred by globalization.

Self-identification and the Other amid Globalization

The construction of the dominant narrative of Friend/Enemy is a recurring historical phenomenon but is socially constructed through specific rhetorical and cultural stimuli, in which the media play a central role. Historical memory, the use of violence, and invoking collective memory were central to creating collective identity and social solidarity. *Asabiyah*, a term coined by Muslim intellectual Ibn Khaldun in the fourteenth century, refers to the development of social solidarity in which the individual identity is subsumed to that of the group and, when reinforced by religion, can become a motor for change.[4] Refrains of this idea are found in Durkheim's work on the collective conscience and in contemporary works on imagined communities and national identity.[5] The *umma* is a collective identity and form of society that hearkens back to the time of Mohammed, when "mankind was uplifted in its social order, in its morals, in all of its life, to a zenith of perfection which had never been attained before and which cannot be attained afterwards except through Islam."[6] For Al Qaeda "the Islamic *umma* is the greatest human power, if only the religion were properly established."[7] This could only happen within a state, the caliphate, where there is no distinction between politics, economics, religion, and governance. The establishment of the caliphate must come through the efforts of the Islamic nation to establish such a unified entity.

The concept of *umma* can thus be understood in a sense as a notion of civil society emerging from the chasm between contested state authority and social order in the Middle East. This could easily be extrapolated to other regions where governments are considered illegitimate and the people lack outlets for expression of their identities. In this respect Cox's notion of the gap between the retreat of the state and the development of civil society in the process of globalization is useful for seeing how Al Qaeda filled a void in the early twenty-first century.[8] Thus, the "exclusionary populism" of Al Qaeda and development of group consciousness can be seen less as an aberrant fluke than as an anticipated episode in the process of globalization.

The "enemy" distinction can be a rhetorical and psychological device used to evoke social cohesion and the collective imagining of identity, based on an us/them, friend/enemy antithesis. After the 2001 attacks on New York and Washington, George W. Bush used the concept of the enemy to create social solidarity and reconstruct collective conscience to allow him to invade Iraq and restrict civil liberties. Thus if you weren't with him, you were against him and belonged in the enemy category.[9] For Al Qaeda, in addition to America the enemy, Jews and Israelis were also the enemy. The Jew as enemy was based on both religious interpretation and the political realities of the Palestinian-Israeli conflict. In the polemics of Al Qaeda members, Jews were identified as the enemy of Islam and as the perpetrators of great crimes against the Palestinians and the greater Arab community.[10] Similarly, Al Jazeera gave significant and sustained coverage to the Israeli-Palestinian conflict and the plight of Palestinians, which helped it build its fan base in the region and connect disparate Arabs and even Muslims more broadly around their collective struggle. By adopting the plight of the Palestinians as their own, both the terrorists and the television network evoked solidarity with the Palestinians and their sympathizers, which include most of the Arab and Islamic world.

Al Jazeera challenged the dominant Western narrative of global media and provided a new means of reaching and portraying a pan-Arab, and often pan-Islamic, audience. Al Jazeera's on-the-ground coverage of Afghanistan during the fall of the Taliban, its broadcasts of taped messages from Osama bin Laden, its comprehensive coverage of the 2003 U.S.-led invasion of Iraq, and the ongoing conflict between Palestine and Israel resonated with Arab viewers. Al Jazeera, furthermore, regularly featured interviews with and presented sympathetic, anti-imperialist coverage of bin Laden and Al Qaeda sympathizers. The symbiosis between Al Jazeera and Al Qaeda help account for the success of both networks in an increasingly globalized political sphere that sought alternatives to U.S. leadership. Al Qaeda used the global network to convey his missives not only to an Arab audience but also to the wider Islamic world via global news flows as Al Jazeera scoops were picked up and rebroadcast. Al Jazeera capitalized on bin Laden's notoriety and its exclusive access to the most wanted man in the world to compete with the major global news networks. According to Kepel, bin Laden represented "the most complete and media-conscious drift into terrorism" of any among the radical Islamist extremist groups, and by 1996 he was "worldwide public enemy number one" from the point of view of the American intelligence services (although it was not until 2001 that the Western public adopted the same perspective).[11]

The station's portrayal of bin Laden differed significantly from that of American media and was more in line with public opinion in the Arab region regarding the U.S. role in the Israeli-Palestinian conflict and withdrawal from Iraq and the Arabian Peninsula.[12] Indeed the U.S. portrayal of bin Laden as public enemy number one helped cement his role as the "poster child" or "hero" for anti-Americanism and anti-Western jihadism thanks to all the media coverage, particularly on Al Jazeera's Arabic channel.

Yet most Arabs perceived the international media as pro-Western and biased in its coverage of Arabs, Islam, and other important issues, and indeed polls from 2004 to 2010 found that Al Jazeera was consistently the preferred international news station in nearly every Middle Eastern country.[13] Its audience was actually larger, however, since Western media outlets routinely quoted the station and rebroadcast its footage, particularly when bin Laden or other Al Qaeda figureheads released a tape. Al Jazeera became a contender with the top global networks with its launch of Al Jazeera English, competing to set the news agenda and present an alternative view to the Western-dominated global media agenda. Al Qaeda, meanwhile, offered an alternative vision of globalization in which the creation of an Islamic nation is the ultimate goal as opposed to complete economic or political integration for the purposes of perpetual peace.[14] Neither vision would have generated the traction it did without the transnational public spheres created by satellite television, the Internet, and social media.

The relative legitimacy and credibility of Al Jazeera in the Middle East reflected "Arab dissatisfaction with both Western and governmental media coverage of the region and its issues" rather than an anti-American editorial policy.[15] The station's emphasis on giving voice to the voiceless and speaking truth to power was certainly anti-establishment and often not in the interests of the U.S. military-industrial complex, but it was only anti-American according to a particular status-quo conservative reading of what being "American" meant. As one public intellectual wrote, Al Jazeera was chosen by Saddam Hussein for an interview in 1999 "because of its credibility . . . wide audience [and] reputation for independence."[16] Like American news, Arab news reflects the values and perspectives of its audience. Al Jazeera, much like Fox News, reflects the ideological commitments and discourse of its audience in its depiction of certain issues.[17] Al Jazeera gained an avid following by adopting a sympathetic view of the Palestinian cause, opposing the Iraq war, and giving voice to young people and other typically disenfranchised voices without access to the state-owned mainstream media in the Arab world.[18] It also garnered viewers because the implicit narrative in the struggle between Al Jazeera and the United States was akin to that of David versus Goliath. The allegedly deliberate bombings of its bureaus and its subsequent expulsion from Iraq further consolidated Al Jazeera's popularity in the region and its enemy complex with respect to the United States.[19]

U.S. officials, furthermore, validated the narrative of Al Jazeera as culturally authentic when they portrayed Al Jazeera as representative of Arabs and Arabness. The role of Arabic satellite television in the formation of Arab identity is evident in the stories the stations tell about themselves and the symbols deployed to create this imagined community. The major global news networks compete through a discourse of "we-ness," often equating Al Jazeera with the Arab world or portraying it as the Arab world's representative. Audience surveys show that Muslims and Christians spend an equal amount of time watching Al Jazeera, indicating that the network appeals to both denominations and that the Arab identity constructed through its broadcasts transcends religious division.[20] Similarly, Al Qaeda clearly identified Al Jazeera as speaking to the community it wanted to reach, and gave the station many exclusives that helped propel its rise to international prominence.

Just as Al Jazeera's narrative resonated with many Arab and Islamic publics, Al Qaeda's narrative resonated with a much smaller subsection of this public. Al Qaeda's religio-political ideology created a framework for unity in an uncertain world and strengthened the bonds of the group through individual devotion manifested through *jihad*. The development of Al Qaeda began with a close-knit group of extremist Arab Salafists bound through their experience fighting the Soviets in Afghanistan. After they defeated the superpower and drove the Soviets out of Afghanistan, the dream of an Islamic victory, and state, became a reality. Many of them returned home while others stayed, emboldened by their success, and worked on establishing their utopian Islamic state in Afghanistan.[21] Meanwhile, thanks to technological advancements online and on mobile platforms, the movement migrated online, where religious *fatwas* (rulings) and improved organizational capabilities attracted new members from around the world. New technologies and networked communication were integral to Al Qaeda's development and expansion. Members of Al Qaeda constituted a virtual community online through websites, chat rooms, and similar communal areas in cyberspace. Online chat rooms, video sharing sites, and websites for jihadists emerged as a virtual place to meet and engage with people who shared each other's viewpoints. Virtual *asabiyah* created a virtual public sphere among extremist Islamist ideologues in which they could construct a common identity, discover shared grievances, and even mobilize collective action. The constant refrain of the American government about the importance of "winning hearts and minds" underscores the importance of imaginary psychological factors, which can become more important than numerical or weapons superiority, in winning a war.[22]

The media, of course, are the platform through which such imagination is given collective representation and voice in the public sphere. The reaction of the United States to Al Jazeera over the years reflects an elision in public perception between bin Laden and the Qatari network, which was at times referred to as the "terror network" and seen as inextricably linked with Al Qaeda and terrorism. One commentator went so far as to claim that "if the U.S. loses the global war on terrorism, Al-Jazeera, the influential anti-American Arab television network primarily known as a mouthpiece for al-Qaeda, could claim responsibility."[23]

In fact, the American government was accused of deliberately bombing Al Jazeera headquarters in Afghanistan and Iraq and of pressuring the station on its editorial policies, both of which contribute to perceptions of hypocrisy by Arabs, Europeans, and even the occasional American.[24] Indeed, the military attacks on Al Jazeera contravened international law that protects civilian broadcasting services as well as Article 79 of the Geneva Convention, which requires that journalists be accorded treatment as civilians. Such attacks did little to undermine Al Jazeera's standing, but rather they underscored U.S. hypocrisy in promulgating the American way of life, exemplified by the First Amendment protections for free expression, while attacking a media outlet that was neither owned by nor affiliated with Al Qaeda.

Shifting Narratives

The U.S. narrative about Arab satellite news and Al Jazeera in particular started out as a positive one. From its inception in 1996 until 2001, Al Jazeera was viewed as a constructive influence for reform.[25] U.S. discourse about Arab satellite media was primarily positive and uncritical. After September 11, 2001, the discourse shifted and became far more contentious. The debates about pan-Arab satellite news largely revolved around two axes of contention. First is the role of the Arab satellite media in political reform and liberalization in the Middle East. Within this debate were discussions about the culture of Arab journalism, which are situated within the larger debate on globalization in terms of its homogenizing versus empowering impact. The values of Arab journalism and the political economy of satellite networks reflect these debates on cultural relativism and universality. Second is the issue of whether Arab satellite news is anti-American.[26]

English, French, Chinese, and other news services routinely use some stock version of the phrase "Al Jazeera, known as the 'CNN of the Arab World'" to provide context. Al Jazeera has routinely been quoted and its footage used by the major Western media outlets, especially given its unique access to sources close to Al Qaeda in the wake of the 9/11 attacks, and more recently its coverage of the 2011 Arab uprisings. Having equated Al Jazeera with CNN made it difficult, but not impossible, for the U.S. government to reverse itself and criticize the station for bias when its coverage of the Iraq War became overwhelmingly negative. Furthermore, quoting and referring to Al Jazeera as an influential news network enhanced its legitimacy and highlighted U.S. hypocrisy, a common theme in the region. In fact, the station made a name for itself with an anti-establishment, antihegemonic approach that was just as critical of many ruling Arab leaders as it was of American foreign policy.

The *New York Times'* Thomas Friedman exemplified how perceptions of Al Jazeera shifted from "beacon of freedom" to "harbinger of hate" following its coverage of bin Laden and the War on Terror. Friedman first wrote about Al Jazeera in 1999 as a hopeful sign of liberalization and globalization in the Middle East. He praised the network as a force for reform and democracy, a political phenomenon, holding it up as an exemplar and positive influence in the region.[27] In 2002, he debated democratization on its airwaves.[28] By 2003, however, Al Jazeera was no longer the miracle of the Middle East but rather the nefarious network responsible for anti-American public opinion.[29] By 2005, Friedman had turned into an avid opponent of the network, making it synonymous with anti-Americanism and bad journalism.[30] The network became the antagonist for every American project in Iraq, the straw man for whatever Friedman was propounding on that week, from torture to public diplomacy.[31] This trajectory mirrored that of U.S. government and public opinion over the same time period as well as the protracted nature of the War on Terror and ongoing hunt for bin Laden.

Al Jazeera's focus on bin Laden and Al Qaeda after 2001, not to mention the Israeli-Palestinian conflict, led to charges of anti-Americanism.[32] When Al Jazeera aired a series of audio and videotapes from Osama bin Laden in the first half of the new millennium, the U.S. government, the mainstream media, and thus the American public became convinced that Al Jazeera was in cahoots with "the terrorists." In April 2004 Secretary of State Colin Powell told Qatar's foreign minister that Al Jazeera coverage "intrudes on the relationship between the two states."[33] The government's position and its characterization of the station, reiterated by Undersecretary Richard Boucher, who said there was "an endemic pattern in this network of reporting false information and using it to try to inflame the situation,"[34] were debated on Al Jazeera's own programs. Shortly thereafter CIA director George Tenet went to Doha to demand that the channel become "more professional."[35] Yet even though voices shouting about anti-Americanism dominated, there was also vocal opposition among analysts, media critics, and the Arab public that argued an alternative narrative in which Al Jazeera wants the "scoop" just like any other (Western) media outlet. The political implications of Arab audiences turning to Arabic-language news first, instead of foreign media, were also hailed as a positive trend because of the greater potential for political and societal change coming from domestic rather than foreign sources.[36]

Implicitly the question of anti-Americanism prompted similar discussion of whether the American media were anti-Arab, a comparison often explicitly brought up by those who wish to demonstrate the hypocrisy of the question.[37] As a director of the Committee to Protect Journalists put it, "lost in the criticism is that Al Jazeera is also a serious news organization whose reporting is regularly cited by the best news organizations. And for Al Jazeera, which has built its reputation on defiantly reporting in the face of official harassment, each criticism adds to its legend in the region."[38] While Al Jazeera's legend is irrefutable, whether it is a villain or a hero is still being negotiated on the airwaves and in the presses, most recently with its purchase of Al Gore's cable station Current TV in January 2013 as part of it efforts to create Al Jazeera America.

On the other side of the debate were commentators, primarily in the Middle East, like Rami Khoury, editor of the *Daily Star*, who is routinely featured as the "Arab media expert" in both the American and Arab media. As a Jordanian editor of a major English daily distributed throughout the Middle East, he is the perfect credible, English-speaking Arab able to serve as a spokesperson for the Arab point of view when American media need to understand what is happening during times of crisis (Abu Ghraib, the Muslim cartoon scandal in the Danish press, messages from bin Laden). In an opinion article published in the *Daily Star* Khoury gave sage advice to Americans skeptical of Arab TV news: "we must not confuse the messenger that carries the bad news—that most Arabs are deeply critical of American and Israeli policies—with the reality and causes of that bad news for the U.S. and Israel."[39] And this, of course, was the crux of contention over Al Jazeera's relationship with the War on Terror: whether Al Jazeera was anti-American or whether American policies in the Middle East actually provoked these sentiments, with Al Jazeera simply playing the role of messenger. Either way, the pan-Arab news network and the global terrorist network Al Qaeda often found a sympathetic audience with those who opposed U.S. policies in the region.

Dueling Ideologies and Airwaves

Al Qaeda's primary political and ideological goals, namely to exorcise the U.S. military from Islamic lands and to reconstitute the Islamic *umma,* had little to do with "American" ideals of democracy and justice. Yet the rhetoric of the Bush administration and the military-industrial complex framed Al Qaeda as an existential enemy that represented a fundamental threat to the "American way of life" and replaced communism as America's imagined antithesis. Indeed, in rhetorically constructing Al Qaeda as an existential threat to the United States and its very way of life, the United States turned the group from a physical security threat into an ideological enemy. Through Al Qaeda, the actions of a few religious extremists came to threaten America's preeminent position as the global superpower, caused billions of dollars in economic and psychological damage, and provoked a backlash that has undermined the very foundation of America's esteem in the world community. "As the twin towers of New York collapsed, something even greater and more enormous collapsed with them," preached Al Qaeda's figurehead in a 2003 sermon, "the myth of the great America and the myth of democracy."[40] Al Jazeera's coverage complimented the view that American support for democracy was indeed a myth as it gave extensive coverage to the massive global demonstrations against the Iraq War.

Radical Islamists and neoliberals served each other's political needs since each group was strengthened and identified in opposition to its ideological Other, its enemy. Such a "strategic image" representing "a subject's cognitive construction or mental representation of another actor in the political world" has powerful effects on their behavior.[41] Such cognitive and psychological approaches allow for the construction of explanation in situations of ambiguity and uncertainty,[42] like that of a post–Cold War world lacking a dominant paradigm or in the feelings of American vulnerability following the September 11, 2001, attacks. Thus, President Bush and other conservative Republicans characterized the War on Terror as a crusade, just as bin Laden did, couching the conflict in religious, sexualized, and deeply historical terms.

The violence with which bin Laden railed against the U.S. intrusion into Muslim lands reflected a religious fervor made even more intense by equating the land with the female body. His condemnation of the presence of foreign troops used sexual imagery when he wrote in the same message from the mid-1990s that "the enemy invaded the land of our *umma*, violated her honor, shed her blood, and occupied her sanctuaries."[43] In fundamentalist interpretations of Islam, women should never be seen by men outside their family, much less interact or copulate with them.[44] The intrusion of foreign troops into the sacred motherland thus constituted a dual violation of honor and domination.

In the Western legalistic tradition one does not hear much about honor. But in the Middle East, where colonial powers divvied up the region into dominions of control, residual feelings of humiliation and vulnerability from its interactions with the West linger close to the surface, and Al Jazeera played no small role in this.[45] The power of this paradigm, as Edward Said might say, is that it has been passed along and transmitted from generation to generation through the collective memory and historical narrative of Muslims who have felt oppressed.[46] Al Jazeera amplified the idea of an Arab collective identity and historical narrative, particularly around Palestine and Iraq, through the mediated Arab public sphere. Similarly, when bin Laden spoke of the *umma* suffering eighty years of "humiliation and contempt" and American hypocrisy in Palestine and Iraq, it resonated with some Muslims who felt that the United States had violated their land and their people.[47] Al Jazeera's antagonistic and critical coverage of the U.S. role in the region echoed the same general sentiment and drew on the historical memory of a collective Arab community that was far older than the station itself. This only intensified after the U.S. invasion of Iraq in April 2003. Former secretary of defense Donald Rumsfeld commented that "even if you were an American you would begin to believe that America was bad" if you consistently watched Al Jazeera.[48] The suffering at the hands of westerners, especially Americans, has been one of the "motivating myths" or stories on which both Al Qaeda and Al Jazeera drew to create unity within an imagined community of Muslims and Arabs and propel these communities toward social transformation.[49] And it is this myth that could transcend extremist ideology and find expression in the global media through Al Jazeera.

Bin Laden was an entrepreneurial fundamentalist Islamist with specific political goals, who inspired and led the movement until 2011. His was an alternative myth of a "pure" Islamic *umma* ruled by Islamic tenets of justice and responsibility. Bin Laden apparently believed that although "America is a superpower, with enormous military strength and vast economic power . . . all this is built on foundations of straw." Al Qaeda would need only focus on the weakest parts, and "then the whole edifice will totter and sway, and relinquish its unjust leadership of the world."[50] Al Jazeera and many of its viewers were sympathetic to this message. Al Qaeda's explicit rejection of American political and economic hegemony posed the first real threat to world order since the end of the Cold War, but not because of the terrorist network itself but rather because of the ideology it espoused and the backlash it provoked from the United States. As bin Laden put it: "the situation is not as the West portrays it: that there exists an 'organization' with a specific name, such as 'al-Qaeda', and so on." Rather, Al Qaeda is "the conscience of our *umma*."[51]

In the wake of the Cold War, American hegemony was achieved through the neoliberal ethic of free markets and consumerism, and the apparatuses of America's global dominance largely went unchallenged. Most states seemed to accept the doctrines promoted by the World Bank, International Monetary Fund, multinational corporations, and other institutions of American economic and political influence as the epitome of economic and political development.[52] Neoliberalism was largely unchallenged. Hegemony, what Mittelman calls "a dynamic lived process in which social identities, relations, organizations, and structures based on asymmetrical distributions of power and influence are constituted by the dominant classes" and thus shape "relations of domination and subordination," is in turn perpetuated by globalization, further entrenching it in the international system.[53] Resistance, therefore, is conceived of as opposition to American hegemony and identification of America as the enemy.[54]

The secular economic and liberal values of neoliberalism are often promoted by mainstream media as universal values and reflect a declining relevance of religion and collectivity. Culture, in turn, becomes indistinguishable from capitalism.[55] But, in fact, these values are not universal. An Al Qaeda training manual found in a member's house in England, for example, noted the importance of collective action and "teamwork," which were emphasized as both a duty to god and as essential for reconstituting unity and the imaginary collective. The final section warned that "abandoning 'team work' for individual and haphazard work means disobeying their orders of God and the prophet and falling victim to disunity."[56] The marketization of daily life, the high value placed on consumerism, and competition based on each man for himself that are characteristic of neoliberalism are fundamentally at odds with the daily lives of many in the less developed, less globalized world. Al Jazeera has "given voice to the voiceless" (as it notes in its tagline) in these regions by covering issues that do not fit within the dominant neoliberal story of progress. From these areas in Southeast Asia, the Middle East, and Africa, not to mention the pockets of poverty and inequality within the more developed countries, Al Qaeda has gotten its recruits. Al Qaeda rejects capitalism and usury, personal freedom over duty to god, the individual over the community.[57] Bin Laden reflected the consensus of his supporters when he explicitly rejected the "evils of materialism" and capitalists, along with democracy, elections, and "polytheistic laws."[58] As Robert Cox aptly pointed out, the ideological hegemony of globalization comes from the inevitability and imperative of competitiveness, which becomes the ultimate form of alienation because it is created by people who come to wield absolute power over everybody else.[59] If the neoliberal ethic is the criteria for "success" and "progress" in the contemporary world, those who cannot or do not wish to compete according to its precepts had other options: Al Jazeera or Al Qaeda.

Conclusion

Perceptions of bin Laden and American understanding of Al Qaeda were intricately and inextricably linked with how global media, particularly Al Jazeera, covered the transnational terrorist movement. Indeed, media plays a role in constructing the friend/enemy dynamic but also become targets of warfare in their own right, as the U.S. physical and rhetorical attacks on Al Jazeera illustrate. Within this paradigm, both Al Qaeda and Al Jazeera have had profoundly disruptive effects on interpersonal, intercommunal, and interstate relations.

The influence of Al Jazeera and Al Qaeda was inextricably linked with the increasing popularity of pan-Arab satellite news and the Internet, which enabled the networks to expand their reach and construct transnational collectives of supporters. Online social media use among Arab youth, who made up a majority of the region's population, challenged the traditional authority of parents, mosques, and religio-cultural norms.[60] Religious leaders have climbed to fame using new media, while imams debate religious teachings and issue *fatwas*, or religious rulings, through the mass media as well as directly on their websites or via text messages. Mainstream mass media convey a dominant narrative while the small media created online enable individuals to form contingent collectivities and identity relationships irrespective of territorial frontiers or the space-time continuum. Al Jazeera was at the forefront of adopting social media into its programming, linking these deterritorialized, contingent identities through programs like "The Stream" to create a global conversation.

The challenge to American hegemony may come from loose-knit, transnational networks like Al Qaeda, but it is through the airwaves that the true battle will be fought. Al Jazeera regularly covers challenges to and defiance of American power, which in turns gives strength and inspiration to other movements. The importance of imaginary psychological factors, such as questioning U.S. moral leadership or its role as the world's sole superpower, becomes more important than numerical or physical superiority in winning an ideological war. Al Jazeera's recent attempt to break into the American media market with the creation of Al Jazeera America is taking this ideological struggle to the United States itself. The assertion that "the significance of hegemony is that it is unquestioned" could imply that anti-American movements like Al Qaeda or media networks like Al Jazeera demonstrate a decline in hegemonic power by the very nature that the United States as superpower is now contested.[61] But hegemonic power is distinctive in that even if it is declining, it is still dominant. As such, it creates the structures and institutions through which politics and international affairs are mediated. As Cox points out, structures represent a picture of reality that necessarily defines reality and thus reproduces it.[62] If the power of hegemony is in the consent of the masses, the question becomes how to reconstruct the hegemonic apparatus, and to do so without using force. For as Gramsci noted, when coercion takes precedent over consent, then there is no hegemony.[63] The use of force, in Iraq and elsewhere, undermined consent and the legitimacy of values, norms, and other such intangibles. Al Qaeda brought this contestation to the forefront while Al Jazeera ensured the world was aware of these challenges.

The explicit rejection of American political and economic hegemony by both Al Qaeda and Al Jazeera posed the first real threat to world order since the end of the Cold War. The powerful blend of religious dogma, political grievance, social morass, and high technology on which both networks thrive provided Al Qaeda's adherents with the justifications that their goals were legitimate and worth dying for and provided Al Jazeera's supporters with an alternative worldview to that presented by global Western media. Although it will take a lot more to destroy America than a few attacks, the U.S. and Western *response* to Al Qaeda's terrorism and Al Jazeera's coverage may be what ultimately undoes American hegemony by weakening America's moral authority and consent to its normative ideals. The attacks on Al Jazeera are emblematic, as was Abu Ghraib, extralegal imprisonment of "enemy combatants" in Guantanamo, and warrantless spying on Americans under the Patriot Act. If hegemony is the maintenance of spontaneous consent by society to the status quo through intellectual and moral leadership,[64] then torture, restrictions of civil liberties, unilateral violations of sovereignty, and the like may be the beginning of the end of moral leadership. We are already seeing a decline of American hegemony as consent shrinks and feelings of hypocrisy swell. Although Al Qaeda certainly threatened the United States, it was the Bush administration's overblown response to the September 11, 2001 attacks, as epitomized by the War on Terror, that represented an existential threat to American hegemony. Polanyi, though describing a different era, put it aptly when he wrote that "secular tenets of social organization embracing the whole civilized world are not dislodged by the events of a decade."[65] But the questions and challenges raised by the reification of economics and the concurrent devaluation of moral and religious principles that supposedly have no place in economics or politics need to be addressed, or the events of the last decade will stretch even further into the next decade. Both the United States and Al Qaeda used each other as the enemy in their rhetoric of war. Thus while bin Laden may have finally been killed, the War on Terror and Al Jazeera's efforts to present an ideological alternative to U.S. hegemony continue.

Notes

1. Al Jazeera consistently ranked as the most watched station for international news in surveys of Arab public opinion. Sidney Telhami, Arab Public Opinion Polls for 2004, 2005, 2006, 2008, 2010, Brookings Institution and the University of Maryland, available from http://www.sadat.umd.edu/.

2. Courtney Radsch, "How Al Jazeera Is Challenging and Improving Egyptian Journalism," *Reset: Dialogue on Civilizations*, October/November 2007.

3. Marc Lynch, *Voices of the New Arab Public: Iraq, Al-Jazeera, and Middle East Politics Today* (New York: Columbia University Press, 2006).

4. Fuad Baali, *Society, State, and Urbanism: Ibn Khaldun's Sociological Thought* (Albany: State University of New York Press, 1988), 43–48; Stephen Gill and James H. Mittelman, eds., *Innovation and Transformation in International Studies* (Cambridge: Cambridge University Press, 1997), 61.

5. Emile Durkheim, *The Division of Labour in Society*, trans. W. D. Halls (Houndmills, Basingstoke, Hampshire: Macmillan, 1984); Benedict R. O'G. Anderson, *Imagined Communities: Reflections on the Origin and Spread of Nationalism*, rev. and extended ed. (London: Verso, 1991).

6. Sayyid Qutb, *Milestones*, rev. ed. (Cedar Rapids, Iowa: Unity, 1981), 30.

7. Osama bin Laden and Bruce Lawrence, *Messages to the World: The Statements of Osama bin Laden* (London: Verso, 2005), 191.

8. Robert W. Cox, with Michael G. Schechter, *Political Economy of a Plural World: Critical Reflections on Power, Morals and Civilization* (London: Routledge, 2002), 103.

9. Network, Cable News, "'You Are Either with Us or against Us,'" in *War against Terror*, ed. CNN.com, 6 Nov. 2001.

10. Bin Laden and Lawrence, *Messages to the World*, 9–10, 17, 29, 123, 125–26, 190.

11. Gilles Kepel, *Jihad: The Trail of Political Islam*, trans. Anthony F. Roberts (Cambridge, Mass.: Belknap Press of Harvard University Press, 2002), 313.

12. Telhami, Arab Public Opinion Polls, 2010.

13. Telhami, Arab Public Opinion Polls, 2004, 2005, 2007, 2008, 2010.

14. Audrey Kurth Cronin, "Behind the Curve: Globalization and International Terrorism," *International Security* 27, no. 3 (2002/03): 30–58. She argues, as many others

have, that Al Qaeda and other terrorist groups like it are "part of a larger phenomenon of antiglobalization" (35). My view of Al Qaeda et al. as a response to and product of globalization was influenced by Olivier Roy, *Globalized Islam: The Search for a New Ummah* (New York: Columbia University Press, 2004); and Peter L. Bergen, *Holy War, Inc.: Inside the Secret World of Osama bin Laden* (New York: Simon and Schuster, 2002). Also, on crime and the covert world as products and processes of globalization, see James H. Mittelman, *The Globalization Syndrome: Transformation and Resistance* (Princeton, N.J.: Princeton University Press, 2000).

15. "Made in Arabia: The Rise of Arab Media and the Challenges of a Post-9/11 World," conference, American University, Washington, D.C., April 25, 2006.

16. Edmund Ghareeb, "New Media and the Information Revolution in the Arab World: An Assessment," *Middle East Journal* 54, no. 3 (2000), 395.

17. Joel Campagna, "Between Two Worlds: Qatar's al-Jazeera Satellite Channel Faces Conflicting Expectations," CPJ (Committee to Protect Journalists) Freedom Reports, October 2001, http://www.cpj.org.

18. Courtney C. Radsch, "Digital Dissidence and Political Change: Cyberactivism and Citizen Journalism in Egypt," doctoral diss., American University, Washington, D.C., 2013.

19. James Gooder, "Al-Arabiya Denies Inciting Attacks" Al Jazeera, November 25, 2003, http://english.aljazeera.net, accessed April 11, 2006; *Media and Authority: Timeline*, March 16, 2004, http://english.aljazeera.net, accessed 11 April 2006; Robert Fisk, "No Wonder al-Jazeera Was a Target," *Independent* (London), November 26, 2005.

20. Philip Auter, Mohamed M. Arafa, and Khaled Al-Jaber, "Who Is Al Jazeera's Audience? Deconstructing the Demographics and Psychographics of an Arab Satellite News Network," *Transnational Broadcasting Studies* 12 (2004).

21. Steve Coll, *Ghost Wars: The Secret History of the CIA, Afghanistan, and bin Laden, from the Soviet Invasion to September 10, 2001* (New York: Penguin Press, 2004).

22. Ibn Khaldun, *The Muqaddimah: An Introduction to History*, trans. Franz Rosenthal, vol. 2 (New York: Pantheon Books, 1958), 130–31; Ibn Khaldun and Philip Issawi, *An Arab Philosophy of History: Selections from the Prolegomena of Ibn Khaldun of Tunis (1332–1406)*, trans. Charles Philip Issawi (Princeton, N.J.: Darwin Press, 1987).

23. This statement is featured at the top of the website http://www.ww.w.toprelateds.com/site/www.stopaljazeera.org, created by the ultra conservative group Accuracy in the Media.

24. Gooder, "Al-Arabiya Denies"; Courtney C. Radsch, "Al Jazeera's Effect on American Foreign Policy," unpublished article, Georgetown University, 2004; Fisk, "No Wonder al-Jazeera"; "Aljazeera Demands Answers from Blair," November 26, 2005, http://www.aljazeera.com/archive/2005/11/200849133237766762.html. My fieldwork and conversations with people in Lebanon, Jordan, Syria, and Egypt, as well as throughout Europe and in the United States, have demonstrated these perceptions of hypocrisy to be widespread and pervasive.

25. Campagna, "Between Two Worlds"; Mohammed El-Nawawy and Adel Iskander, *Al-Jazeera: The Story of the Network That Is Rattling Governments and Redefining Modern*

Journalism (Boulder, Colo.: Westview Press, 2003); Thomas L Friedman, *The Lexus and the Olive Tree: Understanding Globalization*, rev. ed., (New York: Farrar, Straus and Giroux 2000); Sharon Waxman, "Arab TV's Strong Signal: The al-Jazeera Network Offers News the Mideast Never Had Before, and Views That Are All Too Common," *Washington Post*, December 4, 2001.

26. Throughout this chapter I am specifically referring to Arab satellite news networks, not terrestrial news stations nor nonnews satellite programming unless specifically noted.

27. Thomas Friedman, "Foreign Affairs; Glasnost in the Gulf," *New York Times*, February 27, 2001; Thomas Friedman, "Foreign Affairs; Fighting bin Ladenism," *New York Times*, November 6, 2001.

28. Thomas Friedman, "The Democracy Thing," *New York Times*, October 30, 2002.

29. See, for example, Thomas Friedman, "Come the Revolution," *New York Times*, April 2, 2003; Thomas Friedman, "Telling the Truth in Iraq," *New York Times*, August 17, 2003.

30. See, for example, Thomas Friedman, "A Day to Remember," *New York Times*, February 3, 2005.

31. Thomas Friedman, "Restoring Our Honor," *New York Times*, May 6, 2004; Thomas Friedman, "The Last Mile," *New York Times*, November 28, 2004.

32. Even posing this question, of course, assumes that the media are the cause of anti-American sentiments.

33. "Made in Arabia."

34. Ibid.

35. Mireille Duteil, "Al-jezira: Ondes de choc en terre arabe," *Le Point*, May 19, 2005.

36. Naomi Sakr Hafez, ed., *Satellite Realm: Transnational Television, Globalization, and the Middle East* (London: I.B. Tauris, 2001); Lynch, "Voices of the New."

37. The author heard these types of comments many times while conducting research in Egypt and working for Al Arabiya in Dubai, UAE.

38. Joel Campagna, "Al Jazeera: Leave It to Viewers," *International Herald Tribune*, re-published on the Committee to Protect Journalists' website, https://www.cpj.org/, 2004.

39. Rami Khouri, "Facts and Fantasies about Arab Satellite TV," *Daily Star* (London), December 24, 2005.

40. Bin Laden and Lawrence, "Messages to the World," 194.

41. Richard K. Herrmann and Michael P. Fischerkeller, "Beyond the Enemy Image and Spiral Model: Cognitive-Strategic Research after the Cold War," *International Organization* 49, no. 3 (1995), 415–50, quote from 415.

42. Arthur T. Denzau and Douglass C. North, "Shared Mental Models: Ideologies and Institutions," *Kyklos* 47, no. 1 (1994): 3–29, quote from 12.

43. Bin Laden and Lawrence, "Messages to the World," 15.

44. In addition to numerous books and articles on this subject, my experience traveling in Jordan, Syria, Egypt, and Lebanon reinforced the importance in traditional families of keeping women separate from men. During a visit to Petra I was invited, along with the rest of the group of journalists I was with, to the home of a Bedouin man who allowed only the female journalists to see or meet his daughters while the male journalists took

tea outside in the garden. In an interview in April 2005 with a representative from the Jordanian government, the practice of separating men from women was acknowledged to be a normal custom, with the practice of honor killings in the cases where women were perceived as violating their honor being extreme, but nonetheless real, extensions of this. For a fictionalized but apt account of the phenomenon of honor killing see Norma Khouri, *Honor Lost: Love and Death in Modern-Day Jordan* (New York: Atria Books, 2003).

45. See, for example, Ibrahim M. Abu-Rabi, *Intellectual Origins of Islamic Resurgence in the Modern Arab World* (Albany: State University of New York Press, 1996); John L. Esposito, *The Islamic Threat: Myth or Reality?*, 3rd ed. (New York: Oxford University Press, 1999); Bernard Lewis, *The Middle East: A Brief History of the Last 2,000 Years* (New York: Scribner, 1995). The theme of humiliation at the hand of the West is a recurring one felt strongly by both religious and secular Arabs and Muslims. See, for example, a recent quote on the front page on the *New York Times* in which an Egyptian Muslim referred to the humiliation of Muslims everywhere. See Neil MacFarquhar, "Will Politics Tame Egypt's Muslim Brotherhood?," *New York Times*, December 8, 2005. Fundamentalism as a response to humiliation is also discussed in Cox, *Political Economy*, xxi.

46. Edward W. Said, *Orientalism* (New York: Vintage Books, 1979). For a lyrical appraisal of how these feelings have been incorporated into cultural production see Fouad Ajami, *The Dream Palace of the Arabs: A Generation's Odyssey* (New York: Pantheon Books, 1998).

47. Bin Laden and Lawrence, "Messages to the World," 104.

48. Donald Rumsfeld, qtd. in Lynch, *Voices of the New*, 36.

49. Gill and Mittelman, *Innovation and Transformation*, 28.

50. Bin Laden and Lawrence, "Messages to the World," 195.

51. Ibid., 120.

52. Francis Fukuyama, "The End of History?," *National Interest* 16 (1989), 3–18; Francis Fukuyama, *The End of History and the Last Man* (New York: Free Press, 1992).

53. Mittelman, *Globalization Syndrome*, 167.

54. Cox, *Political Economy*, 120–21.

55. Terry Eagleton, *After Theory* (New York: Basic Books, 2003), 48.

56. Last page of final lesson in *Al Qaeda Training Manual: Declaration of Jihad against the Country's Tyrants*, military series, English translation, U.S. Department of Justice, http://www.justice.gov/sites/default/files/ag/legacy/2002/10/08/manualpart1_1.pdf.

57. Usury, or the prohibition against charging interest, is specifically prohibited in the Quran. See Abdullah Yusuf Ali, *The Meaning of the Holy Qur'an: Explanatory English Translation*, 11th ed. (Beltsville, Md.: Amana, 2004, 115–16, 161, 237). The editor points out, with reference to Surah 2:275, that "owing to the fact that interest occupies a central position in modern economic life and especially since interest is the very life blood of the existing financial institutions, a number of Muslims have been inclined to interpret it in a manner which is radically different from the understanding of Muslim scholars throughout the last fourteen centuries and is also sharply in conflict with the categorical statements of the Prophet." Thus modern neoliberalism and capitalism in general put Muslims in direct

conflict with a tenet of their religion. Osama bin Laden refers often to this dilemma. Bin Laden and Lawrence, 2005, 7–8, 181. Regarding personal freedom see Sayyid Qutb, *Milestones*, rev. ed. (Cedar Rapids, Iowa: Unity, 1981), 36. Regarding individualism, one of the five pillars of Islam is the payment of religious taxes or alms to help the poor.

58. Bin Laden and Lawrence, "Messages to the World," 181, 250.

59. Cox, *Political Economy*, 92.

60. Courtney C. Radsch, "Unveiling the Revolutionaries: Cyberactivism and the Role of Women in the Arab Uprisings," James A. Baker III Institute for Public Policy Research Paper, Rice University, May 17, 2012; Courtney C. Radsch, "Blogosphere and Social Media," in *Seismic Shift: Understanding Change in the Middle East* (Washington, D.C.: Stimson Center, May 2011).

61. Robert W. Cox and Björn Hettne, eds., *International Political Economy: Understanding Global Disorder* (Atlantic Highlands, N.J.: Zed Books, 1995), 14–15.

62. Ibid., 33.

63. Antonio Gramsci, *Selections from the Prison Notebooks of Antonio Gramsci*, ed. Quintin Hoare and Geoffrey Nowell-Smith (London: Lawrence and Wishart, 1971), 12–13.

64. Renate Holub, *Antonio Gramsci: Beyond Marxism and Postmodernism* (London: Routledge, 1992).

65. Karl Polanyi, *The Great Transformation: The Political and Economic Origins of Our Time*, 2nd ed. (Boston: Beacon Press, 2001), 149.

5

Metaphorizing Terrorism

Al Qaeda in German and British Tabloids

ALEXANDER SPENCER

The media are considered vital for a terrorist group because they provide the means of attracting attention and spreading the group's message.[1] Considering the strategic communication aspect of terrorism, the media have often been considered the terrorist's "accomplices" or even their "best friend" for providing the "oxygen of publicity."[2] At the same time, it has been noted that terrorists provide media with emotional, exciting, and bloody news that helps them sell their product.[3] Therefore there are mutual benefits for both, and the relationship could be described as "symbiotic."[4] To date, terrorism research has predominantly focused on this relationship and its effects and implications for counterterrorism. Unfortunately, until fairly recently there has been little interest in the perception of terrorism and role of language and discourse in the construction of "the terrorist."[5]

It is widely accepted, not only in academia but also in policy circles, that the media greatly influence public opinion.[6] This chapter considers the implications of how knowledge about terrorism is presented in the media and how the choice of language influences public perceptions. In particular, I focus on the linguistic device of metaphors by illustrating the metaphorization of terrorism in the German *Bild* and British *Sun* tabloid newspapers. Using approaches based in cognitive linguistics, I aim to illustrate how particular metaphorical constructions of Al Qaeda and Osama bin Laden in the tabloid media in both countries make certain countermeasures seem most appropriate by fostering four particular conceptual understandings of terrorism:

Terrorism is war
Terrorism is crime
Terrorism is uncivilized evil
Terrorism is a disease

Thereby, the chapter shows that metaphors in the media actively take part in the construction of the world as we see it, think of it, and ultimately react to it. By projecting understandings from one conceptual area, such as war, to a different area, such as terrorism, metaphors naturalize specific countermeasures while placing other options outside of the mainstream debate. Metaphors are mechanisms for cognitive engagement by making abstract concepts and phenomena that are difficult to grasp, such as terrorism, comprehendible.[7]

I begin by illustrating the concept of metaphors, reflect on what metaphors do, and thereby outline a method of metaphorical analysis. The second part is an application of this method to tabloid news media discourse in two countries and an examination of the four dominant conceptual metaphors that construct the terrorism of al Qaeda and Osama bin Laden in these media. Of particular note are some of the "consequences" of using these metaphors to construct reality in a particular way and thereby make certain reactions in both countries seem most appropriate. I conclude by briefly reflecting on some of the differences between media representations in Germany and the UK and outline some possible explanations for varying metaphor usage.

Metaphor Analysis as a Method

Traditionally, metaphors were, on the one hand, considered "convenient labels that accurately describe the nature of world politics."[8] On the other hand, they were deemed to be a purely rhetorical tool for replacing one word with another and serving little purpose other than eloquence.[9] In contrast to the rhetorical understanding of metaphors, cognitive linguistics goes further and argues that metaphors are more than just words. In particular, George Lakoff and Mark Johnson are among the most influential scholars in this respect to have exported the study of metaphor from linguistics to other disciplines such as psychology, sociology, and political science.[10] As they describe it, the "essence of metaphor is understanding and experiencing one kind of thing in terms of another."[11] In their book *Metaphors We Live By,* they argue that metaphors structure the way people think and that the human conceptual system, as such, is fundamentally metaphorical. They maintain that metaphors make humans understand one conceptual domain of experience in terms of another by projecting knowledge about the first familiar domain onto the second more abstract domain. The central idea here is that metaphors map a source domain—for example, *war*—onto a target domain—for example, *terrorism*—and thereby make the target domain appear in a new light.

Here we have to distinguish between two kinds of metaphors: the *metaphoric expression* and the *conceptual metaphor*. The conceptual metaphor—for example, *terrorism is war*—involves the abstract connection between one "conceptual domain" to another by mapping a source domain (*war*) and a target domain (*terrorism*).[12] Mapping here refers to "a set of systematic correspondences between the source and the target in the sense that constituent conceptual elements of B correspond to constituent elements of A."[13] "Thus, the conceptual metaphor makes us apply what we know about one area of our experience (source domain) to another area of our experience (target domain)."[14] Conceptual metaphors do not have to be explicitly visible in discourse. However, metaphorical expressions are directly visible and represent the specific statements found in the text on which the conceptual metaphor draws. "The conceptual metaphor represents the conceptual basis, idea or image" that underlies a set of metaphorical expressions.[15] In the following sections the empirical analysis draws out the metaphorical expressions (for example, *battlefield*) that are the basis of the conceptual metaphors such as *terrorism is war*.

Metaphors draw attention to certain aspects of a phenomenon and invite the listener or reader to think of one thing in the light of another. Thereby, we can assume they influence policymakers' conceptions of events and the policies they create, which in our case concerns counterterrorism policy. Metaphors "limit what we notice, highlight what we do see, and provide part of the inferential structure that we reason with."[16] As Paul Chilton and George Lakoff point out, metaphors "are concepts that can be and often are acted upon. As such, they define in significant part, what one takes as 'reality', and thus form the basis and the justification for the formulation of policy and its potential execution."[17] Metaphors structure the way people define a phenomenon and thereby influence how they react to it; consequently, they limit and bias our perceived policy choices as they determine basic assumptions and attitudes on which policy making depends.[18]

It is important to realize that metaphors do not cause a certain counterterrorism policy in a direct sense wherein the metaphor is the independent variable upon which the policies are dependent. Metaphors do not entail a clear set of policies but open up space for policy possibilities. Metaphors offer a discursive construct that frames the situation in a certain way. Metaphor "defines the pattern of perception to which people respond."[19] As metaphors help construct reality in a certain way they are able to define the limits of common sense, the limits of what is considered possible and logical while excluding other options from consideration.[20]

There are a number of scholars who offer a range of different detailed plans of how to carry out a metaphorical analysis.[21] Although their emphasis varies, the key components remain similar. First, one selects a text, or rather a series of texts such as works or speeches of a particular author or politician, news reports, or television programs.[22] Second, the researcher starts identifying narrative elements that provide the context for metaphors, such as actors, actions, or settings. Third, one starts collecting the metaphorical expressions used in this corpus to talk about the narrative elements. In a fourth step, one notes common and recurring metaphors and organizes them into clusters that are then generalized into conceptual metaphors underlying the discourse. The frequency of the different conceptual metaphors is crucial as an indicator for their importance in the discourse. The more common the metaphor is, the more influence it is bound to have on the construction of reality and ultimately on policy.[23] In the final step these metaphors are inductively interpreted. This interpretation is intuitive and undoubtedly subjective.[24] But there have been a number of suggestions of how such an interpretation of metaphors could be carried out in a "scientific" and controlled way. For example, Ronald Hitzler has used what he refers to as "artificial stupidity," while Rainer Hülsse takes up Umberto Eco's suggestion to interpret a metaphor like someone who would encounter it for the very first time.[25] As Hülsse points out, with such techniques that spell out "what appears to be obvious, i.e. the deautomatisation of the usually automatic projection from source to target, one can reconstruct the reality constructions of metaphors."[26]

Al Qaeda in German and British Tabloids

Metaphors provide a means of analyzing news coverage as "metaphors provide colorful and accessible means of explaining abstract notions."[27] Consequently, this chapter wants to disregard the "high data" of the political elite and investigate the "low data" produced by the tabloid press in Germany and Britain in order to gain insight into the social construction of terrorism in two different countries and cultures.[28] Therefore, I focus on the metaphorization of terrorism in the *Bild* and the *Sun* newspapers by analyzing one month of articles following four large attacks perpetrated by Al Qaeda: 9/11 in 2001, the bombings in Bali in 2002, the train bombings in Madrid in 2004, and the London tube attacks in 2005. These events were chosen due to their fairly large nature and their focus on a Western target. The time frame of one month after each incident for selecting articles was chosen as further research beyond this time period did not add further kinds of conceptual metaphors. The central idea behind looking at the tabloid media is that they offer an insight into a broad socially shared understanding of terrorism. As very few people follow parliamentary debates or listen to the speeches of politicians, most people get their information about the world from the media. The *Sun* and the *Bild* are particularly important in this regard as they are both the largest national newspapers in their respective countries with a readership of 6.7 million (*Sun*) and 12 million (*Bild*).[29] It is widely accepted that both newspapers are among the most important agenda setters in their countries.[30]

In this section, I outline each of the four overarching conceptual metaphors and provide examples of the types of metaphorical expressions that are the basis of these conceptual metaphors. In each case, I follow this with a description of the responses these metaphors invoked and the resultant policies. I then discuss the ascent of these four constructions in relation to possible alternatives that were marginalized in the mainstream discourse and conclude with some reflections on the implications of terrorism's mediated construction.

TERRORISM IS WAR

A very common conceptual metaphor found in the media discourse following all four events between 2001 and 2005 in both the German and the British tabloids understood terrorism as a war.[31] Although the most famous incarnation is the War on Terror metaphor, there are a large number of other metaphorical expressions that reinforce this understanding. For example, in Germany the attacks of 9/11 were considered "kamikaze attacks," and the event was metaphorized as a second "Pearl Harbor."[32] This understanding of terrorism as a war was further strengthened by describing the terrorists as "al Qaeda warriors" or "terror commandos" in a "terrorist army" made up not only of "soldiers" but also "battle-hardened" "veterans."[33] The attacks are considered a "declaration of war" to the Western "alliance" in a conflict that includes "battlefields" or "war zones."[34] Like a general, Osama bin Laden is "commanding" his "private army" made up of "terror-" or "combat troops" from the safety of his "camouflaged" "command center."[35] In the UK, similar to Germany, one frequently encounters metaphorical expressions that draw comparisons to the Second World War. While 9/11 was also likened to Pearl Harbor and the use of "kamikaze" tactics, there were also a number of metaphors related to Nazi Germany, as the attacks in Bali and Madrid were commonly referred to as a "blitz" by "islamona-zis" motivated by "islamofascism."[36] This understanding of terrorism as war in Britain was further strengthened by metaphors that described the conflict as including "battles," "sieges," and "war zones" demarcated by "frontlines."[37] Here Osama bin Laden is metaphorized to be a "terror warlord" who, together with his "second in command," has "declared war" and, similar to the metaphors in Germany, is now "mobilizing" his "troops" on the "battlefield" from the safety of his "command center."[38] Terrorists are often metaphorized as "suicide squads" in a terror "army."[39] These Al Qaeda "forces," similarly to any normal military, are hierarchically organized and include "footsoldiers," "lieutenants," and "commanders," with bin Laden at the helm.[40] They used their "military training" and their "military arsenal" to conduct "operations" and "missions" as part of a large Al Qaeda "campaign" supervised by a "council of war" from "bases" and "fortresses" in Afghanistan paid for by a "war chest."[41]

Most obviously, constituting *terrorism is war* calls for a military response. As early as 1987 Jeffrey Simon of the RAND corporation realized the importance of the war metaphor in the fight against terrorism: "Equating terrorism with war effectively ends any debate over whether military responses are justified: If a nation is at war it must respond militarily to attack."[42] So the war metaphor influences the public's perception of the enemy and makes a military response appear logical.[43] The illustrative metaphor constitutes reality. As Sarbin points out: "An important feature of the war metaphor is that problems engendered by terrorist acts can be solved through the deployment of military forces."[44] So more than anything, the public associates war with violence, insecurity, and the application of military force to achieve victory and solve the threat of terrorism. If the problem is considered to have military dimensions, a military solution seems appropriate. Metaphors such as "terror commando," "terror army," or War on Terror outlined above are all part of the language of war and thereby frame the issue of "new terrorism" and the conflict with Al Qaeda as a war that can be won by military means.[45]

Germany's initial reaction to Al Qaeda and Osama bin Laden fits this meta-phorical understanding of terrorism as a war very well, as it openly supported U.S. military action in Afghanistan, and the country quickly offered nearly four thousand troops in support.[46] This "war" understanding was also mirrored by the public. In September 2001, 58 percent favored German military participa-tion in a war against terrorism.[47] Similar to Germany, Britain's military response to terrorism following 9/11 fits the conceptual metaphor *terrorism is war* found in the discourse. Britain was the only other country apart from the United States to deploy forces from the beginning of Operation Enduring Freedom on October 7, 2001, only twenty-six days after the terrorist attacks in New York and Washington.[48] In the first few weeks this military operation to destroy Al Qaeda's "army" included elements of all three military branches of the British Armed Forces, who became involved in both Afghanistan and Iraq.[49] Overall, the general public also seems to share this kind of understanding of terrorism as a number of opinion polls indicate that the United Kingdom's active participation in the War on Terrorism fits into the general public's understanding of what terrorism is and therefore how it should be fought. A survey in October 2001 found that between 67 and 74 percent of those questioned supported or approved of the military action by the United States and Britain against Afghanistan.[50]

TERRORISM IS CRIME

A second conceptual metaphor found in both countries constructs terrorism as a crime. While many in the literature on terrorism point to the almost dichotomous relationship between the war and the criminal justice model of engaging terrorism,[51] the discourse on terrorism in the media contains both metaphorical expressions of war and crime at the same time. So in Germany, the terrorist and Osama bin Laden is not only a soldier but also a "thug," and the Al Qaeda "army" is also a "gang" full of "criminal" "murderers" or "killers."[52] The "criminal attacks" were "murderous" "crimes" that left behind not only a "war zone" but also a "murder" "crime scene."[53] Not only were the "commandos" responsible for these "terror murders," but so were the "offender" bin Laden and his "accomplices."[54] Very similar metaphorical expressions can be found in the UK tabloid the *Sun*. Again the terrorists and bin Laden are metaphorized as "murderers" organized in a "gang" or "mob" of "criminals" who commit "murderous" "crimes" and leave behind a "crime scene."[55] The "casualties of war" are also considered "victims" of "crime."[56] By constituting an act of terrorism as, for example, "murder,"[57] the metaphorical expressions map the source domain *crime* onto the target domain *terrorism*.

The conceptual metaphor *terrorism is crime* makes a judicial response seem appropriate. As Peter Sederberg points out, while "the view that terrorism is war leads its proponents to favor repressive responses; the view that terrorism is crime leads its proponents to favor legal solutions."[58] This, however, does not mean that the two understandings are dichotomously opposed to each other in all aspects. In fact, both conceptual metaphors seem to overlap to a certain extent as a legislative response can make sense in both *terrorism is war* and *terrorism is crime*. Similar to the conceptual metaphor *terrorism is war* and the military responses, the understanding of "new terrorism" as something criminal made a legal response by Germany and the UK appear logical after 9/11. And again the implemented policies are evidence and the result of this interpretation of terrorism as crime.

In Germany the government quickly passed a large number of new antiterror laws and alterations to existing legislation against the terrorist "criminal." Most directly this is noticeable in the first two "security packages" (*Sicherheitspakete*), which made adjustments to more than a hundred regulations in seventeen different laws and a number of administrative decrees.[59] It increased the powers of the intelligence and security services giving the Federal Criminal Police Office a stronger position, removing its reliance on the police forces of the *Länder* for data collection. As the security expert Victor Mauer pointed out, although this prompted concerns about civil liberties and excessive intrusion, the "new legislation reflects that the lion's share of counterterrorism against transnational terrorist threats is to be conducted on the law enforcement and intelligence fronts [. . . after all] terrorists are regarded as criminals."[60] This general understanding of terrorism as something criminal is also visible very clearly in German public opinion. For example, in November 2001 over 70 percent of the German population seemed to support the second security package.[61]

The mapping of the source domain *crime* to the target domain *terrorism* is also clearly visible in the policies implemented in the United Kingdom following 9/11. Although the British government had only just passed a new set of fairly substantial antiterror laws in 2000 (Terrorism Act of 2000), there was an understanding that further legislation would be an appropriate means of responding to this kind of "criminal" terrorism.[62] As Sebastian Payne points out, the government could have responded to 9/11 without making new laws, but it chose to legislate and implement, for example, the Anti-terrorism, Crime and Security Act of 2001 and the Prevention of Terrorism Act of 2005.[63] The opinion of the British public appears to further substantiate the belief that *terrorism is crime* as opinion polls have continuously showed very high support for new antiterror legislation.[64] For example, between 64 and 72 percent of the public in 2005 agreed that the police should have the powers to detain "suspected" terrorists without charge for 90 days.[65]

TERRORISM IS UNCIVILIZED EVIL

A third important conceptual metaphor in both Germany and the UK constitutes terrorism by Al Qaeda as something uncivilized and evil. In Germany, the terrorist and Osama bin Laden become "barbaric" "bomb-barbarians," and terrorism becomes "barbarianism" perpetrated by "inhuman" "terror beasts."[66] In addition, the terrorist and bin Laden are not only constructed as a "monstrous" "hydra" or a "terror monster" but the embodiment of "evil."[67] Osama bin

Laden and his terrorists becomes the "devil," who causes "diabolical" "infernos," "apocalyptic" "terror-hells," or the "apocalypse" itself.[68]

This third conceptual metaphor can also be found in the *Sun* newspaper. This is indicated through metaphorical expressions that establish terrorists and bin Laden as "possessed," "vile," "evil" "hydras" who perform "monstrous" and "barbaric acts."[69] Terrorism is considered to be "savage" "barbarism," and Osama bin Laden is described as an "inhuman" "monster" from a "swamp" with "tentacles" spread around the globe.[70] These "subhuman" "evil beasts" "without a soul" are said to have spun a "web of evil" and have left behind "trails of slime."[71] They are unrivaled in "wickedness" and their "doomsday attacks" created an "inferno" and "hell" on earth likened to "Armageddon" or the "Apocalypse."[72]

The conceptual metaphor *uncivilized evil* does a number of things and predicates terrorism in a number of ways.[73] Most importantly, the metaphors signal a stark political difference. Predicating the terrorists as uncivilized or evil leads to a concrete and clear polarization, as it outcasts the actor and his or her actions and dichotomizes and antagonizes *them* (the out-group) and *us* (the in-group).[74] For example, the metaphor *barbarian* constitutes terrorism not only as something "other" but as something explicitly foreign, something that comes from outside one's own country or cultural hemisphere. Similar to the term *Islamist*, the expression *barbaric* gives the terrorist construction something foreign without assigning a concrete nationality. So in addition to the dehumanization of the evil metaphors, the terrorist actor is de-Westernized. Interestingly, Marina A. Llorente has noted that "most violent acts by Westerners tend not to be labeled 'barbaric.' A good example is the case of Oklahoma City bomber Timothy McVeigh, whose action was not categorized in terms of 'barbarism,' presumably because he belonged to the 'civilized' part of the world."[75]

Therefore, one could also make the argument that the regular use of the term *barbaric* increasingly constructs the terrorist as something "other" and generally alien and foreign, which then makes counterterrorism measures—such as tighter border and immigration controls—possible and appropriate to keep such elements out. The understanding, inherent in the conceptual metaphor *terrorism is uncivilized evil* characterizes terrorism as something foreign that is perpetuated by the barbarian other and makes policies that target this otherness appear appropriate.

In Germany, the notion of linking terrorism to the foreign "other," and with this to the idea of migration, was visible from the beginnings of the political debate after 9/11 as politicians from the conservative parties, the liberals, and the social democrats all immediately linked terrorism to immigration and called for tighter controls.[76] The most obvious means of stopping these "evil" "barbarians" from entering the "civilized" world is the securing of one's borders.

In the time since 9/11 Germany has done precisely that; it has tightened its borders and increased resources for the Federal Border Guards (prior to 2005 known as the Bundesgrenzschutz, BGS) responsible for protecting Germany's borders from "evil" "savages." Following 9/11 the budget for the border guards was substantially increased in 2002 by around 120 million Euros, and Germany purchased new high-tech helicopters and patrol boats and recruited and trained more personnel to patrol Germany's borders and embassies abroad against foreign terrorists. As Thomas Diez and Vicki Squire point out, these policies are "indicative of a direct linkage between terrorism and migration in the German case."[77] This link and the understanding of terrorism can also be seen in opinion polls. For example, 79 percent of the German population agreed with Interior Minister Schilly's idea following the train bombings in Madrid of making the deportation of suspicious foreigners quicker and easier.[78]

Tightening immigration regulations and asylum and border controls have also been a central aspect of British counterterrorism since 9/11. Politicians in both the Labour and Conservative Parties have continuously talked about terrorism in connection to immigration. Most dominantly, this connection was made with the introduction of the Anti-terrorism, Crime and Security Act of 2001 (ATCSA). The ATCSA explicitly deals with immigration matters and links them to terrorism in part 4 of the act, fittingly entitled "Immigration and Asylum." This understanding in the UK of the "terrorist" as something uncivilized and foreign is also visible in public opinion polls. In 2003, for example, 82 percent of those questioned thought that it was certain or likely that "terrorists linked to Al Qaeda are entering Britain as asylum seekers," and a survey conducted after the London bombings in July 2005 showed that 88 percent agreed with using "tighter controls on who comes into the country" as a "measure that could be taken to try and reduce the threat of further terrorist attack."[79]

TERRORISM IS DISEASE

The final conceptual metaphor found in both Germany and the UK underlying the discourse constitutes terrorism as a disease. In the German tabloid one encountered metaphors that constituted terrorism as "sick," "crazy," or even the "plague."[80] By metaphorizing the terrorist and Osama bin Laden as an "insane" "mad man" who plots "terror-insanity" in his "sick head," the source domain *disease* is projected onto the target domain *terrorism*.[81]

In the UK the tabloid discourse constructs terrorism as a "sick" "wicked plague," or as "lunacy" perpetrated by "insane" "psychopaths."[82] One comes across a number of metaphorical expressions that constitute the actor bin Laden and his terrorists as "mad"; for example, terrorists are often metaphorized as "madmen," "lunatics," or "nutters," and terrorism is constructed as "sickening" and "deranged" "madness."[83] Terrorists are considered "maniacs" or "crazed fanatics" who have been "infected" by Osama bin Laden and "poisonous clerics."[84] Thereby, expressions such as "suicide nuts" or "terrorist madness" map the source domain *disease* onto the target domain *terrorism*.[85]

Similar to the metaphors of "uncivilized" "evil," metaphors of *disease* indicate a deep political rift. For example, one should consider the interpretation that disease, similar to the metaphors of *evil* and *uncivilized* mentioned above, is something one cannot reason with. This is especially true when we consider the notion of *madness* as a disease. While negotiations and ceasefire agreements do make sense if we constitute the terrorist as a soldier in a war, they are absurd in a conflict with an army of "lunatics" who lack the ability for rational thought. One can simply not trust the "insane," be they soldiers or criminals. A psychological study by Emily Pronin, Kathleen Kennedy, and Sarah Butsch showed that people were far less likely to advocate the use of diplomacy against terrorists if these terrorists were depicted as irrational. Not only can one not negotiate with the insane or with diseases such as cancer, but many other illnesses such as the plague are in fact contagious.[86] So any kind of contact with the "disease" of terrorism runs the risk of the "disease-riddled" terrorist infecting you. Therefore, terrorists should not be talked to but rather should be isolated and quarantined as "contact with them is polluting."[87] Overall, the construction of terrorism as "evil" or a "disease" rather suggests that certain policies such as engagement or negotiations are not considered as possible options.

In contrast to the other concrete policies mentioned above, it is obviously more difficult to indicate the non-existence of a policy. However, one may gain some insight into the implications of the conceptual metaphor *terrorism is disease* when we consider Osama bin Laden's negotiation offer made in April 2004.[88] Both the German and British governments vehemently rejected any such possibility. In Germany, Chancellor Gerhard Schröder and a large number of other politicians vigorously rejected such a truce because "there cannot be negotiations with terrorists [. . .] like Osama bin Laden."[89] The British government announced that bin Laden's first truce offer to Europe was "absurd" and "ludicrous."[90] A number of government spokesmen stated that "the idea of an armistice with a group that defines itself by violence is an absurdity," and that the peace offer was "evidence for the aberration of al-Qaeda."[91] Individual politicians also strongly rejected the idea of any kind of ceasefire with such a terrorist group. For example, the foreign secretary at the time, Jack Straw, proclaimed: "One has to treat such proposals by al-Qaeda with the contempt they deserve. It is a murderous organization which seeks impossible objectives by the most violent means."[92] So negotiations with "mad" terrorists such as bin

Laden seemed to be considered impossible. As former home secretary David Blunkett put it: "It is ludicrous to think that his suggestion has any sense of reality," and even the Liberal Party leader Charles Kennedy pointed out that "there can be no negotiation with Al Qaeda, and [that] bin Laden's truce offer was repellent."[93]

Conclusion

Metaphors play a vital role in the discursive construction of terrorism and thereby contribute to our understanding of how to react to such phenomena. They may not "cause" certain policies in a positivist sense, but certain metaphorical constructions of terrorism make particular countermeasures feel appropriate while others remain outside the realm of considered options. This chapter applies metaphorical analysis to the discourse on terrorism as found in tabloid newspapers in Germany and the United Kingdom and illustrates how four of the most salient conceptual metaphors constructed terrorism as a war, a crime, an uncivilized evil, and a disease, suggesting the appropriateness of military, judicial, or immigration policies while negating other possibilities such as engagement or negotiations. In particular, the ability of metaphorical analysis to indicate impossibilities is valuable, as it highlights reactions previously ignored and opens up new areas of research that were previously considered taboo, such as engagement and possible reconciliation with Al Qaeda.[94] By considering terrorism as a social construction and reflecting on the idea that there are no externally existing facts about "terrorism," one can start questioning the established absurdity of "unthinkable" policies.

While the main aim of this chapter is to illustrate the metaphorical construction of the terrorism perpetrated by Al Qaeda and Osama bin Laden in order to show how particular countermeasures appear suitable and logical in response, it raises other important questions. Most obviously, the chapter has not enquired into where these particular kinds of conceptual metaphors have come from and why certain constructions manage to become dominant while others fall by the wayside. Why did the understanding *terrorism is war* become dominant rather than, for example, *terrorism is business*, which describes Al Qaeda as a franchise? Why is there a shift, for example, in Germany from *terrorism is war* to *terrorism is crime*? (See figures 5.1 and 5.2, which indicate the percentages of the four major conceptual metaphors; the four locations indicate the time: New York and Washington, 2001; Bali, 2002; Madrid, 2004; and London, 2005.)

Although pinpointing specific reasons for the use of a certain metaphor or other linguistic device over another is extremely difficult if not impossible, the variations and shifts in the usage of particular conceptual understandings

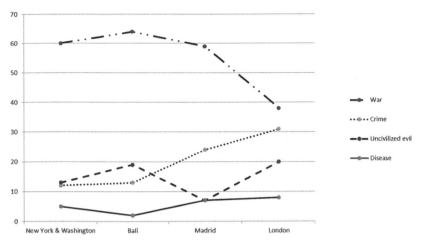

FIGURE 5.1. Percentage of Conceptual Metaphors in the British Newspaper *Sun*.

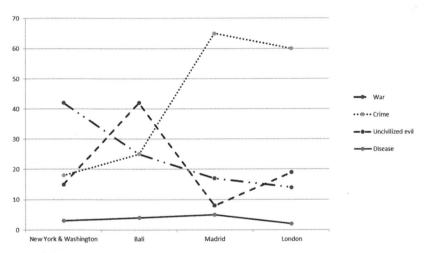

FIGURE 5.2. Percentage of Conceptual Metaphors in the German Newspaper *Bild*.

call for more reflection on the reasons for these differences. The question of why metaphors change has been addressed in a number of ways, and one may briefly consider three possible explanations that could be substantiated by further research.

First, a materialist understanding in line with more traditional approaches to studying terrorism would probably point to "realities" and suggest that changes in metaphor usage reflect the reality of changed circumstances or the specific type of attack that the metaphors describe. From this perspective, as metaphors reflect reality, the change of discourse has to be due to changes on the ground. However, in constructivist thought, discourse cannot simply reflect reality; instead, reality is constituted in discourse. This does not mean that there is no reality or that discourse is independent of the real world, but that such reality has to be interpreted as it cannot speak for itself.

A second more critical perspective on terrorism advanced by authors such as Richard Jackson would probably point to "interests" of those using the metaphors as an explaining variable.[95] In this conception, the changes or shifts of metaphor usage would not be due to the realities on the ground, but rather to the changing interests of the influential elite. Politicians or the media would change their metaphorical language in order to manipulate the public audience and further their interests.[96] Consistently using or changing metaphors, and thereby spreading their implicit understanding of phenomena, would be considered an explicit act of power to maintain or increase the power of those uttering the metaphors. In other words, metaphors are used by someone for some purpose. For example, in the case of the War on Terror a number of scholars claim that discursive devices and narratives were used to serve the interests of the conservative political elite in the United States.[97] Alternatively, in this explanation the war metaphors could be due to the financial interests of the media printing them. So it was a conscious choice of the *Bild* and the *Sun* to print war metaphors, as the notion of "war" sells more newspapers than the notion of "business."

A third possible interpretation focuses less on agency but is rather interested in "experiences." Metaphors arise or change if the inferences they make by mapping one domain to another are supported by physical and cultural experiences.[98] As Christ'l De Landtsheer and Ilse De Vrij point out, new metaphors arise in a time of crisis precisely because they are "powerful agents of cognitive framing."[99] For example, in the case of 9/11, a war metaphor in Germany made sense as it appeared to fit many of the characteristics of war experienced in the past. The number of casualties, the level of destruction, and usage of airplanes as guided bombs made the source domain *war* appropriate. However, over time the war metaphors seemed increasingly at odds with the experiences of terrorism in Germany. With a lack of further 9/11-style attacks the experiences of war no longer seemed an appropriate means of conceptualizing and understanding terrorism. Metaphors of crime were better suited for capturing the general sentiment in Germany. Rather than experiencing terrorism as an exceptional state of affairs with high levels of death and destruction, terrorism was slowly considered something normal to every society. Crime metaphors were better at capturing the notion of terrorism as something that is there all the time without constantly affecting us. The difference to the first kind of explanations rooted in "realities" is that metaphors are not exact mirrors of events. There is no one-to-one relationship between reality and metaphors, as we cannot observe physical events directly but do so in a particular interpretative context and through discourse. Discourse makes us see things in a particular way, but at the same time discourse is not independent of empirical events. For example, the lack of any 9/11-style terrorist attacks in Germany had an effect on the terrorism discourse in Germany. The inferences of a war metaphor were no longer supported by physical and cultural experiences. The central idea of this explanation would be that experiences of empirical events shape discourse, and discourse shapes our experiences. In other words, discourse and experiences are mutually constitutive.

Notes

This chapter draws on Alexander Spencer, *The Tabloid Terrorist: The Predicative Construction of New Terrorism in the Media* (Basingstoke, UK: Palgrave Macmillan, 2010).

1. David L. Paletz and Alex P. Schmid, eds., *Terrorism and the Media,* (London: Sage, 1992); Gabriel Weimann and Conrad Winn, *The Theater of Terror: Mass Media and International Terrorism* (New York: Longman, 1994); Brigitte Nacos, *Terrorism and the Media: From the Iran Hostage Crisis to the World Trade Center Bombing* (New York: Columbia University Press, 1994).

2. Alex Schmid, "Terrorism and the Media: The Ethics of Publicity," *Terrorism and Political Violence* 1, no. 4 (1989): 540; Bruce Hoffman, *Inside Terrorism,* 2nd ed. (New York: Columbia University Press, 2006), 183; Thatcher cited in Paul Wilkinson, *Terrorism versus Democracy: The Liberal State Response* (London: Frank Cass 2000), 175.

3. Boaz Ganor, *The Counter-terrorism Puzzle: A Guide for Decision Makers* (New Brunswick, NJ: Transaction, 2005), 231.

4. Alex Schmid, "Terrorism and the Media: The Ethics of Publicity," *Terrorism and Political Violence* 1, no. 4 (1989): 539–65.

5. Richard Jackson, *Writing the War on Terror: Language, Politics, and Counter-terrorism* (Manchester: Manchester University Press, 2005); Lee Jarvis, *Times of Terror Discourse, Temporality and the War on Terror* (Basingstoke, UK: Palgrave Macmillan, 2009); Alexander Spencer, *The Tabloid Terrorist The Predicative Construction of New Terrorism in the Media* (Basingstoke, UK: Palgrave Macmillan, 2010).

6. Joshua Woods, "What We Talk about When We Talk about Terrorism: Elite Press Coverage of Terrorism Risk from 1997–2005," *International Journal of Press/Politics* 12, no. 3 (2007): 3–20; Kerry G. Herron and Hank C. Jenkins-Smith, *Critical Masses and Critical Choices: Evolving Public Opinion on Nuclear weapons, Terrorism and Security* (Pittsburgh: University of Pittsburgh Press, 2006).

7. See also Aditi Bhatia's chapter in this volume.

8. Paul Chilton and George Lakoff, "Foreign Policy by Metaphor," in *Language and Peace*, ed. Christina Schäffner and Anita Wenden (Amsterdam: Harwood, 1999), 56.

9. Paul Chilton, *Security Metaphors: Cold War Discourse from Containment to Common House* (New York: P. Lang, 1996), 359; Jonathan Charteris-Black, *Corpus Approaches to Critical Metaphor Analysis* (Basingstoke, UK: Palmer Macmillan, 2004), 25.

10. George Lakoff and Mark Johnson, *Metaphors We Live By* (Chicago: University of Chicago Press, 1980).

11. Ibid., 5.

12. George Lakoff, "The Contemporary Theory of Metaphor," in *Metaphor and Thought*, ed. Andrew Ortony, 2nd ed. (Cambridge: Cambridge University Press, 1993), 208–9.

13. Zoltan Kövecses, *Metaphor: A Practical Introduction* (New York: Oxford University Press, 2002), 6.

14. Petr Drulák, "Metaphors and Creativity in International Politics," Institute for Advanced Studies in Management and Social Sciences, Lancaster University, Discourse Politics Identity, Working Paper Series, working paper no. 3, 3.

15. Charteris-Black, *Corpus Approaches*, 9.

16. George Lakoff, "Metaphor and War: The Metaphor System Used to Justify War in the Gulf," in *Thirty Years of Linguistic Evolution: Studies in Honour of René Dirven on the Occasion of His Sixtieth Birthday*, ed. Marin Pütz (Amsterdam: John Benjamins, 1992), 481.

17. Chilton and Lakoff, "Foreign Policy by Metaphor," 57.

18. See, for example, Chilton, *Security Metaphors*; Jeffrey Scott Mio, "Metaphor and Politics," *Metaphor and Symbol* 12, no. 2 (1997): 113–33; Jennifer Milliken, "The Study of Discourse in International Relations: A Critique of Research and Methods," *European Journal of International Relations* 5, no. 2 (1999): 225–54; Alexander Spencer, "Bild Dir Deine Meinung: Die metaphorische Konstruktion des Terrorismus in den Medien," *Zeitschrift für Internationale Beziehungen* 18, no. 1 (2011): 47–76.

19. Murray J. Edelman, *Politics as Symbolic Action: Mass Arousal and Quiescence* (Chicago: Markham, 1971), 67.

20. Rainer Hülsse and Alexander Spencer, "The Metaphor of Terror: Terrorism Studies and the Constructivist Turn," *Security Dialogue* 39, no. 6 (2008): 571–92.

21. Raymond Gibbs, "Researching Metaphor," in *Researching and Applying Metaphor*, ed. Graham Low and Lynne Cameron (Cambridge: Cambridge University Press 1999), 29–47; Rudolf Schmitt, "Systematic Metaphor Analysis as a Method of Qualitative Research," *Qualitative Report* 10, no. 2 (2005): 358–94.

22. Paul Ricoeur, "Metaphor and the Central Problem of Hermeneutics," in *Paul Riceur: Hermeneutics and the Human Sciences*, ed. John B. Thompson (Cambridge: Cambridge University Press, 1981), 165–81.

23. Charteris-Black, *Corpus Approaches*, 34; Petr Drulák, "Identifying and Assessing Metaphors: Discourse on EU Reform," in *Political Language and Metaphor: Interpreting and Changing the World*, ed. Terrell Carver and Jemej Pikalo (London: Routledge, 2008), 112.

24. Jack Lule, "War and Its Metaphors: News Language and the Prelude to War in Iraq, 2003," *Journalism Studies* 5, no. 2 (2004): 182.

25. Ronald Hitzler, "Verstehen: Alltagspraxis und wissenschaftliches Programm," in *"Wirklichkeit" im Deutungsprozeß: Verstehen und Methoden in den Kultur- und Sozialwissenschaften*, ed. Thomas Jung and Stefan Müller-Doohm (Suhrkamp: Frankfurt am Main, 1993), 230; Rainer Hülsse, "Sprache ist mehr als Argumentation: Zur wirklichkeitskonstituierenden Rolle von Metaphern," *Zeitschrift für Internationale Beziehungen* 10, no. 2 (2003): 228; Umberto Eco, *The Limits of Interpretation* (Bloomington: Indiana University Press, 1994).

26. Rainer Hülsse, "Imagine the EU: The Metaphorical Construction of a Supra-Nationalist Identity," *Journal of International Relations and Development* 9, no. 4 (2006): 404.

27. Jonathan Charteris-Black, *Politicians and Rhetoric: The Persuasive Power of Metaphor* (Basingstoke, UK: Palgrave Macmillan, 2005), 16.

28. Jutta Weldes, "High Politics and Low Data: Globalization Discourses and Popular Culture," in *Interpretation and Method: Empirical Research Methods and the Interpretive Turn*, ed. Dvora Yanow and Peregrine Schwartz-Shea (Armonk, NY: M. E. Sharpe, 2006), 176–86.

29. See Media UK, "The Sun: Readership Figures," http://www.mediauk.com/newspapers/1370/the-sun/readership-figures, accessed July 21, 2014; *Bild*, "Bild und die Fakten," http://www.bild.de/digital/bild-zeitung-druck/bildzeitung/bild-und-die-fakten-7356678.bild.html, accessed July 21, 2014.

30. It is important to point out that the social and political context of the data such as the ideological orientation of the newspaper does not play a major role in this chapter's analysis. As mentioned above, it is concerned mainly with the resulting "realities" of metaphor use rather than the reasons for why particular metaphors are used. Furthermore, the *Sun* and the *Bild* newspapers serve as examples, as many of the following metaphors can also be found in other media outlets and political statements. See, for example, Alexander Spencer, "Bild Dir Deine Meinung: Die metaphorische Konstruktion des Terrorismus in den Medien," *Zeitschrift für Internationale Beziehungen* 18, no. 1 (2011): 56.

31. The following metaphors are examples of the various metaphors found in the *Bild* and the *Sun* newspapers. Due to a lack of space only one example reference is noted for each metaphorical expression.

32. *Bild*, "Gibt es jetzt Krieg, Herr Scholl-Latour?," September 12, 2001; *Bild*, "Kriegserklärung an die Menschheit," September 12, 2001.

33. *Bild*, "Die Spur führt zu Al Qaida," March 15, 2004; *Bild*, "Neue Terror-Kommandos unterwegs?," September 15, 2001; *Bild*, "Das FBI jagt bin Laden mit 180 Spionage-Satelliten," September 14, 2001; *Bild*, "Nach 26 Tagen schlage n die US-Streitkräfte zu," October 8, 2001; *Bild*, "Der Bergbunker von Osama bin Laden," September 15, 2001; *Bild*, "Das FBI jagt bin Laden mit 180 Spionage-Satelliten," September 14, 2001.

34. *Bild*, "Das ist bin Ladens Kriegserklärung," September 25, 2001; *Bild*, "Ein abscheuliches Verbrechen," October 25, 2002; *Bild*, "Mitternacht stand das Paradies in Flammen," October 14, 2002; *Bild*, "Großer Gott steh uns bei!" September 12, 2001.

35. *Bild*, "Wir werden Madrid mit Leichen spicken," March 17, 2004; *Bild*, "Wo steckt bin Laden?," September 19, 2001; *Bild*, "Das sind die Pass-Fälscher von Terror-Chef bin Laden," September 28, 2001; *Bild*, "Wir sind bereit zu sterben," October 25, 2002; *Bild*, "Überall blutüberströmte, weinende Menschen," November 21, 2003; *Bild*, "Der Angriff," October 8, 2001.

36. *Sun*, "All the World Must Unite to Defeat These Evil Cowards," September 12, 2001; *Sun*, "Moment the Plane Hit," September 12, 2001; *Sun*, "Spirit of the Blitz," September 14, 2001; *Sun*, "I Thought Ian Blair Was Recruiting Muslims for the Police—Not al-Qaeda," July 12, 2005; *Sun*, "Being Anti-war Won't Save You," March 16, 2004. Interestingly, the *blitz* metaphor is not used in Germany.

37. *Sun*, "Why the World Mustn't Sleep," October 14, 2002; *Sun*, "Let's Hope the Bombers Are on Holiday Too," August 3, 2005; *Sun*, "Deadly Times, Deadly Action," July 23, 2005; *Sun*, "Frontline Europe," March 12, 2004.

38. *Sun*, "Madrid Warlord in Britain," March 18, 2004; *Sun*, "Back in Your Cave, Coward," August 5, 2005; *Sun*, "A Terrible Tragedy Has Just Befallen My Nation," September 12, 2001; *Sun*, "No. 1 Suspect," September 12, 2001; *Sun*, "Gang's Mystery Man," July 14, 2005; *Sun*, "Why Here? Why Now?," July 12, 2005; *Sun*, "Blitz Is Coming . . . ," September 17, 2001.

39. *Sun*, "7/7: Suicide Squad on CCTV at King's Cross," July 13, 2005; *Sun*, "Bush Hits Bin Where It'll Hurt," September 25, 2001.

40. *Sun*, "War to the Death," September 18, 2001; *Sun*, "Nest of Killers," September 26, 2001; *Sun*, "Forces Are Ready to Go," September 28, 2001; *Sun*, "Bombers at Airport on Visit to al-Qaeda," July 19, 2005.

41. *Sun*, "Four Seized in Swoop by Bomb Police," October 17, 2002; *Sun*, "How Could It Happen—Nowhere Is Safe from Terrorists," September 12, 2001; *Sun*, "Operation Death Train," March 12, 2004; *Sun*, "Enemy Would Rather Die Than Be Caught," July 22, 2005; *Sun*, "Hate Britain," July 9, 2005; *Sun*, "Partners in Evil," October 6, 2001; *Sun*, "We Have No Choice, Says Hero's Mum," October 9, 2001; *Sun*, "Battle for Osama No 2," March 19, 2004; *Sun*, "Notting Hill Bank Link to Murders," September 20, 2001.

42. Jeffrey Simon, "Misperceiving the Terrorist Threat," RAND Publication Series, R-3423-RC (June 1987), 9, http://www.rand.org/pubs/reports/R3423.html, accessed June 17, 2014.

43. Benjamin R. Bates, "Audiences, Metaphors, and the Persian Gulf War," *Communication Studies* 55, no. 3 (2004): 447–63.

44. Theodore R. Sarbin, "The Metaphor-to-Myth Transformation with Special Reference to the 'War on Terrorism,'" *Peace and Conflict: Journal of Peace Psychology* 9, no. 2 (2003): 150–51.

45. Keith L. Shimko, "Foreign Policy Metaphors: Falling 'Dominos' and Drug 'Wars,'" in *Foreign Policy Analysis: Continuity and Change in Its Second Generation*, ed. Laura Neack, Jeanne A. K. Hey, and Patrick J. Haney (Englewood Cliffs, NJ: Prentice Hall, 1995), 71–84.

46. Adrian Hyde-Price, Redefining Its Security Role: Germany," in *Global Responses to Terrorism: 9/11, Afghanistan and Beyond*, ed. Mary Buckley and Rick Fawn (London: Routledge, 2003), 101–12.

47. Peter J. Katzenstein, "Same War, Different Views: Germany, Japan, and the War on Terrorism," *Current History* 101, no. 659 (2002): 429.

48. Laura K. Donohue, "Britain's Counterterrorism Policy," in *How States Fight Terrorism: Policy Dynamics in the West*, ed. Doron Zimmermann and Andreas Wenger (Boulder, CO: Lynne Rienner, 2007), 17–58.

49. Bradley Bamford, "The United Kingdom's 'War against Terrorism,'" *Terrorism and Political Violence* 16, no. 4 (2004): 737–56; Andrew Dorman, "Loyal Ally: The United Kingdom," in Buckley and Fawn, *Global Responses to Terrorism*, 66–78.

50. "The Guardian Poll October 2001," *ICM Research*, October 10–11, 2001, http://www.icmresearch.co.uk/pdfs/2001_october_guardian_afghanistan_poll_1.pdf, accessed June 5, 2012; or "Evening Standard London Poll October 2001/ War in Afghanistan," *ICM Research*, October 10–11, 2001, http://www.icmresearch.com/media-centre/polls/evening-standard-war-in-afghanistan, accessed July 21, 2014.

51. Ronald Crelinsten and Alex Schmid, "Western Responses to Terrorism: A Twenty-Five Year Balance Sheet," *Terrorism and Political Violence* 4, no. 4 (1992): 307–40.

52. *Bild*, "Wer steckt hinter dem Anschlag," July 8, 2005; *Bild*, "Terroristen ermorden ägyptischen Botschafter," July 8, 2005; *Bild*, "Mr. President, treffen Sie die Schuldigen, nicht die Unschuldigen," September 17, 2001; *Bild*, "So feige! So sinnlos! Ihr Mörder!," March 12, 2004; *Bild*, "Er war's!," July 14, 2005.

53. *Bild*, "Schily fordert Raster-Fahndung in ganz Europa," March 27, 2004; *Bild*, "Um 8.51 Uhr zerfetzte es die erste U-Bahn," July 8, 2005; *Bild*, "Ein abscheuliches Verbrechen," October 25, 2002; *Bild*, "Das ist Deutschlands gefährlichster Häftling," October 23, 2002; *Bild*, "Ich sah, wie Trümmer eine Frau enthauptet haben," October 14, 2002.

54. *Bild*, "Verdammte 11: Angst vor Attentaten am Ostersonntag," April 7, 2004; *Bild*, "Kriegserklärung an die Menschheit," September 12, 2001; *Bild*, "Was passiert mit den Leichen der zerfetzten Attentäter?," July 19, 2005.

55. *Sun*, "Murderers Damned by the World," March 12, 2004; *Sun*, "Gang 'Return' to Flat to Get More Explosives," July 27, 2005; *Sun*, "Backpack Butchers: Terror Mob Had Bombs in Rucksacks," July 13, 2005; *Sun*, "Two Million Unit to Defy Terrorists," March 13, 2004; *Sun*, "Now Go Get 'em George," September 14, 2001; *Sun*, "Day That Changed the World," September 12, 2001; *Sun*, "Heavenly Island Turned into Hell," October 16, 2002.

56. *Sun*, "A Tragic Casualty of War," July 25, 2005; *Sun*, "Tunnel of Blood," July 8, 2005; *Sun*, "We Shall Prevail . . Terrorists Shall Not," July 8, 2005.

57. *Sun*, "They Must Have Killed Thousands," September 12, 2001.

58. Peter Sederberg, "Conciliation as Counter-terrorist Strategy," *Journal of Peace Research* 32, no. 3 (1995): 299–300.

59. Peter J. Katzenstein, "Sonderbare Sonderwege: Germany and 9/11," AICGS/German-American Dialogue Working Paper Series, American Institute for Contemporary German Studies, Johns Hopkins University, http://www.aicgs.org/site/wp-content/uploads/2011/11/katzenstein.pdf, accessed June 5, 2012.

60. Victor Mauer, "Germany's Counterterrorism Policy," in Zimmermann and Wenger, *How States Fight Terrorism*, 63.

61. "Deutschland TREND: November 2001," conducted by Infratest dimap for the ARD, http://www.infratest-dimap.de/uploads/media/dt0111.pdf, accessed June 5, 2012.

62. Laura K. Donohue, "Britain's Counterterrorism Policy," in Zimmermann and Wenger, *How States Fight Terrorism*, 17–58.

63. Sebastian Payne, "Britain's New Anti-terrorist Legal Framework," *RUSI Journal* 147, no. 3 (2002): 44–52.

64. "BBC Daily Politics Show Poll," Populus, June 6–7, 2007, http://populuslimited .com/uploads/download_pdf-040707-The-Daily-Politics-Fighting-Terrosrism.pdf, accessed June 5, 2012.

65. "Times Poll," Populus, November 4–6, 2005, http://www.populus.co.uk/uploads/ download_pdf-061105-The-Times-Political-Attitudes.pdf, accessed June 5, 2012; "Sky News / YouGov Survey Results," YouGov, November 4–5, 2005, http://www.yougov .co.uk/extranets/ygarchives/content/pdf/DBD050101009_1.pdf, accessed June 5, 2012.

66. *Bild*, "Die Spur führt zu Al Qaida," March 15, 2004; *Bild*, "Jagt auf die Bomben-Barbaren," July 9, 2005; *Bild*, "Jetzt sind wir alle Amerikaner weil . . . ," September 13, 2001; *Bild*, "Terror-Bestie lebte acht Jahre in Deutschland," September 14, 2001.

67. *Bild*, "Putin versetzt Luftabwehr in Gefechtsbereitschaft," September 12, 2001; *Bild*, "Mitten ins stolze Herz Spaniens," March 12, 2004; *Bild*, "Ist bin Laden schon aus Afghanistan geflohen?," September 22, 2001; *Bild*, "Besiegen sie das Böse?," September 19, 2001.

68. *Bild*, "In New York erlebten wir die Handlanger des Teufels," September 21, 2001; *Bild*, "War es Osama bin Laden," October 14, 2002; *Bild*, "Um 8.51 Uhr zerfetzte es die erste U-Bahn," July 8, 2005; *Bild*, "Gibt es jetzt Krieg, Herr Scholl-Latour?," September 12, 2001; *Bild*, "Ich überlebte die Terror-Hölle," October 15, 2002; *Bild*, "Die Woche der Apokalypse," September 17, 2001.

69. *Sun*, "He Mumbled a Prayer, Bag Went Bang; 3 Heroes Piled In," July 22, 2005; *Sun*, "Bali Outrage Shows We Must Win War on Terror," October 15, 2002; *Sun*, "Evil across Our Planet," July 8, 2005; *Sun*, "We're All American Now," September 14, 2001; *Sun*, "Shocked at Evil Attack but Proud and Defiant," July 11, 2005; *Sun*, "Queen Cries along with Us All," September 15, 2001.

70. *Sun*, "UK . . . You will pay . . .Bin Laden's on Way," April 3, 2004; *Sun*, "A Terrible Tragedy Has Just Befallen My Nation," September 12, 2001; *Sun*, "We Shall Prevail . . . Terrorists Shall Not," July 8, 2005; *Sun*, "Abuse of Britain," July 12, 2005; *Sun*, "Riddle of 'fifth hijack' Foiled by Cancellation," September 19, 2001; *Sun*, "Why the World Mustn't Sleep," October 14, 2002.

71. *Sun*, "Our Spirit Will Not Be Broken," July 22, 2005; *Sun*, "I'm So Angry Our Kids Are Growing Up in World of Terror," July 9, 2005; *Sun*, "Bush: Al-Qa'ida Did It," October 15, 2002; *Sun*, "Hook's Web of Evil," March 17, 2004.

72. *Sun*, "Depths of Evil," October 15, 2002; *Sun*, "Did They Learn on Pounds 50 CD Rom?," September 13, 2001; *Sun*, "All the World Must Unite to Defeat These Evil Cowards," September 12, 2001; *Sun*, "56 Minutes of Hell," July 8, 2005; *Sun*, "War Zone . . . It's Armageddon," September 12, 2001; *Sun*, "You Don't Expect Your Boy to Turn into One of the 4 Horsemen of the Apocalypse," July 18, 2005.

73. See Aditi Bhatia's chapter in this volume.

74. Annita Lazar and Michelle Lazar, "The Discourse of the New World Order: 'Outcasting" the Double Face of Threat," *Discourse and Society* 15, no. 2–3 (2004): 223–42.

75. Marina A. Llorente, "Civilization versus Barbarism," in *Collateral Language: A User's Guide to America's New War*, ed. John Collins and Ross Glover (New York: New York University Press, 2002), 45.

76. Thomas Diez and Vicki Squire, "Traditions of Citizenship and the Securitisation of Migration in Germany and Britain," *Citizenship Studies* 12, no. 6 (2008): 574.

77. Ibid., 573.

78. "Deutschland TREND: April 2004," Infratest dimap conducted for the ARD, http://www.infratest-dimap.de/uploads/media/dto404.pdf, accessed June 5, 2012.

79. "Terrorism Poll Conducted for the BBC," *ICM Research*, February 5–6, 2003, http://www.icmresearch.co.uk/pdfs/2003_february_bbc_Radio_five_live_terrorism_poll.pdf, accessed June 5, 2012; "Terrorist Bombings and the Olympics Survey," *Populus*, July 8–10, 2005, http://www.populus.co.uk/uploads/download_pdf-100705-The-Times-Terrorism.pdf, accessed June 5, 2012.

80. *Bild*, "Deutschland weint mit Amerika," September 12, 2001; *Bild*, "Putin versetzt Luftabwehr in Gefechtsbereitschaft," September 12, 2001; *Bild*, "Was uns die Spanier lehren," March 16, 2004.

81. *Bild*, "So quälen sie die Geiseln von Moskau," October 26, 2002; *Bild*, "Wer sind die barbarischen Bombenleger?," March 12, 2004; *Bild*, "Terror-Irrsinn!," March 25, 2004; *Bild*, "Wird heute bin Ladens Gehirn verhaftet?," March 20, 2004.

82. *Sun*, "Disciples of Osama . . . but They Targeted ALL Religions," July 8, 2005; *Sun*, "Blair: We Have Incontrovertible Evidence bin Laden Did It; We Will Get Him, Stop Him," October 1, 2001; *Sun*, "Don't Grass Rant," April 2, 2004; *Sun*, "We're All American Now," September 14, 2001; *Sun*, "Silence That Said It All," July 15, 2005.

83. *Sun*, "If Blair Used the Laws We Have, We Wouldn't Need a Stable Door Act," July 22, 2005; *Sun*, "Slaughter of the Innocent," March 12, 2004; *Sun*, "Siege Ended in Tragedy but Putin Had No Choice," October 29, 2002; *Sun*, "I Thought Ian Blair Was Recruiting Muslims for the Police—Not for al-Qaeda," July 12, 2005; *Sun*, "Horror in My Street," July 8, 2005; *Sun*. "We're All American Now," September 14, 2001; *Sun*, "We've Got Him," July 28, 2005.

84. *Sun*, "Maniac's Passport Is Found in Rubble," September 17, 2001; *Sun*, "Let's Hope the Bombers Are on Holiday Too," August 3, 2005; *Sun*, "Show Them We Are Not Afraid," July 14, 2005; *Sun*, "Send Him Bak," July 20, 2005.

85. *Sun*, "Outrage as Ken Justifies Suicide Nuts," July 20, 2005; *Sun*, "America Thought Pentagon Was Safe; Nobody Counted on a Jet Dropping from the Sky," September 12, 2001.

86. Emily Pronin, Kathleen Kennedy, and Sarah Butsch, "Bombing versus Negotiating: How Preferences for Combating Terrorism Are Affected by Perceived Terrorist Rationality," *Basic and Applied Social Psychology* 28, no. 4 (2006): 385–92.

87. Joseba Zulaika and William A. Douglass, *Terror and Taboo: The Follies, Fables and Faces of Terrorism* (New York: Routledge, 1996), 62.

88. For the full text of bin Laden's audiotape see "Bin Laden Tape," BBC News, April 15, 2004, http://news.bbc.co.uk/2/hi/middle_east/3628069.stm, accessed June 5, 2012.

89. *Süddeutsche Zeitung*, "Keine Verhandlungen mit Terroristen und Schwerver-brechern," April 15, 2004, http://www.sueddeutsche.de/politik/bundesregierung-keine -verhandlungen-mit-terroristen-und-schwerverbrechern-1.439366, accessed June 5, 2012.

90. *Daily Telegraph*, "Bin Laden's Truce Offer Rejected as 'Absurd': Taped Message from al-Qa'eda Chief Calls on Europe to Abandon America," April 16, 2004; *Evening Standard*, "Europe Is Offered a Truce in 'New bin Laden Message,'" April 15, 2004.

91. *Sun*, "Peace off bin Laden," April 16, 2004; *Die Welt*, "'Wenn ihr unser Blut vergießt, vergießen wir eures'; Osama bin Laden meldet sich nach langer Zeit wieder zu Wort und bietet den Europäern einen Waffenstillstand an," April 16, 2004.

92. *Agence France Press*, "Alleged bin Laden Truce Offer Merits 'Contempt': British FM," April 15, 2004.

93. *Sun*, "Peace off bin Laden"; *Observer*, "Blair Has Lost His Grip," April 18, 2004.

94. Judith Renner and Alexander Spencer, eds., *Reconciliation after Terrorism: Strategy, Possibility or Absurdity* (London: Routledge, 2012).

95. Richard Jackson, *Writing the War on Terror: Language, Politics and Counter-terrorism* (Manchester: Manchester University Press, 2005).

96. Petr Drulak and Lugie Königove, "Figuring Out Europe: EU Metaphors in the Minds of Czech Civil Servants," *Perspectives* 15, no. 1 (2007): 5–23.

97. Jackson, *Writing the War on Terror*; Lee Jarvis, *Times of Terror: Discourse, Temporality and the War on Terror* (Basingstoke, UK: Palgrave Macmillan, 2009).

98. David Ritchie, "'ARGUMENT IS WAR'—Or Is It a Game of Chess? Multiple Meanings in the Analysis of Implicit Metaphor," *Metaphor and Symbol* 18, no. 2 (2003): 125–46.

99. Christ'l De Landtsheer and Ilse De Vrij, "Talking about Srebrenica: Dutch Elites and Dutchbat; How Metaphors Change during Crisis," in *Metaphorical World Politics*, ed. Francis A. Beer and Christ'l de Landtsheer (East Lansing: Michigan State University Press, 2004), 166.

6

The Myth of the Terrorist as a Lover

Competing Regional Media Frames

NOHA MELLOR

As the main enemy of the Western world for nearly a decade, Osama bin Laden was the focus of international news media and the topic of several books about his life before and after exile from his homeland. Several of these stories, particularly in the Anglo-American media, illustrated a significant fascination with the Arab male's sexuality, mainly in the most authoritarian states, which contributes to the image of the Arab as a neurotic sexual being.[1] Indeed, this fascination was not confined to bin Laden, as other male authoritarian figures received similar attention; for instance, Saddam Hussein was rumored to be a womanizer who had a number of concubines, and the founder of Saudi Arabia, Ibn Saud, was rumored to have married into over thirty tribes to unify his country.

This chapter zooms in on media coverage of bin Laden and how it depicted his relationship with his wives, particularly the sixth one, Amal Assadah, who was rumored to have shielded bin Laden when the American commandos shot him. I argue that the main difference between the coverage in Arab media versus Anglo-American news media is that the former focused on the *issues* surrounding bin Laden and his family, foregrounding the wives' support of bin Laden as part of their duty as virtuous Muslim women. Anglo-American media, however, chose to focus on the *image* of bin Laden as a sexual being, thereby contributing to the myth of bin Laden as a neurotic evil. Both regions focused on these wives as mainly emotionally or religiously motivated to follow bin Laden rather than on their political and ideological motivations. The following section provides a brief discussion about the role of myth in the news-making process, focusing on the myths surrounding bin Laden's sexuality. The subsequent sections then present examples of pan-Arab and Anglo-American coverage.

Soft News as Myths

News about men like Osama bin Laden or Saddam Hussein does not only feature in the analysis sections in national broadsheets, but in the sensational tabloids as well. For instance, Richard Keeble showed that parallel to the construction of the war myth in Anglo-American media was the "demonization of Saddam Hussein." Such sensational news aimed at "simplifying an enormously complex history, seriously distorting the representation of the conflict and drawing attention away from other important social, political, geostrategic, religious and economic factors."[2] Such demonization entailed the depiction of Saddam as the new Hitler, a mad man, and barbarous creature, which, in turn, contributed to reducing a major political conflict to a fight between good and evil. Similar coverage was given bin Laden in the Anglo-American media, as Samuel P. Winch illustrated in his analysis of the news during the period from 1999 to 2002, arguing that bin Laden was depicted as an archetypal evil genius villain, with a "baffling and frightening personality." The image of bin Laden as "savage, uncivilized barbarian" hinged on journalists' tendency to resort to the mythical archetypes of the formidable opponent because "there is no glory in dealing a weak opponent." As Winch argues, many journalists did "imply a grudging admiration for the perpetrators of the attacks," depicting bin Laden as a "larger-than-life pop culture revolutionary figure." Thus, while drawing on mythical figures, journalists depicted bin Laden as "a formidable foe, terror incarnate, an iconic enemy worth of military attention."[3]

As E. Bird and R. W. Dardenne argue, "Myth reassures by telling tales that explain [...] phenomena and provide acceptable answers; myth does not necessarily reflect an objective reality, but builds a world of its own."[4] Drawing on such myths serves the purpose of attracting audiences while eliminating competing frames of the same story, which may require both efforts and resources to investigate. Myths have "identifiable narrative structures that become formulaic through repeated application, complete with common central actors and predictable outcomes [...] The concept of myth builds upon archetypes by taking archetypal stories and adding social meaning about 'ideals, ideologies, values and beliefs.'"[5] For example, the image of the Palestinian suicide bomber was at times depicted "as the Trickster: a part-human, part-animal being driven by lust and physical appetites. The Trickster has no control over his impulses and is not guided by normal conceptions of good and evil."[6] As shown below, this image of the villain is similar to the way bin Laden was depicted in Anglo-American tabloids.

Because news communicates through narrative, it rests on the construction and dissemination of known cultural myths, understood not as false tales but as narratives that are grounded in specific cultural values and ideologies. Such narratives then reflect a certain (cultural) view of the world, and it inevitably includes archetypes such as heroes, villains, and victims. These characters follow a recurrent pattern in which the hero embarks on a special journey usually involving fighting a villain and facing great challenges. The villain is usually evil beyond redemption, struggles with the protagonist, and tries to spoil the latter's efforts to reach his or her goals. In such storylines, the villain must be defeated in order to restore the balance and end chaos. Such myths and mythical figures are present in the news, such as the narrative of rescuing Jessica Lynch in Iraq in 2003.[7] By resorting to such conventional storylines, journalists manage to reduce the complexity of (political) news while collapsing a long narrative into a short vignette. The telling and retelling of these narratives reinforces predictable ways of interpreting political events while naturalizing these interpretations to make them appear more commonsensical than alternatives. These narratives rest on selected appropriation of events and facts (and even characters) in accordance with the news values in media institutions. These news values are the basis upon which journalists make decisions regarding the newsworthiness of any event. These appropriations, although interweaved in a predefined narrative, still have to rest on the journalistic claims of objectivity and factuality.

Moreover, journalists tend to personalize news because "when stories are told in human terms, they become more accessible," and Anglo-American journalists also tend to show interest in transforming hard news into soft news stories.[8] One major difference between soft and hard news is the value of immediacy; hard news is likely to be an immediate event, while soft news can deal with any topic regardless of its timeliness. Other differences include the topicality and personalization:

> The more a news item is politically relevant, the more it reports in a thematic way, focuses on the societal consequences of events, is impersonal and unemotional in its style, the more it can be regarded as hard news. The more a news item is not politically relevant, the more it reports in an episodic way, focuses on individual consequences of events, is personal and emotional in style, the more it can be regarded as soft news.[9]

The boundaries between hard news and soft news in Western media have become blurred,[10] with the latter becoming a staple of the news diet in the serious (or quality) media, while political news is declining in priority. In fact, this tendency has been the concern of American journalists, who have expressed their concern to report news factually while avoiding sensationalism. Both types of news are linked in journalistic practices, as soft news "reinforces and complements the dominant political consensus articulated in [...] current affairs coverage."[11] For instance, sex scandals can be constructed in a way that turns them into hard news by highlighting the institutional causes and impact of such scandals, thereby "hardening and lengthening ... a soft ... and lower status story."[12] Another reason to personalize the news is the shrinking audience, which has forced the news media to increase their soft news sections in order to attract or at least maintain their share of audience.[13] It was perhaps for this reason that bin Laden's militant actions were not the only concern of the media; the women surrounding bin Laden have received a great deal of attention as well. His niece made headlines when she posed for provocative photographs for the American magazine *GQ*. She grew up in Saudi Arabia but later moved to Geneva and then to the United States, where she was born.[14] His wives were also under journalistic scrutiny after the publication of his son's memoirs in 2009.

In summary, news stories are indeed "stories," and journalists are the "professional storytellers of our age."[15] Storytelling here involves gathering data about certain events that engaged certain characters in a customized sequence of events (or plot). This employment includes selective appropriation of events and characters, and thus is inherently political. The following sections explore the stories and myths attached to bin Laden and his wives in a small random sample of Arab and Anglo-American news.

Comparative Approach

For the purpose of this chapter, I have analyzed a random sample of news articles written in Arabic and English.[16] The articles cover a range of news sources in Arabic, such as Al Jazeera.net, *Laha* women's magazine, Mareb Press online, the Egyptian newspaper *Al Wafd*, the London-based newspapers *Al Hayat* and *Al Quds Al Arabi*, Hashd online source, Adwaa online, Iraq Hurr radio station, and *Saudi Gazette*. The English articles are primarily selected from the British tabloids *Daily Mail* and the *Sun*, the broadsheets the *Telegraph* and the *Independent*, and *Time* magazine, in addition to the *New York Times*, *Vanity Fair*, and AFP agency.

In the following, I analyze the selected news texts as part of a narrative and a grand myth about bin Laden. Anglo-American media presented bin Laden (the villain) as a husband, father, and even lover, while depicting his wives as weak helpers following him out of ignorance or to seek power or sexual satisfaction. Bin Laden was said to have married six times: his first wife was his cousin, Najwa, and they had eleven children together. She followed him to Afghanistan but left right before the 9/11 attacks and moved permanently to Syria. His second wife, Khadijah, had three children with him, and she divorced him while in Sudan and moved back to Saudi Arabia. The third wife is Khairiah, a highly educated woman who had one son with bin Laden. The fourth wife, Siham, had four children with him and is also highly educated. The fifth marriage was in Sudan but was annulled within forty-eight hours. The sixth and last wife was Amal Assadah, who was only seventeen when she married Osama in 2000.[17] She had one daughter with Osama and was with him in Pakistan when he was killed.

What is notable in the selected Arabic news stories is their depiction of women as bearers of culture and tradition with regard to their roles as obedient wives and dedicated mothers. In fact, scholarly debates on the relationship between gender and nation discuss the roles that have been rather rigidly prescribed for women in Middle Eastern societies, including the role of women in biological reproduction and the cultural production of the nation, thereby assigning women the burden of representing the cultural values of the nation.[18] Women often serve as symbols of the collective unity and honor, such as the image of nation as a mother, even if they are excluded from the political process.[19] In the Arab world, there has often been a tension between nationalism and Islamism, or the configuration of an identity for Arab women that can be reconciled with Islamist tradition. In many Arab states, women's citizenship rights are usually required to reconcile with the teachings of Islam. Indeed, "women's struggles in the Middle East—whether around the modernization of family laws, or in the fight against fundamentalism, or around the demands for greater employment opportunities, political participation, or nationality rights—are the central motor of the drive for citizenship."[20]

As bearers of culture, Arab women are encouraged to see their identity as inextricably linked to that of the collective identity governed by kinship; this is what Suad Joseph coined "connectivity."[21] Kinship here does not necessarily refer to the closest family relations but encompasses a large political identity that relates the female self to other kinsmen in the same country or other Arab states. As Suad Joseph argues, "The use of women—or more particularly their status and relations with others—in competing claims to modernity and tradition is further evidence of the symbolic centrality of women as markers of the nation."[22]

Within Islamist teaching, Barbara Stowasser distinguishes between two discourses on women: the modernist discourse, which propagates women's right to sociopolitical equality with men within the teaching of Islam, and the conservative Islamic discourse, which, while not denying women's rights to equality with men, confines women's roles to the family and the private sphere on the grounds that men are more suited to handling the political sphere.[23] Moreover, media play a pivotal role in reproducing and disseminating these Islamic discourses, contributing to the definition of an ideal role for Muslim women. This role has been further enforced by the rise of Islamic media and television channels, which often depict women as symbols of the nation's survival and as self-sacrificing mothers, sisters, and wives.[24]

In the selected Arabic data, bin Laden's women were seen as symbols of the virtuous Muslim woman in their dedication to their husband, even if he keeps more than one wife, and their children. For those women who chose to be on the move with bin Laden, they were depicted as mothers dedicated to the education of their children. For those who chose not to follow bin Laden's path, they were still seen as making a sacrifice for the sake of their children by sacrificing their marriage.

On the other hand, the Anglo-American press demonized the image of bin Laden, focusing on his exaggerated sexual appetite when mentioning his relationship with his wives and mistresses. This depiction is part of the myth of bin Laden as a formidable opponent. It is also part of the news outlets' strategy to personalize the news as a means to attract audiences.

The following sections illustrate how the Anglo-American publications turned the news about these women into soft news that entertains the readers and describes the way bin Laden treated his wives. On the other hand, the Arab news media chose to see these women through humanitarian lenses, namely as victims to be rescued and protected, focusing on the recent events surrounding the detention and release of bin Laden's wives in Pakistan.

Women Following Their Desires

To begin with, the British *Daily Mail* illustrated a concerted interest with bin Laden's sexual relationship with his wives. This is also manifested in the coverage of Omar bin Laden's memoirs in which he said that his father was "a man that no other man can control."[25] He mentioned that his grandfather bin Laden had two passions: work and women: "He was extremely successful in both arenas. His ethic for hard work and total sincerity won him the complete trust of the King. With hard work came financial rewards, which enabled my grandfather to satisfy his second passion: women . . . he not only married four women but continually emptied several of the four marriage positions so that he could fill the vacated slots with new wives."[26] The grandfather was said to have so many children that it was difficult for him to maintain a strong relationship with each one. Omar also complained that he was one of twenty children, and he too had to struggle to get his father's attention. He commented on his father's somber and religious life and said he used to "avert his eyes whenever a woman not of his family came into his view." From his childhood memories, he remembers that his parents "secluded themselves in their bedroom, not to be seen by the family for several days."[27] The *Daily Mail* confirmed this story in one of its reports following the death of bin Laden: "Osama bin Laden used to have sex with his first wife for days on end whenever he came back from waging Jihad [. . .] [A]sked by an interviewer to name her favorite time when living with the terrorist, she replied: 'the sleeping time.'"[28] The report also claimed that the U.S. soldiers who raided bin Laden's compound had "found herbal Viagra." One reader commented on this article sarcastically: "As usual when there is nothing else to report the media sink into the gutter and always fall back on some sex article when there is nothing else to say. The media act like a crowd of pubescent schoolboys."

Bin Laden's second wife was an expert in Islamic theology and Arabic, and she used her expertise to serve bin Laden, thus remaining within her role as a helping wife. The third wife was knowledgeable, offering her knowledge to educate her and other wives' children. Bin Laden's women were not described as beautiful or endowed with attractive looks; it seemed more important for the media to focus on sexuality as the main connection between bin Laden and his wives. His first wife was claimed to have called him a "sex machine."[29] Media reports about his sex life could be used to scandalize the whole institution of clergy and Muslim jihadists and preachers in the same way that they had scandalized Hollywood actors.[30] Thus, bin Laden is depicted as a clergyman who does not practice what he preaches, as he cares about sex but preaches duty and jihad. Moreover, he indulged in sexual adventures although they were deemed *haram,* or forbidden, such as his fantasies about Whitney Houston—who as an American is thus one of his enemies. In so doing, bin Laden is still confined to the role of the barbaric villain who cannot restrain his instincts.

The *Daily Mail* has dedicated entire reports to bin Laden's fantasies about Whitney Houston. In 2012, one such report claimed that "bin Laden is said to have lusted after Houston, dreamed of marrying her and at one point even plotted to murder her husband Bobby Brown."[31] The rumors stemmed from bin Laden's Sudanese mistress, Kola Boof, who released her autobiography in 2006, claiming to have been kept as bin Laden's sex slave in 1996. Boof also claimed that bin Laden would keep copies of *Playboy* in his briefcase and that he used to puff cannabis from a gold hookah pipe.[32]

In another 2010 article in the *Daily Telegraph*, Omar bin Laden was claimed to regard his father, Osama bin Laden, as "neither a jihadist nor a mass murderer," but as a "lost man, a fanatical father who withheld his love, beat and betrayed his children, and destroyed his family chasing his fantasy of becoming a latter-day prophet."[33] *Time* magazine published a feature about Osama and his three wives in Pakistan following his death in 2011. The report claimed that "his family must have driven him nuts. During his last days in Abbotabad, Pakistan, bin Laden had to contend with three wives and 17 noisy children under one roof. He had no escape from the din, save for furtive pacing around the garden late at night or vanishing into his so-called Command and Control Center, a dank, windowless room."[34] It was also claimed that he kept each wife and her children on a separate floor. In another *Daily Mail* story commenting on his tough lifestyle, it was alleged that he used to take his wives and children into the desert and have them dig holes to sleep in.[35] Following his marriage to Amal Assadah, bin Laden was asked why he kept his wives and children with him in hiding rather than keeping them safe in Saudi Arabia or in Yemen, to which he said, "It is my desire that my children grow up in an atmosphere of jihad and absorb Islam in its true spirit […] Believe me, when your children and your life become part of your struggle, life becomes very enjoyable."[36]

His marriage to Amal Assadah is claimed to have shook his relationship with the first three wives, argues Lawrence Wright: "Although the marriage [to Amal] seems to have been a political arrangement between bin Laden and an important Yemeni tribe, meant to boost al-Qaeda recruitment in Yemen, bin Laden's other wives were upset, and even his mother chastised him."[37] One of Amal's relatives told CNN that Amal belonged to a conservative family but was in no way extremist before the wedding, and claimed that the former Yemeni government harassed the family into keeping silent about their terrorist in-law.[38]

Press reports labeled Amal as bin Laden's "youngest and favourite" wife, and U.S. officials were claimed to be determined to talk to her to get as much information as possible about bin Laden's four other sons, who could be anywhere in the world, after his son Hamza, twenty, was shot in the raid.[39] According to these reports, Amal served as a human shield in an attempt to protect her husband as the U.S. forces stormed into his bedroom. She was then shot in the leg and remained in a Pakistani military hospital until her release and extradition to Saudi Arabia. Being the youngest wife, she was depicted in the

Daily Mail as obedient and naive.[41] Her youth was also seen as the reason for jealousy among bin Laden's other wives.

When the wives were captured in Pakistan, the *New York Times* claimed that Amal Assadah was the one who offered "the most detailed account yet of life on the run," although the Arab media claimed that Amal was the one who refused to talk to the investigators.[42] Following the release of bin Laden's wives in Pakistan and prior to their departure to Saudi Arabia, the British newspaper the *Sun* claimed that Amal asked for asylum in the UK with "her five kids fathered by the evil terror master."[43] She is quoted as saying, "I believe the UK people and the government are more polite and friendly than US people. I am sure they believe in peace more than military actions. I would love to meet the UK Royal Family." Thus, she is portrayed as an inconsistent and irrational woman, who, on the one hand, shields bin Laden when he was attacked while, on the other hand, releases information about Al Qaeda and even seeks asylum in a Western country.

In summary, the Anglo-American media sought to focus on bin Laden's sexuality and his relationships with his wives, particularly the last one. Indeed, the focus on sex and sexuality is one strategy of the tabloid journalists to attract readers' attention.[44] Perhaps because it is claimed that these women enjoyed their sexuality with bin Laden, it was not expected of them to remarry after bin Laden's death: "As widows, under Islam, they are free to marry again, if they wish. But few suitors are likely to step forward. Marrying the widow of the world's most wanted man has its own complications."[45]

Feeble Agents to Be Rescued

Writing about bin Laden's wives, Arab news media focused on specific events as they unfolded, particularly the detention and subsequent release of these women in Pakistan. This news was told from a humanitarian perspective as the story of mothers and widows detained in a foreign country and in need of help from the Arab states, particularly Saudi Arabia, to facilitate their release and their return to Saudi Arabia. For instance, Al Jazeera focused on this event as an "ordeal" for bin Laden's family, who were arrested following his death in Pakistan. They published statements by the family's lawyer in Pakistan, saying that family members were relieved to be released and could not wait to leave Pakistan for Saudi Arabia. They also referred to the Taliban's threats to Pakistan of escalating their suicide attacks if the family were not released.[46]

Amal Assadah was the only wife who received much attention from both the Arabic and English news media as the youngest and last wife of bin Laden and who was shot in her leg while allegedly shielding bin Laden. Unlike the image that Anglo-American tabloids chose for Amal, as young and naive for protecting bin Laden, the Arab news media bestowed on her the image of a woman who was following her faith through dedicating her life to serving her husband. As a woman, Amal did not find it possible to join the jihadist call, nor did she show interest in it, according to her relatives, although Al Qaeda had female recruits, and examples of such women were the topic of an exclusive episode of the *Khabaya* (Secrets) program on MBC (Middle East Broadcasting Center) TV on October 4, 2011.[47]

Amal's cousin, Walid Assadah, spoke to the *Al Hayat* newspaper about Amal and her marriage to bin Laden. He said that she was always ambitious and wanted to enter history. Osama loved her and commended her father on her upbringing, telling him, "Thank you for this upbringing. I am very pleased." Assadah asserted that Amal would never remarry even if it was "the Yemeni president himself." "She was an ordinary woman, she did not complete her compulsory studies, but she was very ambitious [...] I used to tell her that without education or qualifications, she could never enter history as she dreamed."[48]

He told the story behind bin Laden's marriage to his cousin, which began when bin Laden asked a friend to find him a wife from the Assadahs, after one of his followers married a girl from the Assadah clan and was pleased with her. At that time (in 1999), the family did not know bin Laden, and as Walid Assadah said, "Amal did not have TV or Internet and did not read newspapers. Perhaps she did not understand who bin Laden was, and she was also an adventure-seeker." Bin Laden invited Amal's father to visit them in Afghanistan in 2000, which he did, but he was not happy with the heavy security around bin Laden. They invited the father to stay with them, and bin Laden offered to arrange a marriage for him, but Amal's father refused and returned to Yemen. Amal's family was claimed to be divided into two groups: one group condemned the marriage once they knew the identity of bin Laden the terrorist, and the other group was proud of bin Laden and this marriage.

Amal's brother, Zakariya Assadah, also spoke to the Arab media, and in a 2012 interview with the newspaper *Adwaa* he blamed the Pakistani authorities for not allowing bin Laden's widows to return to their homelands (Yemen and Saudi Arabia).[49] He suggested that the American administration was behind this delay to complete their investigations. He stressed the physical and emotional suffering of his sister and the other widows and children who were kept under house arrest in a windowless place in Pakistan. During their detention, the newspaper *Al Quds Al Arabi* claimed that Abdullah bin Laden, Osama's eldest brother, was responsible for the widows and their children, and that he was in negotiations with the Pakistani authorities and the Saudi Embassy in

Islamabad to release the family.[50] Ayman Al Zawahiri's wife was also claimed to have made this message public in order to announce her appeal for the release of bin Laden's widows earlier in 2012. She also made headlines as she was said to have published a message on an Islamic website congratulating Muslim women on the Arab Spring and urging them to raise their children on God's love and fighting in his name.[51]

During the investigations with Amal, an Iraqi radio station claimed that bin Laden's widows were "loyal" to him during the investigation and that they refused to reveal any secrets about Al Qaeda. The radio report also claimed that the widows were talking about bin Laden passionately and that Amal in particular was reluctant to speak to the investigator. In these reports, Amal was even compared to the Argentinean activist Che Guevara in that she felt she was fighting for a cause with her silence.[52] The wives' detention in Pakistan motivated Ayman Al Zawahiri's wife to publish a message on an Islamic website appealing for the release of bin Laden's widows earlier in 2012.

When bin Laden's widows arrived in Saudi Arabia, it was reported that their families were overjoyed as these women had not seen their families for years. Amal's family denied the rumors that Amal wanted to seek asylum in the UK, saying that the "bin Laden family would not abandon its sons and daughters." The Saudi authorities are depicted as active agents who took into consideration the widows' needs as a humanitarian case.[53] It was also claimed that the Saudi authorities did not restrict bin Laden's movements inside Saudi Arabia, and the widows, in turn, were looking forward to performing Umrah (pilgrimage to Mecca) in order to gain some inner peace after years of hardship. As *Laha* magazine put it: "They need rehabilitation after what they've been through" (ten months in prison in Pakistan).[54]

Unlike the Anglo-American portrayal of these wives as being in constant argument out of jealousy with one another, the Arab coverage tends to depict these women as virtuous wives who served their husbands and families. The exception was a short article in the Egyptian newspaper *Al Wafd*, where it was claimed that the three youngest wives used to argue and that the older wives were truly upset about bin Laden's decision to marry his last wife, Amal, who was only seventeen at the time of marriage.[55] It also claimed that Osama said that he did not know that the bride was so young and that he asked for a wife between twenty-five and thirty years of age. However, he told his sons, "Now that she's here, we cannot return her to her family, so she should stay with us."[56]

In summary, unlike the Anglo-American media, the Arab media tended to focus on the societal circumstances surrounding bin Laden's family, especially Amal. Their following bin Laden was depicted as an act motivated by their faith rather than sexuality. This is also illustrated in the coverage of Siham, bin Laden's fourth wife, who holds a PhD in Islamic theology and mastered written Arabic. In an interview with the pan-Arab women's magazine *Laha*, Saad el Sharif, Siham's brother, said that Siham was "forced" to follow her husband in order to be close to her children despite her parents' objections. She married bin Laden because she admired his cause and his desire to fight for the jihad in Afghanistan during the 1980s. As el Sharif asserted, she even donated her jewelry and dowry for the cause of jihad and devoted her life and talents to serve bin Laden as part of her sacred duty as a wife.

> Osama treated his wives as wives only and did not allow them to interfere in his Jihad [...] Osama believed that Jihad was to protect women and children so he did not allow his wives to meddle in it [...] My sister invented home schooling before it was even applied in Saudi Arabia, so she managed to educate her daughters at home [...] She used to read him poetry and make him company. She was his teacher, so he used to consult her whenever he wrote anything [in Arabic].[57]

Siham's knowledge then was mobilized to serve her faith by being a faithful companion to her husband and a dedicated mother; her knowledge is justified through Islamist discourse. As one Hezbollah female activist once put it, education is "a huge investment in the service of Islam, especially for women [...] women in Islam do not follow their husbands but their faith."[58]

Thus, bin Laden's wives were defined primarily through a relational lens that saw them as connected to their husband, the jihadist. This form of "connectivity," as defined by Suad Joseph, "entails cultural constructs and structural relations in which persons . . . invite involvement with others in shaping the self."[59] The combination of patriarchy and connectivity feeds into a psychodynamic mechanism where "connectivity can support patriarchal power by crafting selves responding to, requiring, and socialized to initiate involvement with others in shaping the self," and in return patriarchy feeds into connectivity by "crafting" the males to "direct" females and females ready to accept this direction.[60] Connectivity here serves as one rule or schema that helps enforce the patriarchal division between political/public realm and the domestic realm.

Conclusion

This chapter argues that the coverage of bin Laden's wives in the Anglo-American media was confined to the *image* of bin Laden, focusing on his sexuality. As an Arab man, bin Laden was the embodiment of extreme sexual enjoyment as someone who lived an exotic life even in the harshest environments in the desert. Above all, bin Laden was "a great lover" and his amorous prowess triggered his need to marry more than once. This depiction is what Edward Said called the otherness of Arab culture: "the Orient was a place where one could look for sexual experience unobtainable in Europe."[61] The image of bin Laden's wives is almost made synonymous with the image of bin Laden himself as a mythical figure, using references to the personal and familial realms as discursive tools to reproduce the image of the erotic Orient.

On the other hand, the focus of the Arab news media was on the *issues* and difficulties facing these women following bin Laden's death, highlighting these wives' support of bin Laden as part of their duty as Muslim women. Moreover, both Anglo-American and pan-Arab news showed little interest in debating the ideological and political motivations of Amal and bin Laden's other wives. Instead, they were mostly described as motivated by love and respect for their husband and thus being emotionally charged.[62]

It can be argued that Arab women were used as symbols that combine Islamic heritage with Western modernity, measured by Western standards such as education. Thus, women like Siham, for instance, have been called to mobilize their knowledge and education at the service of their families. Paradoxically, Islamic fundamentalism can also be regarded as a response to these very Western standards in that it uses "women's bodies as sites for assertion of cultural authenticity, further reinscribing women's symbolic and real importance in definitions of the nations."[63] It was perhaps for this reason that bin Laden is claimed to have discouraged his widows from remarrying after his death.[64] In any case, the media fascination with the Al Qaeda women is likely to continue, and bin Laden's widows might remain in the news for years to come.

Notes

1. Edward W. Said, *Orientalism: Western Representations of the Orient* (London: Routledge and Kegan Paul, 1978).

2. Richard Keeble, "The Myth of Saddam Hussein: New Militarism and the Propaganda Function of the Human Interest Story," in *Media Ethics*, ed. Matthew Kieran (London: Routledge, 1998), 66–81.

3. Samuel P. Winch, "Constructing an 'Evil Genius': News Uses of Mythic Archetypes to Make Sense of bin Laden," *Journalism Studies* 6, no. 3 (2005): 285–99.

4. E. Bird and R. W. Dardenne, "Myth, Chronicle, and Story: Exploring the Narrative Qualities of News," in *Media, Myths, and Narratives: Television and the Press*, ed. James W. Carey (Beverly Hills, CA: Sage, 1988), 7–87, quote from 70.

5. Dan Berkowitz, "Suicide Bombers as Women Warriors: Making News through Mythical Archetypes," *Journalism and Mass Communication Quarterly* 82, no. 3 (2005): 607–22, quote from 608.

6. Ibid., 612.

7. Deepa Kumar, "War Propaganda and the (Ab)uses of Women: Media Constructions of the Jessica Lynch Story," *Feminist Media Studies* 4, no. 3 (2008): 297–313.

8. Steve M. Barkin, "The Journalist as Storyteller: An Interdisciplinary Perspective," *American Journalism* 1, no. 2 (1984): 27–33, quote from 28; Joshua Gamson, "Normal Sins: Sex Scandal Narratives as Institutional Morality Tales," *Social Problems* 48, no, 2 (2001): 185–205, quote from 188.

9. Carsten Reinemann, James Stanyer, Sebastian Scherr, and Guido Legnante, "Hard and Soft News: A Review of Concepts, Operationalizations and Key Findings," *Journalism* 13, no. 2 (2011): 221–39.

10. Herbert J. Gans, *Democracy and the News* (Oxford: Oxford University Press, 2003).

11. James Curran, Angus Douglas, and Gary Whannel, "The Political Economy of the Human-Interest Story," in *Newspapers and Democracy*, ed. Anthony Smith (Cambridge, MA: MIT Press), 288–316, quote from 316.

12. Gamson, "Normal Sins," 199.

13. Gans, *Democracy and the News*, 23.

14. "Bin Laden Niece in Glamour Shots," December 23, 2005, http://news.bbc.co.uk/1/hi/world/americas/4555430.stm.

15. Allan Bell, *The Language of News Media* (Oxford: Blackwell, 1991), 147.

16. The total number of news items included here is thirty stories. To sample these stories, I've searched for "bin Laden & wives" in Arabic and English online news sources. The search was conducted first in Arabic and then in English. Detailed items about bin Laden and his wives were mainly found in tabloid and women magazines, but a few items from American and British broadsheets are also included. In the Arabic sample, news items were primarily from national and pan-Arab broadsheets. In addition, during the research of stories in Arabic, I came across TV footage from a program called *Khabya* (Secrets) broadcast on MBC about female terrorists, to which I briefly refer in the following section.

17. Najwa bin Laden, Omar bin Laden, and Jean P. Sasson, *Growing Up bin Laden: Osama's Wife and Son Take Us inside Their Secret World* (New York: St Martin's Press, 2009). See also Omar bin Laden, "My Father, the Terrorist," extract from *Growing Up bin Laden, Vanity Fair,* October 28, 2009, http://www.vanityfair.com/politics/features/2009/10/omar-bin-laden-200910.print.

18. See, for example, Nira Yuval-Davis, *Gender and Nation* (London: Sage, 1997), 26, 39.

19. Ibid., 47.

20. Valentine M. Moghadam, "Women and the Changing Political Dynamics in the Middle East and North Africa," in *Middle East at the Crossroads: The Changing Political Dynamics and the Foreign Policy Challenges*, ed. Manochehr Dorraj (Lanham, MD: University Press of America, 1999), 147–71, quote on 155.

21. Suad Joseph, "Connectivity and Patriarchy among Urban Working-Class Arab Families in Lebanon," *Ethos* 21, no. 4 (1993): 452–84.

22. Suad Joseph, *Middle East Report*, no. 198, Gender and Citizenship in the Middle East (January –March 1996), 4–10., quote on 6.

23. Barbara Stowasser, *Women in the Qur'an, Traditions, and Interpretation* (Oxford: Oxford University Press, 1996).

24. See, for example, Ehab Galal, "The Muslim Woman as a Beauty Queen," *Journal of Arab and Muslim Media Research* 3, no. 3 (2010): 159–75.

25. Omar bin Laden, "My Father, the Terrorist," extract from *Growing Up bin Laden, Vanity Fair,* October 28, 2009, http://www.vanityfair.com/politics/features/2009/10/omar-bin-laden-200910.

26. Ibid.

27. Ibid.

28. Daniel Bates, "Osama bin Lothario: Terror Chief 'Was a Sex Machine Who Would Vanish into the Bedroom with His Wife for Days," *Daily Mail* (London), June 10, 2011, http://www.dailymail.co.uk/news/article-2002152/Osama-bin-Laden-sex-machine-vanish-bedroom-wife-days.html.

29. Ibid.

30. Gamson, "Normal Sins," 194.

31. "Osama bin Laden 'Had Stoned Fantasies about Marrying Whitney Houston and Murdering Bobby Brown," *Daily Mail* (London), February 16, 2012, http://www.dailymail.co.uk/news/article-2101634/Whitney-Houston-Osama-bin-Laden-dreamed-marrying-singer-murdering-Bobby-Brown.html.

32. Kola Boof, *Diary of a Lost Girl: The Autobiography of Kola Boof* (Diamond Bar, CA: Door of Kush, 2006).

33. Guy Lawson, "Omar bin Laden Speaks Out," *Telegraph* (London), March 31, 2010, http://www.telegraph.co.uk/news/worldnews/middleeast/7528897/Omar-bin-Laden-speaks-out.html.

34. Tim McGirk, "*Big Love* in Abbottabad: How Osama bin Laden Kept Three Wives under One Roof," *Time* magazine, May 12, 2011, http://www.time.com/time/printout/0,8816,2070880,00.html.

35. Bates, "Osama bin Lothario."

36. Bin Laden, qtd. in Jerome Taylor, "The Six Wives (and Many Children) of Osama bin Laden: What Will Become of the Large and Complicated Family Left Behind by the World's Most Wanted Man?," *Independent* (London), May 5, 2011.

37. Lawrence Wright, *The Looming Tower: Al-Qaeda and the Road to 9/11* (New York: Knopf, 2006), 338.

38. Mohammed Jamjoom and Tim Lister, "Exclusive: Bin Laden's Yemen bride, 18, was confident, conservative," CNN, May 10, 2011; http://www.cnn.com/2011/WORLD/meast/05/07/yemen.bin.laden.wife/.

39. Taylor, "Six Wives."

40. McGirk, "*Big Love* in Abbottabad."

41. "'I want to be martyred with you': Bin Laden's young wife's suicide pledge to terror mastermind," *Daily Mail* (London), May 12, 2011, http://www.dailymail.co.uk/news/article-1386158/Osama-Bin-Laden-wife-Amal-al-Sadas-suicide-pledge-terror-mastermind.html.

42. Declan Walsh, "In Hiding, Bin Laden Had Four Children and Five Houses," *New York Times*, March 29, 2012.

43. Nick Parker, "Mrs Bin: Let Me In—Osama's Widow Wants Asylum in UK; She'd Like to Meet Royal Family," *Sun* (London), April 19, 2012, http://www.thesun.co.uk/sol/homepage/news/4265444/Bin-Laden-widow-wants-asylum-in-UK-hopes-to-meet-Royals.html.

44. Gamson, "Normal Sins," 189.

45. McGirk, *Big Love* in Abbottabad."

46. S. Belal, "The Case of bin Laden's Widows Is to Be Solved," Al Jazeera.net, April 5, 2012, http://www.aljazeera.net/news/pages/5b0c9e83-bf5f-487e-b10b-bff581345657.

47. *Kayaba*, MBC, http://www.mbc.net/ar/mbc1/articles/الحلقة-4--نساء-في-ظل-القاعدة.html#comment7%Clist. These women include, for example, the Saudi Heila Al Qassir, from Al Qassim, who was claimed to have managed three terrorist cells, collected donations, and recruited women to join Al Qaeda. Al Qassir was jailed for fifteen years and was known as "Al-Qaeda lady" for being the first Saudi woman tried for involvement in violence. "'Al-Qaeda Lady' Gets 15-Year Jail," *Saudi Gazette*, October 30, 2011, http://www.saudigazette.com.sa/index.cfm?home.con&contentid=20111030111366.

48. "Amal Assadah—the Women Whom bin Laden Loved Before He Met Her," cited in *Mareb Press*, June 13, 2011, http://marebpress.net/nprint.php?sid=34571.

49. "Al Qaeda Leader Asked Them Not to Talk to the Media—bin Laden's Widows Live under Arrest in Pakistan," *Adwaa*, January 25, 2012, http://www.aladhwaa.net/print.php?no=3810.

50. "Bin Laden Asks His Disciplines to Temporarily Cease the Killings of the Jews and Christians and Beware of Traitors," *Al Quds Al Arabi*, May 3, 2011, http://www.alquds.co.uk/.

51. "Al Qaeda's Wife Congratulates Muslim Women on the Arab Spring," *Al Wasat* (Bahrain), issue 3562, June 8, 2012,http://www.alwasatnews.com/3562/news/read/668949/1.html.

52. "Bin Laden's Widows Loyal to Him," *Iraq Hurr*, May 25, 2012, http://www.iraqhurr.org/archive/news/20120525/1093/1093.html?id=24592990.

53. "The Yemeni Amal and bin Laden's Widows Arrive in Riyadh," *Hashd*, April 27, 2012, http://hshd.net/print14864.html.

54. "Bin Laden's Widows in Saudi Arabia," *Laha*, May 7, 2012, http://www.lahamag.com/printArticle.asp?articleId=20487.

55. N. Hassan, "The Secrets of bin Laden's Three Women," *Al Wafd*, May 9, 2011, http://www.alwafd.org/index.php?option=com_content&view=article&id=43000&catid=100&Itemid=89.

56. Ibid.

57. "Bin Laden's Brother-in-Law: My Sister Had a Different Ideology to Osama's," *Laha*, issue 560, June 15, 2011, http://www.lahamag.com/Details/26167/بعد_أسامة_بن_لادن_وليد_السادة_'أمل'_لن_تتزوج_.

58. Cited in Dalal El Bezri, *The Shadow and Its Double: Muslim Women between Modernity and Tradition* (Beirut: Dar el Nahar, 1996, in Arabic), 91, 150.

59. Joseph, "Connectivity and Patriarchy," 453.

60. Ibid., 453.

61. Said, *Orientalism*, 190.

62. See also Deborah M. Galvin, "The Female Terrorist: A Socio-psychological Perspective," *Behavioral Sciences and the Law* 1, no. 2 (1983): 19–32.

63. Suad Joseph, "Gender and Citizenship in Middle Eastern States," *Middle East Report*, no. 198 (January–March 1996), 4–10.

64. *Al Quds Al Arabi* printed bin Laden's will, which includes the following plea: "Dear wives, May Allah reward you. You were good support and help to me, after God good support. From the first day you knew that the road was full of planted brambles and mines you left your families' luxuries and chose my modest life. You were ascetic during your life with me, so remain ascetic after me, and do not marry after me but take good care of our children and give them your prayers and sacrifice." *Al Quds Al Arabi* 23, issue 6809 (May 4, 2011).

Images of Our Dead Enemies

Visual Representations of bin Laden, Hussein, and el-Qaddafi

SUSAN MOELLER, JOANNA NURMIS,
AND SARANAZ BARFOROUSH

In a nine-minute speech at 11:35 p.m. Eastern time on the evening of Sunday, May 1, 2011, President Barack Obama announced that U.S. Navy SEALs had killed Al Qaeda leader Osama bin Laden in Abbottabad, Pakistan.[1]

How do you know someone is dead unless you see the evidence? If the fact of a death really matters—politically, militarily, even emotionally—is it enough to take someone else's word for it, to just simply hear (or read) a narrative account of that death?

Does a waiting audience want—or *need*—visual confirmation?

In the minutes and hours after the news of Osama bin Laden's killing broke first across social media and then through President Barack Obama's brief May 1 speech to the nation, news outlets across the world scrambled to cover the story of the decade.[2] With no immediately forthcoming photos of bin Laden's corpse (and the White House's subsequent decision not to release any of the Navy SEALs' pictures of the dead bin Laden), mainstream news outlets were excused from the ethical as well as moral binary decision about whether to show or not show images of bin Laden's corpse. Instead, news outlets the world over had a set of decisions to make about what kind of image to select to accompany the announcement of bin Laden's death.

The choice of which visual would lead the news became a complex, even political decision. Some news outlets chose to run archival photos of bin

Laden; others used iconic images of Al Qaeda's attack on the World Trade Center towers on 9/11. Still others used pictures of Americans celebrating the news of bin Laden's death, and some ran photos and tape of President Obama speaking from the East Room of the White House. In essence, through their choices, news outlets decided how to visually "frame" the death of Osama bin Laden, the world's most wanted man.

News media around the world considered their own priorities. What were they most interested in:

Presenting evidence of bin Laden's death?
Reminding their audiences how "evil" bin Laden was—as evident in his masterminding of 9/11 and other terrorist acts?
Gloating over bin Laden's downfall (and not so coincidentally emphasizing American power)?
Articulating the political meaning and consequences of his death for Al Qaeda, for terrorism, for the political fortunes of President Barack Obama?
Marking the historical moment?
Reporting the details of the U.S. raid?

These considerations—and this case study—are a dramatic reminder that framing is one of the most inevitable, yet at the same time most complex, of all media actions. Journalists, whether working in print, broadcast, or digital media and whether covering an event or an issue, must make choices about that event's or issue's most salient elements. In turn, those reported elements influence how audiences perceive and interpret that event or issue.[3] The photographs and videotape that media chose to illustrate the breaking news of bin Laden's death, for example, together with the headlines and stories that contextualized those images, framed bin Laden's death for a watching world. Those frames helped direct the public to a particular understanding of that death.

Picturing the Dead: To Show or Not to Show? Graphic or Not So Graphic?

We live in an immersive, nonstop, localized-globalized world, where a plethora of social media platforms has spawned networks of self-initiated, self-curated bits and strands of information around the nodes of traditional arms-length news outlets. These linkages mean that there are no longer any bright lines between "mainstream" journalism and "citizen" journalism, between breaking news that is first reported by professional journalists and "news" that is published via YouTube, Twitter, Facebook, or a myriad of other social media platforms by people who happen to be "on location." Mainstream news outlets pass on information collected via social media sources; everyday citizens forward stories collected from professional outlets. Increasingly, the sine qua non for today's world is immediate access to uncensored information, no matter the originating platform.

What does this media environment mean for stories about death and destruction? What kind of information is posted and what is shared?

More specifically, what pictures are taken of violent death and what does the "public" want to see of those dead?

That depends on who the dead are.

For obituaries of well-loved family members killed in an accident, for example, it is common to see the dead commemorated with a favorite photograph, where the relative appears happy, healthy, and vibrant.

For memorials of innocents killed in mass catastrophes, by contrast—earthquakes and tsunamis, for instance, or even massacres—news outlets typically select photographs where bodies are evident to suggest the extent of the tragedy, but where faces are obscured and gore is minimized. There is usually (if not always) some line of privacy that is respected and an unarticulated level of graphic horror beyond which "reputable" news outlets and social media sites do not go (at least without a warning label attached). The downing of the Malaysian civilian plane over Ukraine in the summer of 2014, for example, is a case in point. Many "mainstream" media outlets showed photos of the destruction that included clots of bodies in the pictures, but the bodies were not recognizable, showed no evident blood, were not naked—even though the accompanying articles specifically noted that some of the dead were identifiable, were covered with blood, and had had their clothes blown off.

For coverage of the death of an enemy, the inhibitions against showing graphic gore are lifted. When someone has died who is believed to be guilty of violent aggression, war crimes, or crimes against humanity, all too often a blood lust rises among those who consider themselves to be the enemy's victims, even victims by proxy. Audiences want to see the formerly all-powerful persecutor "taken down," and that often means wanting to see unexpurgated photos of corpses, or even of the moments immediately preceding death, as evident in the online rush to view the photos and video of the legal execution by hanging of Iraqi president Saddam Hussein and the preemptive killing of Libyan leader Colonel Muammar el-Qaddafi by rebel forces.

In evaluating the images that appeared in the days and hours following Osama bin Laden's death, it is instructive to consider the photos and video that emerged immediately following the deaths of Saddam Hussein in 2006 and Muammar el-Qaddafi five years later.

The Case Study of Saddam Hussein

President Saddam Hussein's almost quarter century of despotic rule over Iraq began in 1979 and came to a close in 2003, following the American-led invasion in March of that year. With the fall of the capital of Baghdad in April 2003, Hussein fled into the country; U.S. soldiers captured him hiding in a "spider hole" at a farmhouse near his historic stronghold of Tikrit on December 13, 2003. The U.S. military first held him in solitary confinement at a U.S. base in the country, then transferred him to an Iraqi Special Tribunal to be tried for crimes against humanity. Ultimately two trials resulted: the first in 2005 tried him for his role in the executions, torture, and illegal arrests of hundreds of Shiite men and boys in Dujail following a 1982 assassination attempt. A second separate court trial that began in August 2006 tried Hussein on charges of genocide, crimes against humanity, and war crimes for his 1987–88 Anfal campaign against the Kurds, "an operation," the *Washington Post* noted, "that included the use of mustard gas and nerve agents to slaughter entire villages; concentration camps where women and children died after being stuffed 100 to a room; and mass graves dug so shallow that wild animals consumed the corpses. Prosecutors said the campaign claimed 182,000 victims."[4] In November, even as the genocide trial continued, the Iraqi Special Tribunal sentenced Saddam Hussein to death for the willful killings in Dujail—and on other counts the tribunal sentenced Hussein to ten years imprisonment for forcible deportations and another ten years for torture.[5] Saddam Hussein was hanged on December 20, 2006, just before dawn, during the morning call to prayer.

An official video crew attended Hussein's execution and captured footage that aired on Al Iraqiya state television and around the world.[6] The silent video showed Hussein led to the gallows without a struggle by three guards in black masks, and it notably captured Hussein declining to wear a hood before the executioners put the noose around his neck.[7] "It took some three to four hours before official photographs were released by the Iraqi government of Hussein's corpse in a shroud," wrote journalist Vivian Salama in an article for *Arab Media and Society*. "Thereafter, Arab networks began rolling video of Hussein's final moments, showing official government-supervised video of the final moments of the former dictator's life just before the trap door dropped from underneath his feet."

"It is perhaps ironic that the man who controlled the broadcast of his image with an iron grip was executed in one of the most widely watched news events of recent times," observed Salama.[8]

> Networks on both sides of the Atlantic wrangled with questions of ethics leading up to his December 30, 2006 hanging as to what could and what could not be shown on television. The scrutiny was different for both camps. Western networks simply sought to show enough of the final moments of Saddam Hussein's life to captivate viewers without offending them. Middle Eastern networks—particularly those catering to primarily Iraqi audiences—had to prepare for repercussions of a quite different order. So they treaded carefully, attempting to show just enough footage to convince people that he was dead without further inciting sectarian tensions.[9]

Then a low-resolution mobile phone video of the execution taken by a witness was leaked and posted to YouTube and elsewhere.[10] That video, which included sound and the actual hanging of Hussein, was significantly more graphic in what it visually depicted—even considering the poor quality of the footage. Among the riveting aspects of the stealth video was that it "revealed that Mr. Hussein exchanged taunts and jeers with jailers in his final moments, and was told to 'go to hell' by someone witnessing the event," as the *New York Times* reported.[11]

The evidentiary impact of both the government video and the surreptitiously taken mobile phone video from the execution was greater than Iraqi officials had anticipated, argued Al Arabiya's Washington bureau chief Hisham Milhem. The videos "proved" Hussein's death, but they also documented the manner of his dying. "He was not trembling or in a state of panic as some Iraqi officials claimed him to be before the videos were released," said Melhem. As a consequence, he told Salama, Hussein "became a sort of victim or martyr, appearing more dignified than his executioner."[12]

"If mainstream media were to learn one thing from the execution aftermath," noted Salama, "it was this: they are no longer in the reporting game alone. The role of citizen journalists had never been so prominent as in the coverage of Saddam Hussein's demise. Despite efforts—or alleged efforts as the case may be—to secure the premises of the execution so as to prevent leaked footage, international audiences witnessed—many for the first time—a capital punishment online. . . . [F]rom Minnesota to Manila, public opinion addressing the execution and its coverage exploded onto the World Wide Web giving anyone with Internet access the opportunity to take part in history."[13]

The Case Study of Muammar el-Qaddafi

Almost five years later, Colonel Muammar el-Qaddafi, another regional dictator, died at the hands of Libyan rebel forces on October 20, 2011, in his hometown of Sirte. Those captors used mobile phones to film his death and the frenzy immediately preceding his death.[14]

Qaddafi's despotic rule, which lasted forty-two years, had been punctuated with public trials of his critics, executions in public squares, the bombing of eastern Libyan towns harboring the growing Islamist opposition, the shooting of 1,200 prisoners in Tripoli's Abu Salim prison, the bankrolling of terrorist organizations in Europe, the Middle East, and Africa, and the backing of coup attempts in Africa. His agents were believed responsible for the 1988 deaths of 270 people when Pan Am Flight 103 exploded in midair over Lockerbie, Scotland, and the explosion of a French passenger jet over Niger in 1989 that killed 170 people.

As the *New York Times* wrote in its account of his death:

> Col. Muammar el-Qaddafi's last moments Thursday were as violent as the uprising that overthrew him.
>
> In a cellphone video that went viral on the Internet, the deposed Libyan leader is seen splayed on the hood of a truck and then stumbling amid a frenzied crowd, seemingly begging for mercy. He is next seen on the ground, with fighters grabbing his hair. Blood pours down his head, drenching his golden brown khakis, as the crowd shouts, 'God is great!'
>
> Colonel Qaddafi's body was shown in later photographs, with bullet holes apparently fired into his head at what forensic experts said was close range, raising the possibility that he was executed by anti-Qaddafi fighters.
>
> The official version of events offered by Libya's new leaders—that Colonel Qaddafi was killed in a cross-fire—did not appear to be supported by the photographs and videos that streamed over the Internet all day long."[15]

AFP staffer Philippe Desmazes covering the fighting in Libya transmitted the first photograph of a captured and bloodied Qaddafi to the outside world. As Agence France-Presse reported:

> "I was covering the fall of Sirte when I heard gunfire some distance west of where I stood," said Desmazes, adding that it sounded like a celebration rather than fighting.

"I asked the fighters to take me there, and when we reached the site they showed me huge cement culverts in which, they said, Kadhafi had been hiding before his capture."

Desmazes said his lucky break came when he noticed another group of fighters nearby, eyes fixed on a mobile phone and decided to join them.

"I was lucky because I was the only one to notice them," he said. "The owner of the cell phone showed me (a video of) the arrest of Kadhafi which he had taken a few minutes earlier.

"The light at that time made it difficult to take a picture of the screen," he said. But "the fighters moved closer and created a shadow enabling me to take a picture . . . I was very lucky."[16]

Other newscasters, including Al Jazeera, Al Arabiya, and Libya TV, soon followed AFP's breaking of the story with additional images from mobile phones of the rebels. Then Associated Press, Reuters, and other international news outlets transmitted screen grabs from those videos, together with still images of Libyan rebels huddling around Qaddafi's corpse with cell phone cameras, some of them posing for a picture of themselves with the bloodied body of their reviled leader. Several of those images made it to front pages of major newspapers. Other news outlets chose to feature the screen grab of Qaddafi confused and bloodied just before his death, and still others opted to give prominent spots to joyful rebels and civilians celebrating in the streets.[17]

The still grab that Desmazes transmitted of Qaddafi in his final moments was a photo of a photo. That image, other video stills that emerged, and the raw videos themselves were so clearly artless—impulsive, almost instinctively made images by individuals who wanted to record the cataclysmic event transpiring in their midst—that they became especially convincing documents of what really happened.

The uncertainty that shrouded the actual moment of Qaddafi's death brought a special aura to those images. For viewers around the world to become privy to those last seconds of Qaddafi's life, when he was confused, terrified, bloodied, and menaced by a group of fighters, was both astonishingly intrusive and disturbingly cathartic.[18] "A remarkable feature of the Arab revolts is the degree to which almost every incident is documented, usually by cellphone camera images," observed the *New York Times*. "They are almost instantly fed to the Internet and satellite channels, or ferried by e-mail."[19] For millennia the world has vicariously witnessed the fictional and fictionalized ends of dictator's lives, from Aeschylus's *Agamemnon* to Shakespeare's *Julius*

Caesar and beyond, yet the stage and movie iterations have traditionally emphasized tragic, grand, and heroic finales. The reality of a death by violence, as witnessed by mobile phone cameras, by contrast, is seen as brutal, raw, and almost unbearably true.

"Habeas Corpus"? Bin Laden's Death Unobserved and Undocumented by Civilian Spectators

Saddam Hussein was executed at an appointed time at the close of a formal judicial process—yet his neck was broken with such force from the hanging that it almost severed. Muammar el-Qaddafi died in such a scrum of a manhunt that it remains unclear exactly who—or how many—dealt the final shot or blow. The end of Osama bin Laden's life was also brutal—he too was killed at the end of a long manhunt by opposition forces. Yet there was a key difference between the cases of Hussein and Qaddafi and that of bin Laden: the bodies of Qaddafi and Hussein were available for viewing after their deaths by a range of confirming official and citizen spectators. That was not the case for Osama bin Laden. His corpse was whisked away from all eyes and buried at sea.

The public lack of access to the body of bin Laden led news outlets to search for the kind of photographic "evidence" of his death as they had had with Hussein—and as they were to have six months later with Qaddafi.[20] And as if wishing could make it so, a photo quickly surfaced that purported to show the dead Al Qaeda leader. Just hours after bin Laden was killed, Pakistani television ran a photo of an apparently dead bin Laden, a broadcast that led additional news outlets, including both British and Arab media and news agencies such as AFP, to publish the picture—a gory close-up of a bloodied face of a bearded dead man. The appearance of that image, however, soon prompted a statement by U.S. officials asserting that the picture had been forged. Major news outlets, such as the *Guardian*, National Public Radio (NPR), the *New York Times*, and the *Washington Post*, then reported on the surfacing of the fake photo and its dissemination. On the Lens blog of the *New York Times*, for example, David Dunlap noted that the *Guardian* had been quick to catch the doctored photo, although other UK sites had been taken in.[21] The image in question, of a dark-haired, olive-skinned man who was shot in the face, had actually been circulating online on conspiracy forums since 2009. According to the *Washington Post*, the fake image was a composite of another bloodied corpse and an image of Bin Laden from 1998.[22] Forensic investigation of the lighting of the corpse in the photo also suggested that the picture could not have been one of the actual images taken by the Navy SEALs as evidence of bin Laden's death during the raid.[23]

Accepted at Face Value?
Photos Are Not Evidence

In 1974, Princeton historian Bernard Lewis delivered a series of lectures at Yeshiva University on how historical inquiry not only shapes a nation's understanding of its past but also helps determine—and is determined by—national identity and public policies. In Lewis's three speeches collected into a small volume, he noted, "I have endeavored to define and to illustrate the three different types of historical material offered to readers of history—remembered, recovered, and invented history."

Lewis began chapter 3 of his book with these comments: "'Tell it like it was,' runs a common American phrase, echoing, no doubt unconsciously, Leopold von Ranke's famous injunction to write history 'wie es eigentlich gewesen'— how it really was. But this is neither as simple nor as easy as it sounds. What happened, what we recall, what we recover, what we relate, are often sadly different."[24]

Apply Lewis's observations to contemporary events, and consider journalism, rather than history. How does the world "know" what just happened? How can professional journalists or citizen journalists tell it "how it really was"? From Plato to Rene Descartes, James Frederick Ferrier to Edmund Gettier, Charles Sanders Peirce to Karl Popper, philosophers and epistemologists have wrestled with questions such as whether knowledge is justified true belief.[25] Lewis implicitly engages with this question in *History: Remembered, Recovered, Invented* by unwrapping the "truth" of historical evidence. Too often, he notes, those who write history remember only selected bits of it, recover only certain aspects of the past, invent—or "tailor"—history to advance a certain political, religious, or social agenda.

In *History*, Lewis is in accord with other contemporary epistemologists who challenge the view that "evidence" is sufficient to justify beliefs. While "evidence" contributes to the formation of beliefs, Lewis argues, there is a too-facile use of what appears to be evidence. Too often "evidence" is accepted at face value due to cultural, national, and other implicit or active biases—and what appears to be "evidence" is shaped or even actively manipulated to serve certain ends.

Of all the evidence that can be marshaled by journalists to convince a public that something has happened, photographs and videos are commonly considered to be the most trustworthy due to their "indexical" or referential nature—even today in the era of Photoshop, computer-generated pictures, and digital, on-the-fly manipulation of moving images. A photograph appears to be relatively neutral "evidence" of what it portrays; viewers understand a photographic image to be a mechanical documentation of something that "exists." That referential characteristic was more inherent when photography was film-based—then an actual chemical reaction occurred to produce the image that could not have existed if rays of light did not bounce off of that object in the picture. As Columbia University professor Rosalind Krauss has observed: "Every photograph is the result of a physical imprint transferred by light reflections onto a sensitive surface. The photograph is a type of icon, or visual likeness, which bears an indexical relationship to its object."[26] At present, digital technologies have weakened this assumption of indexicality. But the notion that a photograph truthfully replicates what has existed remains a powerful impression, no matter whether the images are created by a chemical or digital process. As Susan Sontag famously observed: "To remember is, more and more, not to recall a story but to be able to call up a picture."[27]

The act of "seeing" appears to confirm the existence and the reality of what one sees. Heraclitus, a Greek philosopher of the late sixth century BCE, wrote that the mass of men learn best through direct sensory experience: "The things of which there is sight, hearing, experience, I prefer." Yet Heraclitus noted that *seeing through direct personal experience* of a deed is what most human beings need.[28] Plato, too, wrote in the *Republic* (Book 4) of Socrates recalling a story of Leontius, who "observed some dead bodies lying on the ground at the place of execution. He felt a desire to see them, and also a dread and abhorrence of them; for a time he struggled and covered his eyes, but at length the desire got the better of him; and forcing them open, he ran up to the dead bodies, saying, Look, ye wretches, take your fill of the fair sight."[29]

Although Heraclitus and Plato did not have an experience of photography, their writings emphasize the authority of "seeing" in person. Only with the advent of photography could later writers observe that published pictures are only simulacra for direct visual knowledge—by themselves photographs cannot serve as documentary evidence; they can neither confirm, for example, that a death has happened, nor can they entirely explain the circumstances of that death.

Photographs are not substitutes for personal witnessing. Upon bin Laden's death, the media's publication of archival photographs of him while he was alive were, of course, inadequate as "justified" formal evidence that he had been killed, but so too would photos of his corpse have been—unless there had been some kind of supra-chain-of-custody documentation that authenticated the taking, custody, control, transfer and disposition of the presumably digital images.

Yet even without a chain-of-custody certainty, the impact of "seeing" some-thing—even via a second-hand-removed photograph—remains persuasive, despite the recognition that captions can distort, still images can be doctored, and live video can be corrupted on the fly.[30] As author Clive Scott has tried to argue: "many news photos are not significant in themselves but are emblematic, or representative: they have the task of establishing a news item, authenticating it rather than depicting it."[31] And as the raw mobile phone videos of Hussein's execution and Qaddafi's last moments suggest, the emotional and political impact of videos taken by civilians who want to document "how it really was" can hold considerable evidentiary sway for the watching public.

Photographic "Evidence": "The Risks of Release Outweigh the Benefits"

There is a lengthy history of governments, media, and even the public attempt-ing to use photographs to make their messages unassailable, yet politicized agendas can undermine that goal. For example, in the summer of 2003, fol-lowing the U.S. invasion of Iraq, the U.S. government released through the provisional authority in Baghdad photographs taken of the dead faces of Uday and Qusay Hussein, the two sons of Saddam Hussein, killed in a firefight with Americans. The authorities distributed the images via CD-ROM to reporters. The CDs also included X-ray photos of the wounds Uday Hussein suffered in a 1996 assassination attempt, which were said to have helped doctors confirm his identity. The next day, July 25, journalists were allowed to view the bodies, and the following day videos of that viewing, which included full-body shots of the two men, were also distributed.

Secretary of Defense Donald Rumsfeld, who had been very critical of Iraq releasing pictures of dead Americans during the war, defended the U.S. actions of releasing the three sorts of images (still photos, X-rays, and video) of Hus-sein's sons: "This is an unusual situation. This regime has been in power for decades. These two individuals were particularly vicious individuals. . . . They are now dead. . . . The Iraqi people have been waiting for confirmation of that and they in my view deserve having confirmation of that."[32]

Were the photos convincing of the deaths and the identity of Uday and Qu-say? Not uniformly. Americans and Europeans accepted the visual testimony as sufficient evidence. But as the macabre photos aired around the world, debate swirled as to whether the photos constituted proof of the men's deaths. For many Iraqis the confirmation came not with the images from the suspect U.S. authorities, but from a TV clip purporting to be from the associates of Saddam's sons. Al Arabiya television aired a tape of a masked man claiming to be from Fedayeen Saddam, which Uday had run, saying: "We pledge to you Iraqi people that we will continue in the jihad against the infidels. The killing of Uday and Qusay will be avenged."[33]

Eight years later, many Americans believed that the publication of post-mortem photographs of bin Laden would confirm his death to the world. CBS News noted on May 2, 2011, for example, "Skeptics at home and abroad are already asking for proof that bin Laden has indeed been killed. 'There is not a shred of evidence that Bin Laden has been killed and, of course, the media are not requiring any,' one American wrote in an email to CBS News. '. . . Is it un-patriotic or un-American to ask how, specifically, we know that he's dead?'" The CBS story then discussed whether photos of bin Laden's corpse should be released as proof: "Any photos of bin Laden are expected to be gruesome in light of the fact that officials say he was shot in the face during the raid on his compound. Though officials say he is easily identifiable post-mortem, the nature of his death suggests that may not be the case—potentially degrading their value as evidence of his death."[34]

ABC News also weighed in that same day about the evidentiary value of photos of bin Laden's corpse: "The argument for releasing them: to ensure that the public knows and can appreciate that he's dead. There is of course skepticism throughout the world that the US government claim that it killed bin Laden is true. The argument against releasing the pictures: they're gruesome. He has a massive head wound above his left eye where he took bullet [*sic*], with brains and blood visible."[35]

In making the case for the release of photos of bin Laden's corpse, many U.S. news outlets referred back to the Pentagon's essentially "indexical" use of the 2003 morgue photographs of Uday and Qusay.[36] As CBS wrote: "The release [of the photos of Uday and Qusay] appeared to be an attempt to convince skeptical Iraqis that the two men were indeed dead," although as ABC noted in its similar article, "but not until after they'd been touched up by a mortician, making them look not quite real."[37]

As the global public processed the announcement of the Abbottabad strike, reports by news outlets continued to take for granted that photos of the dead bin Laden would be significant evidence of both his death and his identity—but they did debate whether the value of the photographic evidence would be out-weighed by both domestic and international reaction to the graphic images.[38]

The *Huffington Post* reported on May 4, 2011, for example: "Senate Intelligence Chair Dianne Feinstein (D-Calif.) has also said that she sees no need to release photos since other evidence has already proven that bin Laden is dead. 'The DNA has been dispositive,' she said. But Senate Homeland Security Chairman Joe Lieberman (I-Conn.) and the panel's top Republican, Sen. Susan Collins (Maine), said during a Monday press briefing that it 'may be necessary' to release photos to prove to the public once and for all that bin Laden is dead."[39]

Then, later that day, CBS News released part of a transcript from an interview with President Barack Obama to be broadcast four days later on *60 Minutes*. In that excerpt, President Obama announced that his administration would not release the photographs taken of Osama bin Laden after Navy SEALs killed him in his compound in Pakistan:

> "It is important to make sure that very graphic photos of somebody who was shot in the head are not floating around as an incitement to additional violence or as a propaganda tool," said the president. "We don't trot out this stuff as trophies," Mr. Obama added. . . . "We discussed this internally," he said. "Keep in mind that we are absolutely certain that this was him. We've done DNA sampling and testing. And so there is no doubt that we killed Osama bin Laden."[40]

The words of the president appeared to close off the possibility of the release of any postmortem bin Laden photos—a decision upheld the following month by a federal judge responding to a Freedom of Information Act–request lawsuit.[41]

The decision by the president, and later by the court, enjoyed surprisingly bipartisan support among policy makers. According to NPR and other news reports, the government's decision not to release the images of bin Laden's corpse was one of the "few unifying factors" between the Obama administration and congressional Republicans during that period. President Obama and congressional leaders believed that releasing the photos could put American troops in Iraq and Afghanistan at greater physical risk. Republican congressman Mike Rogers, chair of the House Permanent Select Committee on Intelligence, the House's primary panel responsible for authorizing the funding for and overseeing the execution of the intelligence activities of the U.S. government, released a statement against publishing the photos:

> I don't want to make the job of our troops serving in places like Iraq and Afghanistan any harder than it already is. The risks of release outweigh the benefits. Conspiracy theorists around the world will just claim the photos are doctored anyway, and there is a real risk that releasing the photos will only serve to inflame public opinion in the Middle East.[42]

As it turned out—as with the aftermath of the deaths of Uday and Qusay Hussein—the confirming evidence for many doubters about bin Laden's death was not a photo, but a verbal confirmation from someone within the "enemy's" inner circle. A top Al Qaeda ideologue posted a long eulogy for bin Laden on multiple websites just hours after President Obama's speech announcing the Pakistan raid—a eulogy that included a promise to "avenge the killing of the Sheik of Islam." The Taliban also de facto confirmed the killing when it publically threatened reprisal for bin Laden's death.[43]

Framing bin Laden's Death
One, Two, or More Ways

The finiteness of time and space in the news business puts journalists under intense deadline pressures to discover and relate breaking news. As Bernard Lewis believed was true about historians, most journalists neither intentionally fabricate stories nor make up sources. But deadline pressures may mean that there is little time for enterprise reporting—with the result that stories may ignore the views of sources beyond the power elites that have shaped the originating news. Such constraints may, over time, shape how a critical event or person is remembered or shape what kind of policy response is believed to be appropriate.

Photographs chosen in deadline haste, without time for sober second thought, can also shape long-term beliefs and strategic policies. Photographs may not be "justified evidence," instead just convincing testimony that shapes the opinions of a mass of people, from the grass roots up to the level of policy makers. As photo historian David Perlmutter observed in *Visions of War*, "whatever the actual power of pictures, the first-person effect can drive the way we make war if political and military leaders base policy on it. . . . [I]f leaders believe that opinion is driven by images, they will act accordingly to encourage or forestall opinion."[44]

The belief that images matter—perhaps especially in stories of great public interest—complicated the decision-making process of the news media as they considered both how to tell the news of bin Laden's death and how to market the news to their audience. What should they show and say?

Late on the evening of May 1, 2011, and into the morning hours of May 2, news outlets, under significant time pressure, evaluated their options for illustrating the breaking news of bin Laden's death. U.S. newspapers especially ran up against their print press deadlines as they determined how to frame the story.

Individually and in juxtaposition, the different subject matter of different images signaled different meanings. The *Daily Beast*, for example, ran a slide show that led with a photo of the breached "Bin Laden's Compound," in effect framing bin Laden's death as a significant military and intelligence victory—yet a victory tempered by Homeland Security's immediate public warnings of "threats of retaliation" following bin Laden's killing.[45]

Those news outlets that broke the story with a photo of the president delivering his late-night speech in the East Room of the White House emphasized that bin Laden's death held political meaning for the country—perhaps as well as consequences for the political fortunes of President Obama himself. Not surprisingly, the Washington-based website *Politico* featured such images.[46]

A substantial number of news outlets decided to run several images on their front and home pages. Quite a few outlets published a file photo of bin Laden on the same page as a photo of President Obama during his speech to the nation; for example, as the *Detroit News* and the *Desert Sun* did.[47] When paired with a photograph of bin Laden, the image of the president marked the signal importance of the historical moment, simply because it coupled the picture of the world's most wanted terrorist with a photo of the world's most powerful leader.

Other news outlets, such as the *Tampa Bay Times* and the *Bakersfield Californian*, ran archival photos of bin Laden together with pictures of gleeful crowds partying outside the lit-up White House.[48] Such images highlighted American power—although not the formal exercise of power at highest levels of government, as the pictures of President Obama suggested, but the chauvinistic power of Americans as they rejoiced over the death of the iconic enemy and gloated over the prowess of the Navy SEALs who had killed bin Laden.

Still other outlets such as the *Washington Post* published a host of images in an attempt to say it all—a snapshot from the historical record of bin Laden's life, a still from President Obama's speech to the nation, a photo of crowds celebrating outside the White House, and an iconic image of the plane crashing into the World Trade Center towers on 9/11.[49]

"Just" bin Laden Photos: *Memento Mori* with a *Schadenfreude* Punch

For all the various options available to them that night of May 1 into May 2, the news media most commonly illustrated the news of bin Laden's death with close-up photographs of bin Laden alive.[50] Oftentimes the historical image was cropped tighter than it had originally appeared so that the image became almost entirely bin Laden's face. As Professor Karen Engel has argued, portraits of faces hold a fascination for audiences because they present both the "face" or "mask" individuals show the world and the "face" or "window" into their being. When the public is presented with the face of someone who is labeled as an enemy, the audience believes both that the image is "hiding" something and that there is something to be "discovered" in the face.[51]

That duality—the tension between the explicit and the implicit—may have encouraged news outlets the world over to put bin Laden's face on their front and home pages. Publication after publication published a photo of bin Laden sitting alone, staring off into middle distance, his eyes slightly averted. In most of the photos selected he was dressed in a white turban, cap, or covering, wearing a traditional Afghan shalwar kameez, usually white as well.[52]

Many media outlets, including the *Chicago Sun-Times, Chicago Tribune, New York Post*, as well as *Newsday*, and papers as far afield as the *Hartford Courant, Philadelphia Inquirer, Kansas City Star, Los Angeles Times*, and *Honolulu Star-Advertiser*, all chose the same image to accompany their story of bin Laden's death: a file photo dating from 1998. In that picture bin Laden's face appears peaceful, even gentle. Bin Laden is slightly smiling in a Mona Lisa fashion, and his eyes look slightly upward and to the right, as if he were listening and contemplating an answer.

On one hand, that Mona Lisa–esque photo appears an odd choice for a news outlet to make: the April 1998 photo not only had no direct connections to his death, but its origin predated both the August 7, 1998, bombings of the U.S. embassies in Dar es Salaam, Tanzania, and Nairobi, Kenya (the attacks that placed bin Laden on the FBI's Most Wanted list[53]) and the September 2001 attacks on the World Trade Center and the Pentagon.

Yet for all photographs' time-out-of-mind quality, there can be a powerful, even if implicit, relationship between a photograph taken while a subject is alive and the announcement of that subject's death, as Roland Barthes wrote in his seminal 1980 work *Camera Lucida*. Photographic prints preserve a specific moment in time—a time that has already passed, never to be again. As a result every photograph essentially is, as Susan Sontag wrote, a memento mori.[54] In *Camera Lucida*, Barthes reflected on the impact of Alexander Gardner's Civil War photograph of prisoner Lewis Payne, a Lincoln assassination conspirator about to be executed. The historical portrait is most powerful and poignant to those viewers who are aware that, while long dead, the man in the picture is "going to die." While looking at the young man's face in the picture, Barthes notes that viewers comprehend that "this will be and this has been."[55] A photograph of someone who a viewer knows is going to die (because that death has already occurred) provides the frisson it does because the viewer, in effect, is privy to a future (albeit in the past) event: Lewis Payne is alive in the photograph; but he will die, and in fact he is already dead.

The desire to trigger such a sentiment was perhaps also part of the rationale behind the choice of news outlets to use seemingly benign photos of bin Laden. When the stories of bin Laden's death appeared in mainstream online, print, and broadcast media, many in the public already knew about the death via Twitter and other immediate sources (including push notifications from the mainstream outlets). As a result, viewers who saw a photograph of bin Laden alive used as an illustration for the story of his death could experience not only a pleasurable shudder of schadenfreude in learning the details, but perhaps even a sense of personal accomplishment. As they saw the archived photo of an "alive" bin Laden that accompanied the breaking news of his death they automatically mentally amended their understanding of the photograph—just as the viewers of Gardner's Lewis Payne photo did.

In effect, after bin Laden's death, viewers of photographs of bin Laden alive had to adjust the "evidence" of those photos, by essentially "killing" the man they saw in the photographs; that is what the headlines in many of the news outlets that ran this photo "helped" their audiences to do. The headlines to the stories of bin Laden's death often included the word *killed*—ranging from the simple headlines of *Houston Chronicle's* "Bin Laden Killed" and *Los Angeles Times'* "US Kills bin Laden," to the more didactic headline of the *Washington Post*: "U.S. Forces Kill Osama bin Laden; Obama: 'Justice Has Been Done.'"

The "Butcher" Is a "Bastard" Who Will "Rot in Hell"

Some news outlets, especially tabloid papers and the more sensationalizing online sites, ran nonthreatening images of bin Laden but paired those photos with dramatic headlines that went beyond the "news" to define the man and his acts as evil, to cement his position as *the* icon of terror—such as the *New York Post's* "Got Him! Vengeance at Last! US Nails the Bastard"; the *New York Daily News'* "Rot in Hell! Obama: U.S. Team Kills bin Laden in Firefight"; and the *San Francisco Examiner's* "The Butcher of 9/11 is DEAD."[56]

Other news outlets chose to "balance" the news in the opposite way, pairing more ominous images of bin Laden with more neutral headlines and text. Media outlets such as the *Daily Herald* (suburban Chicago) and the *Shreveport Times*, for example, ran archived images of bin Laden that more consciously primed viewers to recall his terrorist acts, but that were simply headlined "Bin Laden Killed" or "Bin Laden Dead."[57] Yet even simply worded headlines held nuanced distinctions: "Bin Laden Killed" was a more "passive" past-tense-voiced explanation of what happened compared to the more active present-tense-voiced "US Kills Bin Laden."

Photos used to prompt viewers to think of terrorism included photo grabs from bin Laden's recruiting videos for Al Qaeda, pictures of bin Laden wearing military garb, and images where an automatic weapon is visible. Then there were other outlets, such as the *Tampa Bay Times*, the *Patriot Ledger*, the *Desert Sun*, and the *Detroit News*, that all ran similar undated photos of bin Laden backed by a black background with Arabic calligraphy on it.[58]

Such images did more than just "identify" the enemy; they put a face to the question "Who is a terrorist?" In effect the photos argued: A terrorist is a man in camouflage jacket and a turban. A terrorist is a man with a gun. A terrorist is an Arab. A terrorist is a man with a beard. According to Engle, audiences participate in a practice she calls "facialization": viewers make "unseen interior truths visible by projecting them on to the surface of the body using the medium of photography."[59] A "terrorist," therefore, should look like a terrorist, and the way to confirm that narrative is to select a photograph that corroborates that appellation.

However, photographs of recognizable people—especially of their faces—are also what make a person identifiably human; therefore, to publish an image of an enemy's face is, in some measure at least, to humanize that person. So it is perhaps not surprising that the weekly magazines such as *Time*, *Newsweek*, the *New Yorker*, and the *Economist*, all of which emphasize news analysis, represented bin Laden by "defacing" him. *Time* magazine's cover commemorating his death, for example, published his image with a bloody red X over it—the exact same X (even to the "drips" of blood) as the magazine had superimposed over the cover of Saddam Hussein's face after his execution, and the cover of Adolf Hitler after his suicide.[60] Similarly, *Newsweek* ran a red and black drawing of Osama bin Laden's face on its cover, with a paint roller stripe of white paint over his eyes.[61] The *New Yorker* also ran a drawing of bin Laden on its cover, with his entire face erased.[62] And the *Economist* ran a cover using the iconic Mona Lisa–like smiling bin Laden photograph, but the photograph was actually a photomosaic of terrorism events since 9/11.[63]

Lessons from the Framing of bin Laden

Ever since the invention of photography in the nineteenth century, publishers have used images to "confirm" the deaths of heads of state and other authority figures.[64] Yet media's coverage of bin Laden's death suggests that photographs used to illustrate the breaking news of the death of an enemy—even those that do not show corpses but instead are archival images of the enemy alive—do more than just corroborate death. Photographs are a key means by which media, and through them the public, come to terms with that death.

Images of an innocent in extremis—women, children, those wounded or killed in natural disasters, for example—usually stir sympathy in the eyes of the beholders. This study documents that showing the face of one we define as "the enemy" can be used to provoke the opposite effect, that is, to deny the enemy's humanity—and that the tabloid press especially may try to further destroy any potential sympathy for a dead enemy by using forceful, shocking, and horrible words (instead of forceful, shocking, and horrible images) to confirm and frame an enemy's death.

At the time of bin Laden's death, his public face was one of the most recognizable in the world. His killing in a U.S. secret raid and the immediate burial at sea of his body meant that there were no accessible photos of his corpse—as there had been of Saddam Hussein and as there would be some months later of Muammar el-Qaddafi. But it was only then, after that Navy SEAL raid, that finally the media could "frame" bin Laden without the fear that bin Laden himself would trump their framing of him by masterminding another terrorist attack.

Photos frame our world. What "frame" they put around an event or issue or person matters. How a frame is selected is not happenstance. As this research argues, in cases of breaking news of a dead enemy, the photos that bracket that death are in part a consequence of the circumstances of those specific deaths and in part a consequence of what media believe audiences will find compelling and convincing given the adversarial background of that actor.

The histories of Bin Laden, Qaddafi, and Hussein, including their relations with the "West," shaped the coverage of their deaths as enemies of the "West." The literal circumstances of the three men's capture and death also shaped and constrained the visual telling of those deaths.

Saddam Hussein's story as a man who had once shaken hands with Western officials, as a head of state who was tried in court following his capture, and as a prisoner who died in a rule-of-law sanctioned execution, shaped the official images of the moments leading up to his hanging. Hussein no longer posed a direct threat to those who had captured him; as a result the approved images of his death were moderated at least to a certain degree by standards of justice.

Yet surreptitious video of Hussein's execution emerged, far more graphic and intrusive than the official visual documents. That video, and the screen grabs from it, were not subject to the same vetting as officially sanctioned photos of dead enemies of the past—including those of Hussein's sons, Uday and Qusay. The amateur video emerged via social media, and from there it moved to mainstream outlets. Yet it was that footage that ultimately appeared to be the most accurate in its depiction of Hussein's death. The grainy, handheld production values signaled that the video had been taken by an eyewitness to (and likely participant in) Hussein's death. It further signaled that the taking of the video had not been sanctioned by a state authority or the staff of a particular media outlet—so it appeared relatively "spin-free," not twisted by a national political agenda as images taken by authorized members of those institutions were certain to be.

Then there was the death of Muammar el-Qaddafi. He died as he lived, large, dramatically, disturbingly. President Ronald Reagan's famous words describing him as the "mad dog of the Middle East" were repeated and underlined further in the days following Qaddafi's death; as NPR said in one of its stories: "America's long, complicated history with Libyan leader Moammar Gadhafi goes back three decades. During Ronald Reagan's presidency, Gadhafi was public enemy No. 1—just as President John Kennedy's nemesis had been Cuba's Fidel Castro. 'I find he's not only a barbarian but he's flaky,' Reagan said of Gadhafi."[65] In the years leading up to Qaddafi's death, in the moments surrounding his death, and even postmortem, he appeared in photos as an unstable, arrogant and flamboyant dictator, a dangerous man in large measure because of his delusions of grandeur. The images that surfaced of the minutes surrounding his death were entirely unscripted—taken by amateur photographers who themselves were participating in a treacherous melee where the primary agenda was not to shape Qaddafi's image, but to taunt, humiliate and kill him. Those bloody and disquietingly gleeful images of the torment of a tormentor appeared on front pages and home pages of news outlets around the world. But even months and years later it is difficult to consider mainstream media showcasing, in a manner almost tantamount to endorsement, such images of any other state leader—even an enemy.

Most distinctively there was the death of Osama bin Laden. Of all three leaders, he was the ghost, a man responsible for horrific actions, yet his years in hiding meant that most existing photographs of him had been taken at a time and a place of his own choosing—such as his occasional self-made and globally disseminated videos threatening the "West." As a result, fewer images of Bin Laden exist than of Qaddafi or Hussein; unlike the other two men, bin Laden was not a state leader; there are no "state" photos of him. Bin Laden gave few media interviews over his years as a public figure; there are few pictures of him in front of "Western" cameras. Bin Laden communicated to the world through terrorism. The world was scared of bin Laden, but as he controlled his public face, most existing images of him show him as a calm man smiling or preaching to his followers. It was those images that were framed—and defaced—in the minutes and hours and days surrounding Osama's death. Those images were intended to confirm the killing of a mastermind of terror—but intentionally or otherwise helped media audiences gloat over bin Laden's demise and celebrate the concomitant ascendance of "Western" power and authority.

Notes

The three authors of this study evaluated news sites from the day of the three respective deaths, using a broad range of online Internet archives (including such resources as Pinterest and the Internet Archive Wayback Machine, https://archive.org/web/). The authors also analyzed the front pages of all major U.S. and international newspapers archived on the Newseum's newspaper front-page archive on the day following the respective deaths, or in case the headline didn't come in time for that paper, the next day's front pages as well, in order to compare and contrast the papers' presentation of the three respective deaths. Finally, archives of major papers and outlets were searched via Lexis-Nexis and the online search engines of those news outlets for a week following the deaths of the three leaders. The cases of Saddam Hussein and Muammar el-Qaddafi were used as a context and comparison for the main object of study, the choices media outlets had to make in publishing images that would announce the news of Osama bin Laden's death. The authors put together three Pinterest boards for each of the dead men, which can be consulted at the following URLs as a complement to reading this study:

Saddam Hussein: http://pinterest.com/sdmoeller/saddam-hussein/
Osama bin Laden: http://pinterest.com/sdmoeller/osama-bin-laden/
Muammar el-Qaddafi: http://pinterest.com/sdmoeller/muammar-el-qaddafi/

1. Barack Obama, "President Obama on Death of Osama bin Laden," White House video, May 1, 2011, http://www.whitehouse.gov/photos-and-video/video/2011/05/01/president-obama-death-osama-bin-laden#transcript. For details of the Navy SEALs' raid itself, see Mark Owen with Kevin Maurer, *No Easy Day: The Firsthand Account of the Mission That Killed Osama bin Laden* (New York: Dutton, 2012).

2. Bin Laden was killed shortly after 1:00 a.m. local time on May 2, 2011, in Pakistan, which, given the time difference, allowed many U.S. and Western European newspapers just enough time to remake their May 2 front pages. President Obama announced the news in a televised address on May 1, at 11:35 p.m. East Coast time; social media broke the story more than an hour before: see Alexia Tsotsis, "First Credible Reports of bin Laden's Death Spread like Wildfire on Twitter," techcrunch.com, May 1, 2011, http://techcrunch.com/2011/05/01/news-of-osama-bin-ladens-death-spreads-like-wildfire-on-twitter/.

3. In its consideration of framing, this chapter has been informed by the founding work of Ervin Goffman, Robert Entman, and sociologists William A. Gamson and Andre Modigliani in their 1989 article "Media Discourse and Public Opinion on Nuclear Power:

A Constructionist Approach," *American Journal of Sociology* 95, no. 1 (1989): 1–37. A more recent article of note also informed this work: in 2011 Iowa University media scholars Lulu Rodriguez and Daniela V. Dimitrova emphasized the power of visual framing, a type of framing often overlooked because it may appear to be unintentional. Lulu Rodriguez and Daniela V. Dimitrova, "The Levels of Visual Framing," *Journal of Visual Literacy* 30, no. 1 (2011): 48–65.

4. Amit R. Paley, "As Genocide Trial Begins, Hussein Is Again Defiant," *Washington Post*, August 22, 2006, http://www.washingtonpost.com/wp-dyn/content/article/2006/08/21/AR2006082100058.html.

5. Kirk Semple, "Saddam Hussein Is Sentenced to Death," *New York Times*, November 5, 2006, http://www.nytimes.com/2006/11/05/world/middleeast/05cnd-saddam.html?pagewanted=all.

6. As journalist Vivian Salama noted, however, "Curiously, it was not Al Iraqiya who broke the news of the execution on the Arab end, but rather two networks—Alhurra and Al Arabiya—who were reportedly the first to officially confirm that Hussein was, in fact, dead. This raises questions as to who was calling the shots that early morning in Baghdad since Alhurra is a US government-funded, Arabic-language network, and Al Arabiya is owned by America's top Gulf ally—Saudi Arabia." See Vivian Salama, "Death by Video Phone: Coverage of Saddam Hussein's Execution, *Arab Media and Society* 1 (Spring 2007), http://www.arabmediasociety.com/?article=84.

7. Bill Carter, "How Much Should Be Shown of a Hanging? Network Executives Wonder and Wait," December 30, 2006, http://www.nytimes.com/2006/12/30/business/media/30netw.html?_r=1; and Mark Santora, "On the Gallows, Curses for U.S. and 'Traitors,'" *New York Times*, December 31, 2006, http://www.nytimes.com/2006/12/31/world/middleeast/31gallows.html.

8. Other journalists, too, repeatedly noted Hussein's control of his image. For example, Saddam did not allow himself to be filmed walking more than a few steps, since he had a slight limp, and as reporter Neil MacFarquhar observed in Hussein's *New York Times* obituary, "While Mr. Hussein was in power, his statue guarded the entrance to every village, his portrait watched over each government office and he peered down from at least one wall in every home. His picture was so widespread that a joke quietly circulating among his detractors in 1988 put the country's population at 34 million—17 million people and 17 million portraits of Saddam." Neil MacFarquhar, "Saddam Hussein, Defiant Dictator Who Ruled Iraq with Violence and Fear, Dies," *New York Times*, December 30, 2006, http://www.nytimes.com/2006/12/30/world/middleeast/30saddam.html?pagewanted=1&_r=1.

9. Salama, "Death by Video Phone."

10. Live Leak, "Full Saddam Execution Video Leaked from Cellphone," December 30, 2006, http://www.liveleak.com/view?i=863ce7d4a3.

11. Tom Zeller Jr., "Execution Samizdat Investigated in Iraq," *New York Times*, January 2, 2007, http://thelede.blogs.nytimes.com/2007/01/02/execution-samizdat-investigated-in-iraq/. An even more graphic second cell phone video leaked shortly thereafter, as Salama notes: "Two mobile phone videos surfaced within 48 hours of Saddam Hussein's execution. The first is approximately two and a half minutes long. It appears to

have been recorded from inside the chambers where Hussein was hung. [...] The second video to surface, a 27-second clip, was posted on an Iraq-based website believed to support the late-dictator's Ba'ath Party. Apparently taken shortly after Hussein's death, this video shows a hand pulling down the white shroud to expose a close up of the former-President's face, his neck twisted at a 90 degree angle to the right, with a gaping, bloody neck wound."

12. Salama, "Death by Video Phone."

13. Ibid.

14. Neil MacFarquhar, "An Erratic Leader, Brutal and Defiant to the End," *New York Times*, October 20, 2011, http://www.nytimes.com/2011/10/21/world/africa/qaddafi-killed-as-hometown-falls-to-libyan-rebels.html?_r=1&ref=africa.

As of the writing of this chapter there remains disagreement as to whether the actual moment of Qaddafi's death was captured on camera—or at least whether it has been shown to the public. The *Guardian*, for example, noted that in addition to a three-minute clip that describes the moments after Qaddafi's capture "in the most detail," there were many other videos: "There are other clips that complete much of the story: Gaddafi slumped on a pickup truck, face smeared with blood, apparently unconscious; Gaddafi shirtless and bloody on the ground surrounded by a mob; Gaddafi dead in the back of an ambulance. What is not there is the moment of his death—and how it happened—amid claims that he was killed by fighters with a shot to the head or stomach." Peter Beaumont and Chris Stephen, "Gaddafi's Last Words as He Begged for Mercy: 'What Did I Do to You?,'" October 23, 2011, http://www.guardian.co.uk/world/2011/oct/23/gaddafi-last-words-begged-mercy. The *Guardian's* summary is in line with what the *Daily Mail* noted in an October 21, 2011, story copiously illustrated with videos and screen captures from videos: "A clutch of videos have emerged on the internet in which he is seen begging his captors for mercy. His condition varies dramatically, with later footage showing him rambling and drenched in blood." David Williams, "Who Shot Gaddafi? New Video Shows Blood Pouring from Dictator Immediately before Death but Mystery Surrounds Coup de Grace," October 21, 2011, http://www.dailymail.co.uk/news/article-2051361/GADDAFI-DEAD-VIDEO-Dictator-begs-life-summary-execution.html.

However, in the lead to an article on October 22, the *Daily Mail* asserts that the "moment of death" video may have been found: "The last few moments of Gaddafi's life became clearer today as pictures surfaced of the moment a handgun was pushed to his temple. Seconds later the spluttering dictator can no longer be heard. The next scenes show the tyrant's lifeless body on the ground. His eyes are closed and he's not breathing. Amid reports tonight that the National Transitional Council will hand over the dead dictator's corpse to members of his extended family, the dramatic footage may clear up some of the mystery surrounding Gaddafi's death as his widow calls for an inquiry into how her husband died." That article also included the video as well as multiple screen captures from that video. "Gunshots, Then Silence: Is This the Moment Gaddafi Was Killed by a Bullet in the Head?," *Daily Mail*, October 22, 2011, http://www.dailymail.co.uk/news/article-2052178/GADDAFI-DEATH-VIDEO-Moment-Libyan-dictator-killed-bullet-head.html.

15. Kareem Fahim, Anthony Shadid, and Rick Gladstone, "Violent End to an Era as Qaddafi Dies in Libya," *New York Times*, October 20, 2011, http://www.nytimes.com/2011/10/21/world/africa/qaddafi-is-killed-as-libyan-forces-take-surt.html?pagewanted=all.

16. "AFP in Scoop with Bloodied Khadafi Image," Agence France-Presse, October 21, 2011, http://newsinfo.inquirer.net/80109/afp-in-scoop-with-bloodied-kadhafi-image.

17. The Newseum has collected the front pages of newspapers from Qaddafi's death, which are available for viewing at http://www.newseum.org/todaysfrontpages/default_archive.asp?fpArchive=102111.A HuffingtonPost.com article featured dozens of those: "Muammar Gaddafi Dead: Did Newspapers Go Too Far? (GRAPHIC PHOTOS, POLL)," October 21, 2011 updated December 21, 2011, http://www.huffingtonpost.com/2011/10/21/muammar-gaddafi-dead-newspapers_n_1023665.html#s424620.

18. See Hans Blumenberg, *Shipwreck with Spectator: Paradigm of a Metaphor for Existence* (Cambridge, MA: MIT Press, 1997).

19. Fahim, Shadid, and Gladstone, "Violent End to an Era."

20. As Scott noted: "many news photos are not significant in themselves but are emblematic, or representative: they have the task of establishing a news item, authenticating it rather than depicting it." See Clive Scott, *The Spoken Image: Photography and Language* (London: Reaktion, 1999).

21. Amelia Hill, "Osama bin Laden Corpse Photo Is Fake," *Guardian, May 2, 2011*, http://www.guardian.co.uk/world/2011/may/02/osama-bin-laden-photo-fake; David W. Dunlop, "Wanted—Dead, Alive, or Photoshopped," May 4, 2011, http://lens.blogs.nytimes.com/2011/05/04/wanted-dead-alive-or-photoshopped-2/.

22. Elizabeth Flock, "Osama bin Laden DNA Confirms Death, but Photos Are Fake, *Washington Post*, May 2, 2011, http://www.washingtonpost.com/blogs/blogpost/post/osama-bin-laden-dna-confirms-death-but-photos-are-fake-should-white-house-release-actual-photos/2011/05/02/AFez6naF_blog.html.

23. On May 4, 2011, Reuters released four graphic, bloody pictures showing the faces (at least one with a bullet hole in the face) and the bodies of three unidentified men strewn inside what was claimed to be Osama bin Laden's Abbottabad compound, taken by a Pakistani security officer an hour after the raid. In an explanation released with the pictures, Reuters said it was confident the images were authentic, because it conducted some lighting analysis, and some of the details of the photographs match up with known details of the compound. Reuters, "Photos from the bin Laden Compound," http://www.reuters.com/subjects/bin-laden-compound.

24. Bernard Lewis, *History: Remembered, Recovered, Invented* (New York: Simon and Schuster, 1975), 71.

25. Edmund L. Gettier, "Is Justified True Belief Knowledge?," *Analysis* 23 (1963); 121–23, http://www.ditext.com/gettier/gettier.html.

26. Rosalind Krauss, "Notes on the Index: Seventies Arts in America," *October* 3 (Spring 1977): 68–81.

27. Susan Sontag, *Regarding the Pain of Others* (New York: Farrar, Straus and Giroux, 2003).

28. "Of this Word's being forever do men prove to be uncomprehending, both before they hear and once they have heard it. For although all things happen according to this Word they are like the inexperienced experiencing words and deeds such as I explain when I distinguish each thing according to its nature and declare how it is." DK22b55 and DK22b1. Hermann Diels and Walther Kranz, *Die Fragmente der Vorsokratiker* (Zurich: Weidmann, 1985).

29. Plato, *The Republic*, ed. James Adam, 2nd ed., with intro by D. A. Rees (Cambridge: Cambridge University Press, 1963).

30. Michael Griffin notes that pictures rarely "stand on their own." Herta Wolf also contends that photographs require some sort of narrative contextualization. According to Griffin, this interdependence between images and the words that accompany them is inevitable: "philosophical and theoretical concerns with the subject/spectator [. . .] or with the interpreter/reader [. . .] necessarily imply the analysis of visual signifying systems as codes nested within other sociocultural codes and contexts." See Michael Griffin, "Sociocultural Perspectives on Visual Communication," *Journal of Visual Literacy* 22, no. 1 (2002): 29–52; and Herta Wolf, "The Tears of Photography," *Grey Room* 29 (2007), 66–89.

31. Scott, *Spoken Image*.

32. Donald Rumsfeld, "DoD News Briefing—Secretary Rumsfeld and Ambassador Bremer," July 24, 2003, http://www.defense.gov/transcripts/transcript.aspx?transcriptid=2894.

33. Agencies, "US Releases Photos of Saddam Sons," *Guardian, July 24, 2003*, http://www.theguardian.com/world/2003/jul/24/iraq.usa2; and see Susan Moeller, *Packaging Terrorism: Co-opting the News for Politics and Profit* (Malden, MA: Wiley-Blackwell, 2009), 167–68.

34. Brian Montopoli, "Will U.S. Release Gruesome bin Laden Photos?," CBS News, May 2, 2011, http://www.cbsnews.com/8301-503544_162-20058972-503544.html.

35. Sara Just, "White House Officials Debate Releasing Photographs of bin Laden's Corpse," ABC News, May 2, 2011, http://abcnews.go.com/blogs/politics/2011/05/white-house-officials-debate-releasing-photographs-of-bin-ladens-corpse-1/.

36. See, for example, Moeller, *Packaging Terrorism*, 167–68.

37. Montopoli, "Will U.S. Release"; Just, "White House Officials Debate." See also Wolf, "Tears of Photography," 73: "the patched corpses of the sons of Saddam Hussein [. . .] were presented to press photographers, ensuring the widest possible diffusion of images that were meant—as stated in the captions [. . .]—to confirm the 'contested' death of Hussein's 'cruel' offspring once and for all."

38. There is a long history of public executions, which used to draw thousands of onlookers and provided them an odd sense of vindication and satisfaction, as well as serving to warn them of their fate were they to break the law. Today the equivalent schadenfreude comes from surfing to shock sites that traffic in explicit scenes from war, accidents, and executions. Yet seeing gory corpses of our enemies neither makes us more informed or more clear-sighted about the path ahead—in fact it may do the opposite. According to Andrew Silke, "gruesome pictures lead to increasing emotional arousal in viewers, with

the emotions experienced including anger, fear, anxiety and disgust. As the emotional intensity rises it is accompanied by a decline in frontal lobe cognitive functioning. Cooler, objective consideration of the evidence and issues is undermined." Andrew Silke, "Obama Is Right to Withhold Photos of Bin Laden's Corpse," *New Scientist*, May 6, 2011, http://www.newscientist.com/article/dn20454-obama-is-right-to-withhold-photos-of-bin-ladens-corpse.html?full=true#.U8jckRZqraQ.

That is perhaps why, according to Silke, President Obama prohibited the release of photos of Osama bin Laden's body: "Releasing images of bin Laden's corpse will provoke this effect across the world, many parts of which are already unsympathetic—if not downright hostile—to the US. Among people who identify with Al-Qaida, the images can be expected to increase sympathy and support for militant groups, especially ones that claim to be the defenders of cultural identity. Linked to this will be increased hostility towards the enemies of that identity—the US and its allies, in other words—and an increased willingness to engage in violence. In short, the risks in many parts of the world would go up."

39. Jennifer Bendery, "Osama Bin Laden Pictures Will Not Be Released, Obama Decides," *Huffington Post*, May 4, 2011, http://www.huffingtonpost.com/2011/05/04/osama-bin-laden-pictures_n_857568.html.

40. Brian Montopoli, "Obama: I Won't Release bin Laden Death Photos," CBS News, May 4, 2011, http://www.cbsnews.com/news/obama-i-wont-release-bin-laden-death-photos/.

41. Associated Press, "Judge Denies Freedom of Information Request to Release bin Laden Photos," FOX News, April 26, 2012, http://www.foxnews.com/world/2012/04/26/judge-denies-freedom-information-request-to-release-bin-laden-photos/.

42. "Chairman Rogers Opposes Public Release of Osama Bin Laden Photos," press release, House Permanent Select Committee on Intelligence, May 4, 2011, http://intelligence.house.gov/press-release/chairman-rogers-opposes-public-release-osama-bin-laden-photos, http://intelligence.house.gov/sites/intelligence.house.gov/files/documents/050411RogersOpposesReleaseofBinLadenPhotos.pdf.

43. "Osama bin Laden Killed in Pakistan," Al Jazeera, May 2, 2011, http://www.aljazeera.com/news/americas/2011/05/2011522132275789.html.

44. David D. Perlmutter, *Visions of War: Picturing Warfare from the Stone Age to the Cyber Age* (New York: St. Martin's Press, 1999).

45. "Photos: Bin Laden's Compound," *Daily Beast*, May 2, 2011, Pinterest, http://pinterest.com/pin/143270831866366481/.

46. Ben Smith and Glenn Thrush, "Bin Laden's Death Brings Celebration, Unity—and Questions," *Politico*, May 2, 2011, http://www.politico.com/news/stories/0511/54073.html.

47. "U.S. Kills bin Laden," *Detroit News*, May 2, 2011, Newseum, http://www.newseum.org/todaysfrontpages/hr_archive.asp?fpVname=MI_DN&ref_pge=gal&b_pge=1; "Bin Laden Dead," *Desert Sun*, May 2, 2011, Newseum, http://www.newseum.org/todaysfrontpages/hr_archive.asp?fpVname=CA_DS&ref_pge=gal&b_pge=1.

48. "Got Him (Shot Him) *Tampa Bay Times*, May 2, 2011, Newseum, http://www.newseum.org/todaysfrontpages/hr_archive.asp?fpVname=FL_TBT&ref_pge=gal&b_pge=1; "Justice Served," *Bakersfield Californian*, May 2, 2011, Newseum, http://www.newseum.org/todaysfrontpages/hr_archive.asp?fpVname=CA_BC&ref_pge=gal&b_pge=1.

49. See Bradley Graham, "U.S. Forces Kill Osama bin Laden; Obama: 'Justice Has Been Done,'" *Washington Post*, May 2, 2011, http://bit.ly/oblbook1. The next day media ran tense pictures of President Obama and his senior staff in the White House Situation Room watching the Navy SEALs' raid unfold in real time (released the next day). See the White House's photostream, Flickr,

http://www.flickr.com/photos/whitehouse/5680724572/in/photostream.

50. To see global newspaper front covers announcing bin Laden's death, see the Newseum's archived pages: http://www.newseum.org/todaysfrontpages/default_archive .asp?tfp_show_sort=yes.

51. As Karen Engle noted, "identification [...] can only take place via representation, and the capacity to represent its others is fundamental to State operations." Engle described a process he calls "facialization," "the process of making unseen interior truths visible by projecting them on to the surface of the body using the medium of photography." The very fact that an audience can see and study an enemy's face makes the enemy less frightening; nothing is more fearsome than a faceless enemy. Engle also noted, however, that a face is what makes a person human, what most distinguishes a person from all other human beings—that is why, she observed, that images of an enemy are often defaced. Karen Engle, "The Face of a Terrorist," *Cultural Studies and Critical Methodologies* 7, no. 4 (2007): 397–424.

52. Osama bin Laden, April 1998, Afghanistan, Associated Press photograph, http://bit.ly/oblbook2.

53. FBI, undated, "Wanted: Usama bin Laden", http://www.fbi.gov/wanted/wanted _terrorists/usama-bin-laden.

54. Susan Sontag also notes the odd proximity of photography and death: "Ever since cameras were invented in 1839, photography has kept company with death." Sontag, *Regarding the Pain of Others*.

55. Roland Barthes, *Camera Lucida: Reflections on Photography* (New York: Hill and Wang, 1981), 96.

56. Communication professor Michael Griffin, for example, conducted a study of *Newsweek* images of the War on Terror in 2003. According to his research, Osama bin Laden and Saddam Hussein were among the third most represented visuals in the War on Terror theme, with Osama bin Laden also occupying eighth place by himself. Griffin also noted that *Newsweek* featured Osama bin Laden's face on its cover three times between the dates of September 2001 and January 2002. Griffin concluded that Osama bin Laden was considered the "icon" of terror, "identified in headlines and captions as 'the evil one.'" Michael Griffin, "Picturing America's "War on Terrorism" in Afghanistan and Iraq, *Journalism* 5, no. 4 (2004): 381–402. A fruitful—and related—topic for study would be research that investigated how media reference enemy leaders by name. Do they use the same standards as allies, for example: the full first and last name, possibly with the title (e.g., Colonel Muammar Qaddafi)? Do they use just a first name, which bequeaths a "notorious" and also "familiar" aspect to the character (e.g., Saddam) or just a last name (e.g., bin Laden)? Or do they use some other sobriquet to stand in for

the name (e.g., the bastard). As Scott shows, these choices are not arbitrary, and each carries a significant weight in terms of how the accompanying image will be interpreted. For instance, showing a photo of a notorious murderer with the headline only naming him by his last name, Scott implies, "is not only a way of disowning him, of closing him off from sympathy, but also a convention of the thriller and detective fiction: the world of brutal acts, sadism and cynicism is a male world and maleness expresses itself in the guarded, unyielding aura of the surname." Similarly, as Scott notes, the use of pronouns as well as the voice and tense of headlines and captions, all have significance. Are editors writing "We got him!" or "US Forces Kill . . ." or "Bin Laden Is Dead"? Scott discusses these nuances in much detail. Scott, *Spoken Image.*

57. Osama bin Laden, undated file photo, Associated Press, http://bit.ly/oblbook3; "Bin Laden Killed: 'Justice Has Been Done'," Pinterest, http://pinterest.com/pin/143270831866366914/.

58. Interestingly, the *Detroit News* ("U.S. Kills bin Laden") identified the photo as dating from 1998, and the *Desert Sun* ("Bin Laden Dead") identified an almost identical image (same background, same clothes) as from 2001.

59. Engle, "Face of a Terrorist."

60. Cover art, *Time*, May 20, 2011, Pinterest, http://pinterest.com/pin/143270831866198296/; cover art, *Time*, April 21, 2003, Pinterest, http://pinterest.com/pin/143270831866198346/; Ray Gustini, "A Brief History of Time Magazine's 'X' Covers," *Atlantic Wire*, May 2, 2011, http://www.theatlanticwire.com/entertainment/2011/05/brief-history-time-magazine-red-x-covers/37269/.

61. "Mission Accomplished: But Are We Any Safer?," *Newsweek*, May 10, 2011, Pinterest, http://pinterest.com/pin/143270831866198301/.

62. Cover art, *New Yorker*, May 16, 2011, Pinterest, http://pinterest.com/pin/34058540902426615/.

63. "Now, Kill His Dream," *Economist*, May 7–13, 2011, Pinterest, http://pinterest.com/pin/143270831866198306/.

64. Consider, for example, Francois Aubert's 1867 photograph of Emperor Maximillian's shirt following his execution: World History of Art, http://www.all-art.org/history658_photography13-7.html.

65. Tom Bowman, "For Reagan, Gadhafi Was a Frustrating 'Mad Dog,'" NPR, March 4, 2011, http://www.npr.org/2011/03/04/134228864/for-reagan-gadhafi-was-a-frustrating-mad-dog.

PART III

Engaging Popular Cultures

Without Osama

Tere Bin Laden *and the Critique of the War on Terror*

PURNIMA BOSE

Released in July 2010, *Tere Bin Laden* is a madcap comedy about an ambitious Pakistani journalist, Ali Hassan, who stages a fake video of Osama bin Laden as his golden ticket to immigrate to the United States; the film provides a trenchant critique of global media, the War on Terror, and the capitalist aspirations of lower-middle and middle-class Pakistanis.[1] An Indian independent film in Hindi, written and directed by Abhishek Sharma, it became an instant box office success in the key "metro cities" of Delhi, Mumbai, Chennai, Kolkata, and Bangalore and was thereafter distributed in international markets such as the UK, Middle East, Australia, South Africa, and Mauritius.[2] Adding to the repertoire of popular culture representations of Osama bin Laden, *Tere Bin Laden* contributes a progressive critique of the War on Terror from South Asia, a part of the world often viewed as at risk for generating political violence and terrorism. The film explores the unholy trinity among the transnational bourgeoisie, media, and governments (U.S. and Pakistan) that conspire to produce different versions of Osama bin Laden for their separate purposes. The astuteness of the film's analysis of the War on Terror and global media resides in its insertion of representatives from different segments of Pakistani civil society into a transnational economy of representation and images associated with bin Laden, in which these classes simultaneously critique U.S. foreign policy and become complicit with it. In its ability to manipulate global media and affect geopolitical outcomes, Pakistani civil society emerges in the film as a full media subject in both senses of the term—the subject of media and subjects' making media.

Tere Bin Laden literally means "Your bin Laden," but also yields the pun "Without you, Laden" (Tere *bina* Laden), and the joke of the film centers on the absence of Osama bin Laden himself. The title's double meaning implies that regardless of the actual bin Laden, he becomes whatever "you" (the transnational bourgeoisie, media, and governments) make him. In the mediated landscape of the twenty-first century, Osama bin Laden exists as a handy empty signifier that multiple agents can manipulate for different kinds of economic, professional, and geographic mobility.

In this chapter, I primarily focus on how *Tere Bin Laden* articulates a critique of the War on Terror. I first consider how the opening segments of the film set up its dual concerns with the nature of the U.S. national security state as a racial formation and with an idealized version of the American dream that constitutes the desire for upward mobility in the imagination of elite Pakistanis such as Ali. I then turn to the film's representation of the War on Terror and U.S. foreign policy to analyze how it draws on the speeches of the actual Osama bin Laden and spoofs the U.S. military campaign in Afghanistan by literally rendering it into a cartoon. Evaluating the filmmaker's and lead actor's claims that the film provides a generalized South Asian perspective on the War on Terror, I explore *Tere Bin Laden's* representation of Pakistani civil society as constituted by a range of classes and aspirations that can be persuaded to cooperate with one another only in limited ways and as existing in an uneasy equilibrium with the state.

Throughout this chapter, my methodology derives from that materialist strain of postcolonial studies that understands cultural artifacts to be connected in some way to historical events and geopolitical relationships. Rather than gauge representation in terms of its aesthetic codes and internal logic alone, I situate readings of scenes in their larger referential contexts under the assumption that *Tere Bin Laden* has an analysis to make of actual political realities. This reading of the film is in line with the director's intent: while acknowledging the satirical elements of his film, Sharma also argues for its mimetic accuracy in its representation of a conspiracy about fake bin Laden tapes, which is a strong cultural current in many parts of the world. As part of his research for the film, he watched both real and fake Osama bin Laden footage.[3] If anything, the distinction between "the real" and representation itself concerning the War on Terror was initially blurred by Bush administration officials who falsely claimed that Saddam Hussein had an operational relationship with Al Qaeda and was conspiring to launch terrorist attacks against the United States, and who also exaggerated evidence about the existence of weapons of mass destruction (WMD) as a pretext for going to war against Iraq.[4] Consistent with the permeable border between "the real" and the "representational," historically speaking, my analysis uses close readings of the film to shuttle between the real Osama bin Laden's explanations for geopolitical violence and justifications for terrorism, and the consequences for Afghans of the War on Terror.

"Amreeka": The National Security State and the American Dream

Before an analysis of the opening scene, it may be helpful to briefly summarize the plot of *Tere Bin Laden*. Mistaken for a terrorist on a flight to the United States, Ali has been permanently denied a visa to emigrate to "Amreeka," his destination of choice. In order to acquire a forged passport, he must give a large advance to a shadowy organization, Lashkar-E-Amreeka (a parody of Lashkar-e-Taiba).[5] Unable to afford the advance, he hits on the idea of fooling Noora—a poultry-farmer, simpleton, and Osama bin Laden look-alike—into appearing in footage of the Al Qaeda leader, which he plans to sell for a lucrative amount. First aired on *Live India* and then *News America*, the fake footage acquires a life of its own, gaining global distribution and precipitating political alarm in the United States and financial markets worldwide. In response, the U.S. government initiates a massive bombing campaign of Afghanistan. Stricken by the unleashing of American power on Afghanistan as a consequence of his video, Ali convinces Noora to make a follow-up tape addressed to President Bush in which Osama bin Laden suggests a ceasefire between the two sides. Comedic plot twists conspire to make U.S. and Pakistani intelligence officers and government officials complicit in the production of Ali's Osama video sequel.

Tere Bin Laden's opening scene sequence establishes its twin concerns with the United States as a national security state and the superficiality of segments of the Pakistani bourgeoisie, emphasizing the role played by global media in promoting the government's security agenda and creating an idealized version of the United States among elite Pakistanis' imaginations. The film opens several days after September 11, 2001, in the Karachi airport, where Ali, an intrepid reporter for a down-market local television channel, frantically waits to use the WC in time to make his flight to New York. A fellow traveler, who is wrestling to undo the knot on his kurta pajama, responds to Ali's urgings to hurry by remarking that Ali must be going to New York to become a taxi driver, thereby suggesting that the United States offers limited economic opportunities for South Asian immigrants.

Immediately following this scene, the camera presents a medium close-up shot of Ali on board the flight as he rehearses for an audition as a newscaster; he reads aloud sample headlines, practicing different inflections of an Americanized accent: "America Becomes Suspicious of Muslims," "Bush Ready to Bomb Osama," and "Al Qaeda behind Plane Hijacking." Scared by his repetition of the words *bomb* and *hijack*, the skittish flight attendant screams, prompting a burly male passenger to restrain Ali, who is turned over to U.S. authorities. The film then breaks into a Bollywood song and dance sequence, "Ullu da Pattha," which intersperses shots of Ali being interrogated and tortured by U.S. authorities, gyrating female immigration agents, a "Federal Bureau" panel apparently reviewing his case for deportation, a Karachi bazaar, multiple visits to the American embassy to secure a visa from a dour official, and Ali's fantasy object: a skimpily-clad blond woman in front of a Craftsman style bungalow.

The song sequence explicitly constructs the United States as a national security state that differentially treats those within its borders based on their racial identities and geographical origins. In addition to the racial profiling of Ali as a "terrorist" on the Go America flight that opens the film, after Ali's arrest a continuous series of stills flash across the screen, featuring mug shots of prisoners of different ethnicities. In the first still, a brown man holds a sign reading *Mexican*. He is followed by a mug shot of a black man holding an *African* sign. A white male with a sign lettered *Peter* is next, and Ali and his *South Asian* sign round out the mix. While the others are marked as foreign subjects (*Mexican*, *African*, and *South Asian*), the white male prisoner is the only one granted a unique identity through the use of his first name and the absence of any geographic identification labels. In not marking Peter's geographic origins, the scene implies that the U.S. national security state collapses geographic and racial identity, naturalizing American citizenship as white.

The threat of violence against foreign/ethnic subjects is signified by a large blood splatter in the background of Ali's mug shot. This threat is reinforced by visual references to interrogation that pepper the sequence; the blue shirts initially slap Ali while questioning him, and he is later strapped into a chair with electrodes protruding from his head. These images evoke the controversial U.S. record of using torture in military facilities in Afghanistan and Iraq to interrogate those designated terrorist suspects as their inclusion in the song sequence underscores the idea that terrorist suspects are inevitably racialized subjects in the eyes of the U.S. state. That the state is incapable of discerning the finer distinctions between different political categories that it defines as constituting threats to its national security becomes apparent in the Federal Bureau panelists' responses to Ali. One official deems him an Al Qaeda member, another designates him Taliban, and a third reverts to the more comic label

Ullu da Pattha, a Punjabi phrase that literally translates into "son of an owl" (the equivalent of "son of a jackass") and is an invective used to insult someone's intelligence or judgment.

But if the song sequence aims to expose the United States as a racialized national security state, it also mocks middle-class Pakistanis who buy wholesale into the discourse of the American dream. The Pakistani man who taunts Ali in the men's room with the prospect of becoming a cab driver in New York vocalizes an actual reality for many South Asian immigrants, particularly Pakistanis, who have found employment driving taxis in New York.[6] This scene helps deflate the puffed-up rhetoric of the American dream that Ali has swallowed. His image—in the song sequence when he appears before the Federal Bureau board—features a background collage juxtaposing the Statue of Liberty, an eagle, the U.S. flag, and the words *American Dream*. Later in the sequence, we see him in the midst of a domestic fantasy complete with bungalow and blond babe—an object choice of desire overdetermined by the complex sexual dynamics of colonial history—handing him a glass of milk and a hamburger. The presence of a small, white boy in the frame constructs the American dream as inhering in the marriage between heteronormative reproduction and property ownership. The lyrics of the song emphasize his pursuit of this fiction insofar as the refrain includes the line, "He's running behind the American dream," which implies that he's chasing after a dream that he will be unable to catch.

That Ali's construction of Amreeka is simplistic and almost cartoonish is indicated in the flashbacks to his childhood that represent him as obsessed with the United States from a young age. The Superman bedspread adorning the adult Ali's bed hints that his understanding of the United States has not matured with age. Even more significantly, the title of the song "Ullu da Pattha" is clearly a signifier for Ali himself. His aspirations to attain the American dream, the song's title insinuates, are idiotic and foolish.

This opening song sequence also implicates the global media as being complicit in the promulgation of the War on Terror and with disseminating a hegemonic version of the American dream. In the first scene, Majeed, an executive and reporter for the Pakistani Danka television station, does a "news" spot on the first American flight to depart from Karachi to New York following September 11, apparently newsworthy for the presence of a single Pakistani passenger, Ali, on the flight. At one level, the scene starkly demonstrates the unequal power balance between the United States and Pakistan insofar as the presence of a single Pakistani passenger on the plane would not merit media coverage in the United States. Yet after his detention by U.S. authorities on suspicion of terrorism, the U.S. media pick up the story and run with it. A reporter from News America interviews the flight attendant, who gleefully claims that Ali "had a look of vengeance in his eyes as if he wanted to kill me." Shortly afterward an anchor for the same station solemnly announces that "reports are coming in of bin Laden trying to affect peace in America," thereby implying that Ali is bin Laden's agent. The hyperbole of the news segments both demonstrates media exaggeration of content related to the War on Terror and highlights the speculative nature of U.S. journalism in which all things related to terrorism lead back to Osama bin Laden even in the absence of any causal connections. According to *Tere Bin Laden's* logic, the media—rather than functioning as the Fourth Estate (e.g., the watchdog of democratic processes)—instead acts like the fourth branch of government, promoting views in line with the executive and legislative branches, in effect operating along the lines of what Louis Althusser terms an "ideological state apparatus."[7]

Similar to their U.S. counterparts, Pakistani media, as portrayed in the film and embodied in Danka TV, have a tendency to cover inane human interest stories geared toward entertainment. The song sequence intersperses footage of Ali, at work as a Danka correspondent, interviewing a proprietor of an umbrella shop about the optimum way to open an umbrella and a farmer about his sense of fulfillment from growing white, tubular radishes. Later in the film, Ali's assignment to cover a cock-crowing competition introduces him to Noora, the naive Osama bin Laden look-alike, who will become the unwitting lead in Ali's fake footage.

Two consecutive frames reinforce the sense that the media have played a formative role in Ali's internalization of the American dream. In one, Ali is posed against a background of a wall covered with television screens, all featuring the image of the statue of liberty, with the soundtrack blaring, "He's running blind behind the American dream." The next frame substitutes different stills of Ali's detention and interrogation for the images of the Statue of Liberty on the television monitors. In combination with the other scenes featuring News America and Danka television, these frames point to the power of media and media's capacity to shape individual subjectivity such as Ali's, as well as to exist in a closed loop with the state, beaming propaganda and justifications for the War on Terror on the airwaves and inciting the state to enact more exaggerated forms of coercion against those deemed terrorist suspects.

The Critique of the War on Terror

Tere Bin Laden begins with a standard disclaimer: "The characters and incidents portrayed in the film herein are fictitious and any similarity/resemblance to the name, character, and history of any person living or dead, is entirely coincidental and unintentional. The film is a satire on the difficult times we are living in." This disclaimer is clearly a joke given that the title of the film contains a reference to Osama bin Laden, yet he only appears in the film as his simulacra, his look-alike—the poultry farmer Noora—whom the film crafts as a vehicle to represent the film's critique of the War on Terror. U.S. foreign policy is satirized in several ways: through comic references to George W. Bush, through Noora's speeches in the fake bin Laden videos, and through the cartoonish representation of U.S. military action in Afghanistan. Ali and his cameraman Gul are dispatched to cover a rooster-crowing contest for Danka television, where with a great deal of fanfare the announcer introduces one contestant, "And now straight from the land of Bushes: the mighty Dubya Pardesi [foreigner], last year's champion." An obese rooster struts across the stage, only to issue a puny crow. The rooster's incongruous bodily bulk in conjunction with the feebleness of his voice suggests a parallel with his namesake: in the War on Terror, when push comes to shove, a puffed-up and crowing president is unable to deliver on such basic goods as bin Laden's capture.

Apart from this comic reference to President George W. Bush, the weightiest critique of U.S. foreign policy in the film emerges from the speeches of Osama bin Laden in the fake videos staged by Ali and his gang and in the cartoonish representation of U.S. intelligence officials, who are portrayed as utterly cynical. Tricking Noora into believing that he is making a tape about poultry farming for Saudi television, Latif—an Arab colleague of Ali and Gul's—provides an Arabic script for him to memorize. Unbeknownst to Noora, the crew switches the background images of stacked egg cartons and the accoutrements of poultry farming for visuals of a cave, the setting for many of the actual Osama bin Laden's videotapes. Indeed, the text of Noora's speech echoes the theme of reciprocal violence that is a leitmotif in the actual bin Laden's speeches and interviews. With his arm raised in a gesture characteristic of the real deal, Noora declares: "America will have to pay heavily for its continued atrocities in Iraq, Afghanistan, and the rest of the Middle East. Its hands are red with the blood of innocent Muslim children. America cannot wash away this blood without bleeding itself in return. The sacrifice of our Iraqi brothers and sisters will not go in vain."

As Bruce Lawrence notes, the real bin Laden frequently justifies the use of violence against Western civilians as a form of "reactive terror—a response to what he perceives as the much greater terror exercised by the West over an incomparably longer period of time."[8] Pointing to the lack of equivalence between the violence visited by the United States on other territories—Iraq, Hiroshima and Nagasaki, and Palestine, among others—and that perpetrated by Muslims on the West, bin Laden repeatedly calls for, in his words, a "recalculation" of the human tally of political violence and a "settling of accounts" with the United States, insisting on a moral calculus that recognizes non-Western casualties.[9] He frequently invokes the image of blood alongside references to violence perpetrated against Muslim children. For instance, in an October 20, 2001, interview with Tayser Alluni, then head of the Al Jazeera bureau in Kabul, bin Laden responds to the journalist's question regarding the ethics of "killing innocent civilians" with this rationale:

> It is very strange for Americans and other educated people to talk about the killing of innocent civilians. I mean, who said that our children and civilians are not innocents, and that the shedding of their blood is permissible? Whenever we kill their civilians, the whole world yells at us from east to west, and America starts putting pressure on its allies and puppets. Who said that our blood isn't blood and that their blood is blood? What about the people that have been killed in our lands for decades? More than 1,000,000 children died in Iraq, and they are still dying, so why do we not hear people that cry or protest, or anyone who reassures or anyone who sends condolences?[10]

Particularly abhorrent to bin Laden has been the brutal effects of the U.S.-led UN sanctions against Iraq, which magnified the human misery caused by the earlier destruction of its infrastructure—highways, sanitation and water treatment facilities, and power plants—during the 1991 military campaign headed by the United States. The loss of Iraq's infrastructure, combined with the UN sanctions, resulted in a large number of preventable deaths, especially of children, from malnutrition and water-borne illnesses. The mounting death toll of Muslims as a result of U.S. foreign policy, for bin Laden, requires defensive measures against the United States, which he terms a "defensive *jihad* to protect our land and people."[11] "That's why I have said that if we don't have security," he warns, "neither will the Americans."[12] The themes of U.S. violence against Arabs and Afghans, the deaths of Muslim children, and the threat of retaliatory violence against Americans articulated in Noora's first fake bin Laden tape all have their historical antecedents in Osama bin Laden's actual speeches and interviews.

If the first fake bin Laden tape highlights Muslim grievances against the United States, the second one alludes to the political economy of its foreign policy, expressing a widely held view among South Asians and North American progressives that U.S. foreign policy is largely driven by the desire to exert control over gas and oil energy sources. Rehearsing the script for a second bin Laden tape proposing a ceasefire, Ali addresses the U.S. president as "My beloved [*habibi*], George Bush," and asks, "How long can you use me as an excuse to go oil hunting?" "Stop these atrocities," he orders. Together, the interrogative and imperative sentences assert that Osama bin Laden largely functions as an alibi for the United States to identify new territory and sources of oil to exploit. A third fake bin Laden tape elaborates on the theme of President Bush's desire for oil. Disguised as Osama bin Laden, Noora chides the American leader: "You used to dream of having oil fountains in your backyard. . . . Your sly ways took you straight to oil wells and now you bathe in Iraqi petrol and Afghani [*sic*] diesel every day."

As Eqbal Ahmad, among others, has argued, oil and gas production and distribution have been a consideration of U.S. foreign policy, going back to the early 1970s, as one way for the United States to gain leverage over its allies in Japan and Europe, which needed energy sources to fuel the industrialization of their economies.[13] Moreover, the status of the United States as one of the largest consumers of petroleum (having ceded first place to China in 2010) means that it imports about half its energy requirements. The Middle East, with its vast oil reserves, was the initial focus of U.S. foreign policy, but chronic instability in the region since 1979—including the Iranian Revolution, ongoing tensions over the Israeli Occupation of Gaza and the West Bank, and the rise of Islamist movements in the Arab world, in part, a response to authoritarian states—has prompted the United States to diversify its energy sources.[14] The Central Asian Republics of Azerbaijan, Kazakhstan, Kirghizstan, Turkmenistan, and Uzbekistan are believed to have considerable oil and gas reserves; given that these countries are landlocked, Afghanistan and Pakistan have emerged as a strategically important potential transit route for oil and gas pipelines from Central Asia to the Arabian Sea.[15] Such a route would enable the United States to marginalize Russia and sidestep Iran, which is perceived as generally hostile to U.S. interests. Indeed, the jockeying over strategic partnerships with the Central Asian countries between the United States, UK, and NATO countries, on the one hand, and Russia and the People's Republic of China, on the other hand, has popularized the term *the New Great Game* to capture the new politics of oil, resurrecting the nineteenth-century term used to describe the political rivalry between Britain and Russia in the region.[16]

The third fake Osama bin Laden tape in *Tere Bin Laden* has Noora offering a truce to President Bush and inviting him to share fried foods. References to fried foods bookend Noora's charges that Bush washes in Iraqi and Afghan fuel. He initially remarks, "My beloved Bushie: you've liked your meat deep-fried and oily since you were little," and cautions, "But don't be too greedy or you might end up an oily McBush burger." "Take my advice, drop this war," Noora qua bin Laden advises. "Come to my cave. We'll gorge on fried food [*pakoras*] together." Although clearly ridiculous, the references to fried foods literalize President Bush's—and by extension, America's—insatiable appetite for oil and gas even as Noora's invitation to consume *pakoras,* a savory South Asian fried snack, together alludes to the legendary codes of hospitality in the region.

The War on Terror as Cartoonish

Tere Bin Laden spoofs the War on Terror by using animation stills to signify its cartoonish elements. After the first fake bin Laden tape surfaces, Washington sends Ted Wood, the head of U.S. intelligence, to Pakistan to formulate an appropriate response. Briefing CIA and Pakistan's Inter-Services Intelligence (ISI) officials, Wood announces plans to launch "Operation Kickass:" a campaign to target Afghanistan hourly with cruise missiles and B52 bombers. As he speaks, Wood illustrates his military strategy with visuals that consist of cartoon images of menacing-looking armed Afghans posed against a mountain background. The scene literally renders the War on Terror as a cartoonish enterprise and simultaneously evokes Secretary of State Colin Powell's February 3, 2003, testimony to the UN in which he claimed Iraq possessed weapons of mass destruction. Toggling between actual photographs of Iraqi weapons that no longer existed and line drawings of such weapons and mobile biological weapons labs, Powell made a sober case in support of the Bush administration's plan to go to war with Iraq, a case that he acknowledged was "not solid" a little over a year later.[17]

"Operation Kickass," the name given to this venture, also recalls the absurdity of the designation given to the U.S. military campaign in Afghanistan, "Operation Enduring Freedom" and its ambiguous meaning. Does freedom itself endure, or is freedom that which must be endured?[18] Additionally, the name invokes the U.S. military doctrine of shock and awe and the use of overwhelming force, formulated in 1996 by staff at the National Defense University.[19] In keeping with the farcical nature of the film, *Tere Bin Laden* restricts the lethal effects of Operation Kickass to the deaths of domesticated animals. *Live India's* coverage of the breaking news of the operation reveals "heavy bombing in Afghanistan has caused severe casualties to livestock. America says this onslaught will continue till Osama is captured." In actuality, however, Operation Enduring Freedom has resulted in the deaths of numerous Afghans, though exact figures are impossible to determine given that official tallies of Afghan casualties were not kept until 2007.

The United Nations estimates that the casualty figure for Afghan civilians between 2007 and 2011 is 11,864.[20] Afghan civilian casualties from the start of the war in 2001 to 2007 are probably much higher given the use of aerial power to prosecute the war. A U.S. military pilot remembers that in the initial phases of the war, military aircraft were instructed to return for landings with far fewer bombs than in their initial payload.[21] Lieutenant Commander Morgan recounts, "When this [Operation Enduring Freedom] kicked off, they were launching aircraft with unrecoverable loads. Basically, you had to drop."[22] Military officials now claim that better coordination between ground forces and navy pilots via satellite technology has reduced the number of civilian casualties from aerial bombardment.[23] Since 2009, however, the U.S. military has ramped up its drone program in Afghanistan, both for the purposes of surveillance and for firing missiles and dropping bombs; the surveillance drones are targeted at identifying individuals planting roadside bombs, which are the largest cause of U.S. military casualties.[24] As P. W. Singer, an analyst with the Brookings Institution, has observed, the increased use of drones has the potential to increase civilian casualties. "Not everyone digging by the side of the road is automatically an insurgent," he notes.[25]

Tere Bin Laden's displacement of the violent consequences of the U.S. bombing campaign from Afghan civilians to livestock enables the film to maintain its comedic element and is consistent with its improbable plot, which also exposes U.S. intelligence officials as being callous to the lethal effects of their campaigns. When ISI agent Usman realizes that the Osama tape features a map with Urdu lettering in the background, he concludes that bin Laden is in Pakistan rather than Afghanistan. In response to his question about why the United States is conducting a bombing campaign of Afghanistan when they know bin Laden is in Pakistan, Wood says: "We have a budget of 100 billion dollars for hunting down Osama. I can't spend all of that on sipping coffee." The political economy of foreign intervention, Wood insinuates, becomes geared to its own reproduction regardless of whether its strategic objectives have been met.

From September 11, 2001, until March 2011, Operation Enduring Freedom has cost $444 billion for Afghanistan alone.[26] As a number of analysts have commented, Al Qaeda no longer has a substantial presence in Afghanistan, where instead the Taliban has reinvented itself as a form of Pushtun nationalism in opposition to the U.S. occupation of the country.[27] Just as the ISI agent Usman recognizes that Osama bin Laden's absence from Afghanistan should logically exempt the country from being targeted by the U.S. military, we might ask whether the dwindling numbers of Al Qaeda insurgents there necessitates an ongoing U.S. military presence in that country.

Wood's collaboration with Ali to produce the final fake bin Laden tape amplifies the cynicism of Wood's position on Operation Kickass and the film's representation of the continued military campaign against Afghanistan when intelligence officials know of bin Laden's absence there. After discovering that the Osama bin Laden taken into custody by intelligence officials is Noora, a poultry farmer and not arch enemy number one of the United States, Wood screams at Ali, "What will I say to the world?. . . That we bombed Afghanistan for nothing?" Partly as a face-saving measure for Wood, and partly out of a desire to end the War on Terror and its attendant terror unleashed on Afghans, Ali proposes the ISI, CIA, and his motley crew collaborate to make a final Osama bin Laden tape offering a ceasefire to President Bush. The resulting video has Osama bin Laden proffering an invitation to the president to share fried foods together, which results in negotiations and a cessation to the War on Terror.

That the CIA actively participates in the production of the final fake bin Laden tape in *Tere Bin Laden* will not seem wholly improbable from a plot perspective insofar as numerous actual internet sites, many created by Americans, purport to unmask the agency's role in making the video released by the Bush administration in October 2001 as proof of bin Laden's complicity in the 9/11 attacks. For instance, the website "The Real Proof the Government Released a Fake Video of Osama bin Laden!" walks viewers through points in the tape that do not tally with known aspects of bin Laden's person and character: the Osama in the tape, the narrator claims, is heavier, has a shorter nose, is wearing a ring and wristwatch (ornamentation unlikely in serious believers), and is right-handed (bin Laden was left-handed). This analysis appears on other websites as well, including one featuring an interview with bin Laden's fourth son, Omar, who claims that the man in the tape is not his father.[28] Perhaps because of the popularity of such sites, the BBC even acknowledged, in December 2001, the widespread skepticism toward the authenticity of this tape, particularly in the Arab world.[29]

Five years later, the BBC went on to make a three-part documentary, *The Power of Nightmares*, that historicizes the dialectical relationship between the rise of American neoconservatives and radical Islamists and charts how U.S. foreign policy has shifted from evidence-based decision making to speculative fantasy reliant on the creation of manufactured threats. The final segment, "The Shadows in the Cave" (a joint reference to Plato's parable of the cave in the *Republic* and the setting for many of bin Laden's speeches), presents the view that in pursuing Al Qaeda Western powers are largely chasing a "phantom enemy," whose actual menace is an "illusion" that serves the interests of groups such as politicians in an "age of cynicism" after the end of history and, apparently, of ideology as well.[30] In other words, if Osama bin Laden did not exist, he would have to be invented as a dark fantasy to provide the conditions of possibility

for Western heroics.[31] The invention of imagined threats, of course, also reso-
nates with the actual fabrication of evidence by Bush administration officials
to justify going to war with Iraq.

"The South Asian Perspective" and Pakistani Civil Society

Ali Zafar—the Pakistani pop idol who plays Ali Hassan's character in the film—
insists that *Tere Bin Laden* provides a much-needed Pakistani view of the War on
Terror, and that this element of the film attracted him to the script. Appearing
in an interview on *Dawn*, he claims that the film does not have any content that
is ideological or offensive.[32] The Indian writer and director of *Tere Bin Laden*,
Abhishek Sharma, voices similar sentiments in an interview that aired on the
segment "Is There Room for Humour in the War against Terror?" on the Riz
Khan show, September 6, 2010, on Al-Jazeera. The fictional character of Ali, according to Sharma, represents a generalized "South Asian perspective" on both
the War on Terror and the American Dream. Given the historic rivalry between
Pakistan and India since the partition of the subcontinent in 1947, the collaboration between an Indian director and Pakistani actor itself is remarkable.

The claim, however, that the film represents a generalized South Asian perspective on the War on Terror seems disingenuous given the range of opinions
on the U.S. military campaign in India and Pakistan among diverse communities (religious, ethnic, and territorial, for example), which are positioned
differentially vis-à-vis their respective nation-states and have specific histories
of suffering and entitlement that inform their views of U.S. foreign policy. If
anything, *Tere Bin Laden* demonstrates the complexities of civil society as an
assemblage of voluntary associations, consisting of, among others, faith-based
groups, entrepreneurial units, and ethnic, cultural, and professional organizations that interact in complicated ways with one another and with the state. To
achieve stability, the state must secure a significant degree of popular consent
and exercise hegemony not only through instruments of coercion but also
through the mechanisms and institutions of civil society.[33]

The film portrays the complex interactions between representatives of different elements of Pakistani civil society, who sometimes undermine one another and at other times cooperate in limited ways. Mutual suspicion initially
characterizes the interactions between media operators (Ali and Gul), aspiring
businesswomen and established entrepreneurs (Zoya and Noor), emergent
intellectuals (Latif), and those engaged in oppositional politics (Querishi).
Once they become persuaded that their interests coincide, they become a bloc

that alternates between accommodation and antagonism toward the Pakistani and U.S. governments in much the same way that political theorists such as Antonio Gramsci have posited the relationship between the state and civil society as a moving equilibrium.[34] *Tere Bin Laden's* contribution to discourses about Osama bin Laden and the War on Terror is to insert the Pakistani lower-middle and middle classes, as representatives of civil society, into the nexus of global media by emphasizing their role in producing and disseminating footage pertinent to the War on Terror and, thus, exerting geopolitical agency.

The film concludes with the success of the final fake bin Laden tape. The War on Terror has come to an end. Ted Wood has been promoted to secretary of defense. The Pakistani characters have used the profit from the clandestine sale of their first fake bin Laden tape to realize their dreams for various forms of mobility. Ali becomes a journalist celebrity and goes to the United States accompanied by Gul, his cameraman sidekick; Zoya, the makeup artist who transformed Noora into bin Laden for the tapes, opens a beauty salon; Latif, who masqueraded as a Saudi television executive to fool Noora into making the tape, becomes the best-selling translator of the volume *Osama on Peace*; and Querishi, the leftist who did bin Laden's voice-overs in the fake tapes, founds the Communist Party of Pakistan. Across the ideological spectrum—from the lower-middle class to the professional managerial class to the leftist intellectual class—members of Pakistani civil society act to advance their self-interests even when those are based on complete falsehoods or require the hoodwinking of naive rural subjects. The film represents Pakistanis as opportunistic and concentrated on their own aspirations, whether focused on emigration (Ali and Gul), entrepreneurship (Zoya and Latif), or the amassing of local political power (Querishi); the individual characters, in effect, behave in the same self-serving manner as states.

Noora's identity as a village bumpkin and his appearance (wearing the traditional kurta pajama and *pagari* (turban) and sporting a beard) mark him as a certain kind of Muslim, the manipulated, simple Forrest Gump–like character through whom we see the depravity of the world. His character presents a stark contrast to the constant scheming of Ali, whose clothing and lifestyle identify him as a global cosmopolitan. Yet which subject position is mocked in the film remains unclear, particularly given the opening song sequence, which spoofs Ali and his infatuation with the American Dream, and the ending credits in which Noora's hip haircut, shaving of his beard, and donning of stylish jeans, along with his transformation from rural poultry farmer to urban beauty salon owner, signify his conversion to Western modernity.

By using the vehicle of a simple poultry farmer to be bin Laden's look-alike, the film makes bin Laden into both a figure of ridicule and a spokesperson of a broadly felt negative attitude toward U.S. military power as a cynical cover to monopolize natural resources such as oil and as disproportionate in its realization. Stuart Hall advocates getting inside the image itself as a means of disrupting stereotypical representations of specific communities; new meanings can arise from the gap between the media image and our expectations of how a particular group should be represented, he explains.[35] In associating Osama bin Laden, the paradigmatic face of Islamic terror, with Noora, a simple and affable man, within the generic conventions of a Bollywood comedy, *Tere Bin Laden* presents a counterhegemonic analysis of the War on Terror that unsettles rather than reinforces the dominant narrative of this military intervention. The film, ironically, capitalizes on the figure of Osama bin Laden and the War on Terror even as it stages its critique and, thereby, demonstrates the subversive potential of media. In a final twist of irony, *Tere Bin Laden* anticipates the historical narrative: bin Laden had apparently been in hiding in Pakistan for nearly a decade before the CIA assassinated him there in 2011.

Notes

1. I am grateful to Srimati Basu, Lessie Jo Frazier, Sara Friedman, Susan Jeffords, Jeffrey T. Kenney, Radhika Parameswaran, and Fahed Yahya Al-Sumait for their helpful comments on drafts of this article. All errors are my own.

2. Pooja Shetty Deora and Aarti Shetty (producers), Abhishek Sharma (director), *Tere Bin Laden* (India: Walkwater Media, 2010). While the Pakistani government banned the film—claiming that it would provoke terrorist attacks—pirated copies are readily available in the country.

3. Riz Khan's show "Is There Room for Humour in the War against Terror?," Al-Jazeera,. aired September 10, 2010, http://www.aljazeera.com/programmes/rizkhan/2010/09/2010968455534861.html.

4. For an account of discussions within the Bush administration in the immediate aftermath of 9/11 about linking the attacks to Saddam Hussein and Al Qaeda and the security assessments that disputed such ties, see *The 9/11 Commission Report: Final Report of the National Commission on Terrorist Attacks upon the United States,* particularly section 10.3, "'Phase Two' and the Question of Iraq" (New York: W.W. Norton, 2011). Bob Woodward's *Plan of Attack* details differences among Bush's cabinet members regarding the plausibility of Iraq possessing WMD; he provides an analysis of the exaggerations and contradictions in the 2002 National Intelligence Estimate on "Iraq's Continuing Programs for Weapons of Mass Destruction." Bob Woodward, *Plan of Attack: The Definitive Account of the Decision to Invade Iraq* (New York: Simon and Schuster, 2004).

5. Lashkar-e-Taiba, based in Pakistan, is the military arm of the Islamist organization Markaz-ad-Dawa-wal-Irshad, which seeks to liberate Jammu and Kashmir from India and to establish an Islamic state across South Asia. It has been linked to a number of deadly terrorist acts in India, including the 2001 assault on Parliament and the 2008 attacks in Mumbai. The

Indian government and security experts allege that the organization has ties to Pakistan's Inter-Services Intelligence, though the Pakistani government denies such ties.

6. For more on South Asian taxi drivers and their organizing attempts, see Manisha Das Gupta, *Unruly Immigrants: Rights, Activism, and Transnational South Asian Politics in the United States* (Durham, NC: Duke University Press, 2006).

7. Louis Althusser, "Ideology and Ideological State Apparatuses (Notes towards an Investigation)," *Lenin and Philosophy, and Other Essays*, trans. Ben Brewster (New York: Monthly Review Press, 1972).

8. Bruce Lawrence, ed., introduction to *Messages to the World: The Statements of Osama bin Laden* (London: Verso, 2005), xviii.

9. See, in particular, bin Laden's interviews "The Saudi Regime" and "Terror for Terror" and his open letter "To the Allies of America" in Lawrence, *Messages to the World*.

10. Bin Laden, "Terror for Terror," 117.

11. Bin Laden, "The Example of Vietnam," in Lawrence, *Messages to the World*, 141.

12. Ibid.

13. *Eqbal Ahmad, Confronting Empire*, the transcripts of David Barsamian's interviews with Eqbal Ahmad, has references to the political economy of U.S. foreign policy throughout its pages (Cambridge, MA: South End Press, 2000). For additional critiques of U.S. foreign policy in terms of the scramble to control resources, see Noam Chomsky, *On Power and Ideology: The Managua Lectures* (Boston: South End Press, 1987), and Howard Zinn's classic, *A People's History of the United States: 1492–Present* (New York: HarperCollins, 1980). On the topic of the U.S. attempting to gain leverage over the growing economies of Asia and Europe by controlling access to energy resources, see David Harvey, *The New Imperialism* (Oxford: Oxford University Press, 2003). It is worth noting, however, that considerations over petroleum reserves have a much longer history in geopolitics, dating back to the early twentieth century. Consider, for example, conflicts between the Mexican government and foreign companies such as Mexican Eagle Company (a subsidiary of Royal Dutch/Shell Company) and Jersey Standard and Standard Oil Company of California (now Chevron) over petroleum in the 1920s, the role of corporations such as Standard Oil, Anglo-Persian Oil Company (active in what is today called "Iran" and southern Russia, and the antecedent to British Petroleum Company), and Royal Dutch Shell (a major player in Indonesia and southeast Asia) and their collusion with various imperial powers.

14. For a cogent account of the rise of Islamic movements as a form of "counter nationalism" to authoritarian states in the last several decades, see Jeffrey T. Kenney, "Millennialism and Radical Islamist Movements," in *The Oxford Handbook of Millennialism*, ed. Catherine Wessinger (New York: Oxford University Press, 2011).

15. Ahmad, *Eqbal Ahmad, Confronting Empire*, 48–49. See also Sitaram Yechury, "America, Oil, and Afghanistan," *Hindu Online*, October 13, 2001, http://www.hindu.com/2001/10/13/stories/05132524.htm.

16. The literature on the New Great Game is voluminous: Mohammed E. Ahrari and James Beal, *The New Great Game in Muslim Central Asia* (Washington, DC: Institute for National Strategic Studies, 1996); Shareen Brysac and Karl Meyer, *Tournament of Shadows: The Great Game and the Race for Empire in Asia* (Washington, DC: Counterpoint,

1999); Lutz Kleveman, *The New Great Game: Blood and Oil in Central Asia* (New York: Grove Press, 2004); Rein Mullerson, *Central Asia: A Chessboard and Player in the New Great Game* (New York: Columbia University Press, 2007); Ahmed Rashid, *Taliban: Islam, Oil and the New Great Game in Central Asia* (London: I.B. Tauris, 2000).

17. For a detailed analysis of Powell's UN testimony, see Hugh Gusterson, "The Auditors: Bad Intelligence and the Loss of Public Trust," *Boston Review*, November/December 2005, http://www.bostonreview.net/hugh-gusterson-the-auditors-public-trust. See also Jonathan Schwarz, "The U.N. Deception: What Exactly Colin Powell Knew Five Years Ago and What He Told the World," *Mother Jones*, February 5, 2008, http://www.motherjones.com/mojo/2008/02/un-deception-what-exactly-colin-powell-knew-five-years-ago-and-what-he-told-world. For more on Powell's retraction of his testimony, see "Powell: Some Iraq Testimony Not 'Solid,'" CNN.com, April 3, 2004, http://articles.cnn.com/2004-04-03/us/powell.iraq_1_official-iraqi-organization-biological-weapons-labs-state-colin-powell?_s=PM:US. In a September 2012 address to the UN, Israeli prime minister Benjamin Netanyahu held up a cartoonish drawing of a bomb to dramatize Iran's impending nuclear capability. See Rick Gladstone and David E. Sanger, "Nod to Obama by Netanyahu in Warning to Iran on Bomb," *New York Times*, September 27, 2012, http://www.nytimes.com/2012/09/28/world/middleeast/netanyahu-warns-that-iran-bombmaking-ability-is-nearer.html?pagewanted=all&_r=0.

18. I am grateful to Barbara Harlow for remarking on the ambiguity of the name "Operation Enduring Freedom." Since September 11, 2001, the United States has initiated three operations: Operation Enduring Freedom (primarily focused on Afghanistan, but also targeting smaller operations in areas ranging from the Philippines to Djibouti); Operation Noble Eagle (aimed at enhancing security at U.S. military bases); and Operation Iraqi Freedom (to be renamed Operation New Dawn once the United States transforms its role to an advisory function).

19. See Harlan K. Ullman and James Wade Jr., *Shock and Awe: Achieving Rapid Dominance* prepared by Defense Group Inc. for the National Defense University, http://www.dodccrp.org/files/Ullman_Shock.pdf.

20. United Nations Assistance Mission in Afghanistan and UN Office of the High Commissioner for Human Rights, *Afghanistan: Annual Report 2011: Protection of Civilians in Armed Conflict*, February 2012, http://unama.unmissions.org/Portals/UNAMA/Documents/UNAMA%20POC%202011%20Report_Final_Feb%202012.pdf; Susan G. Chesser, "Afghanistan Casualties: Military Forces and Civilians." Congressional Research Service, 7–5700, R41084, December 6, 2012, http://www.fas.org/sgp/crs/natsec/R41084.pdf.

21. C. J. Chivers, "Afghan Air War May Be Cut Off as U.S. Pulls Out," *New York Times*, July 7, 2012.

22. Morgan, qtd. in ibid.

23. Ibid.

24. Unlike in Pakistan, where the drone program is run by the CIA, the military is in charge of the program in Afghanistan. Christopher Drew, "Drones Are Playing a Growing Role in Afghanistan," *New York Times*, February 19, 2010, http://www.nytimes.com/2010/02/20/world/asia/20drones.html.

25. Singer, qtd. in ibid.

26. For more on the costs of U.S. military operations in the War on Terror, see Amy Belasco, "The Cost of Iraq, Afghanistan, and Other Global War on Terror Operations since 9/11," Congressional Research Service, 7–5700, RL33110, March 29, 2011, http://www.fas.org/sgp/crs/natsec/RL33110.pdf.

27. Robert Greenwald (producer and director) and Jason Zaro (producer), *Rethink Afghanistan* (Culver City, CA: Brave New Foundation, 2009).

28. See, for example, "Real Proof he Government Released a Fake Video of Osama bin Laden!," http://www.youtube.com/watch?v=1W6QLfXE3wA; Max Keiser, "CIA Admit Faking Binladen [*sic*] Video: Interview with Alex Jones," http://www.youtube.com/watch?v=V4a14_LVFtc; "Tim Osman aka Bin Laden," http://www.youtube.com/watch?v=fBIthwLNoiI (removed); "Former CIA Officials Admit to Faking bin Laden Video," May 25, 2010, http://www.prisonplanet.com.

"Bin Laden's Son Says Videos Are Faked," http://www.youtube.com/watch?v=3jXzK5LD3kE&feature=related.

29. "Could the Bin Laden Video Be a Fake?," BBC News, December 14, 2001, http://news .bbc.co.uk/2/hi/1711288.stm.

30. For an analysis of the significance of caves in Islam, along with Osama bin Laden's manipulation of the media, see Faisal Devji, *Landscapes of the Jihad: Militancy, Morality, and Modernity* (London: Hurst, 2005).

31. "The Power of Nightmares: The Shadows in the Cave," BBC News, January 14, 2005, http://news.bbc.co.uk/2/hi/programmes/3970901.stm.

32. "Ali Zafar Interview: Part 1," *Dawn,* http://www.youtube.com/watch?v=Tms2HlBVomE&feature=related.

33. Antonio Gramsci, "State and Civil Society," *Selections from the Prison Notebooks,* ed. and trans. Quintin Hoare and Geoffrey Nowell Smith (New York: International, [1971]1997).

34. Ibid.

35. Stuart Hall in Sut Jhally (producer and director), *Stuart Hall: Representation and the Media* Northampton, MA: Media Education Foundation, 1997).

9

Obama bin Laden [*sic*]

How to Win the War on Terror #likeaboss

RYAN CROKEN

> Bodies inhabit space by how they reach for objects,
> just as objects in turn extend what we can reach.
> We do not have to think where to find such objects;
> our knowledge is implicit and we reach toward them
> without hesitation. Losing things, for this reason,
> can lead to moments of existential crisis: we expect
> to find "it" there, as an expectation that directs an
> action, and if "it" is not there, we might even worry
> that we are losing our minds along with our posses-
> sions.
>
> —Sara Ahmed, *Queer Phenomenology: Orientations,*
>   *Objects, Others*

> Can it be, ladies and gentlemen? Could it be? . . . Bin
> Laden is dead. Confirmed. Urgent confirmed. Multiple
> sources. Osama bin Laden is dead. Happy days!
> Happy days everybody! This is the greatest night
> of my career. The bum is dead. The savage who
> hurt us so grievously . . . I think Osama bin Laden's
> continued existence on this earth has represented
> a continuing humiliation to the United States of
> America. He defied President George W. Bush 43
> and President Barack Obama 44 for all this time. . . .
> Isn't this a brilliant way to start your week?
>
>   —Geraldo Rivera, Fox News Chan-
>   nel broadcast, May 1, 2011

The greatest night of Geraldo Rivera's career: this is worth looking into. To understand Rivera's nationalist ebullience—echoed in the streets and tweets across the United States on the night of bin Laden's death—I'd like to figure Osama bin Laden's body as an object in the Ahmedian sense of the word, that is, as an orientation device with world-mapping capabilities. In this framing, it could be said that bin Laden's fugitive tenure occasioned, among many Americans, a profound and prolonged bout of phenomenological disorientation. Not only did an at-large Osama forestall the realization of "healing" by means of retribution, but this "humiliating," as Rivera put it, disarticulation between the United States and its constitutive nemesis fundamentally unsettled a national subject's ability to read their situation into commonly held folk beliefs (namely, American exceptionalism and unimpeded global omnipotence) and to navigate the existential cartography of the nation's relationship to the rest of the world, in particular, the (Arab/Muslim) East. This being the case, I'd like to suggest that, from September 11, 2001, until his death in May 2011, Osama bin Laden's function in U.S. public culture might usefully be seen as that of a "legend." By *legend* (from the Latin *legenda,* "things to be read"), I refer, firstly, to the term's usage as a "symbolic representation of folk belief and collective experiences" that serves to reaffirm the common values of a group; secondly, to the colloquial designation of an immortalized, larger-than-life historical figure; and, finally, to the idea of *legend* as a key to the symbols and codes on a map.[1] In public imaginaries, the reading of "Osama" dilated the scope of historicity toward legendary bounds—that is, romantic, inaccurate, aesthetically seductive, and totalizing—not only because "Osama" was able to infiltrate and gravely injure a Western homeland, but also because he disrupted this homeland's intuitive facility to move toward and apprehend the "object" upon which its hegemonic motility and coherency relied.

Ahmed notes that subjects move toward objects with the inherited, implicit expectation that they will be found in their place. In the wake of the attacks of September 11, owing to the enduring legacy of Orientalism and its incarnations in the United States, U.S. subjects were highly conditioned to expect that the United States of America would locate and possess the object of bin Laden's Arab/Muslim body. In late modern U.S. cultural production, as Edward Said has observed, "Muslims" are defined by their roles as "eminently killable." Their service as Hollywood villains is mainly to be captured and destroyed: to be brought to justice at the hands of non-Muslim—"white, or even black," Said puts it—American heroes.[2] The critical dissonance between this culturally produced expectation of eminently killable Oriental object-bodies—of which bin Laden stood as perhaps the foremost post-9/11 representative in the minds of many non-Muslim Americans—and the political reality of bin Laden's legendary absent presence is further illuminated by Ahmed's reflections regarding the "reachability" of the Orient. Despite the sublimity of its "farness," the Orient has always been available as a resource for world making, providing an accessible object around which collective Western identities can be, and have been, established. *"The Occident,"* Ahmed writes, *"coheres as that which we are organized around through the very direction of our gaze towards the Orient."*[3] By successfully extending itself outward *toward* the East, the West is able to gather itself *around* the notion that it exists as a definite body against which other bodies may be occupied, sterilized of their subjectivities, and brought back to a "home," a world center, that is made possible by domesticating the distance between what it is not.[4]

Clearly, Osama bin Laden's near-decade of elusion (and the extended wars with which this elusion is associated) defied these foundational tenets of American Orientalist domestication: bin Laden's success at continuing to exist *absconditus* rendered him quintessentially *un*reachable and *un*killable, and the United States found itself staring into a void where a mirror should have stood. With this misplaced object at large in a consequentially unmappable world, many Americans had good reason to believe they might have been losing their minds along with their possessions, among them the War on Terror, exceptionalism, global dominance, moral credibility, financial solvency, and a fundamental belief that the United States could stand at all as a stabilizing point of reference—a "people," a "we," a story of a home and homeland that derived the poetry of its borders from its unfettered expansion beyond them.

It is in this context—amid the crepuscular dimming of "the American Century"—that the object of Osama bin Laden links with that of Barack Obama.[5] Because a nation is, in large part, a contested drama of ongoing narration, the election of a leader is in many ways the practice of modulating the democratic lexicon, of voting in *words* that may be used to speak meaningfully about national subjectivities. This essay is concerned with two such words—*Obama* and *Osama*—and the publicly imagined symbolic relationship between them. Barack Obama and Osama bin Laden are both nonwhite, they were both intent upon attacking (and positioned to do so) the other's body and his respective polities, and their names, it turns out, happen to rhyme quite neatly with one another. These points of connection—and the power of their perceived symmetries—were not ignored by a public in search of a usable legend through which to coordinate their geo-phenomenological orientations. "Osama" and "Obama" were—and continue to be—read into, through, and against one another in an effort to find the world and one's position in it.

The following analysis explores two popular readings of the Osama-Obama nexus. The first reading frames "Obama" and "Osama" as synonymous, a conflation that renders Barack Obama as a foreign infiltration into the heart of what it means to "be an American," post-9/11. This association places the two assonant leaders on the same racial/religious team in a strategic effort to destroy a normative (mainly white and Christian) understanding of "the American way of life." The narrative bond is magnetized on phonetic and phenotypical grounds: Obama's and Osama's nonwhiteness are flushed into the vortex of a particular post-9/11 racial category of "brownness," which—often through some real or imagined connection to "Islam"—marks certain bodies as terroristic threats to the United States and its social fabric. The second reading I explore, which irrupted most prominently at the time and in the wake of the killing of bin Laden, flips this script, casting "Obama" as a providentially entwined antithesis/antidote to "Osama" by fancying Obama to possess a "cool," "badass," and fundamentally all-American ability to protect the homeland specifically on account, not in spite, of his nonwhiteness. In this reading it is the killing power of Obama's Occidental "blackness," made visible against the backdrop of bin Laden's killable Oriental "brownness," that provides a compelling legend to resuscitate America's imperiled sense of exceptionalism and apprehend the object that triggered the disorientation.

My chapter explores how these narratives played out in U.S. public culture across a broad ecology of discursive terrains—memoir, mainstream media commentary, comedic monologue, YouTube posts, hate crime graffiti, T-shirts, underwear, public signage, and elsewhere. I look at the historical-cultural matter(s) that brought these stories into being—how it became possible for them to be told—and examine the real-life repercussions of their telling. In this, I attend to the manner in which the manipulation of "blackness" functioned as a legitimizing discourse to undergird extralegal U.S. military activities in the War on Terror, and the related project of coordinating post-9/11 American "whiteness" vis-à-vis notions of Occidental blackness framed in opposition to imaginings of Oriental brownness. I conclude by providing examples of how this symbolic management has impacted people's lives (particularly the lives of Arab/Muslims) negatively and offer some reflections as to why this may be the case and how and whether it might be otherwise.

"Obama Is Osama," or "It Took Obama to Get Osama"

> Now, folks, we understand our sister stations are saying that Obama was buried. . . . I'm sorry . . . Osama . . . I'm sorry, forgive me . . . Osama . . . was buried at sea at 2 AM Eastern Standard time, roughly. So, that would be 7 in the morning in the UK that Obama was . . . uh . . . O . . . Osama was buried at sea.
>
> —Sky News broadcast, May 2, 2011

In *The Audacity of Hope,* Barack Obama describes a lunch meeting with a media consultant who had been encouraging the then state senator from Illinois to pursue his ambitions to seek higher national office. Obama sketches the encounter, which had been scheduled, coincidentally, to take place shortly after 9/11, thusly:

> "You realize, don't you, that the political dynamics have changed," [the media consultant] said as he picked at his salad.
>
> "What do you mean?" I asked, knowing full well what he meant. We both looked down at the newspaper beside him. There, on the front page, was Osama bin Laden.
>
> "Hell of a thing, isn't it?" he said, shaking his head. "Really bad luck. You can't change your name, of course. Voters are suspicious of that kind of thing. Maybe if you were at the start of your career, you know, you could use a nickname or something. But now . . ." His voice trailed off and he shrugged apologetically before signaling the waiter to bring us the check.[6]

The media consultant's retrospectively myopic inability to foresee the phonetic congruency between "Obama" and "Osama" as a political asset is understandable. While Barack Obama would, of course, go on to propose a translation of his "funny" name in which the very *unlikelihood* of his ascent would itself represent an affirmation of American exceptionalism, perhaps it did take great audacity and hope to envisage this script as having presidentially proportioned viability in late 2001. What Obama and the media consultant were experiencing during their meeting was the undertow of what would become unprecedented waves of anti-Arab/Muslim sentiment, speech, and foreign and domestic policies—part of a phenomenon usefully referred to by Carmen R. Lugo-Lugo and Mary K. Bloodsworth-Lugo as "the browning of terror." This "racial project" paints—or "cooks"—certain bodies as brown to mark them as exogenous threats to the security of the United States and to notions of post-9/11 Americanness.[7] The authors argue that "the process of browning places members of specific groups into a sort of social quarantine, where they are contained and held up for governmental and public scrutiny." Under the clamp of this discursive or physical quarantine, "brown(ed)" bodies are subjected to a "new kind" of public surveillance, interrogation, and sequestration necessitated by the "new kind" of danger confronting the United States in a post-9/11 world.[8]

Since his arrival on the national stage, Barack Obama has, as Lugo-Lugo and Bloodsworth-Lugo suggest, been shaded as a "brown(ed)," as well as black, body. His seeming out-of-nowhere-ness, the ambiguity of his racial inheritance, and his cosmopolitan upbringing presented Americans with a representational puzzle: What could Obama's nonwhite body and name mean? What might his nonwhiteness be *hiding*? One widely endorsed answer is that the concealed object was "brownness," and, therefore, "Islam," and, therefore, the lurkings of terror(ism). This fear—while not sufficiently epidemic to prevent his election—was not fringe. An August 2010 Pew Poll, for example, found that 18 percent of Americans believed that Obama was a Muslim, while 43 percent did not know what his faith was (he's a conspicuously practicing Christian who, as both president and as a presidential candidate, has avoided setting foot inside a mosque on U.S. soil).[9] One of the primary ways in which Obama's brownness was "confirmed" was simply by highlighting the apparent similarities between the words *Obama* and *Osama* (as well as Obama's middle name, Hussein, and its invocation of Sadaam Hussein), thereby using the legends of bin Laden and the Orient to decipher the map of Obama's otherness in an alarming yet narratively coherent fashion.

Examples of efforts to connect Obama to Osama in U.S. public culture are abundant. Vice presidential candidate Sarah Palin, for instance, tapped into and stoked this line of association with her allegations that Barack Obama "pals around with terrorists." The "terrorist" under inquisition is William Ayers, an elementary education theorist and cofounder of the Weather Underground, with whom Obama is unremarkably familiar. Ayers is white, and also only one person, but through the folk-poetic liberty of pluralizing the word *terrorist*, Palin turns the incidental into the representative and routine, conflating specters of 1960s radicalism with "Islamic" terrorism, weaving a hazy yet encompassing web of violently foreign "brownness" into which Obama is ensnared.

Other proposals arguing for an Obama-Osama link claim that Barack Obama is actually Osama bin Laden himself, that the two are literally the same person. Google searches for "Obama is Osama" and related entries reveal thousands of conspiratorial arguments, often culminating with the belief that the hydra-headed "O ama/O ama" figure is a kind of Muslim-incarnated Antichrist (at the time of writing, "Obama is the Antichrist" alone yields 707,000 results, while "Obama is a Muslim" yields 7,650,000). YouTube, meanwhile, presents dozens of videos that have been viewed hundreds of thousands of times that make the Obama-is-Osama case by utilizing amateur "facial recognition technologies" to highlight ostensible similarities through such metrics as mouth and chin alignment, eye distance, finger length and palm line synchronicities. The allegedly empirical impetus for these types of phrenology-reminiscent probings rests entirely on the fact that the faces of Obama and Osama—which are used as comparative canvases upon which the YouTube investigator may circle and paint different body parts—are both tinted the same color, brown.

A related belief holds that while Obama and Osama may not be the same person, they are nevertheless bound by direct lines of kinship, whether spiritual, political, or even familial. One striking example of this mentality manifested itself on a sign outside of Jonesville Church of God in North Carolina in April 2008. The message—which read, "OBAMA . . . OSAMA: HUMM, ARE THEY BROTHERS"—insinuates a fraternal bond between then senator Obama and bin Laden. Playing off white insecurities over imaginings of both African American and Muslim "brotherhoods," this instantiation of inter-legending posits "Obama" as a religious text, demanding exegesis, imbued with inherent meaning by a nationalist Creator, who intentionally tagged a brown body gaining power with a name that conjured "Islam" in an attempt to warn white American Christians that they must defend themselves against an illegitimate infiltration from the Orient. The persuasiveness of this argument lies in the presupposed self-evidence of Islam's evil, as well as the belief that an intervening Christian God speaks the language of racially charged symbols to the "Real Americans" who possess the eyes and ears to decipher the assonant (and thus all-too-obvious) code. Prophecies of this nature warn that a failure to act upon these phonetically verified decryptions of Obama's nonwhite body and name could lead to the end of the United States—and, by national extension and global reduction—the end of the world as we know it. In September of the 2012 presidential campaign season, for example, actor and martial arts expert Chuck Norris and his wife, quoting former president Ronald Regan, warned evangelical Christians and "likeminded American brothers and sisters" that the reelection of Barack Obama would bring about "1,000 years of darkness," intoning a catastrophic lack of light intelligible in both racial and religious registers.[10]

Perhaps—given that an apocalypse is in large part an explanation, a revelation—the eschatological tenor of these readings points towards a widespread desire to "find the world" in its most ultimate sense, by experiencing its end. Along these lines, it is possible to consider this demonization/foreignization of Obama via the transposition of Osama's legend as a productive means of negative self-identification. If the nation—and, thus, national subjectivities— could not be found in part because the object of Osama bin Laden could not be found, perhaps a narrative merging of the two public figures might serve as a strategy for bringing Osama, and the Orient, back within reach. To sentence Obama as Osama is not only to invoke the specter of bin Laden; it is also to give him an actual body in broad daylight. This reification positions Obama as a visible landmark and target within the range of an acutely disoriented post-9/11 American Orientalist scope, and while the proximity of the threat may be frightening, the anxiety may be relished for the sense of purpose and orientation it provides. In this sense, Obama-as-Osama could be viewed as a paradoxically *desired,* even *inspirational,* threat, in that it gives form and location to an otherwise depersonalized fear. Thus, the "browning" of Obama's name and body may alleviate the very terror it presents in the same way a medical diagnosis sometimes helps to assuage the symptoms it carries, by naming them.

Whatever the public or private motivations behind efforts to brown Obama vis-à-vis Osama, the May 1, 2011, death of bin Laden (along with the opportunely timed release of Obama's "long-form birth certificate," just three days prior) diminished the public cache of these religious and racial logics.[11] It seemed, now that bin Laden had been reached and killed by the U.S. government, that a persuasive case could be made that Obama and Osama, rather than being each other's twins, served as perfect foils—diametric difference, not likeness, was the more compelling link. If Obama was Osama's "brother," or Osama himself, how and why would he kill him? The two names, when placed together, lost much of their strength as synonyms and gained currency as antonyms, scripting a doppelgänger romance at the nexus of their relationship in which Obama remained *a kind of* Osama, only pulled out through the other side of his signification. It still seemed a matter of civil-religious destiny that "Obama" and "Osama" appeared so close linguistically, but now the fate resonated with a more familiar Western pop dialectic of an intertwined hero and antihero. Perhaps, legend might have it, it was *only* Obama that could have killed Osama, as, for example, only Luke Skywalker could kill Darth Vader (Anakin Skywalker), only Harry Potter could kill Lord Voldemort, and only Neo could destroy Agent Smith (in *The Matrix*). The seduction of this sublation narrative made its way onto celebratory signs, bumper stickers, and commemorative T-shirts, as shown in figures 9.1–9.3.

FIGURE 9.1. One of the many T-shirts that surfaced to celebrate and capitalize on the killing of Osama bin Laden. Other popular variations on this theme include "Osama got Obama'd," "It takes Obama to kill OSAMA . . . That one letter makes the difference," and "YES WE CAN. YES WE DID, MUTHERFUKA! OBAMA GOT OSAMA. WooT!" (Designed by "expatriate," Zazzle.com, December 1, 2013, http://www.zazzle.com/obama+kills+osama+tshirts)

FIGURE 9.2. Commemorative Obama-over-Osama style bumper sticker. Other paraphernalia of this variety include cocktail plates, mugs, mouse pads, hats, iPhone cases, milk bottles, Christmas ornaments, sweaters, tank tops, license plate frames, coasters, wine charms, boxer brief underwear, teapots, thongs, golf balls, Amazon Kindle kickstands, pet tags, round compact mirrors, women's boy briefs, and dog T-shirts. (Designed by "OneLProductions," Zazzle .com, December 1, 2013, http://www.zazzle.com/obama_got_osama _bumper_sticker-128474450284719384)

These commodified slogans—through which the killing of Osama is literally sold—advertise a coherency of national subjectivity that derives its organizational capabilities by attending to the aforementioned question of what Obama's nonwhite body and name might signify or conceal. In this instance, however, nonwhiteness is not read as "brownness," the color of terror, but rather, I argue, a particular brand of Occidental, vernacular "blackness," projected onto the representational marketplace of Obama's role as head of U.S. *counter*terror. From a legendary vantage, it took "Obama" to get "Osama" because "Obama" could store and circulate a racialized technology that his white predecessors could not: a smooth, effective, decidedly *American* black criminality that could

FIGURE 9.3. One of several "Obama 1, Osama 0" signs held at a spontaneous celebratory rally on the night of bin Laden's killing, Ground Zero, New York City, May 1–2, 2011. (http://jaypgreene.com/2011/05/02/obama-1-osama-0/)

service the Eurocentric drama of American Orientalism as a "secret weapon" of post-9/11 American whiteness and its imperial operations. It is to this process of the mutual "blacking" of Obama and the "blacking" of U.S. counterterror that I now direct my inquiry, paying particular attention to the prefigured templates in which Obama's African American identity was framed in the days and weeks following the death of Osama bin Laden.

From Brown(ed) to Black: How the War on Terror Got Its "Swagga" Back

> You know what the difference is between you and me? I make this look good.
>
> —Agent J (Will Smith), in *Men in Black*

The blacking of U.S. foreign policy and the nonwhite president at its helm found a multitude of satirical, sentimental, and celebratory manifestations in U.S. public culture in the aftermath of the reaching and killing of bin Laden. Perhaps because the drama of Osama's death appeared incomplete without musical accompaniment, it became a popular internet meme to capture footage of President Obama's May 1 Osama-is-dead announcement and lay a soundtrack over his concluding remarks and his memorably cinematic departure from the podium down the long, red-carpeted hallway of the East Room, a spectacular exit that fittingly crowned the Hollywood-esque nature of the military incursion itself. The musical selections of the YouTube mash-up composers reveal something of the racial light in which Obama's "victory" over Osama was cast. The scores can be categorized into three distinct yet interrelated genres:

Hip-hop tracks, such as Soulja Boy's "Turn My Swag On," Rick Ross's "Everyday I'm Hustlin," The Geto Boys' "Damn It Feels Good to Be a Gangsta," Wiz Khalifa's "Money and Hoes," and, of special note, "Like a Boss," originally by Slim Thug but parodied and popularized by the all-white comedy troupe The Lonely Island.[12] The themes of hustling, moneymaking, acting with swagga, and being a boss, thug, or gangsta appropriate the allure of black "street-level" success and situate this fetishized criminality at the historically white locus of the presidency. Through the play of digital minstrelsy ventriloquism, YouTube directors are able to cast the commander-in-chief as an effective "shot caller" deserving of respect, gratitude, and emulation.

Theme songs from blaxploitation flicks such as *Shaft* and the classic Arab-bashing extravaganza, *The Delta Force*.[13] Juxtapositions of this nature celebrate the fulfillment of the culturally produced expectation of a predestined American—"white (or even black)" American, as Edward Said put it—triumph over the brownness of the Orient. In this framing, however, Said's parenthetical observation—"or even black"—becomes *necessarily* black. Imaginings of a black Obama make possible a brand of black "power" that is an essential rather than incidental asset in the struggle for perceived positional superiority between East and West.

A blend of "Asian"-like video game and anime tunes, such as the signature themes of fictional martial arts characters Krillin and Cell (from *Dragonball Z*), and Guile and Ryu (from *Street Fighter II*). Obama's black-American identity and U.S. covert operations are here infused with an alchemical composite of ninja lore, from which is derived the auratics of extralegal honor, discipline, and stealth.

To complement these videos, America's visual ecosystem was flooded with posters, pins, image macros, and banners that reflected a similar type of racial interplay. See, for example, figures 9.4–9.7.

Meanwhile, pundits and sociopolitical observers were offering up commentary that resonated strikingly with these graphics and YouTube productions. Bill Maher, for example, during the May 6 broadcast of his HBO program,

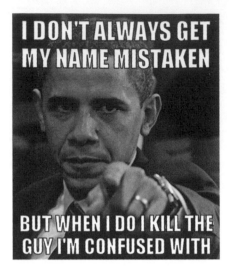

FIGURE 9.4. With his confident, direct gaze and finger-pointing address, Obama's leadership philosophy is presented as unflinchingly American. Note how the pose recalls J. M. Flagg's famous 1917 "I WANT YOU FOR U.S. ARMY" Uncle Sam poster, used to recruit American soldiers for World War I and World War II. By killing Osama and disentangling himself from perceived associations with "Islam," Obama is inducted into the iconic, nationalist Uncle Sam (U.S.) military tradition. (Eat Liver, 2011, accessed July 29, 2011, http://www.memes.com/img/65198)

FIGURE 9.5. This image macro slackens the finger-pointing posture of the previous depiction, so as to add an air of nonchalance, along with a sarcastic "shout-out" style retort to the diminished birther claim that Obama is not an American. (*Boston Phoenix*, May 6, 2011, accessed July 30, 2011, http://thephoenix.com/blogs/photos/news/category40807/picture752199.aspx)

FIGURE 9.6. This image has been altered so as to cap Obama with a (black) cowboy hat, a symbol of the American frontier and the cowboy culture of the Wild West. By associating Obama with the romanced terrain of the American West, the aesthetic argument serves to humiliate claims that Obama is not an American citizen and not, in a related sense, a "Westerner." Perhaps it communicates the sentiment that Obama is in fact *so* American that, with his straight-shooting manner, he has little time or interest in effete East Coast trivialities such as paperwork and certificates. (Social Lunchbox, 2011, accessed July 30, 2011, http://memerial.net/2335-anything-else)

FIGURE 9.7. Visual hyperbole satirizes, and contributes to, the racial superherofication of Obama, equipping the leader with nunchucks and black sunglasses as he escapes from a harrowing combination shark attack/helicopter-and-car crash on a skateboard, with a relaxed smile on his face. (Vi.sualize.us, 2011, accessed July 29, 2011, http://vi.sualize.us/nox/)

Real Time, challenged Republicans to "just admit that Barack Obama is one efficient, steely-nerved, multitasking, black, ninja, gangsta president . . . [who] personally rappelled into bin Laden's secret lair and put a Chinese star down his throat without waking up any of his 13 wives." In this same bit, Maher put forth the following observation, which provocatively highlights the oppositional friction between Obama's American, counterterroristic blackness and his ostensible association with brown "Islamic" terrorism: "It was a Democrat who put a bomb in Gaddafi's bedroom and put a bullet in bin Laden's eye like Moe Green, raising the question: How many Muslims does a black guy have to kill in one weekend before crackers climb down off his ass?"[14]

Maher's question articulates a zero-sum representational inclusivity, in which a racially ambiguous Obama is offered the opportunity to "prove his color(s)" as a black *American*—satisfying white (or "cracker") concerns over his citizenship, patriotism, and racial/religious allegiances—by executing *American* imperial violence against the contrasting arch-brownness of the Orient. Thus, the killing of bin Laden, along with the virtually cotemporaneous release of Obama's long-form birth certificate, had a "naturalizing" effect on the president, a bestowal underwritten by a temporary alliance between white Americanness and black vernacular criminality *on the condition* that such blackness be (con)scripted to direct its threatening energies *outward* against a common Arab/Muslim foe.

In many ways, this conditional reconciliation of blackness and whiteness is simply the realization in American political culture of the common pop-cultural practice of glamorizing the imagined "ghetto" and figuring the black males that emerge from it as possessing extraordinary capabilities to protect the general population. Will Smith's roles in *Independence Day* and *Men in Black,* for example, are illuminating in this regard, as both films cast Smith as an unconventional hero who is able to protect planet Earth—the headquarters of which is stationed in the United States—from ill-intentioned aliens from outer space. (Smith's roles in *I Am Legend* and *I, Robot,* which pit humans against semi-zombies and robots-run-amuck, respectively, might also function in this manner.) A primary distinguishing characteristic of black male protector protagonists (of which Smith is only one of many examples) is their unique, racialized ability—and thus "our" ability as participant consumers[15]—to accomplish the mission with inimitable grace, flow, nonchalance, elegant indifference, and eloquent violence. These aesthetics rely upon conflations of efficacy with violence, ethics with vengeance, status with suave criminality, and dominance with "masculinity."[16] Sanitized black "bosses" are thereby marketed as emblems of the type of coolness that is lacking in predominantly white populations and power structures in need of racial assistance to fend off threats from more othered others, that is, others who may speak a foreign language, worship a foreign-seeming God, and appear not only different but fundamentally alien and unassimilable.

In addition to the rescue and transplantation of ontological mojo, this particular trope of vernacular blackness is serviceable to the mythology of the U.S. War on Terror—with its black sites, black projects, Black Hawks, Blackwaters, missions that take place "in the blackness of night," and so forth—because of the festive permissibility with which black(ed) cultural actors characteristically bend, break, or regard themselves as above the law (even in the relatively hyper-"safe" portrayal of Will Smith in *Men in Black,* his agency still operates without the authorization or awareness of the U.S. government). The type of stylized, blockbuster "gangstas" I have been describing here are recruited onto the scene (in a way, they are voted into culture as Obama was voted into office) specifically for their racially prefigured capacity to achieve their goals "by any means necessary," with a valorized disregard for any form of established jurisdiction that would impede their efforts. This pop-cultural sanctioning of criminal success evidenced itself in the American political imaginary as the public received news of President Obama's decision to covertly send U.S. forces into Pakistan to kill bin Laden without first informing the Pakistani government. By and large, the extralegality of this action was condoned and, in some cases, even appreciated for its very indifference to international boundaries. In the *Real Time* monologue cited above, for example, Bill Maher exclaimed, "In 2008, the candidates were asked, if they knew for sure that bin Laden was in Pakistan, would you send our guys in without permission to get him? McCain said no, because Pakistan is a sovereign nation. Obama said yes, *he'd just do it.* And McCain called him naïve. Who's being naïve now, Kay?"

Maher might have been more critical of this imagined alacrity to violate the territorial sovereignty of a Muslim-majority nation—an impulse whose legitimizing logic appears as a recitation of the perplexingly meaningless but effective Nike slogan, "Just Do It"—were it to emerge from the damn-the-torpedoes machismo of the Bush administration, but as his remarks reveal, Maher approved of not only the philosophy and strategy behind the operation to take bin Laden out, but also the racialized *style* with which it was fantasized to be executed. Here we are presented with an inward-gazing erotics of imperialism, whereby the actions of a black president are publicly savored and delighted in for the lusciously "badass" manner in which they are enacted against a more threatening—in the context of "the War on Terror"—other, the foreignness of brown(ed) Arabs/Muslims. While this exchange between the president and the public rests upon the troubled premise of extralegal violence, the sensual indulgence in the auratics of state-sanctioned "black" criminality are deproblematized for the very reason they are made possible: the imperial nation has heroically elected a member of a historically marginalized population to represent and defend the homeland. As Erica R. Edwards, in her work on portrayals of black leadership, notes, cinematic depictions of African American heads of state in times of crisis demonstrate "how US popular culture manipulates representations of the image of black presidency to affirm the violent operations of American empire even while cleansing its perpetrators of guilt."[17] In an example of reality imitating fiction, the superimposition of vernacular black criminality onto the figure of President Obama serves the purpose of normalizing—perhaps even "white-ing out"—the ironies of exporting "the rule of law" through flagrantly extralegal routes.

The dynamics of this inward-gazing erotic imperialism and the attendant co-generation of blackness/whiteness (at the expense of "brownness") are further illuminated by Toni Morrison's suggestion that the defining attributes of American literature and culture—despite having been authored almost exclusively by white people—came into distinguishable coherence only against the backdrop of "a dark, abiding, signing Africanist presence." Through a process that Morrison refers to as "American Africanism," white American identity is forged amid the tumult of its engagement with and erasure of the experience of an "unsettled and unsettling" black population. Just as an "Orient" is necessary to give rise to an "Occident" in the cartography of American Orientalism, a "real or fabricated Africanist presence" is "crucial to [a] sense of Americanness" in Morrison's conception.[18]

While not engaging directly with Morrison, Ahmed's meditation on the technology of the reproduction of whiteness offers a useful lens through which to examine how the blacking of counterterror was used to coordinate the intertextual exchanges of "Obama" and "Osama" at the crossroads of American Orientalism and American Africanism. Working off bell hooks's notion of appropriation as "eating the other," Ahmed writes: "To *become* black through proximity to others is *not* to *be* black; it is to be 'not black' by the very extension of the body toward blackness. Becoming confirms nonbeing through how it extends the very surface of being toward that which is not it. As an orientation toward others, whiteness gets reproduced even in the moment it acquires some color."[19]

In this manner, in the wake of the killing of bin Laden, sectors of the American Occident were vivified and clarified as "white" through a figuring of Obama as a necessarily black "boss" who could unveil and unleash a lethal, awesome blackness to destroy bin Laden, thereby recuperating the racially encrypted legend of American exceptionalism. By accentuating and harnessing Obama's blackness, U.S. public culture could become more black and, through the workings of Ahmed's paradox, more "white," thereby accumulating an invigorated sense of purpose and capacity to affirm its positional superiority over the brownness of the Orient and find its dominating position in the world.

The widely circulated "Situation Room Photo" (see figure 9.8) provides an intriguing visual dramatization of this process. The killing action that takes place in the Orient, in Pakistan, occurs offscreen. Viewers are not privy to, or perhaps they are guiltlessly spared from, witnessing the impact of U.S. military force in

FIGURE 9.8. "Obama and Biden await updates on bin Laden," popularly referred to as "The Situation Room Photo." Credit: Pete Souza, Official White House Photographer. This image is a work of an employee of the Executive Office of the President of the United States, taken or made as part of that person's official duties. Under the terms of U.S. federal government work, the image is in the public domain.

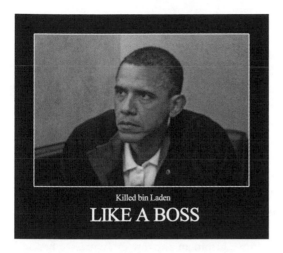

Killed bin Laden

LIKE A BOSS

FIGURE 9.9. Obama's face is cropped into focus in this "Situation Room Photo" appropriation, singling him out as if he were the sole person responsible for the killing of bin Laden, highlighting the legendary connection between the two men. (Retrieved from The Jonestown Blog, May 2, 2011, http://jonestownblog .blogspot.com/2011/05/killed -bin-laden-like-boss.html)

the Orient. This shield of invisibility generates an abstraction of power[20] that preserves the sublimity of the Orient's "farness," yet, through the mediating presence of Obama as an unconventional *axis mundi* of imperial control (the photograph provides a kind of civil-religious headquarters effect), Osama and the Orient are brought within reach, mastered, killed, and, consequentially, domesticated through this death. While President Obama is kept at a remove (he is voyeuristically observed, eaten as he sits crouched—almost hiding, nearly concealed, as if his presence were a trick up the government's sleeve—in the corner of the white room) through the inherent spatiotemporal distance between a photograph and its viewer, Osama and the Orient are *twice* removed, creating a permeable buffer—a tinted two-way mirror—through which white imperial identity is able to engulf the imaginings of blackness and brownness without having to touch either of them. For a pithy and pitch-perfect articulation of this dynamic, see figure 9.9.

Seeing through Legends

> When the sage says: "Go over," he does not mean that we should cross over to some actual place, which we could do anyhow if the labor were worth it; he means some fabulous yonder, something unknown to us, something too that he cannot designate more precisely, and therefore cannot help us here in the very least. All these parables really set out to say merely that the incomprehensible is incomprehensible, and we know that already. But the cares we have to struggle with every day: that is a different matter.
>
> —Franz Kafka, "On Parables"

On May 1, while the majority of Muslims across the United States and around the world were welcoming the news of bin Laden's demise with varying degrees of relief and celebration, graffiti vandals in Portland, Maine, spray-painted the outside of the Maine Muslim Community Center with phrases such as, "Osama today, Islam tomorrow" and "Long live the West."[21] Similar attacks soon followed: in Shreveport, Alabama, pork was hung from the door handle of a mosque; in Sheepshead Bay, Brooklyn, the words "He's Dead" were painted on a mosque construction site; and in Houston, Texas, a group of masked men sneaked into a local mosque, doused prayer rugs with gasoline, and set the building on fire.[22] During these same weeks, eggs were thrown at a nightclub owned by a Muslim man in Anaheim, California; a ninth-grade algebra teacher in Friendswood, Texas, was put on leave after he allegedly asked a student if she was mourning the death of her "uncle," Osama; and two imams on their way to a peace conference were removed from an airplane in Tennessee because their religious garb made passengers feel—according to the pilot who refused to take off with the men on board—"uncomfortable."[23]

One might speculate that these hate crimes represent isolated incidents that are not reflective of popular sentiment, but there is distressing evidence to the contrary. A nationwide poll from the Ohio State University School of Communication found a marked devaluation of non-Muslims' opinion of Muslims, revealing that, in the immediate aftermath of the death of Osama bin Laden, non-Muslims were far more likely to support restrictions on American Muslims' civil liberties, to perceive greater intercultural differences, and to regard American Muslims as the primary source of religious tension in the United States. Table 9.1, taken from the Ohio State poll, indicates general perceptions about American Muslims, both before and after the death of Osama bin Laden.[24]

Table 9.1. Perceptions about American Muslims

Muslims are:	Prior to bin Laden's Death (% agree)	After bin Laden's Death (% agree)
Trustworthy[1]	49	33
Peaceful[1]	48	33
Moderate[1]	39	25
Safe[1]	40	31
Tolerant[1]	45	33

1. Respondents who reported the terms *somewhat* or *very* applied to Muslims.
From Erik Nisbet, Michelle Ortiz, Yasamin Miller, and Andrew Smith, "The 'Bin Laden' Effect: How American Public Opinion about American Muslims Shifted in the Wake of Osama bin Laden's Death," School of Communication, Ohio State University, July 20, 2011.

From one perspective, the exacerbation of the anxiety that Islam is at war with the West and fundamentally counter to notions of American values appears fundamentally at odds with the apparent reality that Muslims were, by and large, equally as satisfied about bin Laden's death as non-Muslims.[25] As President Obama felt compelled to remind his audience during his May 1, 2011 address, "Osama bin Laden was not a Muslim leader; he was a mass murderer of Muslims."[26] Furthermore, these events took place in the midst of the Arab Awakening in North Africa and the Middle East, which demonstrated a monolith-defying array of Arab/Muslim subjectivities that could have opened up space for counter-hegemonic narratives to sever irrational associative linkages between "Islam" and terror. With this in mind, one wonders: Why didn't the bankrupt structures of anti-Muslim prejudice weaken beneath the burden of their own contradictions—and why, in fact, did the exact opposite occur?

The authors of the Ohio State study attribute the rise in anti-Muslim sentiment to a media "focusing event," that is, to the fact that the news of bin Laden's death returned long-simmering thematic concerns over Islam and terrorism back to the front burner of cultural consciousness. To this I would add that 9/11 was a (metaphorical) trauma, which I define as an experience of mortal helplessness and a subsequent misinterpretation of that experience that leads one to believe that the perceived source of the danger (in this case, as evidenced by the spike in anti-Muslim sentiment, the false and fuzzy category of "brownness") is still present as it was at the time of the injury. The media "focus," then, provided a posttraumatic window through which the actual source of the danger (a realistic appraisal of and calibrated response to the threat of terrorist attacks against the United States, rather than the proxy phobia of all things "brown" seeming), could be vividly observed and interrogated from a more reasonable perspective. But by and large, this process—one that I would venture to describe as a legitimate "healing" intervention—did not occur. What instead took place on a mass scale was a deep and bright re-misinterpretation of the threat; the prejudices at play were merely kindled and reoriented—Africanist blackness refracted through the prism of Orientalist brownness—rather than reinterpreted and extinguished.

While "Obama got Osama" may have seemed like a justified, even moral, counterresponse to the insidious claim that Obama *is* Osama, the real-life consequences of this symbolic overturn included, as I hope to have demonstrated in this chapter, increased public support and romanticization of extralegal military operations, a virtual festival of indulgence in fetishized blackness, exacerbation of American nationalist fervor, and overt discrimination and violence against Arabs/Muslims. These serious complications are both revelatory—in that they bring to light cultural matter(s) and dynamics—and cautionary. They raise the question as to how, and when, and whether academics, activists, and anyone with an interest in such things should engage in the production and dissemination of "good" legends of valorized *racialization* ("It Took Obama to Get Osama") in what might be a well-intentioned campaign to combat "bad" legends composed of a purely *racist* poetry ("Obama is Osama"). While the "O ama/O ama" case as I have presented it here does not offer a universal pre-scription regarding the degree to which those with antiracist ambitions should promote legends so seductive that they *seem to speak* entirely from and for themselves with the authority of a transcendent messenger, it does, I believe, demonstrate the critical utility of asking why we tell ourselves these legends in the first place and, observing the conductive manner and the mediums through which they are told, understanding how they entwine and collide and create cultural cartographies as well as the tools with which they are read.

Notes

1. This first definition of *legend* as "a 'symbolic representation of folk belief and collective experiences' that serves to reaffirm the common values of a group" is taken from Timothy R. Tangherlini, "'It Happened Not Too Far from Here . . .': A Survey of Legend Theory and Characterization," *Western Folklore* 49, no. 4 (October 1990): 371–90.

2. Edward W. Said, *Covering Islam: How the Media and the Experts Determine How We See the Rest of the World*, rev. ed. (New York: Vintage Books, 1997), xxvii.

3. Sara Ahmed, *Queer Phenomenology: Orientations, Objects, Others* (Durham, NC: Duke University Press, 2006), 116, emphasis in the original.

4. Ibid., 116–20.

5. Henry Luce, "The American Century," *Life Magazine*, February 17, 1941, 61–65.

6. Barack Obama, *The Audacity of Hope: Thoughts on Reclaiming the American Dream* (New York: Crown, 2006), 7.

7. Carmen R. Lugo-Lugo and Mary K. Bloodsworth-Lugo, "Black as Brown: The 2008 Obama Primary Campaign and the U.S. Browning of Terror," *Journal of African American Studies* 13, no. 2 (2009): 110–20.

8. Mary K. Bloodsworth-Lugo and Carmen R. Lugo-Lugo, "Citizenship and the Browning of Terror." *Peace Review: A Journal of Social Justice* 20, no. 3 (2008): 273–82. The "new kind" of world/threat discourse was deployed consistently throughout the George W. Bush years—promulgated by neoconservative thinkers, War on Terror media analysts, and government officials, including President Bush—as a justification for the unprecedented extralegal practices of the administration. For example, in a January 2002 memo to President Bush, Alberto Gonzales stated: "The war against terrorism is a new kind of war. In my judgment, this new paradigm renders obsolete Geneva's strict limitations on

questioning of enemy prisoners and renders quaint some of its provisions." Gonzales memo found in G. B. Trudeau, *Doonesbury.com's The War in Quotes* (Kansas City, MO: Andrews McMeel, 2008), 84.

9. "Growing Number of Americans Say Obama Is a Muslim," Pew Research Religion & Public Life Project August 18, 2010, http://pewresearch.org/pubs/1701/poll-obama -muslim-christian-church-out-of-politics-political-leaders-religious.

10. "Chuck Norris' dire warning for America–2012," September 1, 2012, MrNorrisVideos, http://www.youtube.com/watch?feature=player_embedded&v=7ud3pK5Wa90#!.

11. On April 27, 2011, the Obama administration released the president's long-form birth certificate from the Hawaii State Department of Health in an effort to ameliorate the concerns of those who felt that Obama might not have been born in the United States (these skeptics are often referred to as "birthers") and would therefore be a noncitizen and illegitimate president. See Dan Pfeiffer, "President Obama's Long Form Birth Certificate," White House Blog, http://www.whitehouse.gov/blog/2011/04/27/president-obamas -long-form-birth-certificate.

12. According to knowyourmeme.com, "'Like a Boss' is a catchphrase often used in image macros or GIFs that feature a person completing an action with authority and finesse. Similar to 'Haters Gonna Hate,' the characters in the macros have an air of supe-riority and do not care how others perceive them." The phrase is also a popular hashtag on Twitter and Tumblr (hence, the title of this essay), used—often in irony and racially inflected mock self-deprecation—to indicate when someone has accomplished a task in said manner.

13. *The Delta Force* was placed on Jack G. Shaheen's "Worst List" in his encyclopedic cataloging of Arab portrayals in American cinema. See Jack G. Shaheen, *Reel Bad Arabs: How Hollywood Vilifies a People* (New York: Olive Branch Press, 2001), 550.

14. Bill Maher (writer and producer) and Paul Casey (director), *Real Time with Bill Maher*, episode 212, May 6, 2011 (Los Angeles: HBO, 2011).

15. While I am focusing primarily on a "white" imaginary, this projection may be partici-pated in by subjects of all races. It could be thought of as a cloud of personality into which one may pass through, or a gear into which one may shift, regardless of the phenotypical markers of the subject. In his August 10, 2011, *Huffington Post* article, for example, African American political commentator Morris O'Kelly encouraged the president to "go 'Samuel L. Jackson' on the Republicans." In this entry, Kelly stated that if Obama were to address Americans "á la 'Julius' citing Ezekiel 25:17, [it] wouldn't only be cool, it would now be ap-propriate." The reference is to the famous *Pulp Fiction* scene in which Jackson's character, Jules Winnfield, intimidates and then murders a group of terrified, green-footed criminals. The execution—delivered with a combination of poised informality and magniloquent fury—involves the recitation of the aforementioned biblical prophecy, highlighting how a connection between "badass," blockbuster blackness and "Christianity" might enable a cross-racial Judeo-Christian alliance against the Orient. Morris W. O'Kelly, "Time for President Obama to Channel Samuel L. Jackson," *Huffington Post*, August 10, 2011, http:// www.huffingtonpost.com/morris-w-okelly/time-for-president-obama-_1_b_922913.html.

16. Pertinent examples of how gendered humiliation factors into the positional struggle between Occident and Orient can be seen in the posthumous "emasculation" of Osama bin Laden, e.g., footage of him rocking back and forth in a distinctly domestic posture, wrapped in a pink blanket (Jon Stewart referred to it as a "jihad Snuggie"), as well as disclosure that he had a stash of pornography and reports—later retracted—that he had used a woman as a human shield.

17. Erica R. Edwards, "The Black President Hokum," *American Quarterly* 63, no. 1 (March 2011): 33–59.

18. Toni Morrison, *Playing in the Dark: Whiteness and the Literary Imagination* (Cambridge, MA: Harvard University Press, 1992), 5–6.

19. Ahmed, *Queer Phenomenology,* 128, emphasis in the original.

20. This recalls the abstraction of power engendered by the usage of drones. The joystick imperialism of dropping bombs through unmanned horizontal (from different continents) and vertical (from the sky) dimensions could be viewed as a modern-day incarnation of the Foucauldian guillotine, the killing power that "takes place almost without touching the body." See Michel Foucault, *Discipline and Punish: The Birth of the Prison,* trans. Alan Sheridan (New York: Vintage Books, 1977), 13.

21. Asma Uddin, "Graffiti Is Illegal; Anti-Islam Remarks are Not," CNN.com, May 13, 2011, http://www.cnn.com/2011/OPINION/05/13/uddin.muslims.post.binladen/index.html?iref=allsearch. Dahr Jamail, "Fomenting Nationalism with Murder," Al Jazeera English, May 3, 2011, http://english.aljazeera.net/indepth/features/2011/05/201153195123966914.html.

22. Marie Diamond, "Attacks on U.S. Mosques Rise following bin Laden's Death," *Think Progress,* May 17, 2011, http://thinkprogress.org/politics/2011/05/17/166778/mosque-hate-crimes-obl/.

23. Nancy Ramsey, "Anti-Muslim Incidents in the U.S. Follow the Death of Osama bin Laden," ABCnews.com, May 6, 2011, http://abcnews.go.com/US/osama-bin-ladens-death-anti-muslim-incidents-us/story?id=13540940.

24. Erik Nisbet, Michelle Ortiz, Yasamin Miller, and Andrew Smith, "The 'Bin Laden' Effect: How American Public Opinion about American Muslims Shifted in the Wake of Osama bin Laden's Death," School of Communication, Ohio State University, July 20, 2011, http://www.eriknisbet.com/files/binladen_report.pdf.

25. Niraj Warikoo, "Arab Americans, Muslims Rejoice at Death of bin Laden," *Detroit Free Press,* May 3, 2011.

26. Macon Phillips, "Osama bin Laden Dead," White House Blog, May 2, 2011, http://www.whitehouse.gov/blog/2011/05/02/osama-bin-laden-dead.

Congratulations! You Have Killed Osama bin Laden!!

SIMON FERRARI

One of the easiest, and most common, ways to begin an academic essay on videogames is to start with an experiential point of view into a gameworld that the reading audience presumably knows little about beforehand. The language is often overwrought, it addresses the reader as if he or she were an interactor, and it exaggerates or omits many details about the game in question. Perhaps we do this because the medium still seems so new and strange to much of the academic community. Maybe it is a holdover from the era when writing about "computer games" could only mean writing about text-based interactive fiction. Or, finally, it could be the ethnographer's penchant for thick description as applied to the study of virtual worlds.

The trick is to convey a feeling of agency and immersion through text, constructing a mental model of the play experience for the benefit of your readers. If I had decided to take this tack, we might have begun with something like this:

> It is only a few weeks after the events of September 11th, 2001. You stand in a curiously casual chamber, perhaps a middle-class dining room, gazing upon the infamous person of Osama bin Laden. Despite being bound to a chair, the man smiles coolly at you. Is he daring you to act? At your right, a variety of tools offer themselves to your contemplation and use. Will you begin the villain's punishment with bolt cutters, a dentist's drill, or the Louisville Slugger?[1]

You can imagine where it goes from there. Reflecting on how to describe these games and their broader cultural implications, it becomes clear that many of the usual methods and stories will not suffice. Many of these early games are flagrantly abhorrent to propriety and taste, but they contain tiny hints at the future development of so-called serious games and design lessons all but lost to the past.

Writing about bin Laden games means writing about one of four virtual activities: whacking Osama bin Laden on the head, shooting bin Laden as he pops out of a hole or hidden lair, torturing bin Laden with blunt and sharp objects, or, bizarrely, playing dress-up with bin Laden. The bulk of these games were published under the "War on Terror" subheading on the popular site Newgrounds within a month of the September 11 attacks.[2] They were made quickly and crudely by amateur designers, angry teens, and young adults. An analysis of these games sits uncomfortably under the heading of "bin Laden in popular culture" because they are "popular" in the sense of "by the people" rather than in that of "played for hundreds of hours by millions of people" (as in the case of, say, the *Call of Duty* series of games).

I say all this because it is important to know that when we talk about "Osama bin Laden videogames," it is not often the equivalent of talking about "bin Laden films," such as Kathryn Bigelow's *Zero Dark Thirty*.[3] Rather, it is more like talking about "bin Laden YouTube videos." Most of the videogames are not mature attempts at interactively articulating the wide range of emotions and ideas we usually encounter when dealing with media about the ongoing War on Terror. They are not really even fun, in most conventional senses of the word. As discussed later in more detail, professional videogame developers in both the mainstream "AAA" and indie industries have largely avoided the subject of bin Laden, despite the recent preponderance of modern warfare-style shooter games.

To be clear: do not take the above description of this genre as neither "mature" nor "fun" as a value judgment. In her analysis of the development of videogames as a medium of expression, Janet H. Murray likens early experiments in new digital genres to *incunabula*; this Latinate word refers to books printed before the establishment of design conventions for the folio and the page.[4] The fact is that many of the bin Laden games were developed well before the indie or serious games industries existed in their current forms. There are still no universally accepted methodologies for the creation of political videogames; the "immature" artifacts explored in this chapter thus represent our medium's first hesitant steps into a new realm of artistic creation and responsibility.

Similarly, the word "fun" represents a significant controversy among game designers and critics—especially in the consideration of politically expressive games. If we take "fun" to mean "enjoyable" or "amusing," and we hold (as many do) that people play games to have fun experiences, then the designers of artistic or political games face a nontrivial conundrum: the War on Terror is not amusing or enjoyable. To get around this problem, we tend to execute one of two common rhetorical moves; either we attempt to broaden the definition of fun, or we argue that fun isn't actually crucial to the definition of play. Because so many laypeople reject the latter, it is much more common to see designers argue along the lines that "fun" means something like "the act of mastering a problem mentally."[5] Robin Hunicke, Marc LeBlanc, and Robert Zubek expound on the many types of fun: sensation, fantasy, narrative, challenge, fellowship, discovery, expression, and submission.[6] So we might say that the bin Laden games are fun in the fantasy, narrative, and challenge registers, but many game enthusiasts and designers would probably remain skeptical.

All of the videogames discussed in this chapter belong to the budding genre of "newsgames."[7] Broadly understood, a newsgame is any game (digital or analog) that embodies one of the functions or goals of journalistic endeavor.[8] These games take current events and ongoing social issues as their subject matter; their creators release them while their embedded narratives might still be considered fresh or relevant. Most of them are created independently of moneyed interests and powerful stakeholders. Their creation contributes to public discourse, though they often embody personal opinions rather than objective truths. Only the most sophisticated examples of the genre are developed through a process derived from traditional reporting, focused on the collection and synthesis of verified information.[9]

In *Newsgames: Journalism at Play*, my coauthors and I establish a rough typology of games that accomplish different modes of newsmaking: *current event games*, including the first wave of bin Laden games, are like playable editorial cartoons or opinion columns; *documentary games* are more complex computational models of the spaces or logics involved in historical events; *literacy games* attempt to teach the practice of journalism or reinforce our collective faith in the value of journalistic labor; *news puzzles* and interactive *infographics* can make current event data playable; and, finally, we identify a number of *community* activities and software *platforms* that might aid in the rapid or ongoing production of journalistic interactives.[10] Since the time of its writing, no new artifacts have given us cause to modify this typology.

This mode of production is dynamic and reactive. The newsgame genre grows cyclically in response to changes in digital journalism and other media involved in the representation of current events. They might take television, photography, cinema, hypertext narrative, and mainstream game design as inspirations and counterpoints. The bin Laden videogames were produced during a time when nearly every representational medium faced a crisis of sustainability. Even though the results often strike one as hopelessly naive or underdeveloped, reflecting a lack of proper journalistic training on the part of these young designers, they embody the struggle of a new medium attempting to remediate prior media while exploring its own formal peculiarities.

I begin with an exploration of games about the news and one method of critiquing them. The second section deals with the first wave of Flash games made after September 11, 2001 (the term *Flash game* denotes any videogame created in Adobe's Flash software development platform). Then I compare and contrast those early offerings with the more refined documentary videogames made after bin Laden's death. Finally, I reflect on how the mainstream industry has capitalized on the War on Terror and what a look back at this tumultuous decade of experimentation tells us about the state of game design and its relation to the broader context of cultural production.

Newsgames and Procedural Rhetoric

One shared critical model and authoring strategy for newsgames research is Ian Bogost's notion of *procedural rhetoric*. Briefly, procedural rhetoric refers to the act of making rule-based models for the purposes of persuasion.[11] The idea of "procedurality" comes from Janet Murray's explication of the essential properties of digital media. According to Murray, the digital medium is *participatory* in that it allows user interaction, *spatial* in that it represents navigable spacetime, possesses an *encyclopedic* data capacity, and is *procedural*.[12] Murray sets procedurality above and apart from the other essential characteristics, as it refers to the computer's "defining ability to execute a series of rules" expressed as algorithms in code.[13]

Bogost's argument is that rules are the primary meaning-making structures in games and other software—the visuals, dialogue, user interface, and other elements merely reinforce or strengthen the basic worldview expressed by the rules. Whenever we perceive that a game's explicit subject matter is matched well with the underlying processes driven by the game's rules, we call it a *tight coupling*.[14] Newsgames are thus a new way of doing journalism in that they do not primarily convey journalistic facts or editorial opinions through text, audio, or video; rather, they "simulate how things work by constructing models that people can interact with."[15]

The most concrete example of procedural rhetoric in a newsgame remains Gonzalo Frasca's *September 12*, which is an experimental meditation on the cyclical causes and effects of terrorist activity.[16] Although the game does not deal explicitly with bin Laden or even Al Qaeda, it exposes a fundamental and tragic logic at work within the War on Terror. Peering down upon an ordinary afternoon in a bustling Middle Eastern marketplace, the game's point of view apes that of the "god game" genre. In games of this kind, players typically have the ability to directly manipulate digital actors or their surroundings in order to influence how the simulation of their lives will play out. But in *September 12*, clicking anywhere on the screen will initiate a countdown to a missile strike.

A player's ostensive task in *September 12* is to rid the marketplace of cartoonish "terrorist" characters interspersed throughout the crowd. The crosshairs of the mouse cursor imply that a projectile will be instantly deployed to the terrorist's location; however, Frasca simulates the lag between missile targeting systems and their payload delivery. By the time the missile reaches the market, it is likely that the terrorist has moved. Whenever a missile strikes, it is likely to take out passersby as well as the stated targets. If a nonterrorist NPC (non-player character) walks past the corpse of an innocent, he or she briefly mourns before morphing into a terrorist.

Players quickly realize that the idea of a "surgical" missile strike is a fairy tale, and they interactively experience Frasca's embedded argument about how the impulse to terrorist activity spreads. There is only one "win" in the game: never fire a missile at all. Bogost labels the procedural rhetoric at work here a "rhetoric of failure," a system in which any allowed action by the player will only ever result in an increasingly negative game state.[17] The underlying systems at work in games drawing upon this rhetoric are arguably "broken," in that they never reach a stable end state. Thus, the rhetoric of failure is often used to reflect the equally broken nature of real-world policies—according to Frasca's simulation, the War on Terror as it has been practiced since the attacks of September 11 will necessarily always fail to achieve its stated goals.

After 9/11: Osama bin Laden Flash Games

The earliest games about Osama bin Laden are curious artifacts, in that they predate the development of political games by academics and artists. Powerful Robot Games didn't publish *September 12* until 2003, nearly two years after the bulk of the War on Terror games hosted by Newgrounds. They also came about before the advent of the burgeoning independent game industry. Although the Independent Games Festival began recognizing the work of smaller game developers in 1999, it didn't come into its own as a cultural force until 2005. That year, The Behemoth's *Alien Hominid* took home a number of prizes—including "technical excellence," "innovation in visual art," and the audience award—and The Behemoth is co-owned by Tom Fulp, who also created and maintained Newgrounds.[18]

Three days after the September 11 attacks, twenty-two-year-old Fulp published one of the first bin Laden games. His mildly interactive *Bad Dudes vs. Bin Laden* has been played over 4.5 million times.[19] The game is a send-up of Data East's cult classic arcade beat-'em-up *Bad Dudes vs. DragonNinja*. A slick-haired Secret Service agent (who is employed by "President Ronnie" in both the original and Fulp's remix) asks Player One if he or she is a "bad enough dude to kick [bin Laden's] ass." Walking into a lavish Middle Eastern marketplace, the player clicks on the upper and lower halves of bin Laden's body to deliver a flurry of punches. Bin Laden fights back erratically, but the player easily overtakes him by rapidly clicking.

When bin Laden's health is reduced to zero, a voice intones to "Finish Him" in the style of *Mortal Kombat,* and Player One automatically kicks bin Laden in the scrotum before knocking his head clean off of his torso. The ability to castrate and decapitate the villain would soon become common to many of the bin Laden games. Ed Halter asserts that these games "play to a more organic desire for retribution" than the multitudinous other violent diversions available on Flash game sites.[20] He variously labels them "goofy," "cathartic," and "jingo-nihilistic," recognizing both the hegemonic ideology embedded within them and their legitimate therapeutic value to the games' creators and players.[21]

WHAC-A-MOLE AND POLITICAL GAMES

Roughly half of the bin Laden videogames made in the latter months of 2001 are simple "re-skinnings" of classic fairground redemption games like Whac-A-Mole and the shooting gallery. In game design terminology, re-skinning refers to the act of maintaining the underlying design (or code) of a game while simply swapping out the art assets like graphics and sound effects. The reason for the dominance of simple skin swaps in the budding genre of political games is self-evident; it's the easiest way to make a videogame. Amateur designers can find the formative code for basic game archetypes in online forums and software hubs. Software such as Flash and Game Maker then allow the quick importing of graphical and audio assets, and the coded markers for these data are almost always human-readable.[22]

In *Osama-Whack*, a sparsely animated dog bashes the heads of bin Laden clones as they emerge from one of five holes in a variety of patterns.[23] The setting is a desert topped by an empty blue sky. These holes resonate with the jingoistic cliché of "terrorists hiding in caves" that remain common today, while the whacking animation supplies ample amounts of gore. Players must achieve a defined number of successful hits to progress through two simple stages. At the end of the game, the story and gameplay morph into a *Godzilla*-like fantasy. Bin Laden grows the extra limbs and third eye of a Vedic god, which the player must shoot at while dodging a toxic spray. This visual rhetoric reflects a youthful (or willful) ignorance on the part of *Osama-Whack*'s designer to the difference between Islam and Hinduism, while the toxic spray invokes popular fears of gas attacks and "dirty" bombs.

When abstracted to digital form, the static shooting gallery is little more than a Whac-A-Mole game with the plane of action tilted upright, while clicking remains the sole means of interacting with the field. *BinLaden—Taste of Anthrax* lets players fire at four clones of bin Laden as he executes action movie–style maneuvers in the ruins of a generic Middle Eastern residence.[24] Despite the crude gameplay and schlocky blood spray, it displays a basic understanding of cinematic conventions like depth of field. As bin Laden attempts to juke the player, he shifts between windows in the background, a staircase in the middle, and some protective debris in the screen's foreground. In a motif that became common in the bin Laden Flash games, players can nihilistically choose at any time to detonate a canister of anthrax and coat the screen in a sickening green ooze to achieve instant "victory."

From a procedural rhetoric standpoint, the basic argument encapsulated within Whac-A-Mole and shooting gallery games is always the same (and so obvious that it's almost embarrassing to state). The subject of the re-skinning— in this case bin Laden—is a nuisance who, despite repeated efforts to root him out, simply will not abate. In some cases these games might have a "boss battle" tacked on to the end, but most Whac-A-Mole variants display a form of the rhetoric of failure. Both the number of "moles" appearing and the speed at which they retreat eventually become such that we cannot hope to succeed. At best, players can only hope for a new high score. Further, much of the tactile joy of slamming a padded hammer against a physical arcade cabinet is lost in these digital incarnations.

Two readings of these Whac-A-Mole games immediately present themselves. First, we can simply write them off as another example of digital revenge against the body of bin Laden. This explanation makes the most sense in the case of the earliest bin Laden Whac-A-Mole games. On the other hand, as consumers of media about the War on Terror who endured a decade of constant media coverage on the subject, it's possible to interpret our play experiences here as a form of counterattack against that rhetorical deluge. Here the act of bopping bin Laden on the head becomes a playful analogue for channel surfing away from network news, or ignoring a 9/11 "truther" at a cafe, or leaving the dinner table when conversation turns, yet again, to the subject of the War on Terror. This certainly isn't the most sophisticated or mature of responses, but it does move us past elementary notions of revenge and catharsis.

Toward the end of the 2000s, designers began to create more sophisticated Whac-A-Mole variants related to the War on Terror and, in some cases, even a broad antagonism to the growth of Islam in the West. For example, in November 2009, the right-leaning Swiss People's Party commissioned *Minarett Attack* [*sic*], a propaganda game advocating for a ban on the construction of minarets in Switzerland.[25] Cinque Hicks describes the game:

> Gold colored minarets emerge slowly at random points throughout the landscape, like missiles emerging from silos. The player fires at the minarets with an aiming reticule, and they recede back into the ground when hit. Predictably, minarets begin to emerge too fast to hit. If a given minaret remains unhit longer than a second or two, it becomes permanent, impervious to any further shooting.[26]

The game builds upon the basic underlying rhetoric of Whac-A-Mole to make a new argument about the impetus of cultural forces. *Minarett Attack*'s graphical skin emphasizes the pristine beauty of Swiss mountains and architecture, contrasting them with what the creators see as visually garish mosques. Meanwhile, its procedural rhetoric adds this idea that once one allows markers of "alien" culture time to establish themselves, they gain permanence and accelerate the societal shift that they represent.

Unlike many of the bin Laden Flash games discussed in this section, *Minarett Attack* represents the public opinion of xenophobic politicians rather than the personal, and often anonymous, expressions of teenagers. Despite its admirable level of craftsmanship and design ingenuity, it draws upon the same repugnant caricatures of Islamic culture. The sheer readability of Whac-A-Mole designs make them particularly amenable to conservative rhetoric, asking little of their players as compared to the more nuanced procedural model in Frasca's *September 12*. It is difficult, if not impossible, to conceive of a Whac-A-Mole variant that could represent the cultural and political decisions that led to the current state of global affairs. It is a game about attacking surface effects, rather than digging deeply into the soil to examine the obfuscated causes of change and upheaval.

TABLOID GAMES AND DIGITAL VOODOO DOLLS

One of Halter's keenest insights is that the early bin Laden games hosted by Newgrounds are re-skinnings of the *celebrity assassination* genre of Flash games. Halter notes that Fulp himself had previously created the "classics titles" *Beat*

Up Backstreet Boys! and *Britney Spears Truck Jump*.[27] The bin Laden shooting range game mentioned earlier, *BinLaden—Taste of Anthrax*, bills itself as "a remake of the Assassin classic *Kill NSYNC!*" In Halter's words, assassin games "give the same basic satisfaction obtained by scribbling over the face of your nemesis in a high school yearbook."[28] The dual acts of creating and playing them harbor no illusion of reflection and rationality.

In the early 2000s, Ian Bogost and Gonzalo Frasca had taken on the task of categorizing and critiquing newsgames on their shared blog *Water Cooler Games*. Many Flash games had been made about sporting figures, including a flurry of interest in Zinedine Zidane's infamous headbutt at the 2006 World Cup finals. In 2007, Zach Whalen reacted to a number of "celebrity sleaze" games published by the Game Show Network, highlighting the escapades of such figures as Mel Gibson and Paris Hilton. GSN's *So You Think You Can Drive, Mel?* presents a compelling simulation of the mind of an anti-Semitic drunk driver suffering from *delirium tremens*: players must swerve back and forth along a road to collect beer bottles, while dodging Stars of David thrown by robed Hasidim.[29] Whalen coined the term "tabloid games" for these artifacts, noting how they combined efficient rhetoric with an unambitious subject matter.[30]

Whalen feared that the popularity of these games would overtake the budding interest in more serious journalistic work via newsgames, but it is worth recognizing that the tabloid game genre had been alive and kicking as early as the late 1990s, in the form of the celebrity assassin games tracked by Halter. Tabloid games do not make any deep editorial claim; they simply reinforce popular attitudes about well-known people.[31] The first wave of bin Laden games fit the bill of the tabloid subgenre, even if they represent its darkest and most chilling examples. Unlike even GSN's portrait of Mel Gibson, these games never attempt to explain the mindset of their subject. They are simply about lampooning and punishing the man, an attempt at warding off the dangerous ideas he represents by rendering his image meek, ridiculous, and deceased.

The creator of *The Torture Chamber: Osama Bin Laden* categorized his game as "Simulation—Pet/Buddy." It's a sparse version of a common formula, a doll suspended upright by chains fastened to its wrists and ankles.[32] Players select either a dagger or a baseball bat, which reveals interaction points when the mouse cursor hovers over selected body parts. The bat produces a dull thud no matter where it hits, causing welts to flower on bin Laden's extremities. Dagger strikes work in the same manner, but they generate a sickening slicing sound effect and deep tissue cuts. After enough hits to any bodily region, it explodes (in the case of the bat) or collapses (from dagger wounds) to simulated fanfare. A guillotine and atom bomb make themselves available to produce instant fatality.

TTC: Osama B.L. and *Torture Osama* (described in the introduction) share the same dream. In the first few weeks after the September 11 attacks, gaming children across America wished to be the one to deliver the killing blow to bin Laden. Unsurprisingly, these games abstract the necessary tracking and capturing of bin Laden—if only the creators had known that this process would take so long and that its toll on their country's economy would be so severe. After dying in these games, bin Laden always instantly reappears without a scratch. This never-ending cycle of rebirth and gruesome end procedurally invokes the popular rhetoric that no punishment could ever be severe enough for the man who threatened the safety and stability of the United States.

Looking back at these torture games and news coverage from the following years, what's most apparent about the visual rhetoric of these works is how it predicts the shocking images of abuse at Abu Ghraib prison. While the stark, empty rooms left much to the imagination at the time, they would eventually find real-world analogues in the banal halls of the infamous detention center. Furthermore, their use and manipulation of bin Laden's photographic image bears a striking resemblance to the digitally composited "death photo" of bin Laden circulated among social media sites and news outlets following his demise—a phenomenon discussed in the Moeller, Nurmis, and Barforoush chapter within this book. As this photographic evidence began proliferating, the number of newly produced torture games fizzled out; we can only guess (or hope) that the young creators were sobered by the actualization of their former fantasies.

While I've been calling these artifacts "torture games," an attempt at reading the procedural rhetoric of these games falls mostly flat. They don't attempt to model the system of "advanced interrogation techniques," the practice of which wouldn't reach widespread public attention until years later. It might make the most sense to label these works toys rather than games, recognizing that they don't possess a goal-based structure or the possibility of losing. *Torture Osama* is nothing more than an operationalization of a personal fantasy, taking the player step-by-step through the designer's conception of a perfect castigation. It is a mash-up of execution scenes ripped from Hollywood cinema and the author's own musings on how to turn everyday implements to the purposes of inflicting harm.

PSYCHOSOCIAL MORATORIA

Tom Fulp's *Bad Dudes vs. Bin Laden* (discussed above) also bears an artist's statement, which on Flash game sites is called the "author comments," containing these brief paragraphs:

I've been very conflicted ever since the attack on NYC . . . I was considering making a tribute movie that portrayed the positive acts that occured [*sic*] during the aftermath, but eventually decided to stick with my roots and make a violent video game. I have a hard time trying new things.

I wasn't sure if a game would be appropriate, but I realized that it really is. You see, America is very sad right now, but it is also very ANGRY. People need a way to vent their frustrations, and I feel this can help.[33]

Fulp also ruminates on his desire to see Americans come together to face this strange new foe. In the pregame text, the author comments, and the game's final screen, he repeatedly implores his players to remember that not every person who wears a turban is an enemy of the state. Considering subsequent attempts to stifle the construction of Islamic cultural centers throughout Europe and North America, it is admirable that Fulp set this tone for the online space he curated (even if it wasn't enforced in the comments section).

Halter gives Fulp's earnest disclaimers a pass, but he reacts cynically to a similar missive embedded within *Bin Laden Liquors*, a first-person shooter featuring bin Laden as the owner of an American booze emporium.[34] Despite the implication that such businesses are often owed by Arab Americans and Indian Americans, who fit the description of "bad guys wearing turbans," *Bin Laden Liquors* claims to make "no attempt to stereotype, condemn or discriminate." Responding to this textual rhetoric, Halter calls the disavowal "lame."[35] He later elaborates, connecting many of the bin Laden Flash games to the niche of racist white power games, explaining that "outside commercial channels [. . .] open hatred can be unleashed freely, without fear of reprisal."[36] As a point of contrast, few if any U.S. politicians would openly endorse the xenophobic propaganda design exemplified by the Swiss *Minarett Attack*.

Earlier on in his discussion, after citing an example of a particularly hateful comment left in the margins beneath a bin Laden torture game, Halter muses that "one of the great joys of the Internet is exploring forbidden desires without real-life repercussions."[37] James Paul Gee has identified these ideas of internet anonymity granting us freedom from reprisal and real-life consequences as one of the key learning principles of digital play. Citing the psychologist Eric Erickson, Gee holds that videogames create a *psychosocial moratorium*, or "learning space in which the learner can take risks where real-world consequences are lowered."[38] When a game focuses on skill-based improvement, this moratorium provides a low risk, high reward loop for players building a new procedural literacy.

In the case of the bin Laden Flash games, we might optimistically assert that the moratorium allows us to play with ideology and intense negative emotions without allowing them to overtake us or spill dangerously into our offline lives. But it is equally likely that these games fed an adolescent hunger for iconoclasm. Halter's exploration of the Newgrounds comments sections reveals that many players felt like the games don't go far enough with their violent fantasies. The social ecology fostered by a multitude of media channels throughout the early years of the War on Terror served to normalize this thirst for blood; therefore, it's not clear that internet anonymity and psychosocial moratoria were even necessary for expressing and exorcising the desire these works represent.

After Death: Abbottabad and Documentary Reality

Although videogames about bin Laden continued to sporadically appear over the course of the next ten years, they never departed significantly from the cartoonish gore of the earliest Flash games. But during the week of extensive news coverage on the Navy SEAL raid on Abbottabad, a new kind of bin Laden videogame gained brief prominence. These *documentary* games render bin Laden's Abbottabad compound in 3D, allowing players a kind of virtual tourism cobbled together from different accounts, videos, and diagrams of the event. Unlike the tabloid games discussed above, the documentary genre doesn't editorialize on the historical events it makes playable. Like the cinematic genre that inspired this type of game, it attempts to capture some fleeting aspect of actuality.[39]

The most basic example of a bin Laden documentary game is the *Counter-Strike: Source* map *Fight Yard Abbottabad*.[40] *Counter-Strike* ranks among the most played multiplayer shooters in the history of PC gaming, following its humble origins as a player mod of Valve's single-player *Half-Life*.[41] Starting in the early days of networked first-person shooter (FPS) games, shrewd game developers realized that they could increase a community's involvement in a game, and its overall lifespan, by releasing its level editing tools and allowing players to distribute their creations online. These software packages often provide a stable of stock objects featured in the official version of the game, while affording the easy importing of custom 3D models and textures. *Fight Yard Abbottabad* is thus doubly "of the people," in that it's a player-created map for a player-created game.

Released just a week after bin Laden's death in May of 2011, *FY Abbottabad* appears to be based upon a Pentagon diagram of the compound and brief video clips of a few interior scenes broadcast by ABC News on May 2.[42] It features two open yards, a communications center topped by a satellite dish, and the three-story house in which bin Laden was slain. In this multiplayer map built for team-based competitive play, bin Laden and his family are absent. *Counter-Strike* does, however, make a decent host to this historical space, because its most common gameplay mode pits a team of "terrorists," whose objective is to plant a bomb at a predetermined location, against a team of "counterterrorist" defenders. All *Fight Yard*–type maps for *CS: Source* have the same basic setup, a deathmatch wherein players can select any of the game's weapons from a stockpile near their spawn point.

FY Abbottabad inverts the conventional logic of *Counter-Strike*'s counterterrorism scenario. The "counterterrorist" team (which we can read as the Navy SEALs) assaults the Abbottabad complex, while the "terrorists" (bin Laden's household guard) defend it. Of course, *FY Abbottabad* doesn't make these identities explicit by renaming the teams. It puts forth no argument about the event, nor does it seek to replicate the step-by-step record of the raid—it doesn't even have a nighttime setting. In *Newsgames*, we name this kind of documentary artifact a *spatial reality*, one that simply seeks to make a historical space navigable by interactors.[43] That the conventions and theme of *Counter-Strike* roughly fit the context of the news coverage is simply a surface effect or happy accident.

OPERATIONAL REALITY
AND THE PROBLEM OF TIMELINESS

Just five days after SEAL Team Six completed its mission in Pakistan, two other independent game developers released a different kind of bin Laden documentary game. Jeremy Alessi and his collaborators at a fledgling project called News+Gameplay had followed the Georgia Tech newsgame group's research; they were familiar with the many types of newsgames that had been made before, the unique problems the medium presented, and common arguments about the characteristic strengths of ludic representation.[44] When the first few details about the raid in Abbottabad began surfacing, the team at News+Gameplay began scouring news sources for video footage and examining the layout of bin Laden's compound using Google Earth.[45]

The result of their fifty-hour flurry of activity, *Bin Laden Raid*, is perhaps the most meditative videogame account of the event.[46] A red light flickers from within a helicopter cabin, accompanied by the constant whirr of its blades spinning above. Burning garbage (derived from the Pentagon diagram) sends sparks into the air next to a chicken coop. The player's camera locks itself tightly to the right shoulder of the soldier he or she controls, whose proximity to the virtual lens takes him slightly out of focus. Navigation of the yard and the sparse interiors proceeds slowly; this isn't a tactically realist shooter, but the soldier still cannot uncharacteristically dash with his rifle lowered. Gun-toting defenders flank the hallways, while bin Laden himself waits unarmed in his second-story bedroom.

At almost the same hour, Kuma Reality Games released the eighty-fifth episode of their Kuma\War series, *The Death of Osama bin Laden* (the official designation of the title is "Mission 107," but they skipped some numbers following a long hiatus).[47] This was hardly the first time Kuma, which bills itself as the "nightly news" of games, had covered the death of a high-priority target in the War on Terror; their first episode chronicled the "last stand" of Uday and Qusay Hussein, and they later documented the capture of Saddam Hussein and the guided bombing of Abu Musab al-Zarqawi. Tracey Fullerton takes note of Kuma's oeuvre in her preliminary research into the idea of a documentary game genre. Through personal interviews with Kuma Games CEO Keith Halper, Fullerton teases out notions of the unique value in simulation-based re-creation and the situational awareness gained via first-person navigation.[48]

Drawn from the same information available during the week after bin Laden's demise, Kuma's spatial re-creation of the scene is almost identical to that of Alessi's. Like the rest of the games in their series, Kuma's rendition features more conventionally entertaining gunplay. There are more enemies waiting inside the compound, including women, and AI-controlled squadmates aid the player in battle. Conflicting with after-action reports of the mission, Kuma's bin Laden shoots back at the SEALs who enter his chambers. In order to imbue the episode with replay value, Kuma randomizes bin Laden's spawn location to either his second-story bedroom or a basement-level studio. Overall, the production values appear significantly higher than *Bin Laden Raid*'s, at the cost of adding needless bombast.

In *Newsgames* we characterize Kuma\War's basic model as capturing a kind of *operational reality*, allowing players to enact events rather than simply exploring their spaces haphazardly.[49] Put another way, operational documentaries feature elements of traditional game design like a goal-based structure, the ability to take on a distinct role or identity, and the possibility of selecting or precipitating variable outcomes. Both *Bin Laden Raid* and *The Death of Osama bin Laden* task players with four objectives: neutralize bin Laden's household guard, retrieve his body, collect laptops and other forms of intelligence, and destroy the malfunctioning helicopter. Neither game questions whether bin Laden should have been taken alive, nor do they satirize the U.S. military for the failure of the secondary Black Hawk helicopter. The games' rhetoric is essentially: "These are the events as reported, and that's all you're allowed to do."

In their race to release these bin Laden documentary games as soon as possible, News+Gameplay and Kuma both invoke the problem of timeliness in journalistic labor. Making videogames isn't easy. Even once a team of artists, programmers, and designers learns the requisite tools and practices of the craft, the developer of a newsgame confronts a significant logistical problem. The core of good design is the iterative loop, wherein a game is honed in the back-and-forth interaction between creators and "playtesters" (impartial players whose task it is to discover problems and ask hard questions about the experience). But the twenty-four-hour news cycle forces game developers to accelerate this process, producing results often riddled with bugs, unintended biases, and meager levels of contextual detail.[50]

Alessi's team wisely built *Bin Laden Raid* in the Unity game engine, meaning that it could be quickly played in an ordinary web browser despite its 3D nature. But the interiors of the Abbottabad complex could only be guessed at from scant video coverage available at the time, their contours painstakingly custom-modeled in 3D Studio Max. The only advantage gained by this tailor-made approach is that the spatial dimensions of the compound aren't distorted to suit conventions of "fun" shooter game design. On the other hand, Kuma came to the project with their own internal set of level editing tools and stock objects, which afforded them more satisfying gunplay, lighting effects, and environmental design. Kuma leverages the power of a personalized software *platform*—or constitutive framework upon which other artifacts can be built—in the rapid production of episodic newsgames content.[51] Further, the independent client Kuma uses to distribute all of its games ensures a built-in audience and a framework for including supplementary material, granting them a slight edge in the appearance of objectivity.

RE-CREATION AND THE PROBLEM OF INDEXICALITY

In July 2012, Madeleine Baran of Minnesota Public Radio explored a fascinating subculture brewing in New Hope, Minnesota.[52] At a company called Sealed Mindset, veteran Navy SEAL Commander Larry Yatch designs defense classes ranging from simple weapon handling to elaborate simulations of real-world crime. Yatch's rhetoric is decidedly survivalist, evidenced by quotes from the interview such as this: "If you spend every weekend shooting or every day at the dojo working on your martial arts, you're halfway to being safe." While many of Yatch's spatial and operational scenarios invoke relatively mundane occurrences such as carjackings, kidnappings, and office shootings, the crown jewel of Sealed Mindset's training studio is what Baran calls a "high-end role-playing game" about the raid on bin Laden's Abbottabad compound.

Sealed Mindset's bin Laden simulation is a complex mélange of successful formulas. LARPing, or live-action roleplaying, is nothing new in the world of gaming, though it usually focuses on fantasy scenarios and calculates the results of player actions with conventional tabletop gaming devices like dice rolls and stats sheets. Also, the historical reenactment of famous battles occurs in communities throughout the United States, typically focusing on the well-documented tactical maneuvers, costumes, lingo, and social mores of bygone eras. And, finally, members of the military constantly drill their skills and decision making in elaborate training protocols, especially in preparation for critical missions wherein logistics teams have studied the layouts and architectural plans of a contentious space beforehand.

Yatch's raid scenario couples introductory live arms training with bin Laden target dummies to a spatial re-creation of the second story of bin Laden's compound. Players enter the hallway with paintball guns designed to look like combat rifles, moving as silently and safely as possible to bin Laden's bedroom doorway. Although Yatch tells his players to take bin Laden alive if they are able, their actual encounter with the actor clad in a bin Laden costume plays out predictably: Baran reports that when the players enter his bedroom, bin Laden begins screaming at them while waving two guns in the air. After a player manages to take out their primary target, happy customers pose for photos with the bin Laden pretender lying in paint-splattered repose.

At the time of Baran's coverage, the evening-long experience would set back its participants $325—a decidedly low fee considering the size of Yatch's training space and the prominence of this shared fantasy. With these documentary games, the medium's overriding desire for bin Laden's blood has come full circle. In late 2001, the bin Laden Flash games primarily represented the violent emotions of mostly anonymous young designers and players experiencing a form of solitary revenge online. After bin Laden's death, we witness middle-aged adults constructing a kind of shared community identity around the same event reenacted and realized in analog space.[53] The participants of Sealed Mindset in Baran's document claim to have grown a new appreciation for the mindset of a SEAL in a dangerous situation, though we can assume that this is something of a foregone conclusion.

This final example of a unique kind of bin Laden documentary game brings our optimistic evaluation of the characteristic strengths and pleasures of the interactive medium into stark contrast with an overriding question: Why should we trust the veracity of any newsgame, especially when its creators are so divorced from the professional context of traditional journalism? Cynthia K. Poremba's research into the crafting of documentary gameplay positions the documentary as "the interrelation of an indexical claim and an expressive framing."[54] All indexical documents make a claim to truth, whether they be audio recordings, video evidence, or firsthand accounts of an event. We also typically assume that primary documents provide a causal bridge between reality and an expressive work.[55] But videogames are not a recording medium. A 3D rendering cannot directly replicate photographic evidence, nor does it unproblematically convert a textual record into an interactive progression of events.

Further, Poremba argues that "it is difficult to escape expressive framing as generally speaking, everything becomes interpretable by virtue of the documentary being a designed work."[56] The cinematic medium has ways to make its labor transparent: it can choose long takes over manipulative montage, interview stakeholders with firsthand accounts of an event, capture an occurrence as it happens in real time, and show viewers how the camera may have affected the flow of action or explication. A newsgame, on the other hand, cannot efface its artificiality. It must re-create the space of a historical event from the ground up, whether by theatrical set design or 3D modeling and texturing. Even in the case of a linear interactive experience, players almost always have the ability to manipulate the timing of key actions. And the bulk of primary documents must be included outside the game proper, displayed in streaming video or a page of links that the player may never actually encounter.

Despite the technical and formal differences between bin Laden Flash and documentary games—and disregarding the time span and actual death of the man between these two periods of development—can we recognize any fundamental distinction between the two? The outcome amounts to the same, and the embedded biases remain identical (which must be noted even if I, as an avid player and American citizen, often share them). Operational and spatial realism is all that separates these later artifacts from the earlier fantasies, and even this distinction has been problematized. The theoretical potential for a new kind of ludic objectivity or editorial hasn't been realized in these games, because they seldom delve to requisite levels of process orientation and due diligence.

But the burden of these shortcomings does not fall entirely on the creators profiled above. Independent and experimental game designers do not exist in a cultural vacuum. To finish our exploration of bin Laden's life and death in ludic history, we must examine the wider media ecology of the past decade.

The Mainstream Industry Keeps (Mostly) Mum

A few years into the twenty-first century, the makers of big budget first-person shooters met with a crisis of subject matter. For many years, World War II– and space-themed shooting games had dominated the PC and console markets. The developers most often associated with the creation and popularization of the FPS genre, id Software, established these two dominant themes with *Wolfenstein 3D* and *Doom*, respectively. Although the sales of games allowing players to decimate alien invaders and Nazi storm troopers never noticeably flagged, enthusiasts repeatedly asked game publishers for more timely subject matter to shoot in the head. In 2008, Infinity Ward released *Call of Duty 4: Modern Warfare* to overwhelming fanfare. It revitalized the genre in the eyes of its dedicated players, initiating a more gritty, photorealistic style while innovating significantly on previous models of networked competitive play.

Modern Warfare's single-player campaign begins with a tantalizing first-person sequence in which the player has no control over his or her avatar.[57] While the credits load, the camera zooms down from a spy satellite into an unnamed Middle Eastern nation. The player enters the body of President Yasir Al-Fulani, who is forced into a waiting car by thugs while the voice of Khaled Al-Asad blares from a helicopter-mounted loudspeaker. Asad is finalizing his coup of the unnamed country with a speech cobbled together from real-world insurgent propaganda, decrying Fulani (and thus the player) for collusion with Western powers. The player is then dragged from the car by masked militia and secured to a post in a public square. After taking a handgun from a mysterious one-armed figure, Asad intones that "this is how [the nation's independence] begins" as he fires point-blank into the player's camera.

For those of us following the development of documentary and current event games at the time, the most disquieting thing about the story that follows from *Modern Warfare*'s opening is that it actually isn't about Middle Eastern insurgency at all. Asad's coup is a red herring, as the one-armed man from the opening scene is eventually revealed to be the leader of an "ultranationalist" Russian political movement seeking to return the region to its former status as a Soviet holding. Although *Modern Warfare* borrows the trappings of contemporary current events, its fictional take on international politics is a fantasy wherein the Cold War never ended. Hopelessly backward in play format as well as narrative, the firefights featured throughout its single-player campaign feel copied over from World War II combat scenarios rather than adapted to fit the changing nature of insurgent struggle.[58]

This disappointing decision on the part of Infinity Ward and the game's publisher, Activision, raises an obvious question: if World War II shooters, dating back to *Wolfenstein 3D*, have allowed players to pull the trigger on a historical villain like Adolf Hitler, why wouldn't a modern warfare-style video-game contextualize its fictional struggle against terrorist forces in a real country and against a real villain (like Osama bin Laden)? The answer is probably a combination of multiple factors: insensitivity to the realities of contemporary relations between Russia and the United States, the design team's inability or unwillingness to experiment with procedural models of insurgency and counterterrorism, and a risk-averse publisher fearful of trivializing the real tragedies of the ongoing War on Terror.

THE PROBLEM WITH "MILITARY PARTNERSHIPS"

The risks involved in selling a videogame about recognizable, real-world enemies of the United States were fully realized when Electronic Arts published its competition to the market dominance of the *Call of Duty* franchise. In an effort to update its flagging *Medal of Honor* series, EA enlisted Danger Close Games to develop a modern shooter based upon the exploits of so-called tier-one operators. *Medal of Honor* takes place during the invasion of Afghanistan, following a number of fictionalized missions undertaken by elite forces such as Navy SEALs, Army Rangers, and Delta Force counterterrorist units.[59] The *Medal of Honor* series is well known for its adherence to accurate details of historical conflicts and for integrating documentary materials such as tactical plans and the personal correspondence of servicemen into its loading screens and extras menus.[60]

When the game came under attack by media outlets and defense secretary Liam Fox after news that *Medal of Honor's* multiplayer mode would allow players to control Taliban units, EA president Frank Gibeau delivered an impassioned defense of Danger Close's creative decision.[61] Gibeau's argument is based on two major assertions. First, he questions why anyone would grant other "art-forms" such as film and literature the liberty to take the war in Afghanistan as their subject matter without question, while decrying any game developer who attempts the same. Second, he appeals to the legitimacy of *Medal of Honor's* depiction as a result of EA's partnership with the "US military and the Medal of Honor Society as well."[62]

Although Electronic Arts eventually bowed to public pressure, renaming the Taliban units in the multiplayer portion of its game the "Opposing Forces," its partnership with members of the U.S. military would raise significant issues directly related to the death of Osama bin Laden two years later. In October 2012, David Martin of CBS News reported that the U.S. Navy had disciplined seven active-duty SEALs for their involvement in the development of *Medal of Honor: Warfighter* (the follow-up to the series' 2010 reboot).[63] On two occasions during the spring and summer of 2012, these seven members of SEAL Team Six worked as consultants on *Warfighter*. Martin's report notes that "one of them was on the raid which killed Osama bin Laden and made SEAL Team Six a household name."[64] Despite this connection, sources asserted that the SEALs provided no confidential information about the raid to designers at Danger Close.

In a turn of events echoing the fairness demanded by Frank Gibeau, Kathryn Bigelow faced similar criticism for factual inaccuracies and deep biases toward the CIA in *Zero Dark Thirty*. In the weeks before the 2013 Academy Awards, an overwhelming number of artists and government officials questioned the film's depiction of torture being implemented to locate bin Laden. Glenn Greenwald of the *Guardian* writes that the film "was a blatant vehicle for CIA propaganda, bolstering a worldview exclusively out of Langley," Virginia, the location of the CIA's headquarters.[65] But no commentators noted that, at the end of 2012, Electronic Arts had quietly released a "*Zero Dark Thirty* map pack" for *Medal of Honor: Warfighter*, linking these controversies in a unique example of transmedia synergy.[66]

As of this writing, there is only incomplete public knowledge of the involvement by individual members of the military in the production of *Warfighter* and *Zero Dark Thirty*, and the ongoing fallout from these collaborations appears far from finished. The map pack for *Warfighter* only features multiplayer combat zones inspired by the Darra gun market and Chitral compound, so it's relatively safe from claims of being based on secrets about the Abbottabad raid. Yet, such opaque relationships between game developers and members of the military go back much further.

MILITARY-INDUSTRIAL-GAMING COMPLEX

In 2004, University of Southern California's Institute for Creative Technologies co-developed *Full Spectrum Warrior* with THQ's Pandemic Studios.[67] Unlike the FPS games described above, *FSW* is a squad tactics simulation based around the practice of suppressive fire and safe movement between cover. *Full Spectrum Warrior* is notable because the project received ample funding from the military, so that THQ could publish two versions of the game—one for military training purposes, the other for the commercial market. Nick Dyer-Witheford and Greig de Peuter's *Games of Empire* tracks the troubled development and public scandals generated by *FSW*'s dual gameplay modes.[68] What's more important to the discussion at hand is their broader critique of gaming's place in the military-industrial-media complex.

As its name suggest, *Games of Empire* analyzes videogames through the lens of "Empire" theory, which posits an all-consuming global power complex composed of economic, military, and media control. Their controversial opening claim is that "virtual games are exemplary media of Empire," embodying its causes and dynamics in the way that other forms of media represented prior historical periods.[69] Empire theory lends itself particularly to a study of bin Laden games, because the global power imbalances it critiques are often held to be the major impetus for Al Qaeda's reactionary politics. In their chapter on modern warfare–style videogames, Dyer-Witheford and de Peuter explicate the idea of a "banalized" war, an ongoing and normalized state of conflict with no distinct boundaries.[70]

Games of Empire excoriates the videogame industry for its contribution to this process of banalization:

> Games such as *FSW* generate subjectivities that tend to war. They prompt not atrocities of gothic delinquency but displays of loyal support for "staying the course." Their virtualities are part of a wider polyphonic cultural chorus supporting militarization, a multimedia drumbeat for war.[71]

Even when mainstream videogames avoid explicitly naming an enemy leader "bin Laden" or an opposing force "the Taliban," players fill in the blanks following dominant ideologies. These games always reinforce the righteous position of American and allied militaries, and they do so while fetishizing the newest implements of war. Just as the bin Laden torture games allow players the "creative" use of everyday household objects, the *Call of Duty* franchise glories in drone strikes, experimental aircraft, and the joy of customizing firearms. The makers of *Medal of Honor: Warfighter* go so far as to license in-game weapons from their real-world manufacturers.[72]

Overriding social theories sometimes threaten to gloss over important distinctions and paint consumers as cultural dupes, but one does not need to subscribe to Empire theory to recognize the problematic nature of the relationship between game development and the military. At the very least, the financial relationships and production modes of the mainstream industry threaten to drown out the multitude of radically different voices contributing to the cultural discourse surrounding the War on Terror. When the investment of time and money into the development of an artifact is so high, as it always is in the case of AAA videogames, the possibilities for experimentation and divergence from accepted norms are diminished. It is always safer to toe the party line or to ignore complex social issues altogether.

In closing, we can recognize that there is a feedback loop in action throughout the entire spectrum of games designed before and during the War on Terror. The original impulse to explore violent fantasies in the first FPS games of the 1990s was carried on by the young game designers reacting to the September 11 attacks. Although they largely predate the artifacts identified by Dyer-Witherford and de Peuter as contributing to the banalization of war, the bin Laden Flash games stem from and reinforce the same cultural attitudes. Meanwhile, academic and experimental game designers react by producing more subtle meditations on the processes and spaces implicated in global current events. These waves of cultural production are cyclical, constantly playing off of each other and adapting themselves to suit changes in taste, style, personal desires, market forces, and research interests.

Conclusion

Time and time again, we have seen examples of bin Laden videogames that simply reinforce the common desire for and celebration of his death. As a survey of a body of work about a person, this chapter strikes one as homogeneous and perhaps disappointing. The most interesting games produced during and about the War on Terror do not focus on bin Laden directly, perhaps because the contemporary videogame ecology is a weak channel for biographical representation. At their best, these games take us through a rough recounting of the night SEAL Team Six raided bin Laden's Abbottabad compound. At their worst, they glorify in the excessive digital mutilation of an infamous man's body. If these were the only videogames that one had ever encountered, then it would be suitable to conclude that the medium could only ever amount to so much blood and gore. They render bin Laden as an object or goal rather than as a person. They are about how he made us feel, about us rather than him.

Instead, it is best to view the discussions above as a window into the theoretical issues and practical problems related to the production of games about the news. How do we distinguish between subjective and objective work in a nonreproducing medium? What are the best ways to make games quickly in response to a current event, and what are the dangers of such rapid production? What are the dangers of financial relationships between the military and cultural producers? How do we talk seriously about "outsider art" or the creations of amateur designers?

Let's return to a line from Fulp's disclaimer on *Bad Dudes vs. Bin Laden*: "I wasn't sure if a game would be appropriate, but I realized that it really is." The fascinating thing about this sentence is that it encapsulates the question that game academics and independent developers of newsgames still ask themselves years later. Its essence also contains the doubt that pundits shed on the legitimacy of any game that dares to address a controversial current event. Fulp may well be the first developer of a newsgame to have asked this of himself, although it is necessarily confronted at the beginning of every design drawn from a real-world system or event. To my knowledge, this query has only been publicly answered in the negative once before: following the untimely death of television personality Steve Irwin, Bogost and Frasca briefly brainstormed how a "Death of the Crocodile Hunter" newsgame might work before "discard[ing] the idea as disrespectful and mov[ing] on."[73]

Today, many designers fear that this attitude—that a videogame can and should be made about anything, by anyone—has been endangered by the growth and refinement of independent game development. Taking Fulp as an example, despite the crude and controversial subject matter of his early creative output, his company The Behemoth has spent the better part of a decade developing wildly popular beat-'em-ups with sci-fi and medieval themes. These more polished, fun-oriented indie games seek broad distribution on corporate channels such as Microsoft's XBOX Live Arcade, the Playstation Network, and Apple's App Store. All of these distribution hubs employ rigorous content policing and quality assurance, and Apple has gone so far as to claim that games are not the place for political or religious critique (it also explicitly bans depictions of torture in its apps).[74]

Our first response to the current state of affairs might be one of relief. Surely it is a good thing that children cannot easily access bloody and often xenophobic media on common devices such as their smart phones and videogame consoles. The bin Laden Whac-A-Mole and torture games, while historically intriguing as objects of study, express no great truths beyond the fact that teenagers and young adults react violently when they feel hemmed in by dangerous situations outside their control. We don't need to play a videogame to learn that many people harbor fear and misunderstanding of exotic others. And perhaps it's best if three-dimensional, action-oriented FPS games recuse themselves from an attempt to represent the motivations or tactics of insurgent combatants. But there is another way to look at this situation.

In her *Rise of the Videogame Zinesters*, Anna Anthropy fervently defends the rights of game designers as artists.[75] Importantly, she argues that contemporary commercial restrictions and standards serve to stifle the creative voices and political speech of many—such as those of women, transgendered individuals, and ethnic and sexual minorities. Anthropy weaves together curatorial opinion, design analysis of her own work, and how-to guides for becoming a game designer with new tools like Twine. Her sensibility harkens a decade back to the time of the early bin Laden games, when youthful creators found large audiences online for their first experiments in Flash development. What we formerly called "amateur" game development is rebranded as "punk" or "do-it-yourself" design, reflecting a much broader spectrum of subject matters and styles than those employed by the young men who allowed their players to virtually punish Osama bin Laden.[76]

We can characterize the past decade of political game development thus: It began violently, yet modestly, in the work of Flash game designers aping the design of popular arcade games to match the context of current events and popular opinion. Soon after, it became almost the sole purview of the academics and advertisers analyzed in Bogost's *Persuasive Games*. All the while, the "core" of mainstream game design remained aloof from political discourse, barring the intermittent episodes when news outlets and political pundits called into question its predilection to graphic violence. Standards for the proper subject matter and style of videogames as commercial products became reified and stagnant, inspiring the recent backlash from punk and minority designers like Anthropy. In 2012 these "radical" games, like Molleindustria's *Unmanned* (a critique of drone warfare) and Richard Hofmeier's *Cart Life* (an exploration of street retail labor) finally gained broader recognition.[77]

In the few years since bin Laden's death, political game design has largely moved away from global news and controversy to focus on identity politics and local activism, such as games made in support of Occupy Wall Street.[78] This flurry of change emphasizes the fact that those of us who study and make videogames still do not know exactly how our medium works and what it can do. This is quite unlike the studies of bin Laden in other artistic and popular media highlighted within this volume. Film, television, and literary nonfiction are old and seemingly wise, formally sure of themselves and given free rein to tackle any subject matter. Videogames, still so young and confused about their identity and best practices, may be the perfect medium to explore phenomena that many of us still struggle to fully comprehend: the War on Terror, gender and sexuality, community activism, and computerized life.

Notes

1. Unknown developer, nicknamed "Narcissus1975." Newgrounds, *Torture Osama* (Glenside, PA: Newgrounds, 2001), http://www.newgrounds.com/portal/view/32463, computer software.

2. Newgrounds website, War on Terror, n.d., http://www.newgrounds.com/collection/waronterror_1.html.

3. Kathryn Bigelow, dir., *Zero Dark Thirty* (Culver City, CA:: Sony Pictures Home Entertainment, 2013), DVD.

4. Janet H. Murray, *Hamlet on the Holodeck: The Future of Narrative in Cyberspace* (Cambridge, MA: MIT Press, 1997), 28.

5. Raph Koster, *A Theory of Fun for Game Design* (Phoenix: Paraglyph Press, 2004), 90.

6. Robin Hunicke, Marc LeBlanc, and Robert Zubek, "MDA: A Formal Approach to Game Design and Game Research," in *Proceedings of the Challenges in Games AI Workshop, Nineteenth National Conference of Artificial Intelligence*, 2004.

7. There were a number of important precursors to this research, of which I name a few. Gonzalo Frasca had coined the term "newsgame" with the release of *September 12*. At the University of Southern California, Tracy Fullerton had established her ongoing research into the development of "documentary games" in the mainstream industry and student game development. And Ed Halter had already published his *From Sun Tzu to Xbox*, one of the first critical examinations of the connection between games and the military industrial complex, following the work of Alexander Galloway.

8. Ian Bogost, Simon Ferrari, and Bobby Schweizer, *Newsgames: Journalism at Play* (Cambridge, MA: MIT Press, 2010).

9. Bill Kovach and Tom Rosenstiel, *The Elements of Journalism: What Newspeople Should Know and the Public Should Expect*, rev. ed. (New York: Three Rivers Press, 2007), 2–6.

10. Bogost, Ferrari, and Schweizer, *Newsgames*, 6–9.

11. Ian Bogost, *Persuasive Games: The Expressive Power of Videogames* (Cambridge, MA: MIT Press, 2007), 28–30.

12. Murray, *Hamlet on the Holodeck*, 71–90.

13. Ibid., 71.

14. Bogost, *Persuasive Games*, 242–43.

15. Bogost, Ferrari, and Schweizer, *Newsgames*, 6.

16. Powerful Robot Games, *September 12* (Montevideo, Uruguay: self-published, 2003), http://www.newsgaming.com/games/index12.htm, computer software.

17. Bogost, *Persuasive Games*, 85.

18. *2005 IGF Finalists and Winners*, Independent Game Festival, n.d., http://www.igf.com/2005finalistswinners.html.

19. Tom Fulp, *Bad Dudes vs. Bin Laden* (Glenside, PA: Newgrounds, 2001), http://www.newgrounds.com/portal/view/31539, computer software.

20. Ed Halter, *From Sun Tzu to Xbox: War and Video Games* (New York: Thunder's Mouth Press, 2006), 294.

21. Ibid., 295.

22. Bogost, Ferrari, and Schweizer, *Newsgames* (2010), 161–162.

23. Thistler, *Osama-Whack* (Glenside, PA: Newgrounds, 2001), http://www.newgrounds.com/portal/view/34996, computer software.

24. Mercifull, *BinLaden–Taste of Anthrax* (Glenside, PA: Newgrounds, 2001), http://www.newgrounds.com/portal/view/34634, computer software.

25. Inter Network Marketing, *Minarett Attack* (Switzerland: Swiss People's Party, 2009), http://dl.dropbox.com/u/2676566/Minarett%20Attack.htm, computer software.

26. Cinque Hicks, "Minarett Attack: Whac-A-Mole and the Culture Wars," http://newsgames.gatech.edu/blog/2009/12/minarett-attack-whac-a-mole-and-the-culture-wars.html, Web blog post.

27. Halter, *From Sun Tzu to Xbox*, 294.

28. Ibid., 293.

29. Game Show Network, *So You Think You Can Drive, Mel?* (Santa Monica, CA: self-published, 2006), http://www.gsn.com/games/game_lobby.php?link_id=G402, computer software.

30. Zach Whalen, "Tabloid Gaming: GSN's The Prison Life," Zach's Blog, June 4, 2007, http://www.gameology.org/node/1509.

31. Bogost, Ferrari, and Schweizer, *Newsgames*, 33–34.

32. Altr, *The Torture Chamber: Osama Bin Laden* (Glenside, PA: Newgrounds, 2001), http://www.newgrounds.com/portal/view/31701, computer software.

33. Fulp, *Bad Dudes*, author notes.

34. Fieler Media, *Bin Laden Liquors* (self-published, 2001), http://arcade.modemhelp.net/play-5155-Bin_Laden_Liquors.html, computer software.

35. Halter, *From Sun Tzu to Xbox*, 296.

36. Ibid., 304.

37. Ibid., 302.

38. James Paul Gee, *What Video Games Have to Teach Us about Learning and Literacy* (New York: Palgrave Macmillan, 2003), 59.

39. Bogost, Ferrari, and Schweizer, *Newsgames*, 62.

40. Fletch, *Fight Yard Abbottabad* (Brooklyn: Machinefloor, 2011), http://css.gamebanana.com/maps/156014, computer software.

41. Valve Corporation. *Counter-Strike: Source* (Bellevue, WA: Valve Corporation, 2004), computer software.

42. George Stephanopoulos (anchor), "Bin Laden Compound Raid: First Look Inside," ABC News Live, May 2, 2011, http://abcnews.go.com/GMA/video/bin-laden-compound-raid-first-look-inside-13507598.

43. Bogost, Ferrari, and Schweizer, *Newsgames*, 64–66.

44. Jeremy Alessi, "News+Gameplay: *Bin Laden Raid*," Gamasutra: The Art & Business of Making Games, May 20, 2011, http://www.gamasutra.com/view/feature/134753/newsgameplay_bin_laden_raid.php. Web log post.

45. Jason Schreier, "*Bin Laden Raid* Puts Osama in Your Cross Hairs," Wired, http://www.wired.com/2011/05/bin-laden-raid/, Web log post.

46. News+Gameplay, *Bin Laden Raid* (self-published, 2011), http://www.newsgameplay.com/?p=36 (computer software no longer available without developer permission).

47. Kuma Reality Games, *Kuma\War Mission 107: The Death of Osama bin Laden* (New York: self-published, 2011), http://www.kumawar.com/osama2011/overview.php, computer software.

48. Tracy Fullerton, "Documentary Games: Putting the Player in the Path of History," in *Playing the Past: History and Nostalgia in Video Games*, ed. Zach Whalen and Laurie N. Taylor (Nashville: Vanderbilt University Press, 2008), 215–38, esp. 227–29.

49. Bogost, Ferrari, and Schweizer, *Newsgames*, 66–69.

50. Ibid., 21–23.

51. Nick Montfort and Ian Bogost, *Racing the Beam: The Atari Video Computer System* (Cambridge, MA: MIT Press, 2009), 2.

52. Madeleine Baran, "Bin Laden Killed Repeatedly in Twin Cities Suburb Game," Minnesota Public Radio, August 17, 2012, http://minnesota.publicradio.org/display/web/2012/08/17/osama-bin-laden-role-playing-game.

53. Bogost, Ferrari, and Schweizer, *Newsgames*, 127–50.

54. Cynthia K., Poremba, "Real|Unreal: Crafting Actuality in the Documentary Videogame" (PhD thesis, Concordia University, Montreal, 2011). 33–34.

55. Ibid., 37.

56. Ibid., 39.

57. Infinity Ward, *Call of Duty 4: Modern Warfare* (Santa Monica, CA: Activision, 2008), computer software.

58. Simon Ferrari, "Popping Smoke," January 12, 2011, Kill Screen, http://killscreendaily.com/articles/popping-smoke/, Web log post.

59. Danger Close Games, *Medal of Honor* (Redwood City, CA: Electronic Arts, 2010), computer software.

60. Fullerton, "Documentary Games," 221–25.

61. Rob Crossley, "EA Boss: MOH Won't Submit to 'Taliban' Outcry," August 23 2010, Develop, http://www.develop-online.net/news/35686/EA-boss-MOH-wont-submit-to-Taliban-outcry, Web log post.

62. Ibid.

63. Danger Close Games, *Medal of Honor: Warfighter* (Redwood City, CA: Electronic Arts, 2012), computer software.

64. David Martin, "7 Navy SEALs Disciplined for Role with Video Game," CBS Evening News, November 8, 2012, http://www.cbsnews.com/8301–18563_162–57547417/7-navy-seals-disciplined-for-role-with-video-game/, Web log post.

65. Glenn Greenwald, *"Zero Dark Thirty*, the CIA and Film Critics Have a Very Bad Evening," *Guardian*, February 25, 2013, http://www.guardian.co.uk/commentisfree/2013/feb/25/zero-dark-thirty-cia-oscars, Web log post.

66. Dean Takahashi, *"Medal of Honor Warfighter's Zero Dark Thirty* Map Pack Debuts," VB Gamesbeat, http://venturebeat.com/2012/12/17/medal-of-honor-warfighters-zero-dark-thirty-map-pack- debuts/, Web log post.

67. Pandemic Studios, *Full Spectrum Warrior* (Agoura Hills, CA: THQ Incorporated, 2004), computer software.

68. Nick Dyer-Witheford and Greig de Peuter, *Games of Empire: Global Capitalism and Video Games* (Minneapolis: University of Minnesota Press, 2009).

69. Ibid., xxix.

70. Ibid., 100.

71. Ibid., 118.

72. Barry Meier and Andrew Martin, "Real and Virtual Firearms Nurture a Marketing Link," *New York Times*, December 24, 2012,http://www.nytimes.com/2012/12/25/business/real-and-virtual-firearms-nurture-marketing-link.html?_r=0, Web log post.

73. Gonzalo Frasca, "Croc Hunter Newsgame," Water Cooler Games, September 7, 2006, http://www.bogost.com/watercoolergames/archives/croc_hunter_new.shtml, Web log post.

74. Jeffrey Grubb, "Apple: 'Want to Criticize Religion? Write a Book'—Don't Make a Game," VB Gamesbeat, January 15, 2013, http://venturebeat.com/2013/01/15/apple-want-to-criticize-religion-write-a-book-dont-make-a- game/, Web log post.

75. Anna Anthropy, *Rise of the Videogame Zinesters: How Freaks, Normals, Amateurs, Artists, Dreamers, Dropouts, Queers, Housewives, and People Like You Are Taking Back an Art Form* (New York: Seven Stories Press, 2012).

76. Joshua Kopstein, "Don't Start a Band: Why Everyone Should Be Making Video Games," *Verge*, April 5, 2012, http://www.theverge.com/2012/4/5/2920131/anna-anthropy-videogame-zinesters-expressive-games, Web log post.

77. "IndieCade East: Featured Games," IndieCade: International Festival of Independent Games, 2013, http://www.indiecade.com/2013/east_games/.

78. Simon, Ferrari, "*Motivating DIY Development for Change: OWS Games,*" June 20 2011, invited presentation at the 8th Annual Games For Change Festival, New York University.

Muslims in America and the Post-9/11 Terrorism Debates

Media and Public Opinion

BRIGITTE L. NACOS

Three years before 9/11, President Clinton's Advisory Board on Race reported a major problem regarding "the representation, coverage, and portrayal of minorities on the news, on television, in film, and in other forms of media." Arab and Muslim Americans were among those minorities. In the words of one Muslim American quoted in the report, "In the United States, we see . . . the Arab and the Muslim have become . . . not only the other, not only the potential terrorist who is a threat to the way of life . . . the Arab and the Muslim have become the enemy."[1] This perception was hardly surprising. After all, Hollywood motion pictures and TV shows had long dwelt on the negative image by casting Arabs and Muslims as violent and barbaric villains.[2] For decades, the authors of crime fiction had taken their plots from media reports of anti-American terrorism in the Middle East perpetrated by Muslim and Arab fanatics.[3] As for the news media, Edward W. Said wrote, "Muslim and Arabs are essentially covered, discussed, apprehended either as suppliers of oil or as potential terrorists."[4]

The horrific attacks of 9/11 by a group of Islamists resulted almost instantly in news narratives reminiscent of typical Hollywood movies in which "the plots are all but spectacular, the villains mostly represent archetypes of 'evil', and ultimately the threat is averted by righteous forces."[5] Based on a qualitative content analysis of Fox News on the afternoon of September 11, 2001, Elisabeth Anker concluded that the reporting was best described as a "melodrama [that] defined America as a heroic redeemer with a mandate to act because of an injury committed by a hostile villain."[6] The other networks told the same story about the eternal clash between good and evil, heroes and villains, freedom-loving victims and ruthless aggressors over and over again. There were metaphors about and references to historic events or fictitious versions of such events. In the fourteen hours or so following the 9/11 attacks, anchors, reporters, experts, and other sources used the terms *evil* sixteen times and *war* or *war on terrorism* ninety-three times in newscasts aired by ABC News, CBS News, and NBC News. The overriding overt or covert message was that just as the nation battled Nazis, Japanese, and Communists in real wars and Hollywood fiction, there was now another evil enemy to be fought—one that fit the most commonly projected profile of modern-day terrorists—Muslims and Arabs. The predominant visuals, too, fit perfectly into the post-9/11 narrative. While the threatening pictures of Osama bin Laden personified the "evil" in particularly dramatic fashion, there were many more visuals of other Arab and Muslim males that reinforced the traditional stereotypes of those groups. While almost all of the depicted men were foreigners, it was their religion and ethnicity, not their citizenship, that fed into the negative connotations associated with Arabs and Muslims in general, including U.S. citizens.[7] As Walter Lippmann recognized, "the subtlest and most pervasive of all influences are those which create and maintain a repertory of stereotypes."[8]

But in the hours, weeks, and months after the terrorist strikes, there were also many voices of reason in the news that emphasized the profound differences between the architects and perpetrators of the 9/11 strikes, who claimed to act in the name of Islam, and the mass of peaceful Muslims and their religion. Hours after the attack, in the midst of destruction and chaos, New York City Mayor Rudy Giuliani said during an ad hoc news conference, "Nobody should engage in group blame."[9] "Nobody should blame any group of people or any nationality or any ethnic group," Giuliani stated.[10] He assured Arabs and Muslims in New York City special police protection and warned that anyone trying to harass them would be arrested.

A few days after 9/11, President Bush visited the Islamic Center of Washington, D.C., and stated:

> The face of terror is not the true faith of Islam. That's not what Islam is all about. Islam is peace. These terrorists don't represent peace. They represent evil and war. When we think of Islam we think of a faith that brings comfort to a billion people around the world. Billions of people find comfort and solace and peace. And that's made brothers and sisters out of every race—out

of every race. America counts millions of Muslims amongst our citizens, and Muslims make an incredibly valuable contribution to our country. Muslims are doctors, lawyers, law professors, members of the military, entrepreneurs, shopkeepers, moms and dads. And they need to be treated with respect. In our anger and emotion, our fellow Americans must treat each other with respect.[11]

A number of media organizations reminded readers of the persecution of Japanese Americans after the Pearl Harbor attacks. The explicit or implicit message here was to not repeat the mistakes of the past. In the six months after 9/11, the U.S. newspapers and wire services represented in the Lexis/Nexis archive published a total of 109 stories. ABC News, CBS News, NBC News, CNN, and NPR combined aired nine segments that recalled the treatment of Japanese Americans in the context of Muslim and Arab Americans' post-9/11 predicament. The *Seattle Post-Intelligencer*'s Joshua Sanders, for example, mentioned in a story about the painful memories of Japanese Americans, like Arab Americans and Muslims who have been the targets of anger and violence during the last week, Japanese Americans—particularly those who survived the internment camps of World War II—remember the same treatment.[12] They, too, were targeted and punished because of their heritage.

In the months immediately after the 9/11 attacks, "voices that defended the civil liberties and rights of American Muslims and Arabs were more numerous in the mass-mediated debate than those who advocated curbing those freedoms."[13] Altogether, a systematic analysis of the textual content of four U.S. newspapers in the six months before and after 9/11 revealed, surprisingly, that "there was a distinct shift from a limited and stereotypical coverage in the pre-9/11 period to more frequent, inclusive, and less stereotypical news presentation thereafter [in the six months after 9/11]."[14]

There were also efforts in the entertainment media to put a human face on the predicament of Muslim and Arab Americans who were falsely suspected of terrorist activities simply because of their ethnicity and religion. The most notable example was an episode of the NBC hit series *The West Wing* that aired three weeks after 9/11 and portrayed a real Muslim American rather than the perennial Hollywood variety. Instead of opening the third season by picking up on the storyline of the second season's finale, there was a special entitled "Isaac and Ishmael," written by Aaron Sorkin, that added up to an effort to understand the complexities of political violence and the human costs of typecasting whole groups as villains. Early on in this episode, the fictitious White House goes once again into a lockdown because of a security breach and possible terror threat. Without ever mentioning the events of 9/11, the program's most gripping subplot is the interrogation of low-level White House staffer Raqim Ali, an Arab-Muslim American, whose name is the same as one of aliases used by a fugitive involved in a plot to bomb New York's La Guardia Airport. White House chief-of-staff Leo McGarry, obviously suspicious, participates in what Ali called "a pitiful [interrogation] exercise." At one point, there is this exchange:

ALI: It's not uncommon for Arab Americans to be the first suspected when that sort of thing happens.
LEO: I can't imagine why.
ALI: Look . . .
LEO: No, I'm trying to figure out why anytime there's any terrorist activity, people always assume its Arabs. I'm racking my brain.
AL: I don't know the answer to that, Mr. McGarry, but I can tell you it's horrible.
LEO: Well, that's the price you pay.
ALI (ANGRY): Excuse me. The price for what? .

When an FBI agent on the scene receives the news that the real suspect has been arrested, Ali is vindicated, and chief-of-staff Leo is left to tell the falsely suspected staffer that he is sorry. In an effort to justify his behavior, Leo explains, "I think, if you talk to people who know me, they'd tell you that . . . that was unlike me, you know? We are obviously all under, um . . . a greater than usual amount of . . . you know . . ." Without spelling it out, Leo obviously alluded to political violence.

To sum up the immediate post-9/11 media content, news and entertainment avoided an overtly biased depiction of Arab and Muslim Americans and even addressed the difficulties that members of those minorities faced as result of the terrorist attacks. But at the same time, the powerful narrative of the existential post-9/11 clash-of-civilization type of confrontation between the evil enemy (Arabs and Muslim) on the one hand and the good, victimized nation (America) persisted in the mass-mediated public debate. If anything, this melodramatic storyline intensified with the beginning of the Afghanistan War some six weeks after 9/11 when the metaphorical war became a real armed conflict.

Rituals of Communication and Excommunication

Communication scholars distinguish between communication as transmission and communication as ritual. Whereas transmission means disseminating information "farther and faster, eclipsing time and transcending space," ritual communication refers to the "sacred ceremony that draws persons together in fellowship and communality."[15] However, there are also "rituals of excommunication" that divide and separate communities rather than draw them together.[16] After the terrorist nightmare of 9/11, the question was: Which one of the media narratives and frames would prevail—those highlighting the voices of commonality and shared values or those dwelling on messages that divide.

As far as the news was concerned, by the time of the first anniversary of 9/11, the more positive reporting patterns of the immediate post-9/11 period survived in two respects only: Muslim Americans were more frequently covered and more often cited than before the events of 9/11. Otherwise "the coverage retreated to the negative and stereotypical patterns of the pre-9/11 period—or worse".[17] This reversal was particularly true for the news media's handling of cases in which the civil rights of Muslim and Arab Americans were violated. In the first six months after 9/11, media sources supporting the civil liberties of those groups outscored the opponents; by the time of the first anniversary, this support had declined sharply, and there was an increase in messages that accused Muslim and Arab Americans of supporting terrorism. Indeed, the greatest flaw here was that the print and broadcast media covered these policies and actions sparingly or not at all. As Anthony Lewis noted,

> Coverage of the administration's record on civil liberties since September 11th has, in my judgment, been sadly inadequate. An example: I first heard about the administration's claim that it could indefinitely detain American citizens simply by calling them enemy combatants . . . I saw it in a story a few paragraphs long in The New York Times. I was bewildered. Why wasn't that claim important news?[18]

News organizations were well aware of the administration's warning that opponents of Washington's counterterrorist measures were unpatriotic and helpful to terrorists. Since the U.S. Department of Justice took the lead in pushing for and justifying curbs on civil liberties as an important weapon in the war on terrorism, Attorney General John Ashcroft was especially vocal in attacking critics as being on the side of terrorists. In his testimony before the Senate Judiciary Committee, for example, Ashcroft said, "To those who scare peace-loving people with phantoms of lost liberty, my message is this: your tactics only aid terrorists, for they erode our national unity and diminish our resolve. They give ammunition to America's enemies, and pause to America's friends."[19] This was certainly an explicit effort to intimidate critics and may have contributed to a press watchdog that was unwilling to bark.

What the news media fail to report or underreport is just as important, or more so, than what is reported. A case in point was the media's lack of interest in publicizing the frequent condemnations of terrorism by Muslim and

Arab American religious and secular leaders in the wake of 9/11.[20] As a result, a plurality or majority of Americans believed that moderate Muslim leaders in the United States had not done enough to support the United States and denounce terrorism. The problem here was that the news media did not report prominently or did not report at all when Muslim leaders did speak out against the attacks of 9-11 and against terrorism in general. The alleged silence of mainstream Muslim American leaders remained high on the agenda of conservative talk shows that perpetuated the myth of a uniformly silent leadership in the Muslim and Arab minorities.

Then, after deadly attacks on the London transit system on July 7, 2005, the Fiqh Council of North America and Canada issued a *fatwa* or religious edict against terrorism. The text was unequivocal in condemning terrorism with the following statements as centerpiece:

1. All acts of terrorism targeting civilians are haram (forbidden) in Islam.
2. It is haram for a Muslim to cooperate with any individual or group that is involved in any act of terrorism or violence.
3. It is a civic and religious duty of Muslims to cooperate with law enforcement authorities to protect the lives of all civilians.

Although released during a press conference at the National Press Club in Washington, D.C., the news coverage in the mainstream media was meager. Both the *New York Times* and the *Washington Post* published stories of modest length (618 and 452 words, respectively) about the forthcoming fatwa's content on pages 14 and 11, respectively, on the day the news conference was held. There were no follow-up stories in the *Times* and *Post* the next day. While National Public Radio carried short news items about the fatwa on several programs and the *News Hour with Jim Lehrer* aired a segment on the responsibilities of mainstream Muslims in America, most media organizations paid little or no attention. Altogether, the hundreds of newspapers that are archived by Lexis/Nexis carried only forty-three news items on the release of the fatwa—many of them buried in short news summaries.

The fatwa served talk show hosts or guests as a launching pad for nasty attacks on American Muslims and their religion. Thus, the Washington, D.C., radio talk show host Michael Graham told his listeners that the "problem is not extremism. The problem is Islam. We are at war with a terrorist organization named Islam." According to the *Washington Post*, "Graham said 'Islam is a terrorist organization' 23 times" in this particular broadcast.[21] On WNYC's *Brian Lehrer Show*, Steven Emerson attacked the fatwa as "bogus" and a public relation trick.[22] As guest host of *The O'Reilly Factor* on Fox News, John Kasich mentioned the antiterrorism pronouncement to introduce a videotaped conversation with Evangelist Franklin Graham. While the audience received no information about the fatwa's content, they learned a great deal about Graham's view on an inherent chasm between Christians and Muslims. At one point, the Reverend Graham said, "But I want the American audience to understand the God that they [Muslims] worship is not the same God we worship. The God that I worship gave his son for me." Obviously speaking of an inevitable Christian-Muslim clash, he added, "I think we have to understand the religious aspect, and we're going to have to continue this war on terrorism. And it's not going to finish in Iraq. There are a number of other countries harboring terrorists right now, that support terrorists, that give to terrorists."[23]

A cartoon in reaction to the fatwa showed the entrance of a mosque, a "Call to Fatwah" sign with daily "Death to the Western Infidels" announcements, the distribution of "balloons & bombs for the kids," and a "Muslims for Peace and Understanding" group in which one member says, "Yes, this is somewhat unfortunate, but if it weren't for U.S. foreign policy . . ."[24]

All of this demonstrated a no-win situation for American Muslim leaders: They were damned for not speaking out against terrorism, and they were damned and doubted as to their sincerity when they did. But mostly, they were ignored when they took stands against terrorism and terrorists.

Questions about the treatment and interrogation of terrorists and suspected terrorists arose soon after 9/11, became more urgent after the arrest of Al Qaeda operative Khalid Sheik Mohammad, and intensified more so once the horrific images of Abu Ghraib detainees were in the public sphere. The following case study explores how the news media dealt with the question whether or not to torture terrorists.

News Media after 9/11:
To Torture or Not to Torture?

Before the shocking visuals and news reports about the human rights violations at the U.S.-run Abu Ghraib prison in Iraq were publicized, the debate about the pros and cons of torture in the War on Terror was not particularly high on the news media's agenda. Typically, the question of how to treat captured terrorists and suspected terrorists was handled in a cavalier fashion by people inside and outside the media. Stuart Taylor Jr., for example, wrote in the *National Journal*:

> Unlike the 1949 Geneva Convention regarding prisoners of war, the torture convention protects even terrorists and other "unlawful combatants." But

its definition of torture—intentional infliction of "severe pain or suffering, whether physical or mental"—leaves room for interpretation. It's a good bet that Khalid Shaikh Mohammed [captured Al Qaeda chief-of-operation in U.S. custody] has felt some pain. And if that's the best chance of making him talk, it's OK by me.[25]

Newsweek columnist Jonathan Alter suggested, "even as we continue to speak out against human-rights violations around the world, we need to keep an open mind about certain measures to fight terrorism, like court-sanctioned psychological interrogation. And we'll have to think about transferring some suspects to our less squeamish allies, even if that's hypocritical. Nobody said this was going to be pretty."[26] In the *Atlantic Monthly*, Mark Bowden wrote, "The Bush Administration has adopted exactly the right posture on the matter. Candor and consistency are not always public virtues. Torture is a crime against humanity, but coercion is an issue that is rightly handled with a wink, or even a touch of hypocrisy; it should be banned but also quietly practiced."[27]

Typically, when such articles were published, the writers were invited to appear on television and radio talk shows. When opponents of torture did appear on such shows, they were typically drawn from human rights and civil liberty organizations and allotted less time to articulate their arguments than were the supporters of any form of some type of torture.

Some of the media's chosen experts were enthusiastic advocates of torture and vilified the opponents of this interrogation method. These voices became more frequent and louder after the capture of Khalid Sheik Mohammed (KSM), a leading Al Qaeda and mastermind of the 9/11 attacks. A law professor emeritus, for example, wrote:

> There are those among us—Jimmy Carter–like pacifists and Ramsey Clark–type America haters come to mind—who would probably stand by idly and endure an atomic holocaust. But most people would doubtless opt for torture, albeit reluctantly.
>
> These realists—and I suspect they are a large majority of the American public—would be correct. In approving the use of torture—or at least accepting it—they needn't suffer even a scintilla of moral guilt. Torture of whatever kind, and no matter how brutal, in defense of human rights and legitimate self-preservation is not only not immoral; it is a moral imperative.[28]

Others, too, claimed that most Americans supported torture. However, such assertions were not borne out by actual public opinion surveys but were based on what Robert M. Entman has called "perceived public opinion."[29] As table 11.1 shows, the U.S. public was not in favor in the months after 9/11 of torturing

Table 11.1. U.S. Public Opinion on the Torture of Terrorists/Suspected Terrorists before the Abu Ghraib Revelations

	Support (%)	Oppose (%)	Depends / Don't Know / Not Sure (%)
Gallup / CNN / USA TODAY, October 5–6, 2001	45	53	3
Fox News / Opinion Dynamics, March 12–13, 2002	41	47	12
Fox News / Opinion Dynamics, March 12–13, 2003	44	42	14

Source: Roper Center, Public Opinion Archives, iPOLL Databank, http://www.ropercenter.uconn.edu/data_access/ipoll/ipoll.htmltab.

terrorists. Instead, a majority or plurality opposed such extreme mistreatment of detainees. It was only after the capture of KSM in early March 2003 and a mass-mediated debate in which proponents of torture took strong stands that the only available survey seemed to reveal a public opinion move toward stronger support of torture. Taking into account the margin of error, there was a tie between supporters and opponents of torture.

Patricia Roberts-Miller has explained that demagoguery "is polarizing propaganda that motivates members of an ingroup to hate and scapegoat some outgroup(s)."[30] This was the approach taken by the most extreme advocates of torture. In that respect, they had a great deal in common with terrorists in that they used the same techniques to push the "they" against "us" divide that is central to terrorist rhetoric. One way to vilify "them" and set "them" apart is a process of moral disengagement during which the enemies "are depersonalized and dehumanized. They are derogated to the ranks of subhuman species. Dehumanization makes it possible for the radicals to be disengaged morally and to commit atrocities without a second thought."[31]

For terrorists, part of the moral disengagement process has long been the practice of looking upon "them" as animals, calling them "pigs" or "dogs." Efforts to dehumanize terrorists or alleged terrorists were also part of the counterterrorism debate before and after the Abu Ghraib revelations. Thus, after the capture of Khalid Sheik Mohammed (KSM), Jack Wheeler of the Freedom Research Foundation appeared on a Fox News *Hannity & Colmes* program, in which the question was raised, what to do in order to get KSM to spill the beans on Osama bin Laden and Al Qaeda. In an exchange with Hannity, Dr. Wheeler said, "I don't care what you do to him. This man is a piece of human garbage." Hannity's answer: "Well I agree with that."[32] A former CIA operative said in a discussion of interrogation methods, "We catch an al Qaeda member, we knows [*sic*] he's al Qaeda, his life as he knows it has got to be over . . . Listen, I lived with these animals. This is a sub-human species of somehow a deviation of the human, of the true human . . . All bets are off. This is an animal that's unlike any we've ever faced.[33] Rush Limbaugh called terrorists and those held as suspected terrorists "subhuman debris."[34]

One wonders whether the perception of real or alleged enemies in the War on Terror as "garbage," "animal," and "subhuman debris" contributed to the attitudes of those who allowed and committed the torturing of detainees in American-controlled facilities. One American soldier who worked at Abu Ghraib prison testified that on one occasion one of the guards had pointed at two naked detainees who were forced to masturbate. "Look what these animals do when you leave them alone for two seconds," he said. According to his sworn statement, one detainee recalled that "they forced us to walk like dogs on our hands and knees. And we had to bark like a dog and if we didn't do that, they start hitting us hard on our face and chest with no mercy."[35] The dehumanization of prisoners was not unique to Abu Ghraib, as the following in the interrogation log of Mohammed al-Qahtani, believed to have been the designated twentieth hijacker in the 9/11 terrorist attacks and held at Guantanamo, attests to: "Told detainee that a dog is held in higher esteem [than he] because dogs know right from wrong, and know how to protect innocent people from bad people. Began teaching the detainee lessons such as stay, come, and bark to elevate his social status up to that of a dog."[36]

The vilification of "them" was more frequently aimed at their religious beliefs and precepts. After the capture of KSM, the *Washington Times* published an op-ed article that described in gruesome details the kind of torture that would make KSM "sing in an hour."[37] The author clearly was out to violate Mohammed's sensitivities related to his Islamic faith. He suggested the Al Qaeda terrorist should be injected with a drug that would paralyze his breathing muscles but not affect his central nervous system and his ability to think and answer questions. He should be put on a mechanical respirator without which he would suffocate and die. After these preliminaries, the interrogation should continue this way:

KSM is asked a series of questions to which the answers are known [e.g., Are you a Muslim? Would you like a drink of pig grease?]. If he lies, the respirator is turned off. Few experiences are more terrifying than that of suffocation. After a sufficiently terrifying period of suffocation, the respirator is turned back on, the question is asked again, and the process repeats itself until he tells the truth.

After all useful information has been extracted from his brain, KSM should be informed that he will now be killed after his body is smeared with pig fat, that his dead body will be handled by women, and all actions taken that prevent a Muslim from entering heaven upon death so that he dies believing he will never get the heavenly wine and virgins, but will burn in Hell instead. Upon his execution, there should be no physical remains. The body should be cremated and the ashes scattered to the winds.[38]

While these remarks were particularly extreme, there were plenty of other attacks on Islam, Muslims in general, and American Muslims. The Reverend Franklin Graham said, for example, "Islam as a whole is evil." And, "It wasn't Methodists flying into those buildings, and it wasn't Lutherans. It was an attack on this country by people of Islamic faith."[39] As ABC News reported, Franklin Graham had plenty of company among leading evangelical preachers when it came to vilifying Muslims and Islam, as shown by the following excerpts from *Tonight with Peter Jennings*:

> JERRY FALWELL, TELEVANGELIST: I think Mohammed is a terrorist.
> REVEREND JERRY VINES, EVANGELIST: Islam was founded by Mohammed, a demon-possessed pedophile who had 12 wives, and his last one was a nine year old girl.
> JIMMY SWAGGART, TELEVANGELIST: We ought to take, we ought to take every single Muslim student in every college in this nation and ship them back to where they came from.[40]

On CNN, the Reverend Anis Shorrosh, suggested that "theologically a Muslim cannot be a true patriotic American citizen, because his allegiance is to Allah, the Moon [*sic*] God of Arabia."[41]

It may never be known whether these rhetorical attacks and the absence of equally prominent rebuttals in the news influenced the practitioners of torture and their enablers. But the investigations of the abuse, torture, and death of detainees at Abu Ghraib and elsewhere uncovered patterns aimed at degrading Muslim inmates' faith and violating the well-known sensitivities of Muslims and Arabs. In his sworn testimony, one Abu Ghraib prisoner described brutal abuse and attacks on his religion and the precepts of Islam:

> They ordered me to curse Islam and because they started to hit my broken leg, I cursed my religion. They ordered me to thank Jesus that I'm alive. And I did what they ordered me. This is against my belief . . . They forced me to eat pork and they put liquor in my mouth.[42]

Before the news of Abu Ghraib, the American news media had no problem using the term *torture* in the hypothetical debate, but thereafter the fourth estate was reluctant to use the t-word. Anchors, correspondents, and reporters themselves preferred terms like "abuse," "alleged abuse," "mistreatment," and "wrongdoing." Here they followed the lead of the Bush administration and its supporters. As Susan Sontag wrote:

> There was also the avoidance of the word "torture" [on the part of the Bush administration]. The prisoners had possibly been the objects of "abuse," eventually of "humiliation"—that was the most to be admitted. "My impression is that what has been charged thus far is abuse, which I believe technically is different from torture," Secretary of Defense Donald Rumsfeld said at a press conference. "And therefore I'm not going to address the 'torture' word."[43]

In the year following the breaking news of the Abu Ghraib scandal, the three major television networks chose the term *abuse* far more often than *torture* in stories about or related to Abu Ghraib. ABC News was a case in point: the network aired 158 pertinent stories that contained the term *abuse*, but only 43 included the term *torture*. The linguistic choices were very similar at CBS News, NBC News, the *New York Times*, and the *Washington Post*. In most instances, anchors, correspondents, and reporters themselves did not speak or write of "torture" in the context of the Abu Ghraib scandal but left this characterization to named or unnamed sources that were critical of the treatment of detainees by Americans. A case in point was the CBS Evening News on April 29, 2004. In introducing the story about the U.S. Army's response "to documented mistreatment of Iraqi prisoners by American soldiers," Dan Rather himself spoke of "mistreatment" and "abuses." In the following correspondent report, David Martin referred to "Iraqi prisoners mistreated and humiliated by their American jailers." He mentions the t-word only in the context of "the Abu Ghraib Prison outside Baghdad, once infamous under Saddam Hussein as a place of torture and death." Or take the NBC Nightly News of May 7, 2004. In introducing the "Iraqi prisoner abuse scandal," anchor Brian Williams asked, "What were military superiors told about the abuse and when were they told?" In the following report, after speaking of "abuses" and "abuse," Lisa Myers mentioned that the International Red Cross warned the U.S. government of the "widespread abuse" of detainees "tantamount to torture."

Summing up, then, the news about torture fit perfectly into the overall post-9/11 narrative of an existential battle between terrorist evildoers and an attacked nation responding with whatever it took to fight and defeat a dangerous enemy. As table 11.2 shows, public support for torturing suspected terrorists to gain information increased in the years after the human rights violations at Abu Ghraib and elsewhere were reported—but most notably during the presidency of Barack Obama.

Table 11.2. Justification of Torture against Suspected Terrorists to Gain Information after Abu Ghraib Revelations

	Often (%)	Sometimes (%)	Rarely (%)	Never (%)	Don't Know / Refuse (%)
July 2004	15	28	21	32	4
March 2005	15	30	24	27	4
October 2005	15	31	17	32	5
September 2006	18	28	19	32	3
February 2008	17	31	20	30	2
May 2009	20	32	18	29	1
January 2010	23	29	19	27	3
May 2011	25	35	14	25	2
July 2011	20	32	19	27	3

Source: Roper Center, Public Opinion Archives, iPOLL Databank, http://www.ropercenter.uconn.edu/data_access/ipoll/ipoll.htmltab.

"Terrortainment," Jack Bauer, and Washington Decision Makers

Similar to their counterparts in news organizations, leading figures in the entertainment media were well aware that the White House expected support in the War on Terrorism. The special episode of *The West Wing*," discussed above, was not the model that people in the White House had in mind. A few weeks after 9/11, senior officials of the Bush administration, led by the president's influential adviser Karl Rove, met with representatives of the film industry to enlist Hollywood's cooperation. As Jack Valenti, president of the Motion Picture Association of America, put it,

> Mr. Rove wanted to come out and have a meeting with the top executives of the studios, the television networks, theater owners, to see what ideas we have that would enable this war to be fought on every front.
>
> The ideas will be lofted at this meeting on Sunday, and then I'll see to it, with my colleagues' help, that we transform these ideas into action.[44]

Whether in response to Karl Rove and his colleagues or not, TV drama series, for example, became far more violent and their torture scenes far more brutal and numerous after the events of 9/11. In the four years before 2001 (1997–2000) there were 47 torture scenes in prime-time network television; in the four years after 9/11 (2002–2005) there were 624 such scenes.[45] Newsrooms seemed aware of this "terrortainment" trend. ABC News opened a *Nightline* town hall meeting about torture and other civil liberty issues by showing a clip from the long-running hit series *NYPD Blues* in which detective Andy Sipowicz brutally "tuned up" a suspect.[46] A broadcast of ABC's *World News Tonight with Peter Jennings* opened a segment on "torture or persuasion" by airing a torture scene from the motion picture *The Siege* with Bruce Willis. In her voice-over Jackie Judd said, "Hollywood's version of torture knows no limits."[47] As Mark McGuire observed, "Today on TV, sanctioned torture and murder are condoned like never before, not only by the individual characters, but also their employers."[48] And whereas before 9/11 those who tortured used to be the bad guys, now the good guys resorted to this interrogation method. According to Robert Thompson, an expert on popular television, "the federal government could not have come up with a better set of [TV] series to prepare its audience for the new order of the day."[49]

Hollywood terror fiction has always embraced the notion that extraordinary events, such as terrorist attacks, call for extraordinary responses. Torture and "harsh interrogation," as officials in the Bush administration called it, qualify as extraordinary measures. While ABC's *Alias*, NBC's *Law and Order*, and a host of other programs showcased brutality, Fox's *24*, featuring the character Jack Bauer as counterterrorism's superhero, went particularly far in its frequent torture scenes. The usual premise was a ticking time bomb or another kind of imminent attack and a captured terrorist who knew details of the planned strike. By torturing the villain, Bauer and other good guys would extract crucial information that would enable them to prevent another human-caused catastrophe. The ticking-time-bomb scenario became part and parcel of America's public debate about the treatment of captured terrorists or suspected terrorists. Never mind that what Jack Bauer faced every week never happened in real life, contrary to what then vice president Richard Cheney and other administration claimed.[50]

Researchers found that participants in focus groups referred slightly more often to fictitious TV shows than newscasts in political discourse. They concluded that "understanding the full impact of television on political conversations and on the public opinions formed during them requires expanding the definition of politically relevant television to include both fictional and nonfictional programing [because] when subjects draw on media in their conversations, they make few distinctions between fictional and nonfictional television."[51]

When the producers of what Sissela Bok has called "entertainment violence" are asked about negative consequences of their work, they tend to insist that they deal in fiction, not reality.[52] Similarly, the lead writer of *24*, Howard Gordon, told an interviewer, "I think people can differentiate between a television show and reality."[53] And Richard Walter, the chair of the graduate screenwriting program at UCLA, rejected the notion that soldiers were getting training from television dramas: "Viewers are able to draw a distinction between entertainment and reality. It's pretend."[54]

But others insist that Hollywood's counterterrorism fiction influences people's attitudes about the treatment of terrorist enemies—and even their actions. Tony Lagouranis, a U.S. military interrogator in Iraq, including at Abu Ghraib prison, said during a panel discussion at the University of California at Berkeley's Law School that he "definitely saw instances where people took specific ideas from TV shows . . . what we took from television was the idea that torture would work."[55] Diane Beaver, the top military lawyer at Guantanamo, told Phillipe Sand that in search for finding an interrogation model that worked, Jack Bauer "gave people lots of ideas."[56] Beaver revealed that while working in the Guantanamo facility, scenes in 24 "contributed to an environment in which those at Guantanamo were encouraged to see themselves as being on the frontline—and go further than they otherwise might."[57] Concerned about rank-and-file-soldiers' enthusiasm for counterterrorism's action hero Jack Bauer, Brigadier General Patrick Finnegan of the West Point Military Academy met producers of the show in Hollywood. He told them that promoting illegal behavior in the series was having a damaging effect on young troops.[58] The general did not succeed in getting torture scenes tuned down, never mind omitted, in subsequent 24 episodes.

Murray Edelman suggested that entertainment and news media affect both the general public and political elites. As he put it,

> The models, scenarios, narratives, and images into which audiences for political news translate that news are social capital, not individual inventions. They come from works of art in all genres: novels, paintings, stories, films, dramas, television sitcoms, striking rumors, even memorable jokes. For each type of news report there is likely to be a small set of striking images that are influential with large numbers of people, both spectators of the political scene and policymakers themselves.[59]

In post-9/11 America, Hollywood fiction and especially Jack Bauer and his actions were not simply feeding conversations at workplaces and dinner tables across the country; they also became part of bare-knuckle politics and public policy discourse, when it came to the treatment of captured terrorists and suspected terrorists. An instructive example occurred during one of the Democratic Party's presidential primary debates in 2008, when moderator Tim Russert of NBC News started out with a ticking-time-bomb case and then asked Hillary Clinton: "Don't we have the right and responsibility to beat it out of him [the terrorist]? You could set up a law where the president could make a finding or could guarantee a pardon."[60] When Senator Clinton rejected the idea, Russert revealed that the hypothetical ticking-time-bomb scenario and the idea of allowing and pardoning the extraordinary treatment of terrorists had been suggested by her husband, ex-president Bill Clinton, during an interview the previous year.

A few days later, during his appearance on *Meet the Press*, Bill Clinton supported his wife's position first and then added,

> The more I think about it, and the more I have seen that, if you have any kind of formal exception, people just drive a truck through it, and they'll say "Well, I thought it was covered by the exception." I think, I think it's better not to have one. And if you happen to be the actor in that moment which, as far as I know, has not occurred in my experience or President Bush's experience since we've been really dealing with this terror, but I—you actually had the Jack Bauer moment, we call it, I think you should be prepared to live with the consequences. And yet, ironically, if you look at the show, every time they get the president to approve something, the president gets in trouble, the country gets in trouble. And when Bauer goes out there on his own and is prepared to live with the consequences, it always seems to work better.[61]

Altogether, the ex-president mentioned Jack Bauer seven times in his lengthy response. Like many in the general public and in the political class, he bought into the ticking-time-bomb justification according to which an imminent threat of catastrophic terrorism calls for an otherwise illegal response—torture. Taking a different stance, a comprehensive expert report on interrogation methods by the Intelligence Science Board noted,

> Most observers, even those within professional circles, have unfortunately been influenced by the media's colorful (and artificial) view of interrogation as almost always involving hostility and the employment of force—be it physical or psychological—by the interrogator against the hapless, often slow-witted subject. This false assumption is belied by historic trends that show the majority of sources (some estimates range as high as 90 percent) have provided meaningful answers to pertinent questions in response to direct questioning (i.e., questions posed in an essentially administrative manner rather than in concert with an orchestrated approach designed to weaken the source's resistance).[62]

Nowhere was the enthusiasm for the show greater than in the White House and the rest of the Bush administration. Even lawyers in the Justice Department who wrote legal opinions in support of "aggressive interrogation" bought into the fictitious ticking-time-bomb premise with an eye on Jack Bauer. John Yoo, one of the lead authors of the infamous "torture memos," for example, wrote in his account of the administration's War on Terrorism: "What if, as the popular Fox television program 24 recently portrayed, a high-level terrorist leader is caught who knows the location of a nuclear weapon in an American city. Should it be illegal for the President to use harsh interrogation short of torture to elicit this information?"[63] And during a panel discussion on terrorism and the law in Ottawa, a Canadian judge said, "Thankfully, security agencies in all our countries do not subscribe to the mantra "What would Jack Bauer do?" U.S. supreme court justice Anthony Scalia disagreed and argued: "Jack Bauer saved Los Angeles . . . He saved hundreds of thousands of lives. Are you going to convict Jack Bauer? Say that criminal law is against him? Is any jury going to convict Jack Bauer? I don't think so!"[64]

In short, Jack Bauer and other heroes on the screen affected public and elite attitudes about torture as an effective weapon in the war on terrorism. Whether the fictitious villains were Muslims here or abroad or of other backgrounds, the post-9/11 "us" versus "them" narrative was likely to affect the stereotypical associations of American audiences, whether consciously or subconsciously.

More Than a Decade after 9/11:
The Negative Muslim Stereotypes Loom Large

As the tenth anniversary of 9/11 drew closer, there were plenty of manifestations of Islamophobia in America. The following is an exchange between talk show host Glenn Beck and Herman Cain, Republican from Georgia and candidate for the presidential nomination, in June 2011:

> BECK: You said you would not appoint a Muslim to anybody in your administration.
> CAIN: The exact language was when I was asked, "would you be comfortable with a Muslim in your cabinet?" And I said, "no, I would not be comfortable." I didn't say I wouldn't appoint one because if they can prove to me that they're putting the Constitution of the United States first then they would be a candidate just like everybody else. My entire career, I've hired good people, great people, regardless of their religious orientation.
> BECK: So wait a minute. Are you saying that Muslims have to prove their, that there has to be some loyalty proof?
> CAIN: Yes, to the Constitution of the United States of America.

BECK: Would you do that to a Catholic or would you do that to a Mormon?

CAIN: Nope, I wouldn't. Because there is a greater dangerous part of the Muslim faith than there is in these other religions. I know that there are some Muslims who talk about, "but we are a peaceful religion." And I'm sure that there are some peace-loving Muslims.[65]

When Cain's remarks came up during the first debate of Republican presidential hopefuls on June 13, 2011 in New Hampshire, Newt Gingrich, a former Speaker of the U.S. House of Representatives, sided with Cain and went even further:

Now, I just want to go out on a limb here. I'm in favor of saying to people, if you're not prepared to be loyal to the United States, you will not serve in my administration, period. We did this in dealing with the Nazis. We did this in dealing with the Communists. And it was controversial both times and both times we discovered after a while, you know, there are some genuinely bad people who would like to infiltrate our country. And we have got to have the guts to stand up and say, "No."[66]

Actually, growing anti-Muslim words and deeds had swept America the previous year.

In August 2010, a bitter controversy over the plan of a Muslim congregation to build a community center some two and one-half street blocks from the site of the World Trade Center bombing in downtown Manhattan reached its highest pitch. Police had to separate demonstrating opponents and supporters of what came to be called the "Park51" project. "No Clubhouse for Terrorists" and similar signs that equated all Muslims and Islam with terrorists and terrorism garnered much more media attention than the signs of those demonstrators who pleaded for religious tolerance.

Also in advance of the ninth anniversary of 9/11, an obscure pastor at the Dove World Outreach Center in Gainesville, Florida, announced that his congregation would stage a public burning of more than two hundred Korans, the Muslim holy book, on September 11. On the lawn next to his church Pastor Terry Jones placed three large posters with words that added up to "Islam is of the Devil." This blasphemy and the pastor's daily news briefings resulted in massive coverage in the national and international media.

There were reports of inflammatory remarks by Allen West, then campaigning for a House seat in Florida's 22nd district. After calling Islam "a very vicious enemy that we have allowed to come in this country," West warned, "We already have a 5th column that is already infiltrating into our colleges, into our universities, into our high schools, into our religious aspect, our cultural aspect, our financial, our political systems in this country. And that enemy represents something called Islam and Islam is a totalitarian theocratic political ideology, it is not a religion."[67]

Seemingly mainstream politicians, too, seized the opportunity to link Islam and Muslims collectively to the 9/11 attacks. Gingrich, then preparing for the 2012 run for the presidency, said: "Nazis don't have the right to put up a sign next to the Holocaust museum in Washington; we would never accept the Japanese putting up a site next to Pearl Harbor . . . There is no reason for us to accept a mosque next to the World Trade Center."[68]

In the midst of all this, on August 24, 2010, twenty-one-year old Michael Enright got into a yellow cab in Manhattan and asked the forty-four-year-old driver, Ahmed Sharif, what country he was from and whether he was a Muslim. Upon learning that Sharif was an immigrant from Bangladesh and, yes, a Muslim, the passenger said, "*Salaam aleikum*" (peace be with you). But peace was not on his mind. After making disparaging remarks about the way Muslims celebrate their holiday of Ramadan, the passenger cursed the cabby and began stabbing him with a knife and slashing his face, throat, and arms.

It is not known whether there were *direct* associations between the heavily reported outbursts of Islamophobia at the heights of the "mosque at Ground Zero" controversy and the headline news about the announced Koran burning on the one hand and the attack on a Muslim cabby in Manhattan and other hate crimes against American Muslims on the other hand. But in her March 2011 testimony before a congressional committee, Farhana Khera linked the growing expressions of anti-Muslim attitudes to hate crimes, when she said, "In 2010, our country experienced a marked uptick in anti-Muslim rhetoric, attitudes and incidents . . . By summer's end, a Muslim cab driver in New York City had been stabbed repeatedly after answering affirmatively when his passenger inquired if he was Muslim. These anti-Muslim activities and incidents continue unabated in 2011."[69]

That the virus of Islamophobia spread within the law enforcement and first responder communities seemed of little interest to mainstream media, as the following example demonstrates: In early 2011, a nonprofit group published an eighty-page research report that exposed anti-Muslim bias in counterterrorism training of security forces and emergency response officials conducted by private firms and paid for by public funds. Although the findings were introduced at the National Press Club, with the exception of National Public Radio, none of the major print and broadcast news media mentioned the shocking revelations.[70]

All this signaled a profound attitudinal change from the immediate aftermath of the 9/11 strikes, when President George W. Bush, New York City mayor Rudy Giuliani, and other leaders had emphasized the profound differences between the 9/11 terrorists, who claimed to act in the name of Islam, and the mass of peaceful Muslims and their religion. During the divisive debate of the "Ground Zero mosque," the provocative voices were louder than the conciliatory ones. Rudy Giuliani opted for rituals of excommunication when he called the planned project "a desecration" and noted that "nobody would allow something like that at Pearl Harbor. Let's have some respect for who died there and why they died there. Let's not put this off on some kind of politically correct theory."[71]

Just as mass-mediated, negative stereotypes of African Americans in news and entertainment media help to explain the white majority's misconceptions about the African American minority in general and in particular about poverty in their own country and their hate of welfare,[72] the stereotypical depiction of Muslims informed post-9/11 public and elite attitudes, counterterrorism policies, and discrimination. How we view the world around us, how we think and talk about issues and problems arising in the public and private spheres is not only affected by the information we receive as news but also by the words, ideas, images, and stereotypes presented in different types of mass media—and person-to-person communications that are also likely to be influenced by various media as well.[73]

In sum, then, while there were both unifying rituals of communication and divisive rituals of excommunication, the "good" versus "evil" narrative and the "us" versus "them" demagoguery of the early post-9/11 period gained ground over time.

Notes

1. President Clinton's Advisory Board on Race, *One America in the 21st Century: The Report of President Bill Clinton's Initiative on Race* (Washington, DC: Initiative, 1998).

2. Jack G. Shaheen, *Reel Bad Arabs: How Hollywood Vilifies a People* (New York: Olive Branch Press, 2009).

3. Reeva S. Simon, *The Middle East in Crime Fiction: Mysteries, Spy Novels, and Thrillers from 1916 to the 1980s* (New York: Lilian Barber Press, 1989),140.

4. Edward W. Said, *Covering Islam: How the Media and the Experts Determine How We See the Rest of the World* (New York: Pantheon Books, 1981), 26.

5. Thomas Riegler, "Through the Lenses of Hollywood: Depictions of Terrorism in American Movies," *Perspectives on Terrorism* 4, no. 2 (2010), 12.

6. Elizabeth Anker, "Villains, Victims, and Heroes: Melodrama, Media, and September 11," *Journal of Communication* 55, no. 1 (2005): 35.

7. While a significant number of Arab Americans are Christians, most Americans are unaware of this and assume that all Arabs are Muslims.

8. Walter Lippmann, *Public Opinion* (New York: Free Press, [1922] 1997), 59.

9. Rudy Giuliani, qtd. in Leslie Casimir, "As Grief Gives Way to Rage, Some Attack Those Resembling Enemy," *New York Daily News*, September 13, 2001, http://paul-altobelli .com/archives/9-11/stars/htm_files/9_13/11.htm.

10. Giuliani, qtd. in David Weigel, "The Liberal Candidate: Is Rudy Giuliani a New Barry Goldwater or a New Bobby Kennedy?," *Reason*, December 2007, http://reason.com/ archives/2007/11/14/the-liberal-candidate/2.

11. George W. Bush, speech at the Islamic Center in Washington, DC, September 17, 2001, *PBS NewsHour*, http://www.pbs.org/newshour/updates/terrorism-july-dec01 -bush_speech_9-17/, accessed June 21, 2014.

12. Joshua Sanders, "Japanese Americas See Similarities to WWII Conditions," *Seattle Post-Intelligencer*, September 18, 2001, A7.

13. Brigitte L. Nacos and Oscar Torres-Reyna, *Fueling Our Fears: Stereotyping, Media Coverage, and Public Opinion of Muslim Americans* (Lanham, MD: Rowman and Littlefield, 2007), 13.

14. Ibid., 17.

15. James W. Carey, *Communication as Culture: Essays on Media and Society* (New York: Routledge, 1992), 17, 18.

16. James W. Carey, "Political Ritual on Television: Episodes in the History of Shame, Degradation and Excommunication," in *Media, Ritual and Identity*, ed. Tamar Liebes and James Curran, 42–70 (London: Routledge, 1998).

17. Nacos and Torres-Reyna, *Fueling Our Fears*, 28.

18. From a speech that Anthony Lewis delivered at the Benjamin N. Cardozo School of Law at Yeshiva University at a conference titled "Weapons of Mass Destruction, National Security, and a Free Press" on March 2, 2004. For the full text see "The Responsibilities of a Free Press," Nieman Reports, Summer 2004, http://www.nieman.harvard.edu/ reportsitem.aspx?id=100829.

19. From Attorney General John Ashcroft's testimony before the Senate Judicial Committee on December 6, 2001, according to the transcript available at Lexis/Nexis.

20. For a list of such statements, see compilations by the Council on American-Islamic Relations (CAIR) at http://www.cair.com/AmericanMuslims/AntiTerrorism.aspx, accessed June 10, 2011.

21. Paul Farhi, "WMAL Suspends Talk Show Host for Comment on Islam," *Washington Post*, July 29, 2005, C1. See also Paul Farhi, "Talk Show Host Graham Fired by WMAL over Islam Remarks," *Washington Post*, August 23, 2005, C1.

22. *Brian Lehrer Show*, WNYC, New York, August 2, 2005.

23. *The O'Reilly Factor*, Fox News Network, July 28, 2005.

24. The cartoon by Steve Benson was published in the *Arizona Republic* on July 31, 2005. See http://www.azcentral.com/arizonarepublic/opinions/benson/ articles/073105bensonhtml, accessed August 8, 2005.

25. Stuart Taylor Jr., "Is It Ever Right to Torture Suspected Terrorists?" *National Journal*, March 8, 2003, http://www.nationaljournal.com/magazine/column-is-it-ever-all-right -to-torture-suspected-terrorists—20030308, accessed June 21, 2014.

26. Jonathan Alter, "Time to Think about Torture," *Newsweek*, November 5, 2001.

27. Mark Bowden, "The Dark Art of Interrogation," *Atlantic Monthly*, October 2003, 76.

28. Henry Mark Holzer, "Terrorism Interrogations and Torture," *Milwaukee Journal Sentinel*, March 16, 2003, 5J.

29. Robert M. Entman, "Declaration of Independence: The Growth of Media Power after the Cold War," In *Decisionmaking in a Glass House: Mass Media, Public Opinion and American and European Foreign Policy in the 21st Century*, ed. Brigitte L. Nacos, Robert Y. Shapiro, and Pierangelo Isernia, 11–26 (Lanham, MD: Rowman and Littlefield, 2000), 21.

30. Patricia Roberts-Miller, "Democracy, Demagoguery, and Critical Rhetoric," *Rhetoric & Public Affairs* 8, no. 3 (2005): 459–476, quote from 462.

31. Ehud Sprinzak, "Extreme Left Terrorism in a Democracy," in *Origins of Terrorism: Psychologies, Ideologies, Theologies, States of Mind*, ed. Walter Reich (New York: Cambridge University Press, 1990), 82.

32. *Hannity & Colmes*, Fox News, March 5, 2003.

33. *Hannity & Colmes*, Fox News, May 13, 2004.

34. Rush Limbaugh, qtd. in Stephen Kinzer and Jim Rutenberg, "Grim Images Seem to Deepen Nation's Polarization on Iraq," *New York Times*, May 13, 2004, 11.

35. Mark Danner, *Torture and Truth: America, Abu Ghraib and the War on Terror* (New York: New York Review of Books, 2004), 245.

36. Adam Zagorin and Michael Duffy, "Inside the Interrogation of Detainee 063," *Time*, June 20, 2004, 33.

37. Jack Wheeler, "Interrogating KSM; How to Make the al Qaeda Terrorist Sing," *Washington Times*, March 5, 2003, 19.

38. Ibid.

39. *NBC Nightly News*, November 16, 2001.

40. *Nightline*, ABC News, March 8, 2002.

41. *Talkback Live*, CNN, August 15, 2002.

42. Danner, *Torture and Truth*, 227.

43. Susan Sontag, "Regarding the Torture of Others," *New York Times Magazine*, May 23, 2004, retrieved from Lexis/Nexis, April 10, 2005.

44. Jack Valenti, qtd. in "Uncle Sam Wants Hollywood," CNN, November 9, 2001, http://articles.cnn.com/2001-11-09/entertainment/hollywood.war_1_war-effort-film -industry-vietnam-movies?_s=PM:SHOWBIZ , accessed June 3, 2011.

45. "The Problem: Torture on TV on the Rise," Human Rights First, http://workers rights.humanrightsfirst.org/us_law/etn/primetime/index.asp, accessed August 3, 2010.

46. The town hall meeting was held and broadcast on *Nightline*, ABC News, on March 8, 2002.

47. *World News with Peter Jennings*, ABC News, March 4, 2003.

48. Mark McGuire, "Good Guys Are Doing Bad Things This Season," *Times Union* (Albany, NY), January 14, 2003, D1.

49. Robert Thompson, qtd. in Mcguire, "Good Guys."

50. John F. Harris, Mike Allen, and Jim Vandehei, "Cheney Warns of New Attacks," *Politico*, February 4, 2009, http://www.politico.com/news/stories/0209/18390.html.

51. Michael X. Delli Carpini and Bruce A. Williams, "Methods, Metaphors, and Media Research: The Uses of Television in Political Conversation," *Communication Research* 21, no. 6 (1994): 793.

52. Sissela Bok, *Mayhem: Violence as Public Entertainment* (Reading, MA: Perseus Books, 1998).

53. Howard Gordon, qtd. in Jane Mayer, "Whatever It Takes," *New Yorker*, February 19, 2007.

54. Richard Walter, qtd. in Barry Bergman, "Prime-Time Torture Gets a Reality Check." *Berkeleyan* (Berkeley, CA), March 5, 2008.

55. Tony Lagouranis, qtd. in ibid.

56. Diane Beaver, qtd. in Jane Mayer, *The Dark Side* (New York: Doubleday, 2008), 196.

57. Beaver, qtd. in Philippe Sands, *Torture Team: Rumsfeld's Memo and the Betrayal of American Values* (New York: Palgrave Macmillan, 2008), 62.

58. Patrick Finnegan, qtd. in Faiz Shakir, "U.S. Military: Television Series '24' Is Promoting Torture in the Ranks," *ThinkProgress*, February 13, 2007.

59. Murray Edelman, *From Art to Politics: How Artistic Creations Shape Political Conceptions* (Chicago: University of Chicago Press, 1996), 1.

60. The debate took place at Dartmouth College, Hanover, New Hampshire, on September 26, 2007. For the full text, see "Democratic Debate Transcript, New Hampshire," Council on Foreign Relations, September 26, 2007, http://www.cfr.org/publication/14313/democratic_debate_transcript_new_hampshire.html, accessed July 20, 2010.

61. Bill Clinton, excerpts taken from the Lexis/Nexis transcript of NBC News *Meet the Press*, aired on September 30, 2007.

62. Intelligence Science Board, *Educing Information* (Washington, DC: National Defense Intelligence College, 2006), http://www.fas.org/irp/dni/educing.pdf, accessed August 10, 2010), 95.

63. John Yoo, *War by Other Means* (New York: Atlantic Monthly Press, 2006), 172.

64. Reported in Peter Lattman, "Justice Scalia Hearts Jack Bauer," Law Blog, *Wall Street Journal*, June 20, 2007, http://blogs.wsj.com/law/2007/06/20/justice-scalia-hearts-jack-bauer/, accessed February 12, 2009.

65. *Glenn Beck Program*, Fox News, June 8, 2011.

66. Newt Gingrich, qtd, on ABC News, June 13, 2011.

67. Allen West, qtd. in George Zornick, "GOP Candidate Allen West: People with 'Coexist' Bumper Stickers Want to 'Give Away Our Country,'" *ThinkProgress*, August 18, 2010, http://thinkprogress.org/politics/2010/08/18/113874/allen-west-islam/, accessed June 6, 2011.

68. Newt Gingrich, qtd. in Andy Barr, "Newt Gingrich Compares Mosque to Nazis," *Politico*, August 16, 2010, http://www.politico.com/news/stories/0810/41112.html, accessed September 21, 2010.

69. Farhana Khera, Written Testimony Hearing on the Civil Rights of American Muslims, U.S. Senate Committee on the Judiciary, Subcommittee on the Constitution, Civil Rights and Human Rights, March 29, 2011.

70. In the UK, the *Guardian* published two stories about the report. Political Research Associates, "Manufacturing the Muslim Menace: Private Firms, Public Servants, and the Threat to Rights and Security," http://www.politicalresearch.org/wp-content/uploads/downloads/2012/11/Muslim_Menace_Complete.pdf, accessed July 2, 2011.

71. Rudi Giuliani, qtd. in Maggie Haberman, "Rudy: GZ Mosque Is a 'Desecration,' 'Decent Muslims' Won't Be Offended." *Politico*, August 2, 2010, http://www.politico.com/blogs/maggiehaberman/0810/Rudy_Mosque_is_a_desecration_.html, accessed June 1, 2011.

72. Robert M. Entman and Andrew Rojeck, *The Black Image in the White Mind* (Chicago: University of Chicago Press, 2000).

73. Ibid.; James Shanahan and Michael Morgan, *Television and Its Viewers: Cultivation Theory and Research* (New York: Cambridge University Press, 1999).

After bin Laden

Zero Dark Thirty

SUSAN JEFFORDS AND FAHED AL-SUMAIT

> The death of bin Laden marks the most significant achievement to date in our nation's effort to defeat al Qaeda.
>
> —President Barack Obama, May 2, 2011

> For a decade we have been at war, a war supposedly launched to find and punish Osama bin Laden and al-Qaeda for the attacks of September 11, 2001. We searched and tried to capture or kill bin Laden, until it proved hard enough that it became easier to pretend he didn't matter after all . . . He was like a ghost, seemingly forgotten. . . . And then came rumors, followed quickly by confirmation, that Osama bin Laden had been found and killed. The man we'd turned into a mythical monster, only to transform him later into an irrelevant missing person, was gone.
>
> —Mark Hughes, *Forbes*, December 2012

Media around the world shared the news of Osama bin Laden's death on May 2, 2011.[1] His death was largely celebrated as a milestone in the Global War on Terrorism. Former president George W. Bush called bin Laden's killing a "victory for America"[2]; former secretary of state Condoleezza Rice echoed these sentiments in calling the death a "tremendous victory."[3] Across the United

States, groups broke into celebratory cheers upon hearing the announcement of bin Laden's death.[4] At the site of the most devastating attack on 9/11—the World Trade Center—crowds waved American flags and burst into choruses of Lee Greenwood's "I'm Proud to Be an American."[5] Four thousand tweets per second were sent during Obama's speech announcing bin Laden's death, so it is not surprising that the sellout crowd at Citizens Bank Field watching the Phillies-Mets baseball game would have erupted into spontaneous chants of "U-S-A!" without any formal announcement in the stadium.[6] Indeed, Obama's announcement was preempted by Twitter, with Keith Urbahn, Donald Rumsfeld's former chief of staff, tweeting five minutes before the president's speech, "So I'm told by a reputable person that they have killed Osama bin Laden. Hot damn."[7] Around the world, reactions were similarly positive, though perhaps not as euphoric. European Union Parliament President Jerzy Buzek, said, "We have woken up in a more secure world," while UN Secretary-General Ban Ki-moon declared bin Laden's death "a watershed moment in our common global fight against terrorism," continuing that he was "personally, very much relieved by the news that justice has been done to such a mastermind of international terrorism."[8] Governments in Ethiopia, Liberia, Libya, Kenya, Somalia, Uganda, Chile, Canada, Albania, Philippines, and more declared bin Laden's death a cause for celebration. Afghanistan president Hamed Karzai noted that bin Laden had been "punished" for his deeds and encouraged members of the Taliban in Pakistan to "learn a lesson" from his death.[9]

Not all reactions were positive. A Taliban commander declared, "the Americans will be happy. . . . In the Islamic countries Osama is a respected person. I hope Muslims join with us after this killing and stand beside us against the Americans."[10] Numerous rallies took place in cities across Pakistan to mourn bin Laden's death and criticize the United States for killing him and violating Pakistan's sovereignty.[11] A mass prayer and rally was held in Khartoum at which Sunni Muslim clerics declared that "Osama bin Laden is our brother" and voiced a hope that "all Arab presidents will become like Osama bin Laden."[12] Prayer meetings mourning bin Laden's death took place around the world, ranging from the Palestinian Territory to London to Egypt to Iran. Rather than lament his passing, Al Qaeda chose to use bin Laden as an example to others, noting, "So if the Americans were able to kill Usama [sic], this is not shame or stigma." Instead, Al Qaeda reminded its followers that the ideas that bin Laden stood for did not die with him: "But can the Americans, with their media, agents, machinery, soldiers, intelligence and agencies kill that for which Sheikh Usama [sic] lived and that for which he was killed?"[13]

Bin Laden's death fulfilled the expectations of many Americans that began with President George Bush's declaration in the days after 9/11: "I want justice. And there's an old poster out West, I recall, that said: Wanted, Dead or Alive."[14] He reiterated this sentiment on December 14, 2001, during a press meeting on the occasion of the visit of the prime minister of Thailand to the Oval Office: "I don't care—dead or alive. It doesn't matter to me."[15] In November 2001, a Gallup poll showed that just over half of U.S. citizens believed that the military actions then beginning in Afghanistan would not be a success unless bin Laden was also killed.[16] Indeed, with the Western genre as a common staple of American culture and media, Americans were quite familiar with what statements about taking someone "dead or alive" meant.

As the time between 9/11 and news of bin Laden's death or capture became longer, and as the wars in Afghanistan and Iraq came to dominate the U.S. media's reporting of the Global War on Terror, less attention was given to bin Laden himself. On the fifth anniversary of 9/11, Bush reminded Americans that "Osama bin Laden and other terrorists are still in hiding. Our message to them is clear: No matter how long it takes, America will find you, and we will bring you to justice."[17] But in the months after 9/11, Bush began to reframe his statements about bin Laden's death. In a press conference in March 2002, he acknowledged: "We haven't heard much from him. And I wouldn't necessarily say he's at the center of any command structure. And, again, I don't know where he is. . . . I'll repeat what I said. I truly am not that concerned about him. I know he is on the run."[18]

With the news of bin Laden's death came questions about the impact of the long-awaited announcement about the discovery of "the most wanted man on earth." The debate is a polarized one. While initial reactions in Western media were positive, Gary Younge of the *Guardian* noted on the first anniversary of bin Laden's death: "beyond avenging the attacks on the world trade centre, the assassination of Bin Laden has achieved precious little. Assassination is not a foreign policy. Nor is it a judicial strategy. Vengeance, however righteous, is not an argument, let alone a plan. The two wars, ostensibly launched in response to September 11, 2001, have been disasters, leaving many more civilians dead than the original act of terror. America's standing around the world has yet to fully recover. The geopolitical relations in the area around Afghanistan and Pakistan remain fragile."[19]

In contrast, Lieutenant Colonel Joe Ruffini (retired), author of *Osama bin Laden: His Death and the Future of Al Qaeda and the Islamist Jihad*, argues that there are several clear impacts of bin Laden's death:

- Intelligence materials gathered in bin Laden's compound by the SEAL Team that killed him
- "Closure" for the American people
- A message to other terrorist groups about American resolve to seek out and address terrorists who have attacked or wish to attack the United States: "Bin Laden's death is all about American pride and honor. It is about national resolve. It is about showing the world and especially our adversaries that harming our nation and its citizens will not be tolerated."[20]

Why does it seem to many that bin Laden's death did not have the impact that was expected from the largest and most expensive manhunt in history? Mark Hughes, writing for *Forbes*, points to an explanation: "All of that tension and aggression, all of that killing and warfare, all of those revelations about the United States engaging in torture and secret prisons and rejection of international law and Geneva Conventions, it was all supposed to be building to this moment. Bin Laden's death was supposed to be worth all of it, the justification for what had come before, and in his death the nation had expected some resolution and fulfillment. And upon the initial reporting of his death, indeed there were crowds cheering in the street and proclamations that at long last the victims of terrorism had been avenged and the survivors could sleep easier." But then, Hughes goes on to say, "the next morning, bin Laden was gone but the rest was still here. The war was still here, the torture and Geneva Convention were still here, and the sense that there was never going to be a definitive end to any of it was still here."[21]

The debate about the film that chronicled the killing of bin Laden, *Zero Dark Thirty*, is equally divided. Billed officially as "The story of history's greatest manhunt for the world's most dangerous man," *Zero Dark Thirty* appeared to much expectation and fanfare in 2012. Reuniting the director and screenwriter who won the Best Picture Oscar for *The Hurt Locker* in 2008—Kathryn Bigelow and Mark Boal—and capitalizing on the celebratory atmosphere of killing Osama bin Laden on May 2 of the year before, the film was the much-anticipated Hollywood narration of the manhunt that had preoccupied the nation for over a decade. What has been called "the narrative of the era of the war on terror" sparked dramatic debates—not about the impact of bin Laden's death, but about the use of torture in gathering the information that led to finding him.[22] Much like the innumerable media representations discussed within this book, the film appropriates (the idea of) bin Laden on terms most favorable to the creators' own objectives. This now familiar exercise appears again to illustrate at least as much about the media producers and their audiences and as it does about bin Laden himself.

Early scenes in *Zero Dark Thirty* show the torture of a prisoner, Ammar al-Baluchi, held at a CIA black site in Pakistan in 2003. The film's central character and viewpoint, Maya (played by Jessica Chastain), witnesses and, as the film goes on, encourages torture techniques that include waterboarding, sexual humiliation, hanging from the ceiling, being confined in a coffin-sized box, and deprivation of food. A key piece of information that becomes crucial to locating bin Laden—the name of bin Laden's courier—is retrieved from Ammar during his interrogation, though in a casual conversation that occurs only after the torture has been applied.

These scenes have been called "unadulterated torture porn" for their depictions of the torture of the prisoner "Ammar," a composite, according to Boal, of different prisoners who were captured during the Global War on Terrorism.[23] Jane Mayer, who has written extensively about the use of torture in the War on Terror, sees the film as "false advertising for waterboarding," because the film's narrative shows torture as instrumental in finding bin Laden.[24] Senator Dianne Feinstein was so disturbed by the interpretation that torture had a role in finding bin Laden that she joined Senator Carl Levin in writing a formal letter to the chairman of Sony Pictures, claiming that the film is "grossly inaccurate and misleading in its suggestion that torture resulted in information that led to the location of Usama [sic] bin Laden."[25] These scenes have led many critics to agree with philosopher Slavo Žižek's conclusion that the film depicts the "normalisation of torture."[26]

Though Bigelow defends the film's depictions as a "first draft of history," and Boal as "a movie not a documentary," critics point less to the question of factuality than to the audience reactions to the film's momentum.[27] Writing for *Rolling Stone*, Matt Taibbi records that when the helicopter carrying bin Laden's dead body took off, "the triumph the characters felt at that moment exploded in the theater, there were gasps and patriotic applause." This sense of triumph makes this movie, for Taibbi, a "straight-up 'hero catches bad guys' movie" with audiences identifying with Maya as the hero. "Are audiences not supposed to cheer at the end of the film, when we get bin Laden?"[28] For this reason, documentary filmmaker Alex Gibney labels the film "fundamentally reckless," because "if we believe that torture 'got' bin Laden, then we will be more prone to accept the view that a good 'end' can justify brutal 'means.'"[29]

In *Zero Dark Thirty*—a film exclusively about the hunt for bin Laden—bin Laden appears only momentarily, as a flash image of a bloodied face as a body bag is quickly unzipped and then zipped again. The film sparked debates—not about bin Laden's motives, his actions, or his role in world politics—but about the torture that became a feature of the U.S. pursuit of the Global War on Terrorism that was the response to the attacks on the United States orchestrated by bin Laden. The film's perspective is unmistakably American and Western, with assumptions that audiences would already know the backstory about who bin Laden is, why the U.S. government invested so much in finding him, and why his death should be an event for celebration. What is remarkable about the debates, the reviews, and the discussions about *Zero Dark Thirty* is that they mimic cultural discourses—such as those reflected upon in this volume—that arose in the decade since 9/11 in an elusive dance with Osama bin Laden.

For several years, powerful forces, including bin Laden himself, worked fervently to define the man and his actions for a global audience. Media producers in particular constructed various narratives attempting to explain what they saw as the most pertinent elements of the bin Laden story. These ranged from the more "objectively" oriented newscasts to openly propagandistic media artifacts arising from Al Qaeda, various war departments, in film, and even among online gamers. Of course, political actors, such as George W. Bush and bin Laden himself, were able to exert their own formidable influence on the messages cascading throughout the world. However, as this book shows, such actors are dependent on mass media to amplify their messages, and this amplification is certainly not without its own idiosyncratic tendencies. As Richard Jackson aptly points out in his chapter, even in light of such a robust discourse surrounding bin Laden, we are still left contemplating exactly who he was and what his life (and death) actually mean.

The essays in this volume contribute to our understanding of how global media figure, represent, construct, and narrate individuals, events, and images around the world. By focusing on the man who has been "a major spectacle of the millennium since the 9/11 terror attacks,"[30] authors in this volume have provided a vantage point for understanding, comparing, and critiquing global media—a vantage point that can also be applied to other media objects. In addition, they have shown how the intersections between global and local media and audiences, that we see in the study of Osama bin Laden, have fundamentally changed media operations and their impacts. The interconnections between the individual tweet that unknowingly announced the raid on Abbottabad ("A huge window shaking bang here in Abbottabad. I hope its not the start of something nasty"[31]), the mainstream media that covered the raid, the films that chronicle bin Laden's death, the video games that allow players to kill bin

Laden over and over—all show the range and complexity of global media that this volume studies.

As *Zero Dark Thirty* shows, the narrative of Osama bin Laden is the narrative of the Global War on Terrorism, and how global culture has changed since 9/11. Identifying, finding, and killing Osama bin Laden came to define the first decade of America's entrance into the twenty-first century and, because of the wars begun in pursuit of him, redefined political, economic, and cultural relations across the globe. None of the other momentous events of that decade— the largest economic crash since the Great Depression, the election of the first African American U.S. president, the transformation of the human-computer interface—surpasses the impact on the United States of 9/11 and the Global War on Terrorism that was started by Osama bin Laden. The United States, redefined as a surveillance and security state, has fundamentally reconfigured its presence around the world, with wars in Iraq and Afghanistan that have had rippling effects across the Middle East and Central Asia and that have hamstrung the American economy. Relationships between governments and citizens have also been redefined across the globe, with a new acceptance of surveillance and personal submission to "security measures"—increased militarization of society, screenings, monitoring of phone records, the largest investment ever made in border security, and the private contracting of protection. It is no wonder that the death of Osama bin Laden has seemed anticlimactic. The War on Terror" shifted the globe—producing the restructuring of the global economy and security state around fear, the increased global tensions around religion and culture, and the new configurations of global media—and none of these disappeared with bin Laden's death. Though he may have been the figure that sparked these changes, and the cause célèbre for enacting them, his death does not eliminate them. Osama bin Laden, who may have seemed like an elusive ghost during the worldwide hunt for him, continues to haunt the world as the man whose life and death redefined the world.

Notes

1. For a selection of forty-five newspaper cover stories of bin Laden's death, see Julie Moos, "Newspaper Front Pages Capture Elation, Relief That Osama bin Laden Was Killed," Poynter Institute, May 2, 2011(updated May 6, 2011), http://www.poynter.org/ latest-news/top-stories/130349/newspaper-front-pages-capture-elation-relief-that-osama -bin-laden-was-captured-killed/.

2. Kevin Hechtkopf, "George W. Bush: Osama bin Laden's Death a 'Victory for America,'" CBSNews, May 2, 2011, http://www.cbsnews.com/news/george-w-bush-osama -bin-ladens-death-a-victory-for-america/.

3. Kevin Hechtkopf, "Politicians from Both Sides of the Aisle Celebrate Osama bin Laden's Death," CBSNews, May 2, 2011, http://www.cbsnews.com/news/politicians-from-both-sides-of-the-aisle-celebrate-osama-bin-ladens-death/.

4. For a sample of photos of U.S. celebrations, see "Celebrating the Death of Osama bin Laden," *Time*, May 2, 2011, http://www.time.com/time/photogallery/0,29307,2068860_2271097,00.html.

5. Fox News, "President George W. Bush Congratulates Obama on bin Laden Killing," May 2, 2011, http://www.foxnews.com/us/2011/05/02/president-george-w-bush-congratulates-obama-bin-laden-killing/.

6. Craig Kanalley, "Twitter Reactions to Osama bin Laden's Death (TWEETS)," *Huffington Post*, May 2, 2011 (updated July 1, 2011), http://www.huffingtonpost.com/2011/05/02/osama-bin-laden-death-tweets_n_856119.html#s272226title=Rosemary_Church; Adam Rubin, "Phillies Crowd Erupts in U-S-A Cheers," ESPN, May 3, 2011, http://sports.espn.go.com/new-york/mlb/news/story?id=6463361.

7. John D. Sutter, "How bin Laden News Spread on Twitter," CNNTech, May 4, 2011, http://www.cnn.com/2011/TECH/social.media/05/02/osama.bin.laden.twitter/index.html.

8. Jerzy Buzek, qtd. in Chris Allbritton, "Bin Laden's Death Makes the World Safer, Leaders Say," Reuters, May 2, 2011, http://www.reuters.com/article/2011/05/02/us-binladen-reaction-idUSTRE7411TN20110502; "U.N. Chief Ban Hails bin Laden Death as 'Watershed,'" Reuters, May 2, 2011, http://www.reuters.com/article/2011/05/02/us-binladen-un-idUSTRE7414W720110502.

9. Terence P. Jeffrey, "Afghan President Karzai: Bin Laden 'Punished' for His Deeds; Taleban Should 'Learn a Lesson,'" CBSNews, May 2, 2001, http://cnsnews.com/news/article/afghan-president-karzai-bin-laden-punished-his-deeds-taleban-should-learn-lesson.

10. Jon Boone, "Osama bin Laden Dead: US Strategy Misconceived, Says Hamid Karzai," *Guardian*, May 2, 2011, http://www.theguardian.com/world/2011/may/02/osama-bin-laden-afghanistan-fears.

11. "First the Tears, Now the Anger: Pakistanis Burn U.S. Flags as Backlash over bin Laden's Death Grows," *Mail Online*, May 4, 2011, http://www.dailymail.co.uk/news/article-1383011/Osama-Bin-Laden-dead-Pakistanis-burn-US-flags-backlash-grows.html.

12. "In Sudan, 1,000 Denounce Killing of bin Laden," Reuters, May 3, 2011, http://www.reuters.com/article/2011/05/03/ozatp-binladen-sudan-idAFJOE7420R020110503.

13. Rita Katz, "Insight into al-Qaeda's Confirmation of bin Laden's Death," SITE Monitoring Service, October 19, 2012 (updated January 15, 2014); http://news.siteintelgroup.com/free-featured-articles/688-insight-into-al-qaedas-confirmation-of-bin-ladens-death.

14. "Bush: Bin Laden Wanted Dead or Alive," ABC News, September 17, 2001, http://abcnews.go.com/US/t/story?id=92483&page=1.

15. "Bush Pledges to Get bin Laden, Dead or Alive," *USA Today*, December 14, 2001, http://usatoday30.usatoday.com/news/attack/2001/12/14/bush-binladen.htm.

16. "Osama bin Laden," Gallup Poll, September 16, 2013, http://www.gallup.com/poll/5266/osama-bin-laden.aspx.

17. Kathy Gill, "President Bush on Fifth Anniversary of 9–11," About.com, http://us politics.about.com/od/speeches/a/9_11_bush.htm.

18. Maura Reynolds, "Bush 'Not Concerned' about bin Laden in '02," *Los Angeles Times*, October 14, 2004, http://articles.latimes.com/2004/oct/14/nation/na-osama14.

19. Gary Younge, "Osama bin Laden's Death Has Had Zero Impact on America's Security," *Guardian*, http://www.theguardian.com/commentisfree/cifamerica/2012/may/01/osama-bin-laden-death-zero-impact.

20. Joe Ruffini, *Osama bin Laden: His Death and the Future of Al Qaeda and the Islamist Jihad* (Beloden Labs, 2011), 25.

21. Mark Hughes, "*Zero Dark Thirty* Review: A Film to Define a Decade," *Forbes*, December 18, 2012, http://www.forbes.com/sites/markhughes/2012/12/18/zero-dark-thirty.

22. Ibid.

23. Ramzi Kassem, "The Controversy around *Zero Dark Thirty*: As Misleading as the Film Itself," Al Jazeera, January 19, 2013, http://www.aljazeera.com/indepth/opinion/2013/01/20131191566253143.htm.

24. Jane Mayer, "Zero Conscience in '*Zero Dark Thirty*,'" *New Yorker*, December 14, 2012.

25. Dianne Feinstein, "Feinstein Releases Statement on 'Zero Dark Thirty,'" press release, http://www.feinstein.senate.gov/public/index.cfm/2012/12/feinstein-releases -statement-on-zero-dark-thirty.

26. Slavo Žižek, "*Zero Dark Thirty*: Hollywood's Gift to American Power," *Guardian*, January 25, 2013, http://www.theguardian.com/commentisfree/2013/jan/25/zero-dark -thirty-normalises-torture-unjustifiable.

27. Kathryn Bigelow interview, *Colbert Report*, January 23, 2013; Mark Boal, qtd. in Dexter Filkins, "Bin Laden, the Movie," *New Yorker*, December 17, 2012, http://www .newyorker.com/talk/2012/12/17/121217ta_talk_filkins.

28. Matt Taibbi, "'Zero Dark Thirty' Is Osama bin Laden's Last Victory over America," *Rolling Stone*, January 16, 2013.

29. Alex Gibney, "*Zero Dark Thirty*'s Wrong and Dangerous Conclusion," *Huffington Post*, December 21, 2012, http://www.huffingtonpost.com/alex-gibney/zero-dark-thirty -torture_b_2345589.html.

30. Douglas Kellner, *Media Spectacle and Insurrection* (London: Bloomsbury, 2012), 147.

31. Doug Gross, "Twitter User Unknowingly Reported bin Laden Attack," CNN Tech, May 2, 2011; http://www.cnn.com/2011/TECH/social.media/05/02/osama.twitter.reports/index.html.

About the Contributors

Editors

SUSAN JEFFORDS is a professor of English and of gender, women, and sexuality studies at the University of Washington. She is author of numerous publications in the field of feminist and masculinity studies, cultural studies, and American popular culture. Among her publications are *The Remasculinization of America: Gender and the Vietnam War* (1989), *Hard Bodies: Hollywood Masculinity in the Reagan Era* (2004), and *Seeing through the Media: The Persian Gulf War* (1994). She is currently serving as the vice chancellor for academic affairs at the University of Washington Bothell.

FAHED AL-SUMAIT is an assistant professor of communication and department chair at the Gulf University for Science and Technology in Kuwait. He was previously a Fulbright-Hays fellow for his research into contested discourses on Arab democratization in the United States and Kuwait and a postdoctoral fellow at the Middle East Institute at the National University of Singapore. Among his notable publications are "Public Opinion Discourses on Democratization in the Arab Middle East" (*Middle East Journal of Culture and Communication*, 2011) and "Terrorism's Cause and Cure: The Rhetorical Regime of Democracy in the U.S. and UK" (*Critical Studies on Terrorism*, 2009). He is also the coeditor of *The Arab Uprisings: Catalysts, Dynamics, and Trajectories* (2014).

Authors

SARANAZ BARFOROUSH is a PhD candidate at the Philip Merrill College of Journalism at the University of Maryland, College Park, where she is studying political communication and news coverage of international conflicts, especially the coverage of enemy states by Western media. She worked as a journalist for Iranian newspapers and weekly magazines for six years, including *HamshahriDaily, Asr-e-ertebat, Zanan,* and *Hayat-e-no.*

ADITI BHATIA is an assistant professor in the Department of English, City University of Hong Kong. She is the author of "Religious Metaphor in the Discourse of Illusion: George W. Bush and Osama bin Laden" (*World Englishes,* 2007); "Discursive Illusions in the American National Strategy for Combating Terrorism" (*Journal of Language and Politics,* 2008); and "Discourses of Terrorism" (*Journal of Pragmatics,* 2009).

PURNIMA BOSE is an associate professor of English and international studies at Indiana University. She is the author of *Organizing Empire: Individualism, Collective Agency, and India* (2003) and coeditor with Laura E. Lyons of *Cultural Critique and the Global Corporation* (2010).

RYAN CROKEN is a doctoral student in the Rhetoric and Public Culture program at Northwestern University. He is also an independent journalist and translator whose work has appeared in the *Philadelphia Inquirer, Tikkun, Religion Dispatches,* and *Truthout.*

SIMON FERRARI is a doctoral student in the Digital Media program at the Georgia Institute of Technology. Currently living in New York, he teaches game criticism at NYU's Game Center while participating in the city's burgeoning independent videogame scene as a writer and producer. For four years Simon was a research assistant on Ian Bogost's Games+Journalism project, culminating in the alpha release of the arcade remix engine Game-o-Matic. Along with Bogost and Bobby Schweizer, he is the coauthor of *Newsgames: Journalism at Play* (2010).

ANDREW HILL is a research fellow in visual culture in the Centre for Research on Socio-Cultural Change (CRESC) at The Open University in the UK. He is the author of *Re-Imagining the War on Terror: Seeing, Waiting, Travelling* (2009).

RICHARD JACKSON is deputy director of the National Centre for Peace and Conflict Studies at the University of Otago, Dunedin, New Zealand, and editor-in-chief of the journal *Critical Studies on Terrorism*. He is the author and coeditor of several books, including *Writing the War on Terrorism: Language, Politics, and Counter-terrorism* (2005), *Contemporary Debates on Terrorism* (2012), *Terrorism: A Critical Introduction* (2011), *Contemporary State Terrorism: Theory and Practice* (2010), *Critical Terrorism Studies: A New Research Agenda* (2009), and, most recently, a novel entitled *Confessions of a Terrorist* (2014).

NOHA MELLOR is a professor of media at the University of Bedfordshire, UK. She is the author of *The Making of Arab News* (2005), *Modern Arab Journalism* (2007), *Arab Media* (2011), and *Arab Journalists in Transnational Media* (2011).

SUSAN MOELLER is a professor of media and international affairs in the Philip Merrill College of Journalism and the School of Public Policy at the University of Maryland, College Park and director of the International Center for Media and the Public Agenda. Her books include *Packaging Terrorism: Co-opting the News for Politics and Profit, Compassion Fatigue: How the Media Sell Disease, Famine, War and Death*, and *Shooting War: Photography and the American Experience of Combat*.

BRIGITTE L. NACOS is adjunct professor in political science at Columbia University. She is the author of several books, including *Terrorism and the Media: From the Iran Hostage Crisis to the World Trade Center Bombing* (1994), *Mass Mediated Terrorism: The Central Role of the Media in Terrorism and Counterterrorism* (2002), and *Terrorism and Counterterrorism: Understanding Threats and Responses in the Post-9/11 World* (2006), and coauthor with Yaeli Bloch-Elkon and Robert Y. Shapiro of *Selling Fear: Counterrorism, the Media, and Public Opinion* (2011).

JOANNA NURMIS is a doctoral candidate at the Philip Merrill College of Journalism at the University of Maryland, College Park, where she is studying visual communication especially as it pertains to international events and policies. Before coming to the United States, she studied international relations (MA from Sciences Po in Paris) and worked as a photo editor in Paris, France.

COURTNEY C. RADSCH, PhD, is an Arab media specialist and the author of several articles and monographs that explore the nexus of technology, gender, and media in the Middle East. She is the editor of several books related to freedom of expression and is frequently invited to speak on these topics. She has been a journalist at *Al Arabiya*, the *New York Times*, and the *Daily Star* and a contributing expert analyst for Oxford Analytics, and she has written blogs for the *Huffington Post*.

ALEXANDER SPENCER is an assistant professor in global governance and public policy at the Ludwig-Maximilians University in Munich, Germany. His research centers on discourse analysis and the potential of constructivist international relations theory for international security and terrorism research, and his work has been published in such journals as *Foreign Policy Analysis, Security Dialogue, International Studies Perspectives,* and *Critical Studies on Terrorism.* He is the author of *The Tabloid Terrorist: The Predictive Construction of New Terrorism in the Media* (2010) and coeditor of *Reconciliation after Terrorism* (2012).

Index

Law and Order, 224
law enforcement, anti-Muslim bias in, 229
Lawrence, Bruce, 149
leaders, charismatic, 35–36
LeBlanc, Marc, 185
legend, definition of, 162
Levin, Carl, 239
Lewis, Anthony, 215
Lewis, Bernard, 120, 125
Lieberman, Joe, 124
"Like a Boss," 181n12
Limbaugh, Rush, 220
literacy games, 185
Llorente, Marina A., 81
London transit system attacks (2005), 43, 216
Lugo-Lugo, Carmen R., 165–66

Mackenzie, J. S., 21, 27
madness, 83
magical thinking in counterterrorism. *See*
    fantasy in counterterrorism thought and
    practice
Maher, Bill, 171, 173
Martin, David, 202, 222
martyrdom, killing as, 46–48
Mayer, Jane, 239
McCain, John, 174
McGuire, Mark, 224
McVeigh, Timothy, 81
Medal of Honor, 201, 202, 203
media: mythological archetypes in, 97; nor-
    malization of violent fantasies by, 194;
    subversive potential of, 157; and terror-
    ism, symbiotic relationship between, ix,
    73; War on Terror role in, xi–xiii
memento mori, photographs as, 127–28
Men in Black, 174
metaphors: analysis of, 76–77; concep-
    tual, 75, 85 *fig 5.1*; constructing reality, 74,
    75–76, 85–86, 87; crime, 79–80, 86–87;
    disease, 82–84; function of, 31n3, 74–75;
    influence of, on counterterrorism policy,
    75–76, 84; uncivilized evil, 80–82; varia-
    tions and shifts in, 84–86; war, 77–79,
    86–87
Metaphors We Live By (Lakoff and John-
    son), 74
Milhem, Hisham, 115

military-industrial-gaming complex, 202–4
military partnerships, videogame, 201–2
Miller, John, vii
Minarett Attack, 190, 193
Mitchell, W. J. T., xii, xiv
Mittelman, James H., 65
Mohammed, Khalid Sheik, 217, 218, 219,
    220–21
moral justice vs. retribution, 27–29
Morrison, Toni, 175
Mortal Kombat, 188
mosque at Ground Zero, 228–29, 230
movies: bias and inaccuracy in, 202; death
    of OBL in, 184, 202, 238–40, 241; expres-
    sive framing in, 199; hero archetype
    in, 174, 175, 181n15; Muslim Americans
    stereotypes in, 211; as terrortainment,
    223–27, 239; torture in, 202; as vehicle for
    propaganda, 202
Murray, Janet H., 184, 186
Muslim Americans: and Bush's "face of ter-
    ror" speech, 212–13, 230; othering of, 211,
    212; patriotism of, questioned, 211, 221;
    post-9/11 media constructions of, 212–16;
    religion of, attacked in media, 217; terrorist
    constructions of, 216–17; and us vs. them
    division, 227–30; violence against, 178, 229
Muslim Americans, stereotypes of: in coun-
    terterrorism policies, 230; discrimination
    and, 227–30; media perpetuation of, 211,
    212, 215; popular culture's influence on,
    213–14
Myers, Lisa, 222
myth, concept of, 96–97
mythological archetypes, 43–45, 96, 97. *See
    also* hero: archetype of; villain, arche-
    type of

Nacos, Brigitte, ix
Nairobi, U.S. embassy attack in, viii
Nakata, Hideo, 41
Nasar, Mustafa Setmariam (al-Suri), viii, ix
Navy SEAL Team Six, x, 45, 112, 120, 124,
    126, 132, 194–96, 202
Nellis, Ashley Marie, xiii
neoliberalism, 65–66, 71n57
news: hard, 97–98; personalization of, 96–
    98, 100; soft, 97–98

The University of Illinois Press
is a founding member of the
Association of American University Presses.

———————————————————

Composed in 10.75/13 Arno Pro
by Lisa Connery
at the University of Illinois Press
Manufactured by Sheridan Books, Inc.

University of Illinois Press
1325 South Oak Street
Champaign, IL 61820-6903
www.press.uillinois.edu